Teacher's Edition

ACCESS

Building Literacy Through Learning™

AMERICAN History

Great Source Education Group

a division of Houghton Mifflin Company

Wilmington, Massachusetts

www.greatsource.com

AUTHORS

Dr. Elva Duran holds a Ph.D. from the University of Oregon in special education and reading disabilities. Duran has been an elementary reading and middle school teacher in Texas and overseas. Currently, she is a professor in the Department of Special Education, Rehabilitation, and School Psychology at California State University, Sacramento, where she teaches beginning reading and language and literacy courses. Duran is co-author of the Leamos Español reading program and has published two textbooks, *Teaching Students with Moderate/Severe Disabilities* and *Systematic Instruction in Reading for Spanish-Speaking Students*.

Jo Gusman grew up in a family of migrants and knows firsthand the complexities surrounding a second-language learner. Gusman's career in bilingual education began in 1974. In 1981, she joined the staff of the Newcomer School in Sacramento. There she developed her brain-based ESL strategies. Her work has garnered national television appearances and awards, including the Presidential Recognition for Excellence in Teaching. Gusman is the author of *Practical Strategies for Accelerating the Literacy Skills and Content Learning of Your ESL Students*. She is a featured video presenter, including "Multiple Intelligences and the Second Language Learner." Currently, she teaches at California State University, Sacramento, and at the Multiple Intelligences Institute at the University of California, Riverside.

Dr. John Shefelbine is a professor in the Department of Teacher Education, California State University, Sacramento. His degrees include a Master of Arts in Teaching in reading and language arts, K-12, from Harvard University and a Ph.D. in educational psychology from Stanford University. During his 11 years as an elementary and middle school teacher, Shefelbine has worked with students from linguistically and culturally diverse populations in Alaska, Arizona, Idaho, and New Mexico. Shefelbine was a contributor to the California Reading Language Arts Framework, the California Reading Initiative, and the California Reading and Literature Project, and has authored a variety of reading materials and programs for developing fluent, confident readers.

EDITORIAL: Developed by Nieman Inc. with Phil LaLeike
DESIGN: Ronan Design

International Standard Book Number: ISBN-13: 978-0-669-50905-2   ISBN-10: 0-669-50905-1

10 11 2266 16   4500594023

CONSULTANTS

Shane Bassett
Mill Park Elementary School
David Douglas School District
Portland, OR

Jeanette Gordon
Senior Educational Consultant
Illinois Resource Center
Des Plaines, IL

Dr. Aixa Perez-Prado
College of Education
Florida International University
Miami, FL

Dennis Terdy
Director of Grants & Special
   Programs/Newcomer Center
Township High School
Arlington Heights, IL

RESEARCH SITE LEADERS

Carmen Concepción
Lawton Chiles Middle School
Miami, FL

Andrea Dabbs
Edendale Middle School
San Lorenzo, CA

Daniel Garcia
Public School 130
Bronx, NY

Bobbi Ciriza Houtchens
Arroyo Valley High School
San Bernardino, CA

Portia McFarland
Wendell Phillips High School
Chicago, IL

RESEARCH SITE HISTORY REVIEWERS

Raquel Aguilar
Lawton Chiles Middle School
Miami, FL

Veronica Hillman
Edendale Middle School
San Lorenzo, CA

Michele Jones
Martin Luther King, Jr.,
   Middle School
San Bernardino, CA

Cheryl Perry
Warren Elementary School
Chicago, IL

Laura Quagliariello
City Island, NY

HISTORY TEACHER REVIEWERS

Michelle Cohen
Pulaski Academy
Chicago, IL

Kimberly Culp
Mount Vernon High School
Alexandria, VA

Martha Freeman
Drummond Elementary
Chicago, IL

Krissy Hanna-Quiring
Sandburg Middle School
Golden Valley, MN

Kathelen Johnson
Oakland, CA

Anne Lowe
St. Paul Minnesota
   Public Schools
St. Paul, MN

Jamie Odeneal
Robinson Secondary School
Fairfax, VA

Kristina Otte
Lincoln Middle School
Berwyn, IL

Melissa Scott
Plymouth Middle School
Plymouth, MN

Jackie Smith
Torrington, CT

TEACHER GROUP REVIEWERS

Harriet Arons
Lincoln Junior High School
Skokie, IL

Andrea Ghetzler
Old Orchard
   Junior High School
Skokie, IL

Lori Miller
Old Orchard
   Junior High School
Skokie, IL

Marsha Robbins Santelli
Chicago Public Schools
Chicago, IL

Tia Sons
Old Orchard
   Junior High School
Skokie, IL

Mina Zimmerman
Deerpath Middle School
Lake Forest, IL

TABLE OF

CONTENTS

ACCESS Develops Basic and Academic Language

The ACCESS program is a standards-based middle-school program for English language learners. It builds students' understanding of the big ideas in English, math, science, and American history while developing their language proficiency in English. The *Newcomers* program gives beginning students survival language and starts them on the way to success in school.

Additional Components Support Each Book

With ACCESS, you have the components you need to support your teaching.

The **Teacher's Edition** provides succinct, informative notes, ▶ along with activity ideas and suggestions for ways to differentiate instruction based on students' language proficiency.

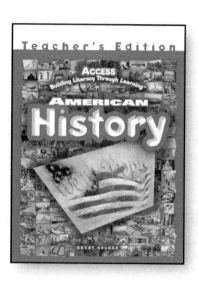

◀ The **Student Activity Journal** helps students build academic vocabulary, master content-area skills, take notes on and understand the lesson, and write about what they have learned.

Overhead Transparencies ▶ provide teachers with 36 graphic organizers to focus students' writing and oral presentations.

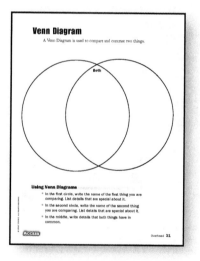

The **Assessment Folder** helps ▶ you track students' language development over the school year.

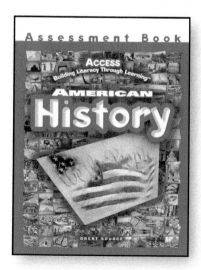

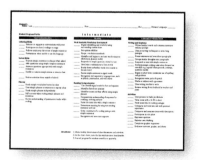

◀ The **Assessment Book** provides tests for each lesson, which assess students' growth in both language development and content knowledge.

Pupil's Edition Features

Each ACCESS Pupil's Edition is organized around lessons specifically designed to meet the needs of English language learners. Each lesson has three parts.

> **1. Talk and Explore**
> **2. Look and Read**
> **3. Develop Language**

1. Talk and Explore

Sets a purpose for students' reading

Gives students the **Big Idea** of the lesson and provides a picture walk-through, so you can build the concepts and language students will need for understanding

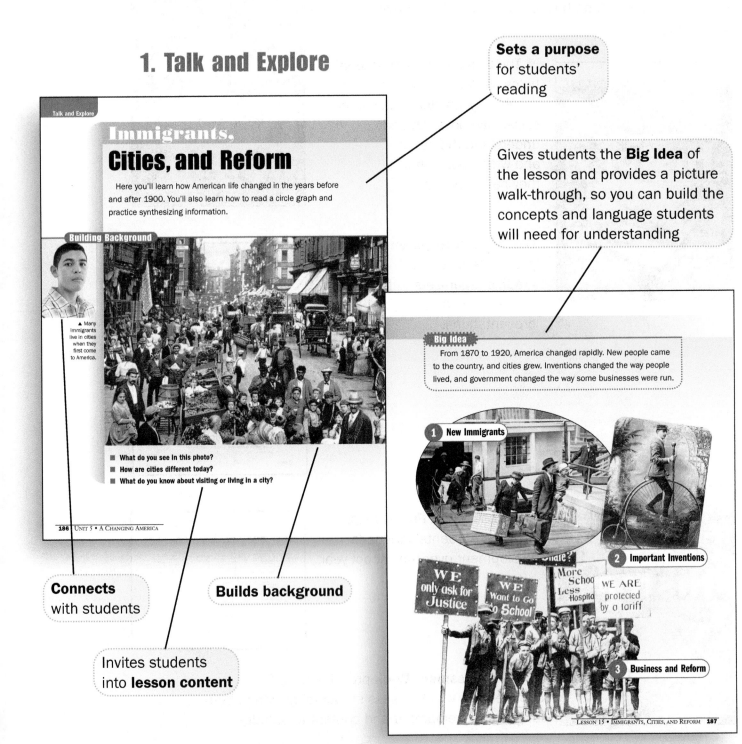

Connects with students

Builds background

Invites students into **lesson content**

Key Concepts

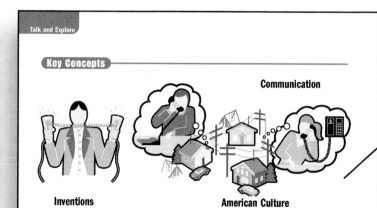

Inventions

Communication

American Culture

Inventions are new things created out of the imagination. The telephone was an invention that changed the way people exchanged news and ideas.

The telephone is one form of **communication.** Inventions in the late 1800s and early 1900s changed American **culture,** or way of life.

Introduces **Key Concepts** needed to understand the lesson

New York City, 1910

Statue of Liberty

Immigrants at Ellis Island

Streetcar

New Fashions

188 UNIT 5 • A CHANGING AMERICA

Includes a **visual aid** to preteach important background for the lesson

Teaches a **skill critical for** both understanding the lesson and for **success in school and on high-stakes tests**

Skill Building

Reading a Circle Graph

A circle graph lets you compare the sizes or importance of things. Circle graphs also are called *pie charts*, because their parts look like slices of a pie. Follow these steps to read a circle graph.

1. Read the title. It tells what the *whole circle* shows.

2. Study the key. This tells you what *each slice* shows.

3. Compare the *sizes* of the slices to each other.

This circle graph shows where immigrants came from between 1891 and 1900. A *homeland* is the land in which one is born. It is the country the people called home. Did more people come from Germany or from Asia?

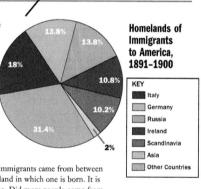

Homelands of Immigrants to America, 1891–1900

13.8%
13.8%
18%
10.8%
10.2%
31.4%
2%

KEY

- Italy
- Germany
- Russia
- Ireland
- Scandinavia
- Asia
- Other Countries

Workers on Strike

Baseball

City Slum

Subway

LESSON 15 • IMMIGRANTS, CITIES, AND REFORM **189**

2. Look and Read

Begins with a **note introducing the main ideas** of the lesson

Presents **standards-based content** in clear, easily managed chunks

Gives **Language Notes** in each lesson to clarify difficult aspects of English

Teaches **academic vocabulary and important everyday words** at the bottom of each page

Focuses on **standards-based content**

Look and Read

Immigrants, Cities, and Reform

Millions of new immigrants came to America between 1870 and 1920. Cities and industry grew. Inventions changed the American way of life. Problems and reforms came with the growth.

A New Wave of Immigration

At the turn of the century, a new **wave** of **immigrants** flooded into America. Earlier in the 19th **century**, most immigrants came from Western Europe. Now most immigrants came from Eastern Europe. They came from such countries as Italy, Russia, and Poland. Other immigrants came from Asia.

ENTERING THE COUNTRY

Immigrants from Europe most often entered the country at New York Harbor. The Statue of Liberty was their first view of America. It seemed to promise what they had come for—freedom and a better life. After landing, **newcomers registered** with the U.S. government at Ellis Island. Immigrants from Asia usually entered the country at Angel Island, in San Francisco Bay. At both these **inspection stations**, newcomers had to show their papers and pass certain tests before they could enter the United States.

▲ These young Polish women carry all they have in cloth bags as they enter America.

Language Notes

Idioms
These sayings don't mean what they seem.

☐ turn of the century: the years near the end of one century and the beginning of the next

☐ fit in: become American; look and act like everyone else

VOCABULARY

wave—a movement of many people coming in, like an ocean
immigrants—people who come into a country to live. The coming in of people is called *immigration*.
century—100 years. The 1800s were the 19th century. We live in the 21st century.
newcomers—people who have just come into a place
registered—signed or filled out a record
inspection stations—places where people are inspected—looked over—to be sure they meet the rules

190 UNIT 5 • A CHANGING AMERICA

THE NEW LIFE IN AMERICAN CITIES

After immigrants passed the inspection, they tried to fit in with American life. It was not easy to be a newcomer. At first, immigrants lived near others from their **homeland**. Many lived in crowded buildings without light and fresh air. **Neighborhoods** full of these buildings were called **slums**.

Immigrants helped **industry** in America grow. In their homelands, many people had farmed. Here they worked in factories. Some Americans feared that immigrants would take their jobs. Fears led to **prejudice**, and in the 1920s, new laws were passed against immigration. The laws ended most immigration to America for many years.

▲ Many immigrants live in poor homes when they first come to America.

◀ Jane Addams comforts immigrant children who come to Hull House.

TALK AND SHARE With your partner, talk about what it was like to come to America in the early 1900s.

VOCABULARY

homeland—land where a person is born; the country a people call home
neighborhoods—areas in a city
slums—the crowded, dirty parts of a city where buildings are old and need repairs and the people are poor
industry—the business of making and selling goods
prejudice—bad and unfair ideas about people based on a group they belong to
horrified—shocked

People in History

Jane Addams

Jane Addams was an American hero. She grew up rich. As an adult, she visited the slums of Chicago. She saw broken-down buildings, crowded apartments, and sick and hungry children. Addams was **horrified!** She bought a house, called Hull House, and set it up to help poor people. Addams brought in nurses to care for the sick. She started classes in English, reading, and music. She set up playgrounds for children. Addams said, "We were asked to wash the newborn babies, and to prepare the dead for burial, to nurse the sick, and to mind the children."

LESSON 15 • IMMIGRANTS, CITIES, AND REFORM 191

REFORMS FOR BIG BUSINESS

Big business caused big problems, but at first the government did nothing. Government leaders believed in a **policy** called **laissez-faire**. This term is French, meaning "let people do what they want."

Then, in 1901, Theodore Roosevelt became president. He started to **regulate** big business. Other presidents had supported owners against the strikers. But Roosevelt made business owners **negotiate** with striking workers. He also worked for new labor laws. Some of these laws made monopolies **illegal**. The big companies had to break up by selling off parts of their business. Other laws raised the pay of workers and lowered the number of hours they had to work. Slowly, **reforms** helped make the American workplace better.

▲ President Theodore Roosevelt

What opinion of Roosevelt does this cartoon show? ▼

TALK AND SHARE With your partner, use the vocabulary words on these two pages to talk about big business and the reforms.

VOCABULARY

big business—the group of large businesses that controlled their industries in the late 1800s and 1900s
policy—a plan that a government makes for the actions it takes
laissez-faire—an economic policy in which the government doesn't make rules about business
regulate—control by giving rules
negotiate—talk in order to settle a conflict
illegal—against the law. It was a crime to have a monopoly.
reforms—changes for the better

Summary

America went through many changes from 1870 to the start of the 1900s. Millions of new immigrants came. New inventions were made. Cities became big, and so did businesses. Then President Theodore Roosevelt brought reform.

LESSON 15 • IMMIGRANTS, CITIES, AND REFORM **195**

Look and Read

Problems and Reform

By the turn of the century, American business began to boom. In time, however, some businesses got too big.

BIG BUSINESS

In the late 1800s, some businesses grew to become **monopolies.** John D. Rockefeller set up the Standard Oil Company. It controlled the whole oil **industry.** Smaller oil companies had to be part of Standard Oil or they were forced out of business. Andrew Carnegie did the same thing in the steel industry. These monopolies ended all **competition.** Buyers had to pay whatever the monopolies charged. There was no one else to buy from.

Standard Oil is a giant octopus crushing other businesses. What opinion about Standard Oil does the cartoon show? ▶

▲ A union leader talks to striking workers.

THE RISE OF UNIONS

As businesses became larger and larger, workers often suffered. The **unions** that began earlier in the century got stronger. Workers **went on strike** more and more often, and many strikes became violent.

▲ Children work long hours in factories.

VOCABULARY

monopolies—businesses that completely control the making and selling of a product
industry—all the companies in a business
competition—the contest between businesses to "win" buyers for their goods
unions—groups of workers who join together to make owners change things
went on strike—stopped working. A strike is a group action taken to make a business owner change things.

194 UNIT 5 • A CHANGING AMERICA

3. Develop Language

Teaches students skills they need to achieve **communicative proficiency** and to produce authentic language

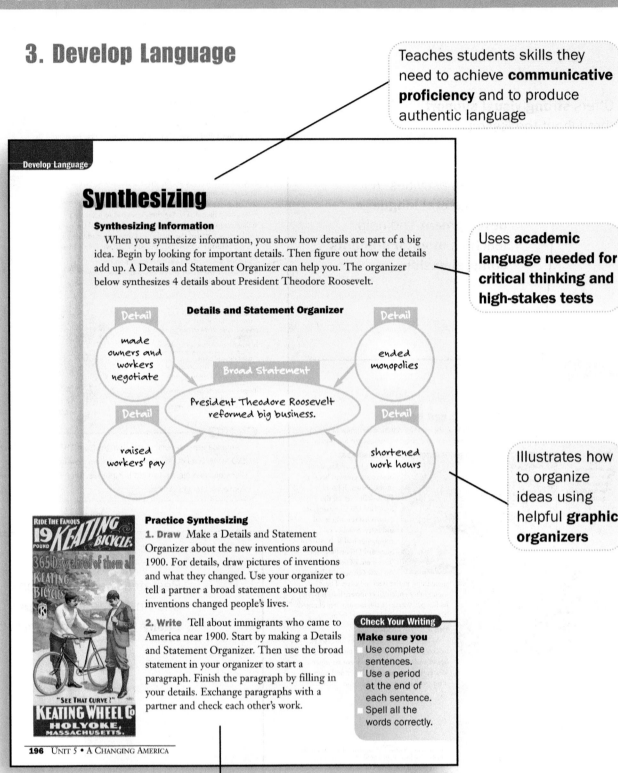

Develop Language

Synthesizing

Synthesizing Information

When you synthesize information, you show how details are part of a big idea. Begin by looking for important details. Then figure out how the details add up. A Details and Statement Organizer can help you. The organizer below synthesizes 4 details about President Theodore Roosevelt.

Details and Statement Organizer

Detail: made owners and workers negotiate

Detail: ended monopolies

Broad Statement: President Theodore Roosevelt reformed big business.

Detail: raised workers' pay

Detail: shortened work hours

Uses **academic language needed for critical thinking and high-stakes tests**

Illustrates how to organize ideas using helpful **graphic organizers**

RIDE THE FAMOUS
19 POUND KEATING BICYCLE.
365 Days ahead of them all
KEATING BICYCLES
"SEE THAT CURVE?"
KEATING WHEEL C.
HOLYOKE, MASSACHUSETTS.

Practice Synthesizing

1. Draw Make a Details and Statement Organizer about the new inventions around 1900. For details, draw pictures of inventions and what they changed. Use your organizer to tell a partner a broad statement about how inventions changed people's lives.

2. Write Tell about immigrants who came to America near 1900. Start by making a Details and Statement Organizer. Then use the broad statement in your organizer to start a paragraph. Finish the paragraph by filling in your details. Exchange paragraphs with a partner and check each other's work.

Check Your Writing

Make sure you
- Use complete sentences.
- Use a period at the end of each sentence.
- Spell all the words correctly.

196   Unit 5 • A Changing America

Differentiates activities for beginning and intermediate/advanced English language learners

Provides activities that build **language development** and give students the opportunity to practice new skills together

Highlights a different aspect of English in each lesson through **Grammar Spotlights**

Oral Language activities build communication skills.

Activities

Grammar Spotlight

Word Order Many English sentences put words in a certain order. The chart shows you examples.

Word Order

Subject ➤ Verb	Subject ➤ Verb ➤ Object
Immigrants came.	*Roosevelt* made *reforms*.
Many *businesses* grew.	*Rockefeller* set up *the Standard Oil Company*.

Write a sentence using these words: *invented   Bell   telephone*.

Partner Practice

On Strike! Imagine that you and your partner are workers on strike in 1900. Make signs. Tell the changes you need at work. List the demands you will make to the business owners.

Oral Language

Show You Know Make a card for each of these words: *immigrants, neighborhood, homeland, slums, prejudice, change*. Turn the cards face down and mix them up. Pick one. Take turns with a partner. Say a sentence using the word. Then your partner picks up a card and says a different sentence using your word *and* the new word. Put those two cards away. Do it again for the next two cards. Then do it again for the last two cards.

Hands On

Graph It With a partner or in a small group, collect information about where the students in your class come from. Then show your data in a circle graph. Give your graph a title. Use a key to show what places the colors stand for. Put the actual percentages inside the parts of the graph.

LESSON 15 • IMMIGRANTS, CITIES, AND REFORM **197**

Practicing with a partner is a safe way to try out English, and students get much-needed practice.

Hands On activities engage students through interactive practice.

Teacher's Edition Features

The Teacher's Edition provides page-by-page support for planning and instruction.

Standards drive each lesson.

Reviews previously taught concepts

Provides suggestions for **differentiating instruction** for students with different levels of language proficiency

Engages students in meaningful ways through **student activities**

Integrates other **Great Source resources** for further reference

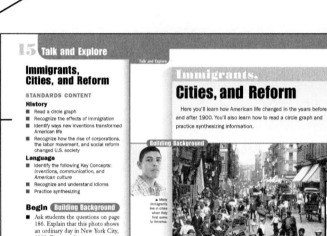

15 Talk and Explore

Immigrants, Cities, and Reform

STANDARDS CONTENT

History
- Read a circle graph
- Recognize the effects of immigration
- Identify ways new inventions transformed American life
- Recognize how the rise of corporations, the labor movement, and social reform changed U.S. society

Language
- Identify the following Key Concepts: inventions, communication, and American culture
- Recognize and understand idioms
- Practice synthesizing

Begin Building Background
- Ask students the questions on page 186. Explain that this photo shows an ordinary day in New York City, 1900. Focus students on:
  - The people's clothing, belongings, and activities
  - Differences and similarities with life today
- Encourage students to share their experiences of cities. Provide students with words as needed (*streets, homes, buildings, busy, marketplace*). Draw out key ideas:
  - Cities often are home to new immigrants.
  - Cities are places where people of different backgrounds can meet.

Activity: City Mural

Have students use markers, paints, or cutout photographs to create a mural showing an American city scene today. Students should decide together where to place buildings, people, and streets. Then have students use sticky notes or index cards to label important parts of the mural. Encourage them to use words and phrases such as *sidewalk, office building, driver, streetlight,* and *store*. Compare the mural to the picture on page 186.

Differentiating Instruction

Beginning
Object Search Focus on building word-picture associations. Have students work in pairs. One student names an object or color in the picture. The second student locates it. Then the two switch roles.

Intermediate
Sentences Have students work in pairs to create three sentences that tell about the picture. They may describe the people or objects they see or tell what the picture makes them think

about. Then have students share their sentences with the class.

Advanced
Describe and Guess Have students work in pairs. One student uses three to five sentences to describe an object in the picture to his or her partner without actually naming it. The partner guesses the object, using the form *Is it a _____?* Then the two switch roles.

186   Unit 5 • A Changing America

Immigrants, Cities, and Reform

Here you'll learn how American life changed in the years before and after 1900. You'll also learn how to read a circle graph and practice synthesizing information.

Building Background

▲ Many immigrants live in cities when they first come to America

- What do you see in this photo?
- How are cities different today?
- What do you know about visiting or living in a city?

186   UNIT 5 • A CHANGING AMERICA

Big Idea

From 1870 to 1920, America changed rapidly. New people came to the country, and cities grew. Inventions changed the way people lived, and government changed the way some businesses were run.

1 New Immigrants

2 Important Inventions

3 Business and Reform

WE only ask for Justice
WE Want to Go to School
More School Less Hospital
WE ARE protected by a tariff

LESSON 15 • IMMIGRANTS, CITIES, AND REFORM   187

Introduce the Big Idea
- Read aloud the Big Idea on page 187.
- Then call students' attention to the three headings listed on the page. Explain that the years around the turn of the century were full of big changes. Immigrants changed the population of the United States. Inventions changed the way people worked and lived. And reforms changed the ways that businesses could operate.
- Have students look carefully at the pictures on the page and form small groups to discuss what they see.

Review

In Lesson 14, students learned about life on farms. Have students compare the images of the Great Plains on pages 176–177 to the images in this lesson. Ask students how life might have been different at the time for children on a Kansas farm and in New York City.

Activity: Changes Chart

Make a Two-column Chart on a bulletin board. Label the left-hand column *Once* and the right-hand column *Now.* Draw a very simple sketch of a baby in the *Once* column and a sketch of an adult in the *Now* column. Say, *Once I was a baby, and now I am a grown-up.*

Invite volunteers to add their own sketches to the chart. They should use a similar format to describe their drawings to the class. Possible sentences include:

- Once I lived in a town, and now I live in a city.
- Once I had a pet dog, and now I have two pet dogs.
- Once I hated to eat eggs, and now I love to eat them.

Write some of these sentences for everyone to see. Point out that these sentences show changes. The chart shows changes in students' own lives; the lesson discusses the changes in American life around 1900. Encourage students to add to the chart throughout the lesson.

Resource Library

Reader's Handbook (red)
Pie Chart 558

Reader's Handbook (yellow)
Circle Graph 427

All Write
Pie Graph 282

Lesson 15 • Immigrants, Cities, and Reform   187

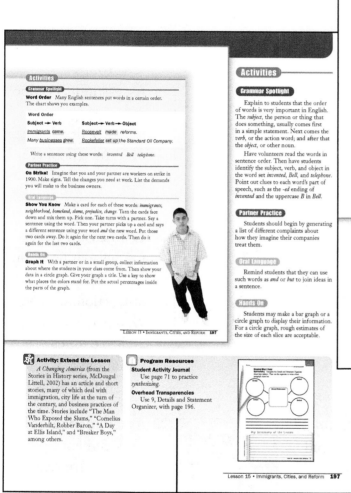

REFORMS FOR BIG BUSINESS

Big business caused big problems, but at first the government did nothing. Government leaders believed in a **policy** called **laissez-faire**. This term is French, meaning "let people do what they want."

Then, in 1901, Theodore Roosevelt became president. He started to **regulate** big business. Other presidents had supported owners against the strikers. But Roosevelt made business owners **negotiate** with striking workers. He also worked for new labor laws. Some of these laws made monopolies **illegal**. The big companies had to break up by selling off parts of their business. Other laws raised the pay of workers and lowered the number of hours they had to work. Slowly, **reforms** helped make the American workplace better.

▲ President Theodore Roosevelt

What opinion of Roosevelt does this cartoon show? ▼

(TALK AND SHARE) With your partner, use the vocabulary words on these two pages to talk about big business and the reforms.

VOCABULARY
big business—the group of large businesses that controlled their industries in the late 1800s and 1900s
policy—a plan that a government makes for the actions it takes
laissez-faire—an economic policy in which the government doesn't make rules about business
regulate—control by giving rules
negotiate—talk in order to settle a conflict
illegal—against the law. It was a crime to have a monopoly.
reforms—changes for the better

Summary

America went through many changes from 1870 to the start of the 1900s. Millions of new immigrants came. New inventions were made. Cities became big, and so did businesses. Then President Theodore Roosevelt brought reform.

LESSON 15 • IMMIGRANTS, CITIES, AND REFORM **195**

Teach About Reforms for Big Business

■ Have students preview the heading and pictures on this page. Ask them what they think will happen to big business.

■ After students finish reading, ask, *What did Roosevelt do to improve the country's business problems?*

(TALK AND SHARE)

Have students work in pairs to discuss the topic. You can use students' responses to check their comprehension of pages 194 and 195.

Discuss the **Summary**

Have a volunteer read the Summary at the end of the lesson while students follow along. Then return to the Big Idea on page 187. Have students state the connections between the Summary and the Big Idea.

☑ Assessment

Assess students' comprehension by asking the following questions:

History
• What were three big changes in the United States at the turn of the century?
• Why did immigrants come to the United States during this time?
• What were some important inventions from 1870–1920?
• What problems did big businesses create? What were Roosevelt's solutions?

Language
Which word does not belong?
• Immigrant, newcomer, homeland, monopoly
• Neighborhood, city, policy, slums
• Union, prejudice, strike, negotiate

Assessment Book
Use page 33 to assess students' comprehension.

Lesson 15 • Immigrants, Cities, and Reform **195**

Activities

Grammar Spotlight

Word Order Many English sentences put words in a certain order. The chart shows you examples.

Word Order

Subject → Verb	Subject → Verb → Object
Immigrants came.	*Roosevelt* made *reforms*.
Many *businesses* grew.	*Rockefeller* set up the Standard Oil Company.

Write a sentence using these words: *invented Bell telephone*.

Partner Practice

On Strike! Imagine that you and your partner are workers on strike in 1900. Make signs. Tell the changes you need at work. List the demands you will make to the business owners.

Oral Language

Show You Know Make a card for each of these words: *immigrants, neighborhood, homeland, slums, prejudice, change.* Turn the cards face down and mix them up. Pick one. Take turns with a partner. Say a sentence using the word. Then your partner picks up a card and says a different sentence using your word *and* the new word. Put those two cards away. Do it again for the next two cards. Then do it again for the last two cards.

Hands On

Graph It With a partner or in a small group, collect information about where the students in your class come from. Then show your data in a circle graph. Give your graph a title. Use a key to show what places the colors stand for. Put the actual percentages inside the parts of the graph.

LESSON 15 • IMMIGRANTS, CITIES, AND REFORM **197**

Activities

Grammar Spotlight

Explain to students that the order of words is very important in English. The *subject*, the person or thing that does something, usually comes first in a simple statement. Next comes the *verb*, or the action word; and after that the *object*, or other noun.

Have volunteers read the words in sentence order. Then have students identify the subject, verb, and object in the word set *invented*, *Bell*, and *telephone*. Point out clues to each word's part of speech, such as the *-ed* ending of *invented* and the uppercase *B* in *Bell*.

Partner Practice

Students should begin by generating a list of different complaints about how they imagine their companies treat them.

Oral Language

Remind students that they can use such words as *and* or *but* to join ideas in a sentence.

Hands On

Students may make a bar graph or a circle graph to display their information. For a circle graph, rough estimates of the size of each slice are acceptable.

🧑 Activity: Extend the Lesson

A Changing America (from the Stories in History series, McDougal Littell, 2002) has an article and short stories, many of which deal with immigration, city life at the turn of the century, and business practices of the time. Stories include "The Man Who Exposed the Slums," "Cornelius Vanderbilt, Robber Baron," "A Day at Ellis Island," and "Breaker Boys," among others.

☐ Program Resources

Student Activity Journal
Use page 71 to practice *synthesizing*.

Overhead Transparencies
Use 9, Details and Statement Organizer, with page 196.

Lesson 15 • Immigrants, Cities, and Reform **197**

> Gives teachers helpful **tools for assessing student progress**

> References relevant exercises in the **Student Activity Journal** for additional practice

ACCESS Newcomers

ACCESS Newcomers is a multi-level program for beginning English language learners. The program offers three progressive stages: Starting Out, Getting Ready, and School Readiness, plus an introductory Readiness unit for those newcomers who arrive with little educational background.

ACCESS Newcomers introduces 2,160 high-frequency vocabulary words, including important academic terms that will get students ready for their content-area subjects. The program includes:

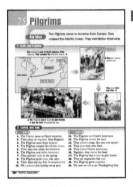

■ **320-page Pupil's Edition** for whole-class instruction

■ **Assessment Folder** for tracking students' language development over the school year

■ **Word Tiles** for hands-on learning

■ **120 Lesson Cards** for pull-out programs and small-group instruction. *Overhead Transparencies* are available for each lesson card.

■ **CD of additional resources,** including printable Word Tiles, Sentence Strips, and take-home activities

■ **Assessment Book** to document student progress

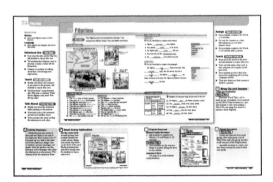

■ **Teacher's Edition** with a four-step lesson plan for giving students practice listening, speaking, reading, and writing vocabulary words in sentence contexts. Additional activities develop students' understanding of English.

Differentiating Instruction

A typical classroom of English language learners includes students at varying levels of language proficiency. ACCESS helps teachers differentiate their instruction to meet these different students' needs. In each of the three lesson parts—Talk and Explore, Look and Read, and Develop Language—you can support your students, as the chart below shows. In addition, teaching notes on every two-page spread give specific activity suggestions for Differentiating Instruction. You can also use the *Assessment Folder* to track students' progress over the course of the year.

Language Proficiency	Talk and Explore	Look and Read	Develop Language
Beginning An effective teaching method for beginning students is to pair them with more proficient partners or with partners who speak the same first language.	Build background by naming objects in the introductory picture. Write key words on the board. Read aloud and have students repeat with you.	Use the introductory paragraph, heads, picture captions, and summaries to help students get a broad overview of the lesson.	Invite students to draw and pantomime to show what they know. Encourage one-word and short-phrase responses.
Intermediate To facilitate learning for intermediate students, you may want to change student partners and form small groups with different combinations of students.	Build background with the picture and encourage students to draw on their own experiences, using short sentences, pantomiming, and labeling to show what they know.	Have students use headings and picture captions to predict what they will learn. Encourage note-taking and K-W-L Charts. Let partners help each other. Over time, raise your expectations for language use.	Relate lesson content to academic expectations in other classes, in assignments, and on tests. Assign the Write activity. Work gradually through lists and numbered sentences to complete paragraph responses.
Advanced At times, pair advanced students together to help them challenge each other.	Build background through a discussion of the picture and how it introduces key ideas of the lesson. Use the questions to stimulate a class or group discussion.	Help students use reading skills, such as predicting, finding main ideas, and comparing and contrasting. Expect silent reading, but check comprehension through the Talk and Share activities.	Encourage written responses. Ask that role-plays be scripted. Help students write descriptive, persuasive, and explanatory paragraphs.

Best Practices for English Language Learners

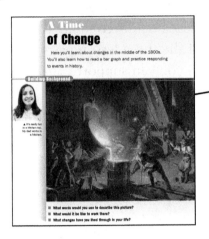

1. An introductory photo helps students connect to the lesson and build language.

2. A Big Idea is taught in every lesson.

Big Idea

From 1870 to 1920, America changed rapidly. New people came to the country, and cities grew. Inventions changed the way people lived, and government changed the way some businesses were run.

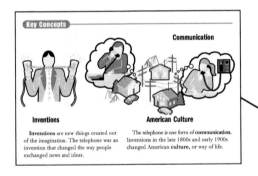

3. Key Concepts establish academic vocabulary and break down the fundamental concepts of each lesson.

4. Content is continuously reinforced by strong visual presentation.

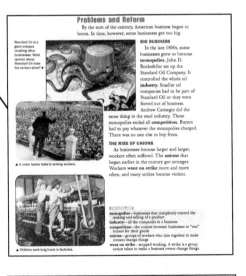

5. Talk and Share activities promote oral language development and help teachers monitor comprehension.

TALK AND SHARE With your partner, talk about what it was like to come to America in the early 1900s.

VOCABULARY

wave—a movement of many people coming in, like an ocean
immigrants—people who come into a country to live. The coming in of people is called *immigration*.
century—100 years. The 1800s were the 19th century. We live in the 21st century.
newcomers—people who have just come into a place
registered—signed or filled out a record
inspection stations—places where people are inspected—looked over—to be sure they meet the rules

6. Vocabulary support is given throughout each lesson and in a comprehensive glossary.

Language Notes

Idioms
These sayings don't mean what they seem.

- **turn of the century:** the years near the end of one century and the beginning of the next
- **fit in:** become American; look and act like everyone else

7. Language Notes teach and help clarify difficult aspects of the English language.

8. Develop Language activities build students' communicative abilities and academic vocabulary for high-stakes tests.

9. Ongoing, consistent instruction in grammar helps students make progress in understanding English.

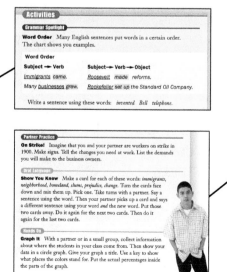

10. Activities promote oral communication and increase the amount of time students are producing and practicing language.

ACCESS gives English language learners the tools they need to develop literacy and build content knowledge in all their school subjects.

Lesson Pacing

ACCESS gives teachers two options for pacing.

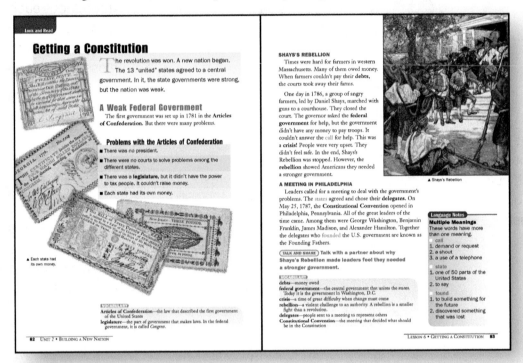

One-year Course

1. The program can be taught in one school year by covering each lesson in one and a half weeks. To complete ACCESS in one year, cover *two pages every day*.

Two-year Course

2. The program can be taught over two school years by covering one lesson every three weeks. To complete ACCESS in two years, move at the pace of *one page per day*.

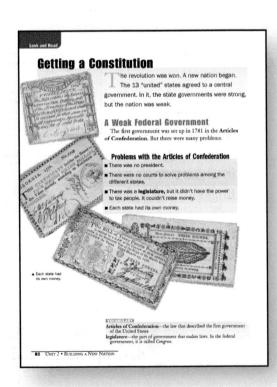

Frequently Asked Questions About ACCESS

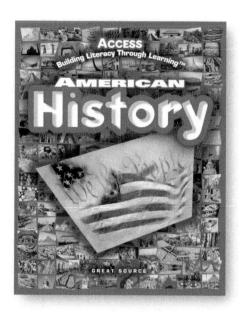

Q: How can ACCESS work for all my English language learners?
A: ACCESS can work for many levels of learners because it targets intermediate and advanced students, and offers *Newcomers* for beginners. ACCESS is also a great resource for students who are transitioning from ESL programs into mainstream classes but who need sheltered content instruction.

Q: How does ACCESS compare to our basal text?
A: ACCESS shelters the content of the subject. It covers the topics and standards of a content area, but with about 10% of the words of other texts. Students need to read texts that are on their reading level. They need comprehensible text, as opposed to frustrating tomes that have considerably more information and complexity than they can currently handle. ACCESS gives ESL students access, or an entry point, making content ACCESSible.

Q: I'm a history teacher. Do you mean, with ACCESS, that I now have to teach language too?
A: ACCESS helps you as a teacher make history more ACCESSible to students by explaining key events in terms and images they can understand. This saves you time and helps you to teach more effectively.

Q: How can ACCESS help my students with little or no educational background?
A: *ACCESS Newcomers* has a readiness unit that covers the basics, such as the alphabet, addition and subtraction, colors, countries of the world, places in America, and other fundamentals. The three levels in *ACCESS Newcomers* become gradually more sophisticated as students are challenged to accelerate their learning and transition to the next proficiency level.

Q: How does ACCESS prepare my students for high-stakes tests and help me show annual yearly progress?
A: ACCESS is a standards-based program. It teaches the language and skills integral to test-taking as well as the standards-based content on the tests themselves. ACCESS gives students the academic language required to understand school assignments and teacher explanations and models how to produce written responses for success.

Lesson	Big Idea
Lesson 1: The First Americans	The first people who settled North America lived in many different regions. They used the resources in each place to create different ways of life.
Lesson 2: European Exploration	Europeans were looking for new trade routes to Asia during the 1400s. Christopher Columbus sailed west and landed in North America instead. Soon, other European explorers followed. They claimed lands for their kings. The Native Americans suffered.
Lesson 3: The Thirteen Colonies	England set up colonies to get American resources. English people came for a better life. People from Africa were brought as slaves. These early years helped shape the way the United States is today.
Lesson 4: Steps to the American Revolution	The colonists grew angry at British rule. Finally, the colonies declared independence from Britain.
Lesson 5: The American Revolution	During the American Revolution, colonial troops fought the British army. Help came from Europe. The colonists won the war, and the United States became a new nation.
Lesson 6: Getting a Constitution	At first, the new government was weak. A meeting was called to plan a stronger government. After a long debate, the Constitution was written. Then the states voted it into law.
Lesson 7: The New Nation	The first presidents gave the United States government a new shape, much more land, and a way of working with other countries.
Lesson 8: Moving West	Around 1800, many Americans began moving to the West. New technology made travel easier. Settlers formed new states. Some new states allowed slavery; others did not.
Lesson 9: The Age of Jackson	Andrew Jackson became president in 1829. Troubles between the North and South grew stronger. More settlers moved to the Far West, and the government forced Native Americans to leave their homelands.
Lesson 10: A Time of Change	After 1830, more Americans began to work in factories. Northern cities grew as people from other countries moved in. Reformers worked to free slaves and gain more rights for women.
Lesson 11: Two New States	Texas and California became states in the mid-1800s. Both areas had once been part of Mexico. A war with Mexico gave land to the United States. Gold was discovered in California. Angry debates about slavery led to a new compromise.
Lesson 12: Seven Years to Civil War	Laws about slavery made problems between the North and the South grow worse and worse. People began killing each other. Then Abraham Lincoln was elected president, and the South left the Union.

Skill Building	Language Notes	Develop Language	Grammar Spotlight
Reading a Chart	Signal Words: Compare/Contrast	Comparing	Comparative Adjectives
Using a Map Key	Multiple Meanings	Identifying Reasons	Prepositions of Time: On, In, At
Reading a Timeline	Homophones	Describing	Simple Past Tense
Cause and Effect	Signal Words: Cause-Effect	Explaining	Irregular Verbs in the Past Tense
Chronological Order	Signal Words: Time Order	Interpreting	Plurals
Evaluating Internet Sources	Multiple Meanings	Synthesizing	Articles
Facts and Opinions	Verb Phrases	Persuading	Subject Pronouns
Reading a Map	Idioms	Evaluating	Object Pronouns
Reading a Timeline	Signal Words: Time Order	Summarizing	Placement of Adjectives
Reading a Bar Graph	Idioms	Responding	Adverbs
Recognizing Cause and Effect	Idioms	Analyzing	Questions with Where, When, and Why
Taking Notes	Multiple Meanings	Interpreting	Using Same and Different

Scope and Sequence of *ACCESS History*

Lesson	Big Idea
Lesson 13: The Civil War	From 1861 to 1865, Americans fought Americans in the Civil War. At the end of the war, the Union was saved, but both sides suffered huge losses, and the South was destroyed.
Lesson 14: After the Civil War	After the Civil War, slavery ended. Former slaves became citizens. At first, African Americans in the South gained power in government. In time, they lost many of their early gains. Many Americans moved west to the Great Plains to start new lives.
Lesson 15: Immigrants, Cities, and Reform	From 1870 to 1920, America changed rapidly. New people came to the country, and cities grew. Inventions changed the way people lived, and government changed the way some businesses were run.
Lesson 16: Becoming a World Power	In the early 1900s, the United States became a world power. It got new lands and used its power to increase its trade.
Lesson 17: Good Times and Bad Times	The United States helped to win World War I, and good times followed. Then the economy crashed. Life was very hard for most Americans, so the government began to help people.
Lesson 18: Fighting World War II	From 1941 to 1945, Americans helped fight and win World War II. The war was fought to stop the spread of empires in Europe and in Asia. It showed how cruel prejudice can be and how deadly atomic weapons are.
Lesson 19: The Cold War	During the Cold War, the Soviet Union controlled half of Europe. Communism spread into countries in Asia. The United States worked with other nations to stop the spread of communism.
Lesson 20: Getting Equality	In the mid-1900s, African Americans across the country began a struggle for equality. Soon other groups began fighting for their civil rights too.
Lesson 21: Into the 21st Century	As the 21st century began, the world changed even faster. New groups threatened world peace. New powers rose based on economic strength, and businesses worked to create a global economy.
Lesson 22: The United States Constitution	The Constitution lays out the plan for the government of the United States. It reflects basic principles and describes 3 branches of government. It also provides checks on the power of government and gives ways to balance power among the different parts of government.
Lesson 23: The Bill of Rights	The Bill of Rights is the first 10 amendments to the U.S. Constitution. It protects freedoms and guarantees rights to all who live in the United States.
Lesson 24: Responsible Citizenship	For the United States to stay strong and free, its citizens must do their duty and meet their responsibilities.

Skill Building	Language Notes	Develop Language	Grammar Spotlight
Reading Primary Sources	Idioms	Comparing	Using *and*, *or*, and *but*
Reading Political Cartoons	Confusing Word Pairs	Explaining	Possessive Nouns
Reading a Circle Graph	Idioms	Synthesizing	Word Order
Recognizing Chronological Order	Verb Phrases	Identifying	Compound Sentences
Analyzing Propaganda	Homophones	Summarizing	Telling How Much
Finding Primary Sources on the Internet	Multiple Meanings	Evaluating	*This*, *That*, *These*, and *Those*
Telling Facts and Opinions Apart	Verb Phrases	Comparing	Comparative Adverbs
Finding Causes in History	Confusing Word Pairs	Explaining	Infinitives
Reading Double Bar Graphs	Figurative Language	Interpreting	Phrases with *Who* and *That*
Taking Notes	Multiple Meanings	Paraphrasing	Passive Verbs
Reading Newspapers Critically	Homophones	Explaining	Clauses with *Because* and *Although*
Separating Fact from Opinion	Multiple Meanings	Persuading	Verbs with *Can*

Lesson	National History Standards
Introduction: Geography, A Key to History	**1:** How to use maps and other geographic representations, tools, and technologies to acquire, process, and report information from a spatial perspective
Lesson 1: The First Americans	**1.1:** Comparative characteristics of societies in the Americas, Western Europe, and Western Africa that increasingly interacted after 1450
	1: How to use maps and other geographic representations, tools, and technologies to acquire, process, and report information from a spatial perspective
Lesson 2: European Exploration	**1.1:** Comparative characteristics of societies in the Americas, Western Europe, and Western Africa that increasingly interacted after 1450
	1.2: How early European exploration and colonization resulted in cultural and ecological interactions among previously unconnected peoples
	2.1: Why the Americas attracted Europeans, why they brought enslaved Africans to their colonies, and how Europeans struggled for control of North America and the Caribbean
	1: How to use maps and other geographic representations, tools, and technologies to acquire, process, and report information from a spatial perspective
Lesson 3: The Thirteen Colonies	**2.1:** Why the Americas attracted Europeans, why they brought enslaved Africans to their colonies, and how Europeans struggled for control of North America and the Caribbean
	2.2: How political, religious, and social institutions emerged in the English colonies
	2.3: How the values and institutions of European economic life took root in the colonies, and how slavery reshaped European and African life in the Americas
	1: How to use maps and other geographic representations, tools, and technologies to acquire, process, and report information from a spatial perspective
Lesson 4: Steps to the American Revolution	**3.1:** The causes of the American Revolution, the ideas and interests involved in forging the revolutionary movement, and the reasons for the American victory
Lesson 5: The American Revolution	**3.1:** The causes of the American Revolution, the ideas and interests involved in forging the revolutionary movement, and the reasons for the American victory
	1: How to use maps and other geographic representations, tools, and technologies to acquire, process, and report information from a spatial perspective
Lesson 6: Getting a Constitution	**3.2:** The impact of the American Revolution on politics, economy, and society
	3.3: The institutions and practices of government created during the Revolution and how they were revised between 1787 and 1815 to create the foundation of the American political system based on the U.S. Constitution and the Bill of Rights
Lesson 7: The New Nation	**3.3:** The institutions and practices of government created during the Revolution and how they were revised between 1787 and 1815 to create the foundation of the American political system based on the U.S. Constitution and the Bill of Rights
	4.1: United States territorial expansion between 1801 and 1861, and how it affected relations with external powers and Native Americans
	1: How to use maps and other geographic representations, tools, and technologies to acquire, process, and report information from a spatial perspective
Lesson 8: Moving West	**4.2:** How the industrial revolution, increasing immigration, the rapid expansion of slavery, and the westward movement changed the lives of Americans and led toward regional tensions
	1: How to use maps and other geographic representations, tools, and technologies to acquire, process, and report information from a spatial perspective
Lesson 9: The Age of Jackson	**4.1:** United States territorial expansion between 1801 and 1861, and how it affected relations with external powers and Native Americans
	4.2: How the industrial revolution, increasing immigration, the rapid expansion of slavery, and the westward movement changed the lives of Americans and led toward regional tensions
	1: How to use maps and other geographic representations, tools, and technologies to acquire, process, and report information from a spatial perspective
Lesson 10: A Time of Change	**4.2:** How the industrial revolution, increasing immigration, the rapid expansion of slavery, and the westward movement changed the lives of Americans and led toward regional tensions
	4.4: The sources and character of cultural, religious, and social reform movements in the antebellum period

All standards

1.1 Social interactions, **1.2** Personal expression, **1.3** Extend communicative competence, **2.1** Interact in classroom, **2.2** Provide subject matter information, **2.3** Apply academic knowledge, **3.2** Use nonverbal communication, **3.3** Extend sociolinguistic competence

1.1 Social interactions, **1.3** Extend communicative competence, **2.1** Interact in classroom, **2.2** Provide subject matter information, **2.3** Apply academic knowledge, **3.2** Use nonverbal communication, **3.3** Extend sociolinguistic competence

1.1 Social interactions, **1.3** Extend communicative competence, **2.1** Interact in classroom, **2.2** Provide subject matter information, **2.3** Apply academic knowledge, **3.2** Use nonverbal communication, **3.3** Extend sociolinguistic competence

1.1 Social interactions, **1.2** Personal expression, **1.3** Extend communicative competence, **2.1** Interact in classroom, **2.2** Provide subject matter information, **2.3** Apply academic knowledge, **3.2** Use nonverbal communication, **3.3** Extend sociolinguistic competence

1.1 Social interactions, **1.3** Extend communicative competence, **2.1** Interact in classroom, **2.2** Provide subject matter information, **2.3** Apply academic knowledge, **3.2** Use nonverbal communication, **3.3** Extend sociolinguistic competence

1.1 Social interactions, **1.2** Personal expression, **1.3** Extend communicative competence, **2.1** Interact in classroom, **2.2** Provide subject matter information, **2.3** Apply academic knowledge, **3.2** Use nonverbal communication, **3.3** Extend sociolinguistic competence

1.1 Social interactions, **1.3** Extend communicative competence, **2.1** Interact in classroom, **2.2** Provide subject matter information, **2.3** Apply academic knowledge, **3.2** Use nonverbal communication, **3.3** Extend sociolinguistic competence

1.1 Social interactions, **1.3** Extend communicative competence, **2.1** Interact in classroom, **2.2** Provide subject matter information, **2.3** Apply academic knowledge, **3.1** Use appropriate language, **3.2** Use nonverbal communication, **3.3** Extend sociolinguistic competence

1.1 Social interactions, **1.3** Extend communicative competence, **2.1** Interact in classroom, **2.2** Provide subject matter information, **2.3** Apply academic knowledge, **3.2** Use nonverbal communication, **3.3** Extend sociolinguistic competence

1.1 Social interactions, **1.3** Extend communicative competence, **2.1** Interact in classroom, **2.2** Provide subject matter information, **2.3** Apply academic knowledge, **3.1** Use appropriate language, **3.2** Use nonverbal communication, **3.3** Extend sociolinguistic competence

Lesson	National History Standards
Lesson 11: Two New States	**4.2:** How the industrial revolution, increasing immigration, the rapid expansion of slavery, and the westward movement changed the lives of Americans and led toward regional tensions **1:** How to use maps and other geographic representations, tools, and technologies to acquire, process, and report information from a spatial perspective
Lesson 12: Seven Years to Civil War	**4.2:** How the industrial revolution, increasing immigration, the rapid expansion of slavery, and the westward movement changed the lives of Americans and led toward regional tensions **5.1:** The causes of the Civil War **1:** How to use maps and other geographic representations, tools, and technologies to acquire, process, and report information from a spatial perspective
Lesson 13: The Civil War	**5.2:** The course and character of the Civil War and its effects on the American people **1:** How to use maps and other geographic representations, tools, and technologies to acquire, process, and report information from a spatial perspective
Lesson 14: After the Civil War	**5.3:** How various reconstruction plans succeeded or failed
Lesson 15: Immigrants, Cities, and Reform	**6.1:** How the rise of corporations, heavy industry, and mechanized farming transformed the American people **6.2:** Massive immigration after 1870 and how new social patterns, conflicts, and ideas of national unity developed amid growing cultural diversity **6.3:** The rise of the American labor movement and how political issues reflected social and economic changes **7.1:** How Progressives and others addressed problems of industrial capitalism, urbanization, and political corruption
Lesson 16: Becoming a World Power	**7.2:** The changing role of the United States in world affairs through World War I **1:** How to use maps and other geographic representations, tools, and technologies to acquire, process, and report information from a spatial perspective.
Lesson 17: Good Times and Bad Times	**7.3:** How the United States changed from the end of World War I to the eve of the Great Depression **8.1:** The causes of the Great Depression and how it affected American society **8.2:** How the New Deal addressed the Great Depression, transformed American federalism, and initiated the welfare state **1:** How to use maps and other geographic representations, tools, and technologies to acquire, process, and report information from a spatial perspective
Lesson 18: World War II	**8.3:** The causes and course of World War II, the character of the war at home and abroad, and its reshaping of the U.S. role in world affairs **1:** How to use maps and other geographic representations, tools, and technologies to acquire, process, and report information from a spatial perspective.
Lesson 19: The Cold War	**9.2:** How the Cold War and conflicts in Korea and Vietnam influenced domestic and international politics **1:** How to use maps and other geographic representations, tools, and technologies to acquire, process, and report information from a spatial perspective.
Lesson 20: Getting Equality	**9.4:** The struggle for racial and gender equality and the extension of civil liberties
Lesson 21: Into the 21st Century	**10.1:** Recent developments in foreign and domestic politics **10.2:** Economic, social, and cultural developments in the contemporary United States
Lesson 22: The U.S. Constitution	**NSCG II.A.1:** The essential ideas of American constitutional government **NSCG II.D.1:** The meaning and importance of the fundamental values and principles of American constitutional democracy **NSCG III.A.1:** How the powers of the national government are distributed, shared, and limited
Lesson 23: The Bill of Rights	**NSCG III.E.3:** Judicial protection of individual rights **NSCG V.B.1:** Issues involving personal rights
Lesson 24: Responsible Citizenship	**NSCG II.B.16:** The importance of voluntarism in American society **NSCG V.A.1:** The meaning of American citizenship **NSCG V.A.3:** How one becomes a citizen of the United States **NSCG V.C.1, 3:** The importance of personal and civic responsibilities to the individual and to society

1.1 Social interactions, **1.3** Extend communicative competence, **2.1** Interact in classroom, **2.2** Provide subject matter information, **2.3** Apply academic knowledge, **3.1** Use appropriate language, **3.2** Use nonverbal communication, **3.3** Extend sociolinguistic competence

1.1 Social interactions, **1.3** Extend communicative competence, **2.1** Interact in classroom, **2.2** Provide subject matter information, **2.3** Apply academic knowledge, **3.2** Use nonverbal communication, **3.3** Extend sociolinguistic competence

All standards

1.1 Social interactions, **1.3** Extend communicative competence, **2.1** Interact in classroom, **2.2** Provide subject matter information, **2.3** Apply academic knowledge, **3.1** Use appropriate language, **3.2** Use nonverbal communication, **3.3** Extend sociolinguistic competence

1.1 Social interactions, **1.3** Extend communicative competence, **2.1** Interact in classroom, **2.2** Provide subject matter information, **2.3** Apply academic knowledge, **3.1** Use appropriate language, **3.2** Use nonverbal communication, **3.3** Extend sociolinguistic competence

1.1 Social interactions, **1.3** Extend communicative competence, **2.1** Interact in classroom, **2.2** Provide subject matter information, **2.3** Apply academic knowledge, **3.1** Use appropriate language, **3.2** Use nonverbal communication, **3.3** Extend sociolinguistic competence

1.1 Social interactions, **1.3** Extend communicative competence, **2.1** Interact in classroom, **2.2** Provide subject matter information, **2.3** Apply academic knowledge, **3.2** Use nonverbal communication, **3.3** Extend sociolinguistic competence

1.1 Social interactions, **1.2** Personal expression, **1.3** Extend communicative competence, **2.1** Interact in classroom, **2.2** Provide subject matter information, **2.3** Apply academic knowledge, **3.2** Use nonverbal communication, **3.3** Extend sociolinguistic competence

1.1 Social interactions, **1.3** Extend communicative competence, **2.1** Interact in classroom, **2.2** Provide subject matter information, **2.3** Apply academic knowledge, **3.2** Use nonverbal communication, **3.3** Extend sociolinguistic competence

1.1 Social interactions, **1.3** Extend communicative competence, **2.1** Interact in classroom, **2.2** Provide subject matter information, Apply academic knowledge, **3.2** Use nonverbal communication, **3.3** Extend sociolinguistic competence

1.1 Social interactions, **1.3** Extend communicative competence, **2.1** Interact in classroom, **2.2** Provide subject matter information, **2.3** Apply academic knowledge, **3.1** Use appropriate language, **3.2** Use nonverbal communication, **3.3** Extend sociolinguistic competence

1.1 Social interactions, **1.3** Extend communicative competence, **2.1** Interact in classroom, **2.2** Provide subject matter information, **2.3** Apply academic knowledge, **3.2** Use nonverbal communication, **3.3** Extend sociolinguistic competence

1.1 Social interactions, **1.2** Personal expression, **1.3** Extend communicative competence, **2.1** Interact in classroom, **2.2** Provide subject matter information, **2.3** Apply academic knowledge, **3.2** Use nonverbal communication, **3.3** Extend sociolinguistic competence

1.1 Social interactions, **1.2** Personal expression, **1.3** Extend communicative competence, **2.1** Interact in classroom, **2.2** Provide subject matter information, **2.3** Apply academic knowledge, **3.2** Use nonverbal communication, **3.3** Extend sociolinguistic competence

Introduction
and
Lessons 1–24

Geography,
A Key to History

STANDARDS CONTENT
Geography
- Read maps to acquire, process, and report information
- Describe physical and human characteristics of the United States
- Recognize the location and characteristics of places and regions of the United States

Language
- Recognize terms related to map reading
- Recognize terms related to geography

Begin `Building Background`

- As an opening activity, have students preview pages 12–15. Post the following Preview Checklist on the board:

  Preview Checklist
  - Titles and headings
  - Words in boldface
  - Labels and captions
  - Map keys and colors

- Then ask students to follow along as you read aloud the introduction. Have a volunteer restate the introduction in his or her own words. Ask:
  - What do you think you will learn from reading this introduction?
  - How can this introduction help you get ready to read history?

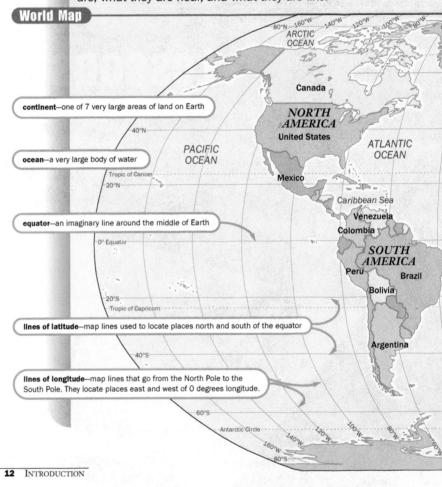

Geography
A Key to History

Everything that happened in history happened somewhere. You can understand history better when you know where the places are, what they are near, and what they are like.

World Map

continent—one of 7 very large areas of land on Earth

ocean—a very large body of water

equator—an imaginary line around the middle of Earth

lines of latitude—map lines used to locate places north and south of the equator

lines of longitude—map lines that go from the North Pole to the South Pole. They locate places east and west of 0 degrees longitude.

ARCTIC OCEAN

Canada

NORTH AMERICA

United States

PACIFIC OCEAN

ATLANTIC OCEAN

Mexico

Caribbean Sea

Venezuela

Colombia

SOUTH AMERICA

Peru

Brazil

Bolivia

Argentina

Tropic of Cancer

Equator

Tropic of Capricorn

Antarctic Circle

12 INTRODUCTION

 Activity: Write Mnemonics

Ask small groups of students to write a mnemonic that can help them remember the names of the seven continents. Begin with the model *Eat An Aspirin After A Nighttime Snack.* Point out the correlation between the first letter or letters of each word and the names of the seven continents: Europe, Antarctica, Asia, Africa, Australia, North America, and South America. Then ask students to write their own mnemonic for the seven continents.

 Differentiating Instruction

Beginning
Names of Places Focus students whose English proficiency is limited on the English names for major areas of the world, such as oceans, continents, and countries of importance to students. Speak slowly and give students time to repeat after you and to each other.

Intermediate
Pair Practice Have partners point to places on the map and identify them in

a sentence. Suggest patterns such as *This is. . . . Jorge comes from. . . .*

Advanced
Memory Test Invite students to close the book and tell a partner as many countries on a continent as they can.

Reading a World Map

A world map is a drawing of the earth. The boxes on these two pages tell you about major parts of the world and how to read a world map.

Teach Reading a World Map

■ Explain that learning key geography terms (*latitude, longitude, equator,* and so on) will make it easier for students to read maps.

- Point out the latitude lines on the world map. Tell the class that latitude runs *flat.* Then have them hold their arms straight out from their sides and say, *Latitude is flat.*

- Next, point to the longitudinal lines. Tell the class that longitude runs up and down, or *long.* Have them hold their hands straight up in the air and say, *Longitude is long.*

■ Then have students look at the world map in its entirety. Invite volunteers to point out continents, bodies of water, and the directional coordinates north, south, east, and west.

Teach the Inset

Direct students' attention to the inset at the bottom of the page. Help them understand that a map inset gives a detailed view of, or specific information about, a particular area.

Have students study the inset of Europe. Which countries have they heard about? Encourage students to share their knowledge.

Activity: Chart a Region

Divide the class into groups. Assign an area of the world to each group.

Students in the group brainstorm facts about their area. A group secretary can list the group's facts on the chart. Then groups take turns explaining their charts to the class.

Our area: _____

Location	Languages	Food

Activity: People Endings

Write these word endings on the board: *-ans, -ians, -eans, -ese.* Tell students that the English names for the people of a place usually add one of these endings to the place name. Offer *China/Chinese,* and *America/Americans* as examples. Using places students choose, help them complete a chart. Invite volunteers to write the name of the people in the appropriate column.

Program Resources
Student Activity Journal

Assign pages 6–7 to practice using a world map.

Teach America's Land Regions

■ Explain the purpose of a physical map: *A physical map shows the elevation (height) of land compared to sea level. It also shows land features.* Ask students to point to features such as mountains and bodies of water (e.g., oceans, lakes, and rivers).

■ Have students look over the entire map. Point out the main parts: title, key, labels, and scale.

■ Work with the class to draw conclusions about this map. Ask questions such as *Is the eastern or the western part of the country more mountainous?*

Teach the Map Key

■ Point out the map key. Explain that it tells what a map's symbols or colors mean.

■ Have students note that this map key tells them they can use color to figure out the elevation (height) of different areas of the country.

■ To give students practice using the key, call out various sea levels in no particular order—e.g., *700–3,000 feet above sea level.* Have students point to one or more corresponding areas of the country.

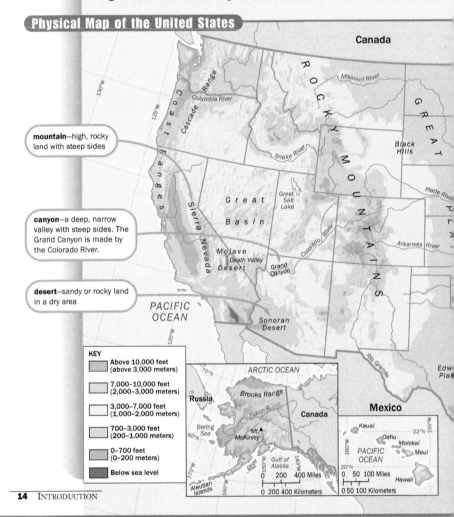

America's Land Regions

A physical map shows the natural regions of a land, such as its mountains and deserts. A physical region is a place that has many things in common. Each region has its own climate, or weather pattern.

Physical Map of the United States

mountain—high, rocky land with steep sides

canyon—a deep, narrow valley with steep sides. The Grand Canyon is made by the Colorado River.

desert—sandy or rocky land in a dry area

KEY
- Above 10,000 feet (above 3,000 meters)
- 7,000–10,000 feet (2,000–3,000 meters)
- 3,000–7,000 feet (1,000–2,000 meters)
- 700–3,000 feet (200–1,000 meters)
- 0–700 feet (0–200 meters)
- Below sea level

14 INTRODUCTION

 Activity: Scavenger Hunt

As a class, locate the compass rose and scale. Have students tell the purpose of each. Then test their ability to use these two map features by asking them to find the following:

- A mountain range west of the Great Basin
- The name of a plain east of the Missouri River
- A desert in the southwestern part of the United States
- The approximate length, in miles, of the Ohio River

 Differentiating Instruction

Beginning
Reading Numbers Direct students' attention to the key. Slowly read aloud the first number shown: *10,000.* Then work with students to say aloud the following numbers: *7,000, 3,000, 700,* and *0; 2,000, 1,000, 200.*

Intermediate
Number Line Create a number line on the board that is marked off in thousands from 0 to 12,000. Work with students to say each number: *1,000, 2,000, 3,000,* and so on. Then

repeat the activity with a new number line that is marked off in hundreds from 0 to 900.

Advanced
Answering Questions Test students' comprehension of the material by asking:

- How high are the Rocky Mountains?
- How high are the Great Plains?
- What region of the country is below sea level?

For example, in the Great Plains, it rains enough for grasses and crops like wheat and corn to grow. But it does not rain enough for forests to grow.

Canada

Lake Superior

Lake Huron

Lake Michigan

L. Ontario

Lake Erie

Mississippi River

Central Plains

Ohio River

Tennessee River

APPALACHIAN MOUNTAINS

Cape Cod

Long Island

Chesapeake Bay

Cape Hatteras

Atlantic Coastal Plain

ATLANTIC OCEAN

Gulf Coastal Plain

Gulf of Mexico

Lake Okeechobee

Cuba

45°N

60°W

40°N

65°W

35°N

30°N

70°W

75°W

25°N

80°W

85°W

90°W

lake—a body of water surrounded by land

plain—an area of flat, grassy land

river—a large stream of water that runs through the land to another body of water

coast—land at the edge of an ocean

compass rose—a map symbol showing the directions north, east, south, and west

plateau—a flat highland

0   200   400 Miles
0   200   400 Kilometers

scale—lets you measure distances on the map

Teach Key Terms

Say the following terms aloud: *mountain, canyon, desert, lake, plain, river, coast, compass rose, plateau,* and *scale.* Have students raise one hand if they have heard the term before, and two hands if they have heard the term and can tell what it means. Have volunteers define the words.

Then walk students through the labels on the page. Have them note the boldfaced words and their definitions.

Have students use the map to tell about the geographical features of their own region of the country.

Teach the Inset

Direct students' attention to the insets. Explain that Alaska and Hawaii are both states but that they are shown differently. Ask students if they can guess why. (*Both states are out of the range shown on the map.*)

 Activity: Measure Distance

Demonstrate how to use a scrap of paper to measure distance on a map. Line up the paper to the scale on page 15 and draw a notch that corresponds with the 400-mile mark. Then take your paper and show how to measure the distance between two points on the map.

Have students practice the technique. Ask them to measure how far they live from a certain geographical feature, such as the Gulf of Mexico.

 **Activity: Visualize a Landform**

Ask students to choose a landform of interest and visualize what it looks like. Have them draw a picture placing themselves in the middle of the landform (*on top of a mountain,* for example, or *in a boat on a lake*). When they finish, ask them to label their landform. Share students' drawings with the class.

Program Resources

Student Activity Journal

Assign pages 8–9 to practice using a physical map.

Teach The 50 States

- Discuss the differences between a physical and a political map. Tell the class that a political map shows human-made divisions of countries or regions.

- Have students look at this map of the United States. Ask them to trace with their fingers the boundary lines of their state.

- Remind students that a physical region has things such as climate and land features in common. People create a way of life that is compatible with their region.

- Connect the discussion to students' own lives by asking them to name physical features of their homelands. How do people in their homeland use the features of the region?

Teach the Map Key

Point out that the map key is different from the one on page 14. Students should know that map keys are map-specific. Then examine the key on page 16 together. Explain why regions are named the way they are. For example, the Mid-Atlantic region is called that because it is located in the middle of the Atlantic Coast. See if students can figure out the name *Midwest*.

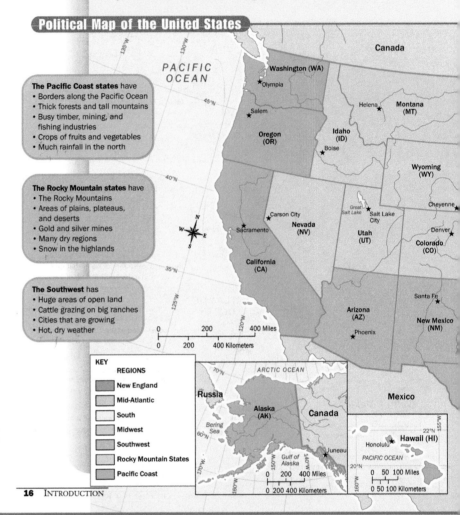

The 50 States

A political map shows countries and states. It also shows capital cities. This is a political map of the United States. The notes below tell you about America's 7 regions.

Political Map of the United States

The Pacific Coast states have
- Borders along the Pacific Ocean
- Thick forests and tall mountains
- Busy timber, mining, and fishing industries
- Crops of fruits and vegetables
- Much rainfall in the north

The Rocky Mountain states have
- The Rocky Mountains
- Areas of plains, plateaus, and deserts
- Gold and silver mines
- Many dry regions
- Snow in the highlands

The Southwest has
- Huge areas of open land
- Cattle grazing on big ranches
- Cities that are growing
- Hot, dry weather

KEY

REGIONS
- New England
- Mid-Atlantic
- South
- Midwest
- Southwest
- Rocky Mountain States
- Pacific Coast

16 INTRODUCTION

 Activity: Team Teach

Divide the class into seven teams. Assign one region of the country to each team. Then have team members work together to memorize the states in their regions, as well as each state's capital. Later, teams can get together and teach each other about their region.

 Differentiating Instruction

Beginning
Pronouncing Words Identify state and capital names that students have a hard time pronouncing and teach them syllabically: /mi-ZOOR-ee/, /PEN-sill-VANE-ya/, /de-MOYNE/.

Intermediate
State Borders Give small groups lists of four states, and ask them to say and then write all of the states that border their assigned states.

Advanced
Lesson Summary On their own, students can list three things they learned from this lesson. Then ask them to get together with a group to share. Ask groups:
- What's the hardest thing about reading maps?
- What's the easiest?

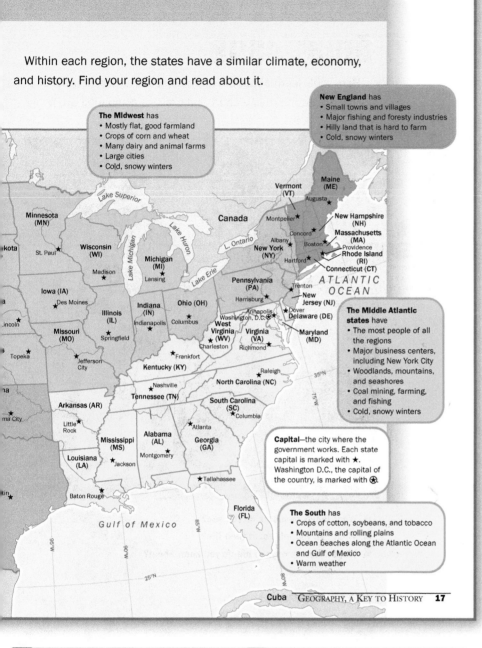

Within each region, the states have a similar climate, economy, and history. Find your region and read about it.

The Midwest has
- Mostly flat, good farmland
- Crops of corn and wheat
- Many dairy and animal farms
- Large cities
- Cold, snowy winters

New England has
- Small towns and villages
- Major fishing and foresty industries
- Hilly land that is hard to farm
- Cold, snowy winters

The Middle Atlantic states have
- The most people of all the regions
- Major business centers, including New York City
- Woodlands, mountains, and seashores
- Coal mining, farming, and fishing
- Cold, snowy winters

Capital—the city where the government works. Each state capital is marked with ★. Washington D.C., the capital of the country, is marked with ⊛.

The South has
- Crops of cotton, soybeans, and tobacco
- Mountains and rolling plains
- Ocean beaches along the Atlantic Ocean and Gulf of Mexico
- Warm weather

GEOGRAPHY, A KEY TO HISTORY   **17**

Teach Key Terms

■ Walk students through the labels on pages 16 and 17. Read aloud each region name, along with its description.

■ Have students make some notes in their history notebooks. Encourage them to take notes in the form of a chart such as the following:

Region	Climate	Land features
New England	cold and snowy	harbors hilly land

■ Remind students of the importance of taking good notes as they read.

Teach the Inset

Have students compare the inset on page 16 with the one on page 14. Then work with the class to use the insets to help them compare the two states. Create a Venn Diagram and have students help you fill out the three sections. Use Overhead Transparency 31, Venn Diagram.

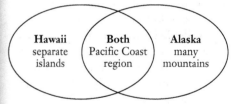

Hawaii
separate islands

Both
Pacific Coast
region

Alaska
many mountains

 Activity: Create a Continent

Have pairs of students create a brand-new continent. First, they should discuss where the continent would be located on the world map. Next, they need to figure out physical features that are in keeping with its location. (*For example, a continent located on the equator would not be covered in ice.*) After that, students can draw political boundaries and place capital cities. When they finish, students can cut out their continents and tape them on the board for the whole class to see.

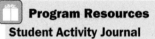 **Activity: Landform Art**

On a sheet of paper, list four landforms: *canyon, river, mountain,* and *desert.* Ask students to sketch what each landform looks like and then write words that describe it. Invite students who are having trouble completing the activity to visit the following Internet site on landforms: http://www.enchantedlearning.com/geography/landforms/glossary.shtml.

Program Resources
Student Activity Journal

Assign pages 10–11 to practice using a political map.

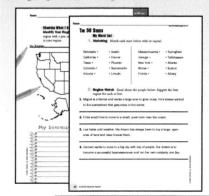

The First Americans

STANDARDS CONTENT

History

■ Read and interpret charts

■ Identify the Native Americans as the first people in the Americas

■ Recognize how Native Americans used the resources of their region to develop their cultures

■ Recognize the differences among Native Americans in the West and the East

Language

■ Identify the following Key Concepts: *resources, region,* and *culture*

■ Recognize words that signal compare-contrast relationships

■ Practice comparing

Begin Building Background

■ Ask students, *Why do we call Native Americans the first Americans?*

■ Ask students the questions under the picture.

  • Invite students to share what they know about Native Americans.

  • Help them talk about details in the photo.

■ Focus students on the special ways people do things with the resources available in different regions. Have a volunteer read aloud the caption below the girl's picture. Ask how they think the family in the picture got and made the following:

  • Clothing • Food
  • Shelter • Tools

The First
Americans

Here you'll learn about the first people in North America. You'll also learn how to read a chart and practice comparing two things.

Building Background

▲ Our family has its own special ways of doing things.

■ **What family members do you see?**

■ **What can you tell about their life?**

■ **What different ways of life do you know about?**

 Activity: Understanding Pictures

Write the words *Native Americans* on an 8½" x 11" sheet. Ask students to name words that tell about the photo. Try to generate such words as *family, beads, blanket, shirt, dress, clothes, mother, father,* and *child.* Have students write the words on index cards and tape them to the wall under *Native Americans.*

Differentiating Instruction

Beginning

Building Associations To build word-picture associations, write the following words on the board: *Native American, clothing, weapon, fur, feathers, made by hand, made from animals.* Ask students to copy the words on sticky notes. Then have them take turns placing the sticky notes where they apply on the picture on page 18, saying each word or phrase aloud.

Intermediate

Asking Questions Have students work in pairs to create two questions about the picture. The questions should start with *who, when, where,* or *what.* Have students exchange and answer each other's questions.

Advanced

Answering Questions Have advanced learners work in pairs to write answers to each question under the picture. Have them write in complete sentences.

1 Settling the Continent

2 Using Resources

3 Ways of Life in the East

4 Ways of Life in the West

Introduce the Big Idea

■ Read aloud the Big Idea and the labels on the four pictures.

■ Use the pictures to encourage a conversation about the different ways of life developed in the different regions. Begin by asking students to tell what they see.

■ Point to the pictures numbered *1, 3,* and *4.* To focus students on the skill of comparing, ask if the houses they see are *similar* or *different.*

■ Ask, *Why do you think Native Americans in different places have different ways of life?*

■ On the board, write these terms:
  • Native Americans
  • American Indians

Tell students that the first Americans are often referred to as *Native Americans* because *native* means *first* or *original.* The people are also called *American Indians.*

Review

Have students look at the map of North America on pages 16–17. Have them point out different regions on the map. Ask them to match the pictures on page 19 to the regions on the map. Ask, *What can you tell about each region from the map and the picture?*

 ## Activity: Three-column Chart

Divide the class into four groups. Assign each group one of the pictures illustrating the Big Idea. To start, have students fold a paper into three columns and label them with the words *who, what,* and *where.*

As guides, write the following prompts on the board:

  • Who are the people?
  • What is happening?
  • Where did they get their things?

Then ask students to "investigate" their picture for clues and write their findings in the appropriate column. Afterward, invite each group to share its findings with the class.

Ask each group to tell how the culture represented in its picture is similar to or different from the cultures in other groups' pictures.

 ### Resource Library

Reader's Handbook (red)
Reading History 66–83

Reader's Handbook (yellow)
Reading Social Studies 58–73

All Write
Reading Tables 283

Teach ⬤Key Concepts

- Pronounce each Key Concept slowly. Have students repeat each word after you.

- Point to the three pictures in turn, asking students to name the details. Then read aloud the Key Concept sentences. Help students connect the relationships among the concepts.

- Ask students to point to places on the map on pages 14–15 where fishing may have been part of Native American life (e.g., *along the seacoasts, lakes,* and *rivers*).

Teach the Visual Aid
⬤American Indian Cultures

Focus students on the gallery of photos across pages 20–21 and help them pronounce the name of each tribe. Invite students to name *resources, regions,* and signs of *culture* that they can see in the pictures—for example, the Iroquois used the timber resources of their northern woodland region to build this house. Encourage students to explore the pictures and talk about what they see.

⬤Key Concepts

Resources
Resources are all the things in a place that people use to help them live.

Region
A **region** is an area of land where many things are the same.

Culture
Groups of people use the resources of the region they live in to develop their **culture,** or way of life.

⬤American Indian Cultures

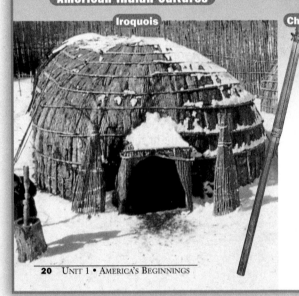

Iroquois   Choctaw   Mound Builders

20   UNIT 1 • AMERICA'S BEGINNINGS

🎭 **Activity: Native American Web**

Create a sample Web on the board with the heading *Native American Groups.* Divide the class into small groups. Have them study the pictures in the visual aid and list one clue from each picture that tells something about the group's culture.

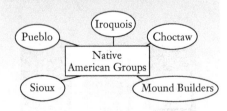

Differentiating Instruction

Beginning
Drawing Pictures Have students work with partners to draw a picture of the region where they live. Have them include at least one resource and show some part of their culture. They can then write labels for their pictures.

Intermediate
Writing Sentences Have pairs use each Key Concept word in a sentence that describes one of the photos above. Ask the pairs to write each sentence on

a sticky note and place it below the appropriate picture as a caption.

Advanced
Writing Captions Ask students to work in pairs to create a caption for each of the photos above. Each caption should include the name of the Native American culture and at least one Key Concept.

Skill Building

Reading a Chart

A chart gives you information. A chart has columns going down and rows going across. This chart has two columns and three rows. Here's how to read a chart.

1. Read the title.

2. Read the heads on the rows and columns.

3. Look down a column or across a row to find a piece of information. Use the heads as your guides.

Study this chart. How did the Plains Indians get food? How did the Pueblo Indians get food? How were their ways of getting food different?

COLUMN HEADS   TITLE

ROW HEADS

Indian Ways of Life

	Plains Indians	Pueblo Indians
HOUSING	Made tipis of buffalo skins	Built apartment houses of adobe
GETTING FOOD	Hunted buffalo, gathered berries, farmed vegetables	Farmed corn and beans, hunted animals such as deer
WHERE THEY LIVED	Moved to follow buffalo	Lived in permanent villages

ROW

COLUMN

Sioux   Pueblo Indians

LESSON 1 • THE FIRST AMERICANS   **21**

Teach   Skill Building

- Read with students the explanation and steps for reading a chart.

- Ask students to point out the following items: title, heads, rows, columns, information.

- Then demonstrate each step for students by using the sample chart to answer the first question.

- Show students how to do Step 3 by pointing to the head *Plains Indians* and running your finger down the chart to the row named *Getting Food*.

- Ask volunteers to demonstrate how to find the answers to the remaining questions.

Teach the Pictures

Tell students that the photographs were taken much later than when the Native Americans first settled. The camera was invented in the 1800s.

Sitting Bull, the Sioux chief pictured on the left, won a famous battle against the U.S. Army in 1876. (He beat General Custer in the Battle of Little Big Horn.) This photograph of Sitting Bull was taken nine years later.

Activity: Make a Culture Chart

Have students create the following Culture Chart to record key information as they progress through the lesson. They can fill out the organizers with words, pictures, or both.

Title: Native Americans

Column headings: Woodland, Plains, Southwest, Coasts

Rows: Housing, Food, Clothing, How They Got Food

Program Resources

Student Activity Journal

Use page 12 to build key vocabulary.

Use page 13 to practice reading a chart.

Overhead Transparencies

Use 33, Web, with page 20.

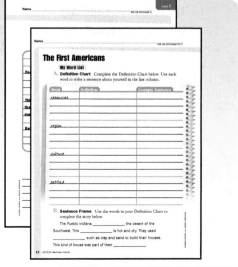

Introduce **The First Americans**

- ■ Ask students what they think they will learn from these two pages. Have them study the pictures and map and read the headings.

- ■ Have students preview the images from pages 22–27. Divide the class into groups of three or four. Have each group talk about a picture, describing what it shows about a tribe's culture or use of resources.

Key Connection: Geography

Write the following on the board and read it aloud with students:

- • **Woodlands**—land filled with trees
- • **Plains**—flat, grassy lands
- • **Desert Region**—dry land
- • **Coastal Region**—land along a body of water

Have students write each region on a sticky note and place notes on the map on this page. The map on pages 14–15 is a reference.

TALK AND SHARE

Ask, *Which Native American group lives near you?* Discuss how to find out more about the groups. Create a master list of research ideas and post it on the class bulletin board.

Look and Read

▲ Native Americans used sharp tools to clean animal skins.

The First Americans

American Indians were the first people in North America. They moved into different regions and developed many different ways of life.

Settling the Continent

American **Indians migrated** from Asia many thousands of years ago. At that time, land connected Asia and North America. America's first people crossed that land. They **settled** the **regions** of North America.

The regions gave the Native Americans **resources** for living. The foods in one region were not like those in others. The things for building homes were not the same. Across America, Native Americans developed different **cultures**.

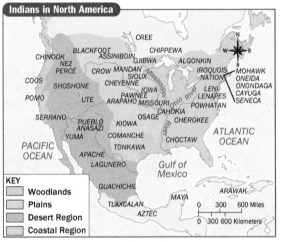

Indians in North America

KEY
- Woodlands
- Plains
- Desert Region
- Coastal Region

(TALK AND SHARE) Look at the map with your partner. Find the Native Americans who lived near where you live. Tell what you know about them. How can you find out more?

VOCABULARY

Indians—a name for the native people of the Americas; Native Americans

migrated—moved from one region to live in another

settled—moved into a place; made a home there

regions—areas of land where many things are the same

resources—things in a place that people use to help them live

cultures—ways of life. *Culture* includes language, foods, beliefs, and ways of doing things.

22 UNIT 1 • AMERICA'S BEGINNINGS

Activity: Teach Vocabulary

Have students work with the vocabulary on each page. Have them keep a word list journal. When possible, they should make Word Wheels.

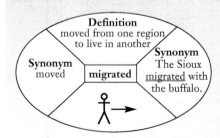

Differentiating Instruction

Beginning

Vocabulary Cards Have students work together to write vocabulary words on 3" x 5" cards. Place the vocabulary cards in a pile. Students take turns picking a card and finding a picture to match it in the lesson. If they cannot find a picture, they should act out the word or draw a picture of it.

Intermediate

Pantomime Have students play a pantomime game. In small groups, students take turns drawing vocabulary

cards and acting out their meanings. The group guesses the terms.

Advanced

Resource Paragraph In pairs, students plan a paragraph describing how they use resources in their area. City dwellers can think about parks or a nearby land or water body (*mountain, river*). Students can present their paragraph to the class.

Using Resources

In each region, Native Americans developed their own way of life with the resources of the place.

IN THE EAST

The East was covered with thick forests. The **Woodland Indians** who settled there hunted deer and rabbits for meat. They used animal fur and skins to make warm clothes to wear in winter. They gathered fruits, nuts, and berries. They grew foods in the forest. They cut trees and built houses made from wood. They lived in **permanent** villages.

IN THE GREAT PLAINS

In contrast, Native Americans who lived in the Great Plains hunted **buffalo** for food. **Plains Indians** lived in tipis made of buffalo skin. These tents were easier to move than houses made from wood. Plains Indians did not stay in villages. They moved, following the great buffalo herds.

IN THE SOUTHWEST

Native Americans who lived in the deserts of the Southwest had few trees. They could not build homes with wood. They made bricks out of clay and ate desert plants and animals.

ALONG THE COASTS

Native Americans who lived on the coasts fished in the ocean. They gathered clams and shrimp and hunted whales. They used shells for money.

(TALK AND SHARE) Talk to your partner about how life was different for Native Americans in the East and in the Southwest.

VOCABULARY

Woodland Indians—the Native Americans who lived in the forests east of the Mississippi River
permanent—lasting; not going away
buffalo—large animals like cattle; also called *bison*
Plains Indians—the Native Americans who lived in the flat parts of the western United States. The Great Plains are shown on the map on page 14.

▲ Northwest coastal Indians carved poles from trees and painted them. They are called *totem poles.*

Teach Using Resources

■ Help students understand how differences in resources resulted in Native Americans around the country forming different ways of life.

■ Explain to students that the locations of these resources—such as herds of buffalo or schools of fish along the coasts—influenced where the Native Americans lived.

■ Connect to students' lives. Ask students to talk about what they know about moving to find better resources for work and living.

(TALK AND SHARE)

Encourage pairs to refer to the Culture Charts they made for page 21, or ask volunteers to contribute to a class list that shows how the Native Americans of the Eastern Woodlands and those of the Southwest were different.

Review

Tell students to look at the map of the United States on pages 14–15. Ask them to point out where the East, Great Plains, Southwest, and Coastal Indian regions are on the map.

 Activity: Making a Map

Divide the class into groups. Give each group poster paper. Have students draw an outline of the United States and label each of the regions listed above. Tell students that they will be using the map throughout the lesson to show where Native American cultures lived.

 Program Resources

Student Activity Journal

Assign page 14:

• To create study notes for students to review

• To provide reinforcement of key vocabulary

Overhead Transparencies

Use 36, Word Wheel, with page 22.

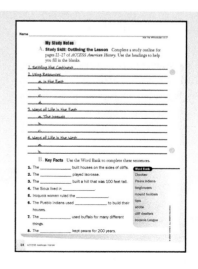

Discuss Ways of Life in the East

On a map of the United States, have students find the Mississippi River and notice how it divides the United States. Invite a volunteer to read aloud the first paragraph on page 24.

Before students read pages 24–25, have them preview the pictures and skim the heads to predict what they will learn. Ask students to share their predictions with the class.

Teach the Pictures

The longhouse on page 24 is made of tree bark. Native Americans in the East used trees from the region's many forests to build longhouses like this one.

A woodland tribe made the rattle pictured to the right by inserting pebbles into a turtle shell.

The illustration on page 25 depicts an artist's recreation of Cahokia buildings. None of the dwellings here have survived.

Look and Read

Ways of Life in the East

The Mississippi River divides the **continent.** Many Native American groups lived east of the river. They used the resources of the land to form their own ways of life.

▲ A longhouse had two doors but no windows.

THE IROQUOIS

The Iroquois were Woodland Indians. Five Iroquois tribes lived in what is now New York State. They were often at war with each other. Then a great leader told the people, "If we came together, we could be strong. Each tribe is like an arrow. No man can break a bundle of arrows." The 5 tribes joined together in the Iroquois League. The League worked to keep peace for more than 200 years.

The Iroquois built wooden **longhouses.** When a woman married, she and her husband moved into her mother's longhouse. More than 10 families could live in one longhouse. The men made peace and war. The women's work was different. They ruled the longhouse and owned most of the property of the group.

THE CHOCTAW

Like the Woodland Indians, the Choctaw Indians of the Southeast lived in the forest. Their life was similar in many ways. The men hunted deer and other animals in the forest. The women grew corn, beans, and squash. Both groups held **ceremonies** to celebrate their **harvests.**

Both groups liked team sports. One of their favorite games was a form of stickball known as "lacrosse." But the way they played the game was not the same. The Iroquois used a single racket or stick; the Choctaw used two rackets.

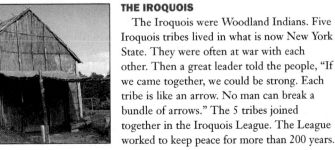

▲ Woodland Indians used rattles in some ceremonies.

VOCABULARY
continent—one of 7 large bodies of land. The continents are Africa, Antarctica, Asia, Australia, Europe, North America, and South America.
longhouses—long, wooden Iroquois houses
ceremonies—events held at a special time, such as when people marry or die or when a new leader is chosen
harvests—the gathering of food crops at the end of the growing seasons

---

Activity: Word Connect

Have students make word cards for the vocabulary words. Then have them lay out their word cards on their desks to look for relationships among them. Ask them to rearrange their words in columns that make sense.

Differentiating Instruction

Beginning
Choral Reading Ask students to do a choral reading with you of the title, introduction, and headings. Review the term *culture.* Then pair beginners with more fluent partners. Have them read a paragraph at a time and talk about what they learned from it. Have them look for information about Iroquois and Choctaw ways of life.

Intermediate
Paraphrasing Ask students to stop at the end of each section and paraphrase

what they just read to their partner. Encourage them to record key words and phrases in their history notebooks.

Advanced
Discovering Dekanawida The Iroquois leader described in paragraph two is Dekanawida. Invite students to use the library or Internet to find out more about him and report back to the class.

▲ Native Americans built the city of Cahokia without metal tools.

THE MOUND BUILDERS

Some Native American groups built giant mounds of earth in and around their towns. They became known as **mound builders.** One of these cultures built the city of Cahokia, near where the Missouri River flows into the Mississippi River. Around A.D. 1200, Cahokia had a **population** of about 20,000 people. They were farmers. Their fields were outside the city. They built a giant mound in the center of the city. It rose to a height of about 100 feet. At the top was a wooden **temple.** It may have taken workers as long as 200 years to build the mound.

(TALK AND SHARE) **Tell your partner how the cultures of the Iroquois and the Choctaw were similar. Make a list of 3 items.**

Language Notes

Signal Words: Compare/Contrast
These words point to ways things are alike and different.

- ☐ different
- ☐ not the same
- ☑ in contrast
- ☐ like
- ☐ same
- ☐ similar

VOCABULARY

mound builders—the Native American cultures of the Ohio and Mississippi Rivers. They built *mounds*, large hills made of earth.
population—all the people who live in an area
temple—a building for religious activities

LESSON 1 • THE FIRST AMERICANS   **25**

Talk About The Mound Builders

- ■ Cahokia is near St. Louis, Missouri. Have students locate it on a map.
- ■ Ask students to imagine that they had to build a city without power tools or metals:
  - • What would they use?
  - • How would they feel?
  - • How long would it take them to finish the job?

Language Notes

Read aloud the Language Notes with students. To demonstrate comparisons, show students two pens that are alike and describe them using the words *like, same,* and *similar.* Then hold up a pen and pencil, describing them with the words *not the same* and *different.* Examples of usage of the terms in the Language Notes appear in red in the lesson text.

TALK AND SHARE

Students who made Culture Charts can use them as they discuss the Talk and Share activity. Otherwise, ask volunteers to contribute to a class list on the board that shows how the Iroquois and the Choctaw were similar.

 Activity: Internet Resources

Have students do Internet research on Native American cultures. Have them work in pairs to locate one of the sites below and print one interesting picture and fact to share with the class:

- • **Iroquois**
  http://www.sixnations.org
- • **Choctaw**
  http://www.choctaw.org
- • **Cahokia**
  http://www.state.il.us/hpa/hs/ Mounds.htm

 Activity: History Notebook

Help students build a notebook for this lesson. The notebook should include items from the Student Activity Journal, pictures, lists, charts, and drawings they've made. Have them share their notebook with a partner.

Discuss Ways of Life in the West

■ Invite a volunteer to point out where the West is on a map of the United States.

■ Ask partners to talk together about what they think they will learn on these two pages.

■ Share with students that huge herds of buffalo once roamed the plains. At the beginning of the 1800s, there were still about sixty million buffalo in North America. By 1889, however, only about 800 remained.

Oral History

Use the feature on Chief Red Cloud to demonstrate the value of oral history. Explain that *oral* means *spoken* and that *oral history* is passed on by word of mouth.

- Tell students that many Native American cultures did not have written languages. They passed on their teachings and beliefs orally.

- Ask, *What stories about history has a family member told you?*

- The rest of the speech by Red Cloud, the Plains Indian quoted on page 26, appears on this website: http://www.unitedearth.com.au/redcloud.html.

Look and Read

Tools made from buffalo and elk bones ▶

▲ Buffalo with calf

Ways of Life in the West

The regions west of the Mississippi River had different resources. The people living in the West had ways of life that were different from those of the groups in the East.

THE SIOUX

The Sioux lived on the plains. They were one of the Plains Indian groups. Sioux men hunted buffalo. A good hunt provided enough meat to last for months. Sioux men and women made **tipis** and robes from buffalo skin. They made spoons and cups from buffalo horns. They made tools and **weapons** from buffalo bones and rope from buffalo hair.

Sioux women made tools and sewed the family's clothing. They cared for the children, carrying them on their backs as they worked. The women built the tipis and often decorated them with beautiful designs.

Both the buffalo and the sun were important in Sioux **religion.** The buffalo **herds** moved according to the **season.** As the Sioux followed the buffalo, they were following the sun. The Sioux believed they were helping to keep the world in order. Once a year, they held a Sun Dance to celebrate life.

VOCABULARY
tipis—tents
weapons—the tools of hunting and war, such as arrows and guns
religion—a belief in and worship of God or spirits
herds—large groups of one kind of animal
season—one of the 4 periods of the year: spring, summer, fall, or winter

Oral History

A Plains Indian described his religion this way.

"Hear me, for this is not the time to tell a lie. The great spirit made us, and gave us this land we live in. He gave us the buffalo, antelope, and deer for food and clothing. Our hunting grounds stretched from the Mississippi to the great mountains."

26 UNIT 1 • AMERICA'S BEGINNINGS

 Activity: Make a History Notebook

Have students research information about Sioux and Pueblo tribes. Ask students to include information and pictures in their history notebooks. They may use library books or the Internet. These websites have useful information:

- http://www.pbs.org/lewisandclark/native/index.html

- http://www.indianpueblo.org/intro/index.cfm

 Differentiating Instruction

Beginning
Finding Key Concepts Have students look at the pictures from the beginning of the lesson to page 28. Then have them connect the three Key Concepts (*resources, region, culture*) to as many pictures as they can.

Intermediate
Summarizing Divide the class into pairs. Have them read aloud the red and blue headings. Then have them give a summary to their partners using the words in the headings.

Advanced
Discussing Questions In a small group, have students discuss the following questions:

- In what regions did Native Americans settle?

- What kind of houses did the different tribes build?

- How do you think the geography of the different regions influenced Native Americans?

THE PUEBLO INDIANS

Some Southwest Indians were Pueblo Indians. *Pueblo* means "town" in Spanish. The first Pueblo people were the Anasazi. They built houses with many levels, like apartment buildings. They made them with **adobe** bricks. Adobe is a mix of clay and straw that is baked. By A.D. 1000, the Anasazi built their houses high on **canyon** walls. Here they were safe from their enemies. We call them **cliff dwellers.**

▲ These cliff houses had more than 150 rooms.

The Southwest is hot and dry. The Pueblo people were farmers. They planted near streams that ran through the dry desert land. There they raised corn, beans, and squash. Pueblo women made beautiful pottery and baskets. The Pueblo believed in Kachinas, or **spirits,** who had the power to bring rain.

(**TALK AND SHARE**) **Find a partner. Together make a chart with two columns. Label the two columns Sioux and Pueblo. Draw or write to show how each group used the resources of its region. Tell your partner what you learned.**

◀ Kachina doll

VOCABULARY
adobe—sun-dried brick made of clay and straw
canyon—a narrow valley with high steep sides and a stream at the bottom
cliff dwellers—Native Americans of the Southwest who built their houses on the sides of cliffs
spirits—supernatural beings. Angels are spirits.

Summary

Native Americans settled across America. In each region, the resources were different. The Native Americans developed different cultures.

Teach About The Pueblo Indians

Ask students to share what they know about the desert. Then tell them some Native Americans of the Southwest built towns there.

Next, invite pairs to take turns reading aloud to each other. Encourage them to work together to figure out difficult words but to keep going if they cannot. Afterward, the class can talk together about parts they had trouble with. Encourage them to use context clues. Supply answers by saying *yes* to their closest guesses and then amplifying the meaning in an example.

(**TALK AND SHARE**)

For partners who need help, provide these prompts: *How did the Sioux use the buffalo? How did the Pueblo use their clay soil?*

Discuss the Summary

Read the Summary aloud with students. Then return to the Big Idea on page 19. Help students compare the Summary and the Big Idea. Then ask volunteers to put what they learned from this lesson into their own words.

✔ Assessment

Assess students' comprehension by asking the following questions:

History

- Where did Native Americans migrate from?
- How did Native Americans in the following regions use resources?
  - East
  - Southwest
  - Great Plains
  - Coastal regions
- What are two differences between life in the East and the West?

Language

Write or say sentences to show how the paired words are related:

- Resources
- Region
- Migrated
- Settled
- Religion
- Culture

Assessment Book

Use page 19 to assess students' comprehension.

Teach **Comparing**

Tell students that many times in school and on tests they will be asked to compare things. This page will give them a strategy, or plan, for doing that.

Model the Organizer

■ Review the skill of reading charts by asking volunteers to read the headings for the columns. Ask other volunteers to read the rows. Ask students which columns in the chart list how the Sioux and Iroquois are different (*first* and *last*).

■ Help students navigate the chart by asking:
  • Did the Sioux hunt buffalo?
  • What did the Iroquois make out of wood?
  • How were the tribes similar?

Give Practice **Comparing**

Assign students to work in pairs to complete one activity.

■ **Draw** Help beginning students find these key words in the third paragraph of page 24: *she and her husband moved; the men made; they ruled.*

■ **Write** Remind intermediate and advanced students to use the signal words for comparisons listed in the Language Notes on page 25.

Develop Language

Comparing

Comparing Two Things

When you compare things, you tell how they are similar. A chart can help you organize your ideas. For example, this Comparison Chart compares the Sioux and the Iroquois. It shows 3 ways they are similar and 3 ways they are different.

Comparison Chart

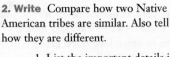

Sioux	Similarities	Iroquois
hunted buffalo	Both hunted animals for food.	hunted deer
made tipis out of animal skins	Both made houses out of their resources.	made longhouses out of wood
often moved	Both developed their own way of life.	stayed in permanent villages

Practice Comparing

1. Draw Draw pictures in a Comparison Chart to compare what Iroquois men and women did. Use your chart to tell how their work was the same and different.

2. Write Compare how two Native American tribes are similar. Also tell how they are different.

1. List the important details in a Comparison Chart.

2. Use those details to write a paragraph of 3 to 4 sentences.

3. Exchange paragraphs with a partner and check each other's writing.

Check Your Writing

Make sure you
- [ ] Use complete sentences.
- [ ] Use a period at the end of each sentence.
- [ ] Spell all the words correctly.

▲ Painted buffalo skin

Activity: Summary Chart

Write the three Key Concepts as heads in a chart on the chalkboard (*resources, region, culture*). Invite students to contribute information they learned in the lesson. Add it to the chart.

Differentiating Instruction

Beginning
Naming Differences Invite students to share their drawings or writings in a class presentation. Have less fluent students name the pictures in their charts.

Intermediate
Fluency Practice Have intermediate students read aloud their paragraphs. To help students gain fluency, encourage them to read their parts several times before their class presentations.

Advanced
Researching Native Americans Invite students to pick one of the groups on the map on page 22 and discover how the activities of the men and women of that group were alike and different. Students should work together to present their information to the class.

Grammar Spotlight

Comparative Adjectives Adjectives describe people, places, or things. When you compare two things, you add the ending *er* to many adjectives. When a word ends with *y*, change the *y* to an *i* before you add *er*.

Example: *These tents were eas*<u>*ier*</u> *to move than houses made from wood.*

Describing One Thing	Comparing Two Things
A deer is small.	A deer is *smaller than* a buffalo.
Longhouses were tall.	Pueblos were *taller than* longhouses.
The Great Plains are dry.	The desert is *drier than* the Great Plains.
Deer skin is warm.	Buffalo skin is *warmer than* deer skin.

Now write a sentence comparing the height of a longhouse and the giant mound at Cahokia. Tell which is higher.

Hands On

Comparing Cultures With a partner or small group, make a picture of the region where you live. Draw or cut pictures out of magazines to show foods, buildings, kinds of work people do, and language. Talk about what you showed. Then compare your region to another region. Use a Comparison Chart to show things that are the same and things that are different. Talk about your chart.

Oral Language

Region Rap With a partner or small group, make a list of things found in your region. Do you have lakes or mountains? Are there tall trees or big cities or farms? Look over your list. See what rhymes. Make a rap to share with the class. Here's an example. Say it aloud with your group.

The lakes
In our states
Are great. We
Live near the great
Great Lakes.

Grammar Spotlight

Provide examples of comparative sentences with *than* using objects in the classroom. Speak slowly, and emphasize *than*. Ask volunteers to compare one object with another. Allow partners to practice with each other before assigning the written sentence at the end of the Grammar Spotlight.

Evaluate students' sentences by looking for the use of a comparative adjective such as *taller* or *smaller* and the correct placement of the word *than*. You may wish to let some students say, rather than write, their sentences.

Hands On

Observe partners or small groups at work and encourage them to use what they learned in the Language Notes on page 25.

Oral Language

Divide the class into small groups to compose raps. When they're done, have groups rehearse their raps. Then stage a Rap Fest, having each group perform for the class.

 Activity: Extend the Lesson

Encourage interested students to work in pairs or groups to make a diorama of a shelter or activity of one Native American culture. A shoebox without the lid is a good container. In addition, students can use both natural and handmade items such as the following: markers, paints, colored construction paper, modeling clay, pipe cleaners, fabric pieces, rocks, grasses, and pine needles.

Program Resources

Student Activity Journal
Use page 15 to practice *comparing*.

Lesson 1 • The First Americans   **29**

European Exploration

STANDARDS CONTENT

History

- ■ Use a map key
- ■ Identify the causes that led to European exploration of the Americas
- ■ Recognize key events and people related to European exploration
- ■ Explain the interactions between European explorers and Native Americans

Language

- ■ Identify the following Key Concepts: *New World, exploration,* and *trade routes*
- ■ Recognize multiple-meaning words
- ■ Practice identifying key ideas

Begin Building Background

- ■ Ask students the questions below the painting. Focus students on:
  - • How people feel when they come to a new land
  - • How people already living on the land feel about strangers arriving
- ■ Ask a volunteer to read aloud the caption below the boy's picture. Ask other students to share their thoughts about arriving in a new country. Draw out their ideas about being in a new place and meeting people who already live there.

Talk and Explore

European Exploration

Here you'll learn why European explorers came to America. You'll also learn how to use a map key, and you'll practice identifying the reasons why something happens.

Building Background

▲ When we came to America, I saw my grandma and grandpa for the very first time.

- ■ **What's happening in this picture?**
- ■ **How do you think the people feel about it?**
- ■ **How would you feel if you came to a new land?**

30   Unit 1 • America's Beginnings

Activity: Word Wall

Write the word *exploration* on an 8½" x 11" sheet. Ask students to name words they think of when they look at the painting. Try to generate words such as *land, ocean, ship,* and *route.* Have students write the words on index cards and tape them to the wall under *exploration.*

Differentiating Instruction

Beginning

Reviewing Key Words On the board, write these words: *Native Americans, Europeans, ships, canoe, weapons, clothes, ocean, explorers.* Have students copy the words on sticky notes and work in groups to place them on the correct part of the picture, saying each word aloud.

Intermediate/Advanced

Talking About It Have students study the map and pictures. They should work with partners to predict why Europeans came to the Americas. Have pairs share their ideas with the class.

Europeans were looking for new trade routes to Asia during the 1400s. Christopher Columbus sailed west and landed in North America instead. Soon other European explorers followed. They claimed lands for their kings. The Native Americans suffered.

1 Looking for New Trade Routes

Trade Routes to Asia

EUROPE ASIA

NORTH AMERICA

2 Christopher Columbus Sails to the Americas

AFRICA

SOUTH AMERICA

KEY
Old trade routes
New trade route

3 Europeans Claim Lands

4 Native Americans Suffer

LESSON 2 • EUROPEAN EXPLORATION **31**

Introduce the Big Idea

- Read aloud the Big Idea on page 31. Then go through the titles on the pictures.
- Use the pictures to encourage a conversation about what European explorers did. Begin by asking students what they see in the pictures.
- Point to the arrows on the map. Ask students if they know how to figure out what the arrows mean.
- Explain that Columbus was looking for new trade routes when he sailed to the Americas.

Teach the Pictures

The third Big Idea image is of Christopher Columbus arriving in North America. He claimed the lands for Spain. King Ferdinand and Queen Isabella of Spain had supported his decision to look for new trade routes.

Review

In the last lesson, students learned about the cultures of several Native American groups. In Lesson 2, students will learn how the arrival of Europeans affected Native Americans.

Activity: Role-Play

Using a volunteer, role-play a scenario between a foreigner who comes to a new land and a native who already lives there. The foreigner and native have very different cultures. Make up a script like the one below.

Foreigner: *I like this land. I will make a home here.*

Native: *What? You can't stay here. This is our hunting ground.*

Foreigner: *This land is huge. Hunt in another place. I am going to build a big home here.*

Native: *We live in small houses. You are in our land now. You should do things our way.*

Tie the discussion back to the lesson topic of European exploration. Ask students how they think the arrival of Europeans made the Native Americans feel. Ask, *How did the new land make the Europeans feel?*

Resource Library

Reader's Handbook (red)
Maps 163–164, 555–556

Reader's Handbook (yellow)
Maps 121, 431

All Write
Using Maps 465–480

Teach — Key Concepts

- To model correct pronunciation, say each term slowly. Ask students to repeat after you. Then read aloud the Key Concept sentences and talk about what they mean.

- To teach *trade routes*, point to the people trading in the picture and the arrow that indicates the route that traders followed to get from Europe to the Far East.

- Have students study the map below to see the waterways and lands that European traders crossed.

Teach the Visual Aid
European Explorations

Focus students on the map to the right.

- Write the terms *Europe* and *European* on the board, and connect their meanings. Invite a volunteer to point out the continent of Europe on the map.

- Call attention to the map's color coding (matching colors for countries and their routes to the Americas).

- Provide students with this sentence prompt: *Explorers from __ went to __ in the year __.* Call on volunteers to complete the sentence while pointing out the routes on the map.

Talk and Explore

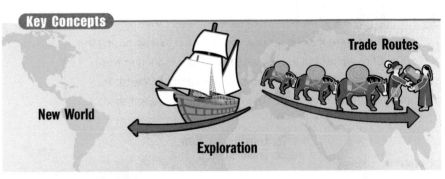

Key Concepts

New World · Exploration · Trade Routes

Trade routes are the paths across land and water that traders use to get to the places where they buy and sell things.

An **exploration** is a trip taken to search for something.

On an exploration for new trade routes to Asia, Christopher Columbus landed in the Americas in 1492. To people from Europe, these continents were a **New World**.

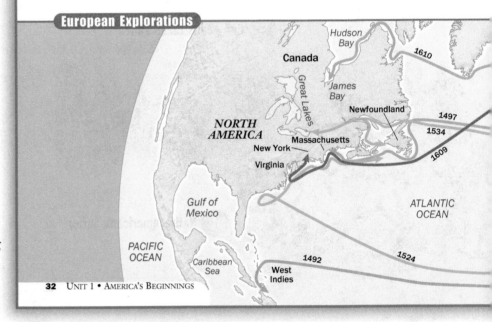

European Explorations

Hudson Bay · Canada · James Bay · Great Lakes · 1610 · Newfoundland · 1497 · 1534 · NORTH AMERICA · Massachusetts · New York · 1609 · Virginia · ATLANTIC OCEAN · Gulf of Mexico · PACIFIC OCEAN · Caribbean Sea · 1492 · West Indies · 1524

32 UNIT 1 • AMERICA'S BEGINNINGS

Activity: Definition Game

Have students preview the Look and Read section on pages 34–39. Divide the class into two groups: terms and definitions. Have students write one file card for each of the terms or definitions. Collect cards, shuffle them, and pass them out.

Have a student with a term stand and say the term. Ask for the student with the definition that matches that term to stand and read the definition. Continue until all cards have been read.

Differentiating Instruction

Beginning
Answering Questions Focus less fluent learners on correctly answering *yes/no* questions about the Key Concepts and visual aid. Use the following example:

Teacher: *Is this a trade route?*

Student: *Yes, this is a trade route.*

Intermediate
Using the Map Have students write the dates on the map on 3" x 5" index cards. Then ask them to take turns drawing a card and explaining what happened in that year while pointing to the appropriate places on the map.

Advanced
K-W-L Chart Have students create K-W-L Charts for European Explorations. Ask them to fill in the two left columns.

Using a Map Key

A map key, or legend, helps you get information from a map. Follow these steps to read a map key.

1. Read the title of the map.
2. Find the key on the map. It is usually in a box.
3. Study the symbols or colors in the key.
4. Locate the symbols or colors on the map.

Here's an example. Find the key for the map below. It is on the right side. The first color is pink for England. Look for England on the map. It is colored pink. Two pink lines go out from England. They show where English explorers went in the New World. Look at the map again. Where did English explorers go?

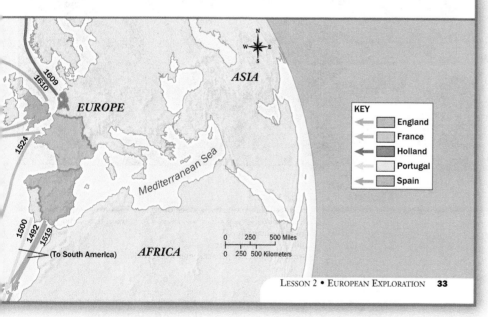

KEY

	England
	France
	Holland
	Portugal
	Spain

ASIA

EUROPE

Mediterranean Sea

AFRICA

(To South America)

1609
1610
1524
1500
1492
1519

0   250   500 Miles
0   250 500 Kilometers

Teach   Skill Building

- Read with students the explanation of what a map key does.
- Be sure that students understand the meanings of *key*, *symbols*, and *colors*.
- Then demonstrate how to follow the steps by using the map key at the bottom of the page. Point to the pink box labeled *England*. Then trace the pink arrow from England to Massachusetts. Say that the label *1497* tells us that explorers from England followed this route in the year 1497.
- Read through the steps once more, this time calling on volunteers to demonstrate each of the steps.

Teach the Pictures

Christopher Columbus and other European explorers wanted to find a shorter route from European countries such as Spain and Portugal to Asia. (Have students find Asia on the map.) After Columbus, explorers from several nations traveled to the Americas to learn about the resources there.

Activity: Internet Resources

Suggest that some of the most exciting ongoing explorations today are in outer space. Invite students to share information they know about space exploration. Record their ideas on the board.

Interested students can check out NASA's website for kids: http://kids.msfc.nasa.gov.

Encourage them to report findings from their online explorations to the class.

Program Resources

Student Activity Journal

Use page 16 to build key vocabulary.

Use page 17 to practice using a map key.

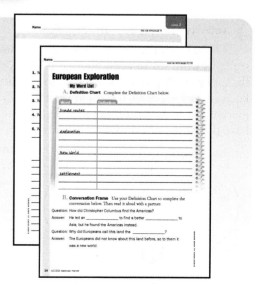

European Exploration

My Word List

A. **Definition Chart** Complete the Definition Chart below.

Word	Definition
trade routes	
exploration	
New World	
settlement	

B. **Conversation Frame** Use your Definition Chart to complete the conversation below. Then read it aloud with a partner.

Question: How did Christopher Columbus find the Americas?

Answer: He led an _____ to find a better _____ to Asia, but he found the Americas instead.

Question: Why did Europeans call this land the _____?

Answer: The Europeans did not know about this land before, so to them it was a new world.

Introduce European Exploration

- Explain that in the 1400s, trade with Asia brought important goods to Europe. Because of the long, difficult journey to Asia, Europeans wanted to find a faster route.

- Cover up the Western Hemisphere on a map or globe. Tell students, *To Europeans at the time, the world looked like this. Why do you think most of them avoided sailing west?* Elicit the concept of fear of the unknown.

Key Connection: Geography

Develop understanding of world geography by using a globe. (If you use an inflatable globe, you can toss the globe to responding students.)

Have pairs of students find the answers to the questions below on a globe. They should demonstrate their answers to the class.

- Where are the seven continents?

- What route could traders take from Spain to India? Is it possible to get there by sea only? By land only?

- Review the cardinal directions: *north, south, east, west.* Then ask, *Can you find a way from Spain to India going west? What countries or continents would you cross?*

Look and Read

European Exploration

During the 1400s, European nations were looking for faster and easier trade routes to Asia. This led them to find a world new to them. They claimed lands and met the native people.

The Search for New Trade Routes

By the 1400s, Europeans wanted things that came from Asia. **Traders** from Europe made long trips to Asia. Their **trade routes** took them east across land. They brought back **goods,** such as **silk** and **spices.** Many Europeans became rich from this Asian trade.

▲ Silk

▲ Spices

VOCABULARY
traders—people who buy and sell things
trade routes—the paths or waterways traders travel to buy and sell goods
goods—things for sale
silk—a fine, shiny cloth
spices—plants like peppers, ginger, and cinnamon that add flavor to food

34 UNIT 1 • AMERICA'S BEGINNINGS

Activity: Teach Vocabulary

Throughout the lesson, have students work with the vocabulary at the end of each page. Ask students to keep a word list of each term in their journal or notebook. When possible, have their lists include Word Wheels.

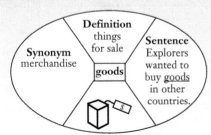

Differentiating Instruction

Beginning
Connections On these two pages, call attention to the title and key words *Europeans, explorers, trade route, Asia,* and *goods.*

Draw a Word Web to emphasize these connections: *Traders from Europe went to Asia on trade routes. Explorers looked for new trade routes. They wanted to bring goods back to Europe.*

Intermediate
Paired Reading Have students read one paragraph at a time. In pairs, have them discuss what they have read. Encourage them to take notes on the Key Concepts in each paragraph (*trade routes, exploration, New World*).

Advanced
Note-taking Have students take notes about the key ideas in each paragraph. Encourage them to use their notes to complete the Talk and Share activity at the bottom of page 35.

DANGEROUS ROUTES

The land routes east to Asia were **dangerous.** **Thieves** attacked traders. Wars broke out along the trade routes. The traders needed to find another way. They started looking for sea routes to Asia. Some rulers of European countries paid **explorers** to search the seas for new routes. Paying for ships, sailors, and supplies was costly, but rulers were willing to **take the risk.** If the explorers found a safer route to Asia, the rulers could get rich.

PORTUGAL LEADS THE SEARCH

In 1419, Prince Henry the Navigator of Portugal started a school for sailors. He invited the best scientists and mathematicians to study there. They **invented** a new sailing ship called a *caravel.* It was strong and fast and could travel long distances. They invented tools for making excellent maps.

Prince Henry's sailors explored the Atlantic Ocean along the west coast of Africa. By 1488, Portuguese sailors reached the southern tip of Africa. Ten years later, they sailed around Africa all the way up to India. They had found an all-water route to Asia, but it was very long, dangerous, and costly.

(**TALK AND SHARE**) **Explain to your partner why the Europeans started looking for a way to Asia by sea.**

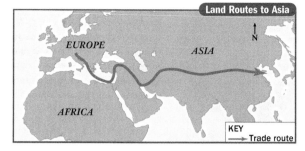
Land Routes to Asia

EUROPE | ASIA

AFRICA

N

KEY
→ Trade route

▲ Prince Henry the Navigator

Language Notes

Multiple Meanings
These words have more than one meaning.

☐ trip
1. a voyage
2. to fall or stumble

☐ key
1. a list on a map explaining the colors or symbols
2. a small tool for locking a door

☐ ruler
1. the leader of a nation
2. a measuring tool

LESSON 2 • EUROPEAN EXPLORATION **35**

Teach About The Search for New Trade Routes

■ Talk about the different goods Europeans wanted to buy from Asia. Ask about the spices found in students' favorite foods. Ask, *Why do you think Europeans wanted spices from other countries?*

■ Connect to students' lives. Ask students to think about things they encounter that come from other countries.

Language Notes

Draw students' attention to the Language Notes. Read through the words and definitions in the Language Notes box. Explain the different meanings of the word *key* by comparing the map key on page 33 to a door key. Then help students find the multiple-meaning words in the reading and identify which definition is used in each sentence.

TALK AND SHARE

Have students complete the Talk and Share activity with a partner. Then, as a class, ask students to share their responses.

Activity: Sentence Patterns

Invite students to answer the following *why* question using complete sentences and words such as *because* and *as a result.*

Q: *Why were the land routes to Asia dangerous?*

A: *The land routes to Asia were dangerous because of thieves and war.*

Program Resources

Student Activity Journal
Assign page 18:
• To create study notes for students to review
• To provide reinforcement of key vocabulary

Overhead Transparencies
Use 36, Word Wheel, with page 34.

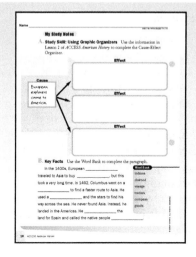

Discuss Christopher Columbus

Read aloud the first heading and emphasize Columbus's importance in history. Explain that his voyage led to enormous changes in the world—both in Europe and in the Americas. To help students remember the key date, provide the following rhyme:

In fourteen hundred and ninety-two, Columbus sailed the ocean blue.

Teach the Pictures

To the right is a photograph of ships built today in the style of Columbus's ships. People built these so they could trace Columbus's route from Spain to North America. The ship in front displays Spain's flag as it looked in 1492.

Also pictured is a compass. Its invention by the Chinese allowed explorers to explore far from home with less fear of getting lost. Because of compasses and strong ships, Europeans were able to explore far-off lands in the 1400s.

TALK AND SHARE

Direct students to the activity in red on this page. Have students discuss it with their partners. Then come together as a class to discuss their responses. Ensure that students understand the reasons for Columbus's journey.

Look and Read

▲ Christopher Columbus

Christopher Columbus

Christopher Columbus was an Italian sea captain. He thought he could get to Asia another way—by sailing *west* across the Atlantic Ocean. Columbus asked the rulers of Spain, King Ferdinand and Queen Isabella, to pay for this **voyage.** They agreed, hoping that Columbus would bring them Asian gold and spices.

On August 3, 1492, Columbus set sail with 3 ships: the *Niña,* the *Pinta,* and the *Santa María.* To find his way across the sea, Columbus used a **compass** and the stars. He sailed for 3,000 miles across the Atlantic. It took many weeks. At last, on October 12, 1492, a lookout shouted "*Tierra, tierra!*" It means "Land, land!" Columbus and his men had arrived at an island in the Bahamas. They went on shore and **claimed** the island for Spain. A people called the Taino lived in the Bahamas. Columbus called them **"Indians,"** because he believed he was in India, a part of Asia.

In fact, Columbus had not arrived in Asia. Instead, he had reached **the Americas.** This part of the world was not on any maps. The Europeans called it the "New World."

TALK AND SHARE **Explain to your partner what Columbus thought he would find when he sailed to the Americas.**

▲ Modern copies of the *Niña, Pinta,* and *Santa María*

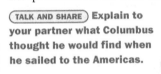

Compass ▶

voyage—a long journey or trip
compass—a tool for finding direction. It uses a magnetic needle that points north.
claimed—said that something belonged to them
Indians—a name for the native people of the Americas; Native Americans
the Americas—the continents of North and South America

36 UNIT 1 • AMERICA'S BEGINNINGS

🏃 Activity: Map Notebooks

Pair students and give each pair two 8½" x 11" blank sheets of paper. Have the pairs draw an outline of North and South America on one sheet and an outline of Europe and Asia on the other. Refer them to the world map on pages 12–13 as a guide. Tell them that they will be using their maps as graphic organizers to take notes throughout the lesson. Have them begin by recording trade routes to Asia and Prince Henry's exploration of Africa.

📖 Differentiating Instruction

Beginning
Describing Pictures Have students choose three pictures from the beginning of the lesson to page 37. Ask them to describe each picture. They should use at least one vocabulary word in each description. Provide them with sentence starters such as *It is_____, He is_____,* and *They are_____.*

Intermediate
Vocabulary Snap Have students choose three pictures from the beginning of the lesson and tell their partners about them. Ask partners to snap their fingers each time they hear a vocabulary word. Students at this level may use descriptive phrases or approximate sentences.

Advanced
Using Sentences Have students choose three pictures from the beginning of the lesson and describe them in complete sentences. Each sentence should identify who or what the picture is about and where, when, or how it took place.

Claiming Lands

The voyages of Columbus began an age of great wealth and power for Spain. Soon other European nations also sent explorers to claim lands in the New World.

SPAIN IN THE NEW WORLD

Spanish explorers after Columbus started a huge Spanish **empire** in the Americas. The Spanish claimed lands in Central and South America and in the southern parts of North America. In 1565, Spain built a fort at St. Augustine, Florida. It was the first permanent European **settlement** in North America.

The Spanish overpowered the Native Americans they met. The Spanish had guns and cannons, but the Native Americans had only arrows, knives, and stones. So even mighty native empires fell. The Spanish took their lands and forced the Native Americans to be their slaves. They stole their gold. The Native Americans **suffered** terribly.

The rulers of Spain were **religious** people. They wanted to spread **Christianity.** They sent Spanish priests to build **missions** in the Americas. Some priests taught the Native Americans with love. Others were very cruel.

The Spanish fort at St. Augustine ▼

VOCABULARY

empire—a group of lands or countries under one government
settlement—a place where people live
suffered—felt pain or loss
religious—believing in God or spirits
Christianity—the religion based on the teachings of Jesus Christ
missions—churches and other buildings where priests live and teach their religious beliefs

LESSON 2 • EUROPEAN EXPLORATION **37**

Talk About
Claiming Lands

- Emphasize that the goal of European explorers changed after Columbus's trip.
- Work with the class to fill in a Before-and-After Chart that shows European trade goals before and after Columbus's journey. Have students illustrate their organizers with maps and pictures. Use Overhead Transparency 2, Before-and-After Chart.

European Explorers

Before Columbus	After Columbus
find trade route	claim new lands find gold

Teach the Pictures

The photo on page 37 is of the fort Castillo de San Marcos at St. Augustine. The Spanish began constructing it in 1672 and finished twenty-three years later in 1695. St. Augustine is the oldest continually occupied city in the United States. The fort has been used by many countries but never has been taken by force.

 Activity: Scavenger Hunt

Have partners search the text to find as many words with suffixes as they can. Ask them to list the words as they appear and then to write the root words. Demonstrate with these vocabulary words:

Word with Ending	Root Word
settlement	settle
Christianity	Christ
claimed	claim

Activity: History Notebook

Help students build a notebook for this lesson. The notebook should include items from the Student Activity Journal, pictures, lists, and drawings they've made about the events. Have them share their notebook with a partner.

Discuss Other Europeans in the New World

■ Ask for five volunteers to point out land claimed by the different European countries.

■ Point out the location of New York. Tell students that it was a colony of Holland (land of the Dutch people).

TALK AND SHARE

Have partners complete the Talk and Share activity. Then, as a class, ask students to share their responses.

Primary Source

An Aztec Poem

Use the Aztec poem to show the value of eyewitness accounts of history.

• Tell students that the Aztec Indians of Mexico had an advanced culture, including large cities, a written language, and beautiful arts.

• Explain that many Aztecs died trying to save their capital city from the Spanish in 1521. This poem describes the event.

• Practice choral readings of the poem, having students repeat each line after you.

• Ask students to share their thoughts on the poem.

Look and Read

European Claims in the New World

KEY
☐ Spanish
☐ French
☐ English
☐ Portuguese
■ Dutch
● New York (1625–1664)
☐ Unclaimed Land

OTHER EUROPEANS IN THE NEW WORLD

The rulers of England, France, Portugal, and Holland also sent explorers to claim lands. Each nation went to a different part of the Americas. Each nation claimed land.

England's **claim** became very important in the years to come. As early as 1497, an English explorer claimed land in North America for the king of England. Then, in the 1580s, Queen Elizabeth I of England sent people to start **colonies** along the east coast of North America. In time, these colonies became the United States of America.

TALK AND SHARE Talk about the map with your partner. Which nation claimed the most land?

VOCABULARY
claim—saying that land is theirs. That land also can be called their *claim*.
colonies—areas that are ruled by another country

Primary Source

An Aztec Poem

In the 1500s, the Aztecs had a mighty nation in Mexico. Then the Spanish arrived and killed the Aztec ruler Moctezuma and other leaders. The Aztecs bravely fought back, but still the Spanish crushed them. An Aztec poem tells about their defeat.

> *Without roofs are the houses,*
> *And red are their walls with blood.*
> *Weep, my friends,*
> *We have lost our Mexican nation.*

Ornament worn by Aztec priests ▶

 Activity: Map Notebooks

Have partners add new key information to their map outlines. They should include land claimed by different countries.

 Differentiating Instruction

Beginning
Reviewing Have students use the Summary on page 39 to review key points in the lesson. Ask students to work with a partner to locate key words in the Summary, such as *Europeans, trade routes, Asia,* and *Christopher Columbus.* As they locate a key word, have them find a correlating picture in the lesson and identify it to their partner using the word.

Intermediate
Map Notebooks Have partners take turns pointing out one piece of information in their maps and explaining it to each other. Encourage partners to ask each other questions about their maps.

Advanced
K-W-L Chart Have students use complete sentences to complete the right column of the charts they made earlier in the lesson.

Bringing Hardship to Native Americans

Europeans in the Americas brought terrible changes to the lives of the native people. At first, many Native Americans welcomed the Europeans. Some showed Europeans how to grow food and hunt animals. Over time, however, the Europeans and the Native Americans became enemies.

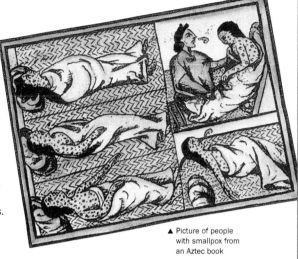

▲ Picture of people with smallpox from an Aztec book

Native American Suffering

Land	The people lost lands they had lived on for a very long time.
Slavery	Some Native Americans became slaves. They had to do hard labor with no pay and no rights.
Disease	Millions of native people died from European diseases—smallpox, measles, flu—they had never seen before. Their bodies had no defenses against these diseases.
Loss of Riches	The treasures of great empires—huge amounts of gold and jewels—were taken to Europe. Native-American books were destroyed. Statues and art objects were melted for their gold.

(**TALK AND SHARE**) Look at the chart and picture above. Tell your partner how the Europeans changed the lives of the Native Americans.

Summary

Europeans searched for new trade routes to Asia during the 1400s. One of them, Christopher Columbus, landed in the Americas. Other European explorers followed him and claimed lands in the New World. The Native Americans suffered after the Europeans came to their land.

Discuss Bringing Hardship to Native Americans

Ask students what they see in the picture on page 39. Explain to students how the Europeans brought diseases that killed many Native Americans. The chart on page 39 lists some of the other ways that Native Americans suffered.

(**TALK AND SHARE**)

Have students read the chart on page 39 aloud with their partners. As a class, discuss the ways that Native Americans suffered hardship.

Discuss the Summary

- Direct students to read the Summary at the end of the lesson.
- Then return to the Big Idea on page 31. Help students see the connection between the Summary and the Big Idea.
- Then ask volunteers to put into their own words what they learned from this lesson.

Assessment

Assess students' comprehension by asking the following questions:

History

- Why did Europeans want to find new trade routes?
- Why did Columbus come to the New World?
- What countries claimed land in the New World?
- How did Native Americans suffer?

Language

Match each word to its definition:

Words	Definitions
1. Goods	**A.** Areas that are ruled by another country
2. Empire	**B.** Things for sale
3. Colonies	**C.** A group of lands or countries under one government

Assessment Book

Use page 20 to assess students' comprehension.

Teach Identifying

Tell students that, in any subject, it is important to understand the reasons behind events. This page will explain how to identify those reasons.

Model the Organizer

■ Ask volunteers to read aloud the three Reasons for European Exploration. Give them the prompt *Europeans wanted to explore _____.*

■ A Web like this one can help students identify reasons something happened.

Give Practice Identifying

Have students work in pairs to complete one activity.

■ **Draw** Have beginning learners complete the Draw activity.

■ **Write** Have intermediate and advanced students complete the Write activity. Guide them in using the first set of words in the Word Bank.

Develop Language

Identifying

Identifying Reasons

In class or on a test, you may be asked to identify, or pick out, reasons. Here's an example: *Identify reasons that Europeans explored the New World*. Ask yourself, "Why did Europeans explore the New World? How many reasons can I think of?" Use a Web to organize your thoughts.

Web

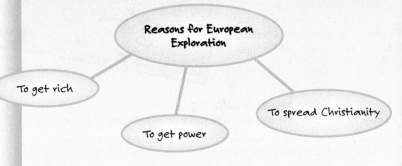

Practice Identifying

1. Draw Make a Web. Draw the reasons that Europeans wanted a sea route to Asia. Use your Web to tell your partner the reasons you identified.

▲ Mask of an Aztec god

2. Write Identify reasons that the Native Americans suffered when Europeans came. First, list the reasons in a Web. Then, use those reasons to write a paragraph of 3 to 4 sentences. Be sure to write a sentence using the word *because*. The Word Bank may help you.

Word Bank
Spanish
land
slavery
disease

steal
stole

killed
destroyed
infected

 Activity: Internet Resources

Have students search the Internet for information on key people in Lesson 2. Have them work in pairs to locate websites of their choosing and make a poster of their subject to share with the class. Encourage them to copy pictures from the site for their posters.

 Differentiating Instruction

Beginning
Key Words Prompt students in identifying key words by writing this text on the board: *Reasons the Europeans Wanted a Sea Route to Asia*. Have students copy the text in the center circles of their own Webs.

Intermediate
Main idea Ask partners to work together to write a sentence that tells the main idea of a paragraph about Native American suffering. It should

include the words in one of the outer circles of their Webs.

Advanced
Expository Paragraph Help students construct their paragraphs.

Suggest that students' paragraphs follow the following format:

1. **Main Idea**
2. **Detail**
3. **Detail**

Activities

Grammar Spotlight

Prepositions of Time: *On, In, At* The words *on*, *in*, and *at* can tell about time.

When to use *on, in,* and *at*	Example
Use *on* with days.	On August 3, 1492, Columbus set sail.
Use *in* for months and years.	Columbus found the Americas in 1492.
Use *at* with clock times.	He arrived at noon.

Show what you know. Write 3 sentences. Tell when the lookout on Columbus's ship shouted, "*Tierra, tierra!*" Tell when Prince Henry started a school for sailors. Tell the time you came to school today.

Hands On

Find a New Route Work with a partner to draw a map. Show the route from the front door of the school to your classroom. Now find another route to the classroom. Can you make a better route? You can add doors or stairs. Make a map key to explain the symbols you use. Tell your partner about your route. Use direction words such as *left* and *right* or *north* and *south*.

Partner Practice

Word Sort Fold and tear a piece of paper into 6 cards. Pick 6 vocabulary words from this lesson and write one on each of the 6 cards. Your partner should choose 6 different words and make 6 cards too. Then, put all 12 cards on the table so you both can see the words. Together, put them into groups. The groups should make sense. Explain your groups to your teacher.

Oral Language

In 1492 Read this poem aloud with a partner. Then write a poem about how Native Americans might have seen the arrival of Columbus. Read your poem aloud with a partner.

In fourteen hundred ninety-two,
Columbus sailed the ocean blue.
Day after day they looked for land;
They dreamed of trees and rocks and sand.
On October 12 their dream came true.
You never saw a happier crew!

Activities

Grammar Spotlight

Provide extra practice by asking students questions such as these and having them answer in full phrases:

- When did you eat breakfast today?
- When did you come to America?

Evaluate student answers by looking for the use of prepositional phrases.

Hands On

Have students practice this lesson's skill by creating symbols for a map key. Prompt them by providing this symbol for stairs:

Partner Practice

Encourage intermediate and advanced learners to write new cards that name each group.

Oral Language

Have students practice the rhyme in several different ways:

- Students clap out the rhythm.
- Volunteers take turns leading a choral reading.

 Activity: Extend the Lesson

For students' additional reading, suggest these books:

- *Meet Christopher Columbus* by James T. DeKay and John Edens (illustrator) (Random House, 2001)
- *How Would You Survive as an Aztec?* by F. MacDonald and M. Bergin (Franklin Watts, 1997)
- *Christopher Columbus and the Age of Exploration in World History* by Al Sundel (Enslow Publishers, 2002)

 Program Resources

Student Activity Journal
Use page 19 to practice *identifying*.

Overhead Transparencies
Use 33, Web, with page 40.

The Thirteen Colonies

STANDARDS CONTENT

History

- Read a timeline
- Identify the motives, hardships, and experiences of the English colonists
- Recognize that U.S. traditions of religious freedom, representative government, and self-government had their roots in the early English colonies
- Recognize the causes and effects of slavery in the English colonies

Language

- Identify the following Key Concepts: *persecution, religion,* and *religious freedom*
- Recognize homophones
- Practice describing people, things, and events

Begin Building Background

- Ask students the questions below the picture. Focus students on:
  - How these people differ from the European explorers in Lesson 2 (*They are settlers.*)
  - The hardships these new settlers might face
- Encourage students to share their understanding of similar events. Provide students with words as needed (*freedom, new, arrive*).
- Ask a volunteer to read aloud the caption below the boy's picture. Ask other students to talk about adapting to a new place.

Talk and Explore

The Thirteen Colonies

Here you'll learn how England started 13 colonies along the east coast of North America. You'll also learn how to read a timeline and practice describing life in one of the colonies.

Building Background

▲ It was hard when we moved to a new place. At first, I didn't have any friends.

- **How would you describe what's happening here?**
- **How do you think they feel?**
- **What do you think is hard about coming to a new place?**

42 Unit 1 • America's Beginnings

 Activity: Word Wall

Write the word *colony* on an 8½" x 11" sheet. Ask students to name words they think of when they look at the picture. Try to generate words such as *new life, difficult,* and *freedom.* Have students write the words on index cards and tape them to the wall under *colony.*

Differentiating Instruction

Beginning

Picture Associations Read the lesson title aloud. Then write the word *colonists* on the board. Explain that the colonists were English people who moved to America to live. Build word-picture associations by having students point out colonists they see on the pages above. Ask students to write the words on sticky notes and place them on all pictures of colonists in the lesson.

Intermediate

Captions Have students work in pairs to write a descriptive caption for the picture above. Invite them to share their captions with the class.

Advanced

Answering the Questions Have students work in small groups to write an answer to one of the questions below the picture. Afterward, have them share their answers with the class. Encourage them to point out details in the picture that support their answers.

England

1 The Early Colonies

2 Religious Freedom

Slavery **3**

4 Growth of the Colonies

Introduce the Big Idea

- Read aloud the Big Idea on page 43.
- Have students go through the labels on the four pictures and use the pictures to tell what they think they will learn about life in the thirteen colonies.
- Point to the map of England and ask a volunteer to identify it.
- Explain that the story of the colonies begins with the English wanting to use resources from North America.

Teach the Pictures

The top image on page 43 shows settlers beginning to export barrels of tobacco from Jamestown, Virginia, around the year 1615. Tobacco was a very important crop for the early settlers. Selling tobacco helped their new colonies thrive.

Review

Connect to the key content that students learned in Lesson 2. Build on their knowledge that Europeans wanted to settle in North America because of natural resources and new opportunities.

Activity: Role-Play

For two minutes, have student pairs role-play an interview with someone who has immigrated to the United States. The interviewer should ask questions such as:

- What do you like about the United States?
- How is it different from your homeland?
- What things were hard for you to get used to?

Activity: Culture Connection

Invite students to talk about experiences with leaving a homeland and coming to the United States. Provide these discussion prompts:

- How did people travel?
- How did the people and their families feel?
- What were some reasons they had for leaving their homeland?

Resource Library

Reader's Handbook (red)
Timeline 561, 681

Reader's Handbook (yellow)
Timeline 64, 434–435, 557

All Write
Timeline 273, 489–500

Teach Key Concepts

- To model correct pronunciation, say each term slowly. Ask students to repeat after you. Then read aloud the Key Concept sentences and talk about what they mean.

- Ask students if they can connect the Key Concepts to a different historical event or to a current event.

- Have them write a sentence about the event using one of the Key Concept terms.

Teach the Visual Aid

Timeline About the Early Colonies

Focus students on the timeline.

- Have a volunteer read aloud the date labels and picture captions.
- Then briefly explain each event in three to five sentences.
- Ask, *What story is the visual aid telling?*

Key Concepts

Persecution	**Religion**	**Religious Freedom**
Persecution is the harm people suffer because of who they are.	Often people are persecuted because of their **religion.**	They want to get away from persecution and have **religious freedom.**

Timeline About the Early Colonies

1607
Settlers land at Jamestown.

1619
Africans are brought to work as slaves.
The House of Burgesses meets.

44   UNIT 1 • AMERICA'S BEGINNINGS

Activity: Word Wheel

Divide the class into three groups and assign each one a Key Concept. Ask each group to create a Word Wheel about their Key Concept. Write these suggestions for categories on the board:

- Examples
- Synonyms
- Opposites
- Pictures
- Sentences Using Word

Differentiating Instruction

Beginning

Answering the Questions Present *either/or* questions about the pictures in the Key Concepts and timeline. Guide students in using your words in their answers.

Teacher: *Is he an African slave or a colonist?*

Student: *He is an African slave.*

Intermediate

Explaining the Events Have students explain the events in the timeline using the date and the words in each heading. Provide this sentence prompt: *In 1607, settlers landed at Jamestown.*

Advanced

Partner Interview Ask pairs to interview each other about the Key Concepts and timeline. One student should point to a Key Concept or timeline event, and the partner can describe it. Encourage students to use complete sentences. Have them each take several turns.

Reading a Timeline

A timeline shows events in the order they happened. We call this *chronological* order. A timeline shows which events happened first, next, and so on. The earliest dates are on the left. The later dates are on the right.

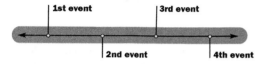

Look at the timeline at the bottom of these pages.

1. Did the slaves arrive after Thanksgiving?
2. Did the Pilgrims come before the Puritans?
3. When was the Mayflower Compact signed?

1620
The Mayflower Compact is signed.

1621
Pilgrims have the first Thanksgiving.

1630
Puritans land at Massachusetts Bay.

Teach Skill Building

■ Read with students the explanation of reading a timeline.

■ Help students see that the events occurred in chronological order.

■ Model using signal words to discuss chronological events by telling students the story that the timeline on pages 44–45 shows.

■ Use signal words, such as *first, next, after that, soon, the next year,* and *then.*

■ Then call on volunteers to answer the questions. Have them demonstrate their answers by pointing out the events on the timeline.

Teach the Pictures

The painting of the first Thanksgiving ceremony with the Native Americans and the Pilgrims in 1621 was painted long after the event and shows how the artist imagined it looked. Pilgrims wanted to celebrate their first harvest and invited a Native American group who lived nearby. Many countries have similar festivals when people finish harvesting crops.

Activity: Current Events Timeline

Have students work in groups to list five important recent events, either in the news or at school. Then have them create a timeline for the events on an 8½" x 11" sheet of paper. Afterward, have the groups tell the story of their timeline to the class. Encourage them to rehearse their story beforehand, using the words *first, second, third,* and so on for chronological order.

Program Resources

Student Activity Journal

Use page 20 to build key vocabulary.

Use page 21 to practice reading a timeline.

Overhead Transparencies

Use 36, Word Wheel, with page 44.

Use 28, Timeline, with page 45.

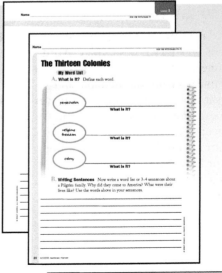

Introduce The Thirteen Colonies

- Have students turn to the world map on pages 12–13. Ask a volunteer to locate England. Have another volunteer trace a path with a finger to the United States. Ask, *On what American coast would settlers from England land?*

- Read aloud the introduction. Then engage students in previewing the lesson by reading all the headings on pages 46–51. Ask students to find pictures that they think relate to the headings. Then have students read in pairs.

Key Connection: Economics

To help students understand *mercantilism*, point to easier words, such as *merchant* and *market* (or *mercado* in Spanish). Europeans wanted resources to use in making goods to sell and markets where they could sell their goods. They got both by setting up colonies.

Look and Read

The Thirteen Colonies

nglish people came to the colonies for wealth, religious freedom, and a better life. Africans did not come freely. They were kidnapped. Many parts of American life today began in the 13 colonies.

▲ Coin used in the colonies in the 1600s

The Early Colonies

The rulers and **merchants** of Europe wanted to use the natural resources in America to get rich. They had a plan for getting rich known as **mercantilism.** First, countries set up colonies. Next, they sent people to look for gold and silver. Then, they sent people to live and work in their colonies.

JAMESTOWN

In 1607, English **settlers** came to Jamestown. The area later became the **colony** of Virginia. A daring soldier, Captain John Smith, led the colonists. A group of wealthy English merchants, called the Virginia Company, paid for the ship, food, and all the supplies.

Life was very difficult at first. Some colonists wouldn't work. They came to find gold, not to grow food. To avoid **starvation,** Captain Smith set up a trade with the Indians. The Indians gave corn and other food. The settlers gave steel knives and copper coins. Then Smith ordered the colonists to plant crops.

▲ Winter in Jamestown

> **VOCABULARY**
>
> **merchants**—business people who make a living buying and selling things
> **mercantilism**—a way nations grew wealthy. They used the resources of colonies to make and sell more goods than they bought.
> **settlers**—people who move into a land to live
> **colony**—an area that is ruled by another country. People who live in a colony are called *colonists*.
> **starvation**—death from not having enough food

 Activity: Word Connect

Have pairs write the vocabulary words on sticky notes to play Word Connect. The first player places a vocabulary word on the table and uses it in a sentence. The next player places a word beside the first and uses both words in a sentence. Play continues until a player cannot find a word to create a logical sentence using all the words previously played. Pairs can play several rounds.

 Differentiating Instruction

Beginning

Words and Pictures Show students how to use headings and pictures as text clues. Help them read the headings aloud together and then match them to the pictures. Write these words on the board: *colonists, settlers, Jamestown, English, Native Americans.* Invite pairs of students to practice saying the words while showing their partners which pictures they go with.

Intermediate

Paired Reading Have students read one paragraph at a time, taking turns with their partners. Tell them to stop after each paragraph and identify at least two key facts, including important people, dates, and places.

Advanced

Note-taking Have students take notes about the key ideas in each paragraph. Encourage them to use their notes to answer the Talk and Share.

▲ Virginia colonists trade with Indians.

THE VIRGINIA COLONY

Jamestown became the first **permanent** English settlement in North America. It was a town in the Virginia Colony. To get more colonists, the Virginia Company promised land to English farmers. Many of them came. The tobacco they grew made many of the merchants rich.

HOUSE OF BURGESSES

England ruled the colonies, but it was far away. In England, elected **representatives** were part of the government. The colonists in Virginia wanted this right too. In 1619, they set up the **House of Burgesses.** It met in Jamestown. This marked the beginning of **representative government** in America.

TALK AND SHARE With a partner, talk about why the English set up colonies in America. Use some of the vocabulary in this lesson and use the word *because*.

VOCABULARY

permanent—lasting; not going away
representatives—the people in government who make decisions for the people who elect them
House of Burgesses—the lawmaking body in the Virginia Colony
representative government—a government run by elected officials. The United States has a representative government.

Language Notes
Homophones
These words sound alike, but their spellings and meanings differ.

☐ some: a few
☐ **sum:** a number that results from adding numbers

☐ steel: a hard kind of iron
☐ **steal:** to take something without permission

☐ right: something a person has a claim to
☐ **write:** to put words down with a tool, such as a pen

Teach About Jamestown and the Virginia Colony

■ Explain that the very first English colonies were not successful. The first *permanent* English colony, Jamestown, was established in 1607. Point out that the pictures on these two pages show Jamestown.

■ Ask, *What clues in these pictures tell you that Jamestown was a permanent settlement?*

Language Notes

Draw students' attention to the Language Notes. Have students find the red words in the text. Read aloud the sentences in which the words are used.

As a class, brainstorm other pairs of homophones. Have volunteers write them on the board.

TALK AND SHARE

Encourage students to take turns reading through the Talk and Share activity on page 47. Have them write down questions they have about unfamiliar words or ideas. Have students work in pairs.

Review

Have students make a Web to identify reasons the English set up colonies.

 ## Activity: Memory Rhymes

The founding of Jamestown in 1607 is an important event in history. Have student pairs work to write a rhyme that helps them remember this event. Tell them that rhyming words have the same ending sound. Demonstrate with *came/name; old/gold; steel/meal; crops/shops; town/gown; plan/man.* Post students' rhymes on the bulletin board. Continue to have students compose memory rhymes for key ideas throughout the lesson.

 ## Program Resources

Student Activity Journal
Assign page 22:

• To create study notes for students to review

• To provide reinforcement of key vocabulary

Overhead Transparencies
Use 33, Web, with page 47.

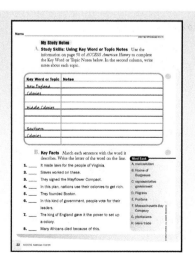

Discuss Religious Freedom

Tell students that many people in England were persecuted for their religion. Discuss the idea of religious persecution. Have students give examples they might know from history or current events.

Teach the Pictures

The picture on the lower half of the page is of the Pilgrims signing the Mayflower Compact. Their signatures are on the facing page. Ask students what they see in the picture. Point out the women and children in the background and explain that the men signed for everyone in the family.

Look and Read

▲ The *Mayflower*

Religious Freedom

Some groups of people in England were **persecuted** because of their religion. They chose to be colonists to escape persecution. The **Pilgrims** were one of these groups.

THE PILGRIMS AND THE MAYFLOWER COMPACT

In September 1620, a group of Pilgrims and other settlers sailed for Virginia on a ship called the *Mayflower*. After two long months, the *Mayflower* reached land, but it wasn't Virginia. The ship had been blown north.

Since they were not in Virginia, they had no government. So, before the **passengers** left the ship, they signed an agreement. It was called the Mayflower Compact. All agreed to obey the laws of the government they would set up. This is what **"self-government"** means. The people freely chose to obey their government. Then they left the ship and went out on the land. They named their settlement Plymouth.

▲ Forty-one men signed the Mayflower Compact in 1620.

VOCABULARY

persecuted—treated badly and unfairly, usually because of religion, politics, or race
Pilgrims—the *Mayflower* colonists
passengers—the people who travel in a ship, plane, train, or bus
self-government—a government that gets its power from the people, not from kings or from force

48 Unit 1 • America's Beginnings

 Activity: Word Sort

Have students make twelve cards for the following vocabulary words and sort them:

- Words for people: *merchants, settlers, representatives, Pilgrims, passengers, Puritans*
- Words about government: *House of Burgesses, representative government, self-government*
- Words about economics: *colony, mercantilism, Massachusetts Bay Company*

Differentiating Instruction

Beginning
Quiz List the vocabulary words from pages 48–49 on the board: *persecuted, Pilgrims, Mayflower Compact, self-government, Puritans, Massachusetts Bay Company*. Have students copy the words on a sheet of paper. Then have them create a quiz by writing definitions or pictures for the words in random order. Have partners exchange quizzes and match each word to its correct definition or picture.

Intermediate
Oral Summary Divide the class into groups of three. Assign each person in a group a blue heading. Have students find the main ideas and then give an oral summary of their passages to their group.

Advanced
Written Summary Repeat the activity above, asking students to write their summaries. Suggest they begin with a sentence that states the main idea of the passage.

THE FIRST THANKSGIVING

During the first winter, the Pilgrims did not have enough food. Many got sick and many died. The next spring was better. Indians helped the Pilgrims find food. They taught them how to plant corn. When fall came, the Pilgrims had plenty of food. They invited their Indian friends to a feast. They gave thanks to God. This feast was the first Thanksgiving.

THE PURITANS

Other groups also were persecuted in England. One was the **Puritans.** In 1629, a group of Puritan merchants formed the **Massachusetts Bay Company.** They wanted to set up another colony in America. In 1630, more than 1,000 Puritans arrived in Massachusetts. They founded Boston.

TALK AND SHARE Talk with your partner about why religious freedom was important. Make a poster about it.

VOCABULARY

Puritans—a group of English colonists who wanted religious freedom
Massachusetts Bay Company—a business with power from the king of England to set up a colony, pay for it, and make money from it

Primary Source

The Mayflower Compact

William Bradford was one of the Pilgrim leaders. He was governor of the Plymouth Colony for about 30 years. Bradford wrote about the colony in a book called *Of Plimoth Plantation.* He put a copy of the Mayflower Compact in it.

The Compact says that the signers are loyal to England's King James. It says they agree in front of each other and God. It says they are making a "civil body politic." That means a government of citizens ruled by law. It was the beginning of self-government in America.

▲ Pilgrims worked hard to build Plymouth.

Talk About The First Thanksgiving and The Puritans

■ Ask students to imagine that they were Pilgrims. Ask them such questions as:
  • What would you do?
  • How would you feel?
  • How would you feed your family?

  Then ask students to read to find out what the Pilgrims did.

■ Another group of English people came to America in the 1600s. Invite students to read about the Puritans.

TALK AND SHARE

Give each pair of students a piece of posterboard and ask them to draw or list why religious freedom is important. Allow time for pairs to share their reasons with the class.

Primary Source

The Mayflower Compact

Explain that primary sources give us information about events in history. We know a lot about the Plymouth Colony because of Bradford's book.

 Activity: Internet Resources

Students can see pictures and learn more about the first Thanksgiving and life at Plymouth Rock at the multilingual websites below. Encourage interested students to create a colorful poster of their findings and present it to the class:

• **English**
http://www.plimoth.org/learn

• **Spanish**
http://www.plimoth.org/about/foreign/spanish.asp

 Activity: Role-Play

Give student pairs one minute each to role-play the first Thanksgiving. One partner should play a Pilgrim; the other, a Native American. Give them five minutes to plan their role-plays. Encourage them to convey historical information—such as kinds of food served, the place, the year—as well as the feasters' emotions and thoughts.

Discuss Growth of the Colonies

- Ask students to use the map key to describe the three groups of colonies shown on the map. Provide the prompt *The _____ colonies are _____.*

- To prepare students for reading, tell them the colonies grew different crops, such as tobacco and rice. Some used slaves on large farms called plantations. Others set up self-government and practiced religious freedom.

- Have students read the paragraphs describing the three groups of colonies. As a class, discuss the differences in the regions.

TALK AND SHARE

Allow time for each pair to share their lists with another pair. Have them highlight details that appeared in both pairs' lists.

Look and Read

England's 13 Colonies

KEY
New England Colonies
Middle Colonies
Southern Colonies

ATLANTIC OCEAN

Growth of the Colonies

In time, England had 13 colonies along the Atlantic Coast. They developed into 3 different groups: the New England Colonies, the Middle Colonies, and the Southern Colonies.

NEW ENGLAND COLONIES

The Puritans **created** New England. Other religious groups found freedom in these colonies too. For example, the first Jewish settlement in America was in Rhode Island.

The New England colonists lived on small farms. Towns were run by town meetings. The largest city was Boston in the Massachusetts Bay Colony.

MIDDLE COLONIES

Here the Dutch started a colony in New York. In 1664, the English took it. In Pennsylvania, a Quaker leader named William Penn started another colony. The Quakers also had come seeking freedom of religion. Over time, New York City and Philadelphia, Pennsylvania, grew into large cities. Jobs in the cities **attracted** many young people from the farms.

SOUTHERN COLONIES

Many farms in the Southern Colonies were huge. The owners of these **plantations** were rich. Their plantations were like small villages. Most of the things people needed were made there. The workers were African **slaves.** Tobacco was the most important crop in Virginia and Maryland. Plantations farther south grew rice.

TALK AND SHARE With your partner, make 3 lists. Label them with the 3 groups of colonies. In each list, put details about life in those colonies. Talk about your lists.

VOCABULARY
created—built or made
attracted—drew or brought people in
plantations—large farms
slaves—people who are owned and forced to work by someone else

50   UNIT 1 • AMERICA'S BEGINNINGS

Activity: Write a Quiz

Divide the class into two groups. Have students use the lists they made for Talk and Share to create a six-question quiz for the other team. Their quizzes should be multiple-choice, with each answer choice being one of the headings on page 50. For example:

Which colonies had plantations?

a. New England Colonies

b. Middle Colonies

c. Southern Colonies

Differentiating Instruction

Beginning
Working with Words Have students copy the vocabulary words on 3" x 5" cards. Ask them to find a picture that relates to each word. Then have students group the words in pairs that make sense, such as those shown here:

settlers   Pilgrims   plantations
colony   Puritans   slaves

Intermediate
City vs. Country Invite partners to brainstorm three reasons people move to cities.

Advanced
Word Wheel Demonstrate using this Word Wheel for *plantation.* Then invite students to make and explain their own Word Wheels for *slavery.*

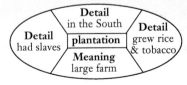

Slavery in America

In the 1500s and later, European merchants entered the **slave trade.** They bought **kidnapped** men, women, and children from merchants in Africa. They sold the Africans in the Americas. Thousands of Africans died during the awful voyage on the slave ships.

The first African slaves to arrive in the English colonies were brought to Jamestown in 1619. In time, slaves worked in all 13 colonies. Most slaves lived in the Southern Colonies, where they worked on the plantations.

Slaves had no rights. By law, they were **property,** not people. Children could be sold away from parents. Slaves could not marry without **permission. Cruel** punishments, such as whippings, kept slaves obeying their masters.

Slavery was a terrible evil. It left a permanent mark on American life. Even today, the harm done by slavery is felt in the way people think about each other.

(TALK AND SHARE) **To your partner, explain what the life of a slave was like.**

▲ Slaves for sale

VOCABULARY
slave trade—the business of buying and selling slaves
kidnapped—taken away by force
property—something that is owned
permission—an agreement from someone with power
cruel—causing pain and suffering. *Cruelty* refers to the act of hurting others.

▲ Chains for holding slaves

Summary

To grow rich, England set up 13 colonies in North America. English people came for wealth, religious freedom, and a better life. Africans were brought as slaves. The United States today is shaped by the ideas the colonists had about freedom and self-government and by slavery.

Teach About Slavery in America

■ Create a K-W-L Chart titled *Slavery* on the board. Read aloud the definition of *slaves* on page 50. Then ask students what they know about slavery and what they want to learn. After reading the section, students should list what they learned.

■ Ask students:
   • Why did English people come to the Americas?
   • Why were African people brought to the Americas?

(TALK AND SHARE)

Ask students to study the pictures on this page. They should discuss with their partners what they think life was like for slaves.

Discuss the Summary

■ Direct students to read the Summary at the end of the lesson.

■ Help students see the connection between the Summary and the Big Idea on page 43.

■ Then ask volunteers to put into their own words what they learned from this lesson.

Assessment

Assess students' comprehension by asking the following questions:

History
• What was the main reason the first colony was founded?
• Why did the Pilgrims come to the colonies?
• What was the slave trade?
• How were the three groups of colonies different?

Language
Define the words in each pair of homophones:
• Some/sum
• Steel/steal
• Right/write

Assessment Book
Use page 21 to assess students' comprehension.

Teach Describing

Explain to students that describing is a skill they will use in all subjects. A Web can help them list the details they could use to describe a person, thing, or event.

Model the Organizer

- Ask volunteers to read aloud the details about the New England Colonies.

- Tell students that a Web like this one can help them list details.

Give Practice Describing

Have students work with partners to complete one activity.

- **Draw** Have beginning learners complete the Draw activity. Encourage them to use key words from the text with the heading *Middle Colonies* on page 50.

- **Write** Have intermediate and advanced students complete the Write activity. Suggest that students work in pairs to brainstorm ideas for a descriptive Web. Then have them work individually to write their paragraphs. Afterward, have them read their paragraphs to their partners.

Develop Language

Describing

Describing Colonial Life

When you are asked to describe something, you give details. Here's an example: *Describe life in the New England Colonies.* Ask yourself, "What were the New England Colonies like? What details tell about religion, about towns, about farms, and so on?" List as many details as you can in a Web.

Web

They were created by the Puritans.

Puritans came for religious freedom.

THE NEW ENGLAND COLONIES

Jews had religious freedom in Rhode Island.

People lived on small farms.

People lived in towns.

Boston was the most important city.

Practice Describing

1. Draw Think of the details you have learned about life in the Middle Colonies. Make a Web and write or draw your details. Then draw a picture of colonial life. Explain your picture to your partner.

2. Write Describe life in the Southern Colonies. First, list the important details in a Web. Then, use those details to write a paragraph of 3 to 4 sentences. The Word Bank may help you.

Word Bank

plantation
village

tobacco
rice

owners
slaves

 Activity: Summary Chart

Write the three Key Concepts as headings on a chart on the chalkboard. Invite students to contribute information they learned in the lesson. Add it to the chart.

 Differentiating Instruction

Beginning
Web Help Provide support by asking the questions below:

- Was one of the Middle Colonies started by the Spanish or the Dutch?

- Did the Middle Colonies include large cities or plantations?

- What big cities were in the Middle Colonies?

Intermediate
Paragraph Help Students may need help seeing the main idea about the Southern Colonies. These colonies were characterized by large farms called *plantations*.

Advanced
Peer Editing Have partners check each other's writing. They should ask:

- What is the main idea sentence?

- How do the details support the main idea?

Grammar Spotlight

Simple Past Tense How do you tell about something that happened in the past? To most verbs, just add *ed*.

Verb	Simple Past Tense
work	Colonists worked hard in early times.
want	The rulers of Europe wanted to use America to get richer.
order	Then Smith ordered the colonists to work planting crops.

Write a sentence using the past tense of one of the verbs in the chart.

Partner Practice

Make a Timeline With a partner, go back to the lesson and pick 4 events. Put the events on a timeline. Draw a picture for each event. Then share your timeline with the class.

Oral Language

Arriving at Jamestown Three students each take a part. Practice your lines. Then perform for your group or class.

Father: At last we are here.

Mother: I'm so glad. I was so sick on that ship! I thought I would die.

Father: We should pray to God to thank him.

Mother: Yes, we should pray. *(They all pray.)*

Father: You and the children stay on the ship. I am going with Captain Smith to look for a place to build our home.

Son: Can I come with you?

Father: No. Your mother will need you. Goodbye.

Mother and Son together: Goodbye.

LESSON 3 • THE THIRTEEN COLONIES **53**

Activities

Grammar Spotlight

Explain to students that in the past tense, most verbs end in -*ed*.

Read aloud each example in the chart and ask students to repeat after you. Then ask them to go back into the reading selection and find examples of past tense verbs.

Partner Practice

Ask students to write a heading and the date for each event in their timelines. Check that events on the timeline are in chronological order.

Oral Language

Encourage trios of students to rehearse their lines. Model how to read the exclamatory sentence with expression and how to lift the voice at the end of the question. After practice, have each group perform their role-plays for the class.

 Activity: Extend the Lesson

For additional reading, recommend the following books:

- *The Settling of Jamestown* by Marylee Knowlton and Janet Riehecky (Gareth Stevens Publishing, 2002)

- *Roanoke: The Lost Colony—An Unsolved Mystery from History* by Jane Yolen and Heidi Yolen Stemple (Simon & Schuster, 2003)

Program Resources

Student Activity Journal
Use page 23 to practice *describing*.

Overhead Transparencies
Use 33, Web, with page 52.

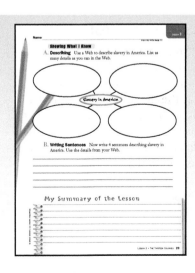

Steps to the American Revolution

STANDARDS CONTENT

History

■ Recognize causes and effects

■ Identify the steps that led to the American Revolution

■ Recognize key events and people related to the American Revolution

■ Recognize important ideas in the Declaration of Independence

Language

■ Identify the following Key Concepts: *power, control,* and *independence*

■ Recognize words that signal cause-effect relationships

■ Practice explaining an event

Begin ▸ Building Background

■ Ask students the questions below the photo. Focus students on:

• Why armed soldiers might fire on a crowd of people

• How this would make people feel about the government that did it

■ Provide students with words as needed (*rifles, soldiers, colonists*).

■ Ask a volunteer to read aloud the caption below the boy's picture. Ask students to share what they know about revolutions.

■ Then draw out these key ideas about revolutions:

• They can be violent.

• They are about power and control.

Talk and Explore

Steps to the American Revolution

Here you'll learn the steps that led to the American Revolution. You'll also learn about cause-effect relationships and practice explaining why something happened.

Building Background

▲ We had a revolution in Nicaragua too. My father said it happened because people were not being treated fairly.

■ What's happening in this picture?

■ Who are these people, and why are they fighting?

■ How do you think Americans felt when they saw this picture?

 Activity: Word Wall

Write the word *revolution* on an 8½" x 11" sheet. Ask students to name words they think of when they look at the picture. Try to generate words such as *fighting, shooting, angry,* and *colonies.* Have students write the words on index cards and tape them to the wall under *revolution.*

 Differentiating Instruction

Beginning
Building Vocabulary Have partners practice saying any new words they learned from the discussion of the picture. Ask them to write the words on sticky notes and label related pictures in the lesson.

Intermediate
Look and Write Have partners create three sentences about the picture: who they see, what is happening, and how they feel about it. Ask students to share their sentences with the class.

Advanced
Write and Share Have students consider how people would feel if soldiers of their own government attacked them. Have them respond in three to four sentences. Ask them to share their responses with a partner.

The colonists grew angry at British rule. Finally, the colonies declared independence from Britain.

1 **Trouble with Britain**

2 **Start of Fighting**

In CONGRESS, July 4, 1776.
A DECLARATION
By the Representatives of the
UNITED STATES OF AMERICA,
In GENERAL CONGRESS ASSEMBLED.

3 **Declaration of Independence**

LESSON 4 • STEPS TO THE AMERICAN REVOLUTION **55**

Introduce the Big Idea

- Read aloud the Big Idea and go through the three steps.
- Explain that the story of the steps to the American Revolution is one of British control and growing anger on the part of the colonists. Eventually, things became violent, and the colonists said they would no longer be part of Britain.

Teach the Pictures

On page 54, the image shows British troops shooting Crispus Attucks in the Boston Massacre. Attucks was a runaway slave of African and Native American descent. He was the first of five Americans killed by British gunfire. Even though there were laws regulating the burial of African Americans, Attucks was buried alongside the other honored men.

At the top of page 55, the image shows the impressment of Boston colonists by the British. Tell students that *impressment* means the act of seizing people for public service or use.

Review

Review words introduced in previous lessons, such as *colonist*, *representative government*, and *self-government*.

Activity: Role-Play

Role-play a scene between an unfair landlord and a tenant.

Landlord: *I'm putting a tax on the heat. Each time you use heat, you have to pay me $1.*

Tenant: *What? It's very cold outside! I don't have a lot of money.*

Landlord: *Too bad. I own the building, and you have to do what I say.*

Tenant: *No way! I'm going to talk to the other tenants, and we're going to fight!*

Then process the role-play with students. Ask them questions such as:

- Did the tenant have any say in what happened to him?
- Who has the power?

Tell students that the colonists were like the tenant. They had no power when Britain said, *I'm putting a tax on you.* Ask them to predict what happened when Britain taxed the colonists.

Resource Library

***Reader's Handbook* (red)**
Looking for Cause and Effect 644–645

***Reader's Handbook* (yellow)**
Looking for Cause and Effect 524–525

All Write
Cause and Effect 270–271

Teach [Key Concepts]

■ To model correct pronunciation, say each term slowly. Ask students to repeat after you. Then read aloud the Key Concept sentences and talk about what they mean.

■ Have students work with a partner to connect the Key Concepts to a different historical event or to a current event.

■ Have partners create a short sentence about the event using some of the Key Concepts.

Teach the Visual Aid

[Steps to War]

Focus students on the visual aid. Help them see that the events occurred in chronological order. Have them talk about what they see in the pictures. Then briefly explain each event and how it led to the next one. Ask students, *What does the visual aid tell us about the events leading up to the American Revolution?*

• Britain angered the colonists.

• Colonists rebelled.

• Colonists met to decide what to do.

• The two sides started fighting.

• Colonists wrote the Declaration of Independence.

[Key Concepts]

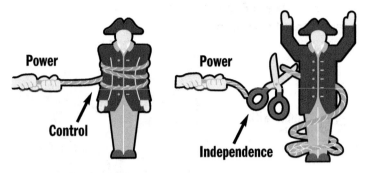

Power is the strength or force that can make people do things. The British used their power over the colonists to **control** them and to keep them down.

The colonists wanted **independence.** That is, they wanted to be free from British control.

[Steps to War]

1765
Stamp Act

1770
Boston Massacre

1773
Boston Tea Party

▲ Tax stamps

56 UNIT 2 • BUILDING A NEW NATION

Activity: Definition Game

Have students preview the Look and Read section on pages 58–63. Divide the class into two groups: terms and definitions. Have students write one file card for each of the terms or definitions. Collect cards, shuffle them, and pass them out.

Have a student with a term stand and say the term. Ask the student with the definition that matches that term to stand and read aloud the definition. Continue until all cards have been read.

Differentiating Instruction

Beginning
Word-Picture Associations Focus on the pictures with less fluent learners. Ask students to name or describe the pictures they see in Key Concepts and in the visual aid. In a small group, encourage students to use words they know to talk about each picture.

Intermediate
Signal Words Have students explain each event in the visual aid in sequence using *first, then,* and *finally.*

Advanced
Partner Quiz Ask students to work in pairs to create a quiz about four to five people or terms. Then have one student read aloud the first question and set of answers. The partner has to listen carefully and choose the correct answer. Students take turns quizzing each other until they complete the quiz.

Cause and Effect

To understand *why* events happen in history, look for causes and effects. The **cause** is what makes something happen. The **effect** is what happens as a result.

The chart below shows the cause of the Stamp Act and its effect. In other words, it tells *why* the Stamp Act happened and *what* result it had in history.

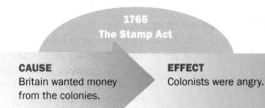

▲ This teapot was made to protest the Stamp Act of 1765.

**1765
The Stamp Act**

CAUSE
Britain wanted money from the colonies.

EFFECT
Colonists were angry.

1774
First Continental Congress

1775
Battles of Lexington & Concord

1776
Declaration of Independence

LESSON 4 • STEPS TO THE AMERICAN REVOLUTION **57**

Teach Skill Building

■ Read with students the explanation of *cause* and *effect*.

■ Then demonstrate a cause-effect relationship. Pretend to pour a little water from a cup onto the floor. Then pretend to walk over it and slip. Write on the board: *cause* (spilled water) and *effect* (slipped and fell).

■ Be sure that students understand the following academic vocabulary: *event, cause, effect*.

■ Walk through the example of the Stamp Act. Explain words such as *tax*, *goods* (like tea), and *king* and the history leading up to the Stamp Act.

■ Then ask volunteers to identify the event (*the Stamp Act*) and describe in their own words its cause and its effect.

Activity: Culture Connection

Invite students to tell what they know about revolutions. Be sensitive to students who do not wish to relive personal horrors.

Tell students that other countries have experienced revolution and many have had to fight for independence: France (1789), Mexico (1821), Colombia (1810), Venezuela (1821), Ecuador (1822), and Panama (1821).

Program Resources

Student Activity Journal

Use page 24 to build key vocabulary.

Use page 25 to practice identifying cause and effect.

Overhead Transparencies

Use 3, Cause-effect Organizer, with page 57.

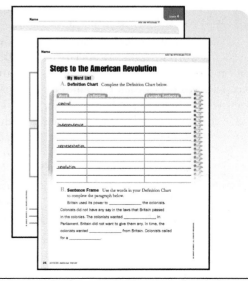

Introduce Steps to the American Revolution

Draw a Multiple-cause Organizer on the board. After the class has finished the lesson, ask volunteers to fill in the Cause boxes.

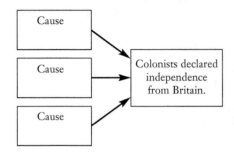

Key Connection: Economics

- Develop an understanding of taxation as a source of revenue for a government.

- Discover what students know about taxes. Ask students:
  - When do we pay them?
  - How do people generally feel about paying them?
  - Why do governments tax people?

- Explain that in this lesson, students will learn that the real problem was not that the colonists were taxed but that they had no say in it.

Steps to the American Revolution

Over time, trouble grew between the colonists and Britain. At first, it was about taxes. Then, it was about control. Finally, the colonists fought back and declared independence.

Growing Trouble with Britain

For many years, **Britain** let the colonies run themselves. When that changed, the colonists grew unhappy.

THE STAMP ACT

In 1765, Britain's **Parliament** passed the Stamp Act. It was a **tax** on paper products, like newspapers. The colonists had no vote in Parliament. Therefore, they thought the tax was unfair. "No taxation without **representation!**" they cried.

THE BOSTON MASSACRE

By 1770, there were more taxes. Many colonists **protested,** and Britain sent soldiers to control the colonies. One winter evening in Boston, a crowd of more than 50 people gathered to protest. Fewer than 12 British soldiers were on guard. People yelled at them and threw rocks and snowballs. The soldiers shot into the crowd because they were frightened. Eleven people were shot. Three were only 17 years old. Five colonists died. As a result, newspapers called the event a **massacre.** Still, a colonial court said the British soldiers were "not guilty."

▲ American colonists

▲ Paul Revere's famous picture of the Boston Massacre helped make the colonists angrier.

VOCABULARY

Britain—the name of the country that includes England, Scotland, and Wales. The people are the *British*.
Parliament—the highest lawmaking group in Britain
tax—the money people must pay to a government

representation—having someone in government speak for you
protested—publicly showed strong opinions against something
massacre—the killing of a large number of people who can't defend themselves

58 Unit 2 • Building a New Nation

Activity: Teach Vocabulary

Throughout the lesson, have students work with the vocabulary at the end of each page. Ask students to keep a word list of each term in their journal or notebook. When possible, have their lists include Word Wheels.

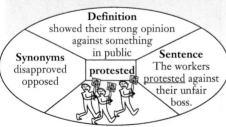

Definition
showed their strong opinion against something in public
Synonyms
disapproved opposed
protested
Sentence
The workers protested against their unfair boss.

Differentiating Instruction

Beginning
Connecting Ideas Focus students' attention on the introductory paragraph and the headings. Ask, *What trouble grew?* Show students how these ideas connect with one another: *The tax (Stamp Act) made the colonists angry. They got angrier when they heard about the Boston Massacre. The Boston Tea Party was their protest, their way of showing how mad they were.*

Intermediate
Read and Share With a partner, students should read aloud one paragraph at a time. Ask them to share one thing they learned from each paragraph.

Advanced
Building Vocabulary Have students read through to the question on page 59 and jot down unfamiliar words. Then, in small groups, have them discuss what they read and work together to find the definitions.

THE BOSTON TEA PARTY

In December 1773, another **event** made things worse. It was called the Boston Tea Party. Britain had put a tax on tea. One reason was to show the colonists that the British were in control. Tea was a favorite drink in the colonies, so many colonists became angry. A British company had 3 ships full of tea in Boston Harbor. After dark, a crowd of colonists dressed up like Indians and boarded the ships. They dumped the tea overboard. Townspeople came out to watch.

News of the event spread. Soon other colonists began to protest too. The Boston Tea Party had two important effects. It helped join the colonists together, and it made Parliament very angry.

(**TALK AND SHARE**) **With your partner, talk about the trouble between Britain and the colonies. How did it start? How did it get worse?**

VOCABULARY
event—something that happens

Language Notes

Signal Words:
Cause-effect
These words are clues to discovering why something happened.

☐ therefore
☐ because
☐ as a result
☐ reason
☐ so
☐ effect

At the Boston Tea Party in 1773, colonists threw British tea into the water to protest taxes. ▼

Teach About Growing Trouble with Britain

- Ask students how a tax might cause trouble, how a massacre would affect people's opinions, and what the reaction might be to protests such as the Boston Tea Party.

- Explain to students that the Boston Massacre was basically media "spin." The event was bad. The newspapers made it seem worse.

- Explore what students know personally about the effect that news reports have on them and on others.

Language Notes

Draw students' attention to the Language Notes. Point out how the (red) words and phrases are used in the text. Help students understand that these words and phrases often signal cause-effect relationships.

TALK AND SHARE

Ask students the questions in the Talk and Share activity. Have students work in pairs to answer the questions. Ask volunteers to share their answers with the class.

Activity: Sentence Patterns

Practice sentence patterns for describing cause-effect relationships.

- What caused the _____?
- The _____ happened because _____.
- The reason the _____ happened was _____.
- As a result of _____, the _____ happened.

First, relate the sentences to classroom events. Then, use the content of the lesson.

Program Resources

Student Activity Journal
Assign page 26:
- To create study notes for students to review
- To provide reinforcement of key vocabulary

Overhead Transparencies
Use 36, Word Wheel, with page 58.

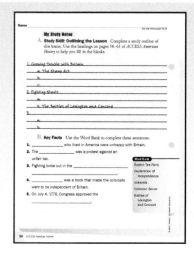

Discuss Fighting Starts

Ask students to predict what they will read next. Encourage them to use the pictures and heads to help with their predictions.

Teach the Skill: Cause and Effect

- Have students look for the signal words *caused* and *because*.

- Have students find the dates 1774 and April 18, 1775, and identify the events associated with each.

- Ask why time order is important in figuring out causes and their effects.

Look and Read

Fighting Starts

The Boston Tea Party caused the king and Parliament to get very angry. Parliament **punished** the colonists. It closed Boston Harbor so no ships could go in or out. It put Boston under the rule of the British army.

Philadelphia, Pennsylvania, was the richest city in the colonies. ▼

THE FIRST CONTINENTAL CONGRESS

A group of leaders from all over the colonies met in Philadelphia in 1774. We call this group the **Continental Congress.** These leaders said the colonies had the right to say what their laws should be. They said if Britain used **force,** the colonists would fight back.

J O U R N A L
OF THE
PROCEEDINGS
OF THE
CONGRESS,
Held at PHILADELPHIA,
September 5, 1774

PHILADELPHIA:
Printed by William and Thomas Bradford,
at the London Coffee House.
M.DC.C.LXXIV.

VOCABULARY

punished—hurt someone for doing something wrong
Continental Congress—a group of men who led the American colonies to independence from Britain
force—soldiers and guns

60 UNIT 2 • BUILDING A NEW NATION

Activity: Oral Story String

Have small groups create an oral story using cause-effect signal words. Provide them with a prompt like the one below or use the content of the lesson. (Example prompt: *The Boston Tea Party occurred.*)

Prompt: *The girl forgot to bring her homework to class . . .*

Student A: *. . . because she was in a hurry this morning.*

Student B: *As a result, her teacher made her stay after school.*

Differentiating Instruction

Beginning
Word-Picture Associations Have students look at the pictures from the beginning of the lesson to page 61. Then have them connect the three vocabulary terms on the bottom of page 60 to as many pictures as they can.

Intermediate
Summarizing the Story Divide the class into pairs. Have students read aloud the red and blue headings. Ask them to give a summary to their partners using the headings.

Advanced
Talk About It In a small group, students should discuss the following questions:

- What events led to the First Continental Congress?

- What happened as a result of the meeting in Philadelphia?

- What do you think will happen next?

THE BATTLES OF LEXINGTON AND CONCORD

Many colonial farmers and businessmen began to arm themselves. They called themselves **minutemen,** because they were ready to fight in a minute.

British troops were called **redcoats.** They feared the colonists were getting ready for war. Redcoats marched from Boston to Concord to take the weapons the colonists were keeping. On the night of April 18, 1775, Paul Revere rode from farm to farm. He called to the minutemen, "The British are coming!"

On the next day, the colonists went out to fight the British. They fought the Battles of Lexington and Concord. People on both sides died. The **revolution** had begun. The colonists were fighting to be a free country.

▲ Paul Revere warned colonists that British soldiers were coming.

(TALK AND SHARE) **With a partner, make a list of events that led to the revolution. Talk about their effects.**

VOCABULARY

minutemen—the colonists who were ready to be soldiers
redcoats—British soldiers during the American Revolution
revolution—a war against your own government

The Battle of Lexington lasted only 15 minutes. Eight minutemen were killed, and 9 were wounded. Only one redcoat was hurt. ▼

Talk About The Battles of Lexington and Concord

- Use the pictures to encourage a discussion of the Battles of Lexington and Concord.

- Invite volunteers to read the captions.

- In the battle picture, ask students to identify the British troops and the colonial forces. Ask:
  - Which side looks stronger?
  - Who has the better chance of winning?
  - Why would the colonists fight against such a force?

(TALK AND SHARE)

Have students complete the Talk and Share activity with a partner. Ask them to write their answers in a list. Then gather as a class and ask a volunteer to name the event that happened in 1774. Ask another volunteer to name the 1775 event. Have a third volunteer write the answers on the board as the students say them.

 Activity: Internet Resources

Have students use the Internet to research these topics and questions:

First Continental Congress
- What colonies did leaders come from?
- Where did they meet?
- What did they decide?

Battles of Lexington and Concord
- Who were some of the key players from both armies?
- Who was Paul Revere?

 Activity: History Notebook

Help students build a notebook for this lesson. The notebook should include items from the Student Activity Journal, pictures, lists, and drawings they've made about the events. Have them share their notebook with a partner.

Discuss The Declaration of Independence

■ Tell students that as a result of the increasing fighting, a second group of leaders met at the Second Continental Congress.

■ Ask students why they think leaders might have written the Declaration of Independence.

■ Encourage students to predict what the declaration says.

Primary Source

Common Sense

Use the feature on *Common Sense* to demonstrate the value of primary source documents in history.

• Show students the Op-Ed section of a newspaper. Read aloud an editorial about a subject that students will understand.

• Explain to students that Thomas Paine wrote *Common Sense* for the same reason editorial writers write today: to win the hearts and minds of the people.

• Help students understand how influential Paine's book was and how it increased colonists' anger toward the king.

The Declaration of Independence

Fighting spread to other colonies. Many colonists believed it was time to **separate** from British rule.

THE SECOND CONTINENTAL CONGRESS

A second meeting of leaders took place in Philadelphia. This meeting was called the Second Continental Congress.

American leaders agree to sign the Declaration of Independence. ▼

The leaders talked about what they should do about their problems with the British. Many **argued** that the time had come to separate from Britain. They wanted **independence**.

VOCABULARY

separate—move away from or leave
argued—led people to believe something by giving reasons
independence—the freedom from control

Primary Source

Common Sense

Common Sense was a little book, but it had a big effect. Thomas Paine wrote it in 1776. Paine was an Englishman who lived in America.

Paine believed the colonies should be independent. He used plain "common sense" in his writing. He attacked the idea of having kings. He said the king was a fool. He said the only thing that made a person a king was that he was born one.

Thousands of colonists read his little book. It made "common sense" to them, and it made them angry at British rule. But most of all, it made them strongly want their independence.

▲ Thomas Paine

62 UNIT 2 • BUILDING A NEW NATION

 Activity: Paired Writing

Divide the class into pairs. Ask students to pick two to three vocabulary terms. Then have them think about another event that would involve those terms. Ask them to write a short paragraph about it using the terms they picked.

Differentiating Instruction

Beginning

Word Meanings For *independence*, have students pantomime *free* vs. *not free*. Then have the students break *independence* into syllables. The prefix *in-* means *not*. *Independence* is *not under someone's control*.

Continental and *Congress* both begin with *con-*. This word part means *come together* or *join*. A *continent* is a large land mass that is *held together*. A *congress* is a meeting of people who have *come together*.

Intermediate

Word Sleuths Have students use their dictionaries to explore the differences between *liberty* and *independence*. *Liberty* suggests free choice. *Independence* signals an end to outside control.

Advanced

Talk About It Have students discuss the ideas in the Declaration of Independence. Ask students, *How did the colonists use these ideas to explain breaking away from Britain?*

WRITING THE DECLARATION OF INDEPENDENCE

The Congress decided to write a **document.** In it, the colonies would **declare** their independence from Britain. They would tell the world that the colonies had a right to be free and independent. The leaders chose young Thomas Jefferson to lead the writing team. John Adams, one of the older leaders, explained to Jefferson, "You are a Virginian and very popular. Also, you can write 10 times better than I can."

After Jefferson wrote it, the whole Congress discussed it. On July 4, 1776, Congress approved the **Declaration of Independence.** That date became an important holiday.

▲ Thomas Jefferson

Important Ideas in the Declaration of Independence

All people are created equal.

People have rights that come from God; these can't be taken away from them.

People have the right to live, to be free, and to seek happiness.

Governments get their power from the people.

People have the right to get rid of an unfair government.

▲ John Adams

(TALK AND SHARE) **Talk with your partner about which ideas in the Declaration of Independence seem most important to you.**

VOCABULARY
document—a written paper
declare—say in an official way
Declaration of Independence—the document that said the colonies were free from British rule

Summary

Colonists thought British control was unfair. They protested against British taxes, and fighting broke out. The American Revolution began. Finally, in 1776, the Continental Congress approved the Declaration of Independence.

Teach About Writing the Declaration of Independence

Explain to students why the colonists decided to write the Declaration of Independence. This document "declared" they were free, effectively starting the revolution. They wanted to explain their actions to the world, not just to Britain.

(TALK AND SHARE)

Have partners complete the Talk and Share activity. Then ask students to share their responses with the class.

Discuss the Summary

■ Direct students to read the Summary at the end of the lesson.

■ Then return to the Big Idea on page 55. Help students see the connection between the Summary and the Big Idea.

■ Then ask volunteers to put into their own words what they learned from this lesson.

✓ Assessment

Assess students' comprehension by asking the following questions:

History

• What were the main problems or troubles between Britain and the colonists?

• What did the colonists do about these problems?

• What were the main ideas in the Declaration of Independence?

Language

Write or say sentences using these cause-effect signal words:

• As a result

• Because

• Effect

• Reason

• Therefore

• So

Assessment Book

Use page 22 to assess students' comprehension.

Develop Language

Teach Explaining

Tell students that often test questions ask you to explain the reasons behind an event. This page teaches them how to explain why something happened.

Model the Organizer

- Ask volunteers to read aloud the three causes for the Second Continental Congress.

- Point to the parts of the Cause-effect Organizer and show how the organizer relates important causes to an event.

Give Practice Explaining

- **Draw** Ask beginning students to complete the Draw activity:

  - Suggest students first find the place in the lesson that tells about the Boston Massacre.

  - Then ask them how many things they can find that led to it. (Answers might include *taxes, a crowd, soldiers on guard, rocks and snowballs.*)

  - Check students' organizers for correct placement of labels.

- **Write** Intermediate and advanced students can complete the Write activity. Check for use of cause-effect signal words.

Develop Language

Explaining

Explaining Why Something Happened

When you explain *why* an event happened, you tell its causes. An organizer can help you keep track of causes. For example, this organizer lists 3 events that caused the colonists to call the Second Continental Congress.

Cause-effect Organizer

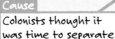

Cause
Colonists fought Battles of Lexington and Concord.

Cause
Fighting spread to other colonies.

Cause
Colonists thought it was time to separate from Britain.

Effect
Colonists called the Second Continental Congress.

Practice Explaining

1. Draw Draw pictures in a Cause-effect Organizer to explain why the Boston Massacre happened. Use your organizer to explain its causes to your partner or group.

2. Write Explain why the colonists decided to declare their independence from Britain. First, list the causes in an organizer. Then, use those causes to write a paragraph of 3 to 4 sentences. You can use words from the Word Bank in your writing.

Word Bank
vote
control
shoot
protest

Parliament
soldiers
tax
crowd

unfair
violent

 Activity: Internet Resources

Have partners search the Internet for information on key events from the lesson. Ask them to find one item below and present a summary about it to the class:

- Pictures
- Timelines
- Short stories
- Music
- First-person accounts
- Video reenactments
- Women's role in the revolution

Some useful websites are:

- http://memory.loc.gov
- http://www.pbs.org

Differentiating Instruction

Beginning
Creating an Organizer Focus students on the words *cause* and *effect*. Ask them to come up with two to three examples of cause-effect relationships. Give students the option of drawing or writing their examples in a Cause-effect Organizer.

Intermediate/Advanced
Checking Your Writing More fluent English language learners may also need help in explaining what happened leading up to the American Revolution.

Remind students to use a Cause-effect Organizer as a way of organizing their thoughts before they begin to write.

After they have finished writing, remind students to read over their paragraphs and check for missing words and misspellings. Refer them to the Grammar Spotlight on page 65 if they need help with irregular verbs.

Grammar Spotlight

Irregular Verbs in the Past Tense To form the past tense for most verbs, you add *ed*. Some verbs are irregular. With them, you need to change the whole word to form the past tense. You'll need to memorize irregular verbs.

	Verb	Present Tense	Past Tense
Regular Verbs	to happen	happen	happened
	to punish	punish	punished
	to protest	protest	protested
Irregular Verbs	to begin	begin	began
	to fight	fight	fought
	to meet	meet	met

Think of one regular and two irregular verbs. Write a sentence using each verb in the past tense.

Oral Language

Sharing Family Ideas At home, talk to your parents about revolution. Ask them what they know about it. Tell them what you are learning. Then share what they said with the class.

Hands On

Freedom Wall Make a poster about freedom and revolution. Draw what you know about these words. Use words and pictures. Share your poster with your group.

Partner Practice

Look What Happened! Draw 3 big circles. With a partner, think of something that happened this week. Write that event in the middle circle. What caused it? Write that in the circle on the left. Draw an arrow from your cause to the event. What do you think will happen because of the event? Decide together. Then write that in the right-hand circle. Draw an arrow from the event to this effect. Tell the class.

Cause → Event → Effect

LESSON 4 • STEPS TO THE AMERICAN REVOLUTION **65**

Activities

Grammar Spotlight

Explain to students that most verbs end in *-ed* when they are used in the past tense. Tell them that some verbs have special forms in the past tense. These verbs are called *irregular verbs.* Explain that irregular verbs have no special rules to remember and that they will have to memorize each verb.

Have volunteers read aloud the examples in the chart. Then ask students to go back into the reading selection and find examples of irregular verbs.

Oral Language

Have students come up with a list or poster of things they learned from the lesson. Have them write two or three questions they would ask their family. Then have them share their list or poster with the class.

Hands On

Ask students to work in small groups. Have them draw pictures or cut them from old magazines. Give them twenty minutes to make their posters.

Partner Practice

Have students cover up the effect and show their organizer to the class. Have the class guess the effect.

Activity: Extend the Lesson

Forging a New Nation (Stories in History series: McDougal Littell, 2003) includes an article and several short pieces of historical fiction that give intermediate and advanced students opportunities to explore this period in more detail: "The Road to Revolution," "Patrick Henry Protests the Stamp Act," "The Daughters of Liberty Stage a Boycott," "Trouble in Boston," "The Boston Tea Party," and "*Common Sense* Changes Minds."

Program Resources

Student Activity Journal
Use page 27 to practice *explaining.*

Overhead Transparencies
Use 3, Cause-effect Organizer, with page 64.

The American Revolution

STANDARDS CONTENT

History
- Recognize chronological order
- Identify the causes and effects of the American Revolution
- Name major events of the American Revolution
- Give reasons for America's victory

Language
- Identify the following Key Concepts: *forces*, *outnumbered*, and *surrender*
- Recognize words that signal time order
- Practice interpreting events

Begin Building Background

- Ask students the questions below the picture.
- Provide students with words as needed (*armies, fighting, independence*).
- Ask a volunteer to read aloud the caption below the girl's picture. Ask students to share thoughts.
- Then draw out key ideas about revolutions for independence:
  - People fighting for their freedom are willing to take big risks.
  - Small armies sometimes can win by using special tactics.
  - Often wars involve face-to-face combat.

The American Revolution

Here you'll learn how the colonists beat the British in the American Revolution. You'll also learn about chronological order and how to interpret major events.

Building Background

▲ A lot has changed since they fought wars a long time ago.

- **What's happening in this picture?**
- **Why are these soldiers ready to fight?**
- **What do you know about soldiers who faced hard times?**

66 UNIT 2 • BUILDING A NEW NATION

 Activity: K-W-L Chart

Have students draw three-column K-W-L Charts for the American Revolution. Review information from Lesson 4. Then ask volunteers to share additional prior knowledge of the war. Students should fill in the first column with the facts that they hear. Then they can write questions they have in the second column. When they have finished the lesson, they should fill in the last column with answers to their questions.

 Differentiating Instruction

Beginning
Key Term Review Review these words and concepts with students: *colonists, revolution, British, soldiers, army, fighting, freedom*. Ask volunteers to describe something in the picture using one of the words. Have them act out or draw concepts they don't have words to describe.

Intermediate
Look and Predict Have students work in pairs to write four sentences. Two sentences should describe the picture,

and two sentences should predict what will happen in the American Revolution. Have students use picture clues in their predictions.

Advanced
Making Comparisons Ask partners to consider how wars are fought. What is needed? Which side, British or American, do they think is better prepared to win?

During the American Revolution, colonial troops fought the British army. Help came from Europe. The colonists won the war, and the United States became a new nation.

1 Two Very Different Armies

LAFAYETTE, Lieutenant Général

2 Help from Overseas

3 Independence

Introduce the Big Idea

■ Use the pictures to encourage conversation about war. Have students identify what they see and share their background knowledge.

■ During the discussion, add information to an American Revolution Web. Then summarize the story of the American Revolution with these four points:

• Britain sent troops to America to stop the revolution.

• At first, the poorly trained Patriots were losing.

• Then France sent important help.

• The Patriots won the war, and America became a free nation.

Teach the Pictures

The third Big Idea shows colonists pulling down a statue of King George III. They were protesting his unfair treatment of the colonists. Ask, *How did the colonists feel when this happened?*

Review

In the last lesson, students learned about what can cause people to have a *revolution*. Ask students to give reasons people have fought revolutions.

Activity: Role-Play

Have students do a role-play that takes place soon after the Battles of Lexington and Concord. Divide the class into two teams. One half of the class will play the roles of colonial newspaper reporters, and the other half will play Patriots ready to fight England for independence.

Stage a news conference in which reporters ask Patriots their reasons for going to war. Prepare a short script, such as the one opposite, to model an example for students. Use a volunteer to play the role of a Patriot.

Reporter: *Why are you so angry?*

Patriot: *The government killed eight of our people! That would anger anyone!*

Reporter: *What will you do now?*

Patriot: *Keep fighting! We want independence!*

Resource Library

***Reader's Handbook* (red)**
Reading History 66–83

***Reader's Handbook* (yellow)**
Reading Social Studies 58–73

All Write
Chronological Order 272–273

Teach `Key Concepts`

- To model correct pronunciation, say each term slowly. Ask students to repeat after you. Then read aloud the Key Concept sentences and talk about what they mean.

- Have students connect the Key Concepts to a different historical event or to a current event.

- Have them write a short description about the event using the three terms.

Teach the Visual Aid
`The American Revolution`

Walk students through the timeline by having volunteers read aloud the dates and captions. Help students see how the timeline shows the story of the American Revolution.

- The British won many battles, but the Americans won the important Battle of Saratoga.
- The Continental Army spent a hard winter camped at Valley Forge.
- Other countries agreed to help the Americans.
- The Americans won the war.

`Key Concepts`

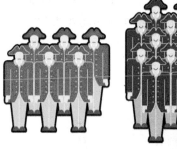 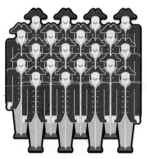 

Forces + **Outnumbered** = **Surrender**

The **forces** of a country are the groups of people organized to fight for it, like its army and navy. When the forces are **outnumbered,** that means there are more people on the other side. Sometimes, then, a general will **surrender,** or give up.

`The American Revolution`

1775-1777	October 1777	Winter 1777-1778	February 1778
British win most battles. ▼	Americans win Battle of Saratoga.	Continental Army suffers at Valley Forge. ▼	France agrees to help. Von Steuben trains Washington's army.

68 UNIT 2 • BUILDING A NEW NATION

Activity: Key Concept Pantomime

Divide the class into three groups and secretly assign each one a Key Concept term. Have the groups rehearse a pantomime of their Key Concept. Then ask each team to act out their term while the other teams guess what it is.

Differentiating Instruction

Beginning
Describing Pictures Ask questions about the Key Concepts and timeline. Provide cue words in your questions that students can repeat in their answers. Ask students to point to the correct pictures.

Intermediate
Explaining the Events Have students explain the events in the timeline using the dates and the words in the captions. Provide this sentence model:

In 1780, the British won the Battle of Charleston.

Advanced
Chronological Order On 3" x 5" cards, have students write the dates and captions from the timeline on the American Revolution. Ask them to shuffle the cards. Then have them take turns arranging the cards in order and explaining the events to their partners.

Chronological Order

Chronological order is the order in which things happen. Here's how to understand chronological order when you read history.

Look for dates.
Washington became leader of the army in 1775.

Look for words that tell about time.
At first, the Continental Army lost battles. Later, it began to win.

Look for the word *had*. Usually events are told in the order they happened. *Had* signals an earlier event.
In 1778, France agreed to help the Patriots. France had been an enemy of Britain for a long time.

George Washington ▶

December	**May**	**October**	**September**
1779	**1780**	**1781**	**1783**
British take control of Georgia.	British win Battle of Charleston. ▼	British surrender at Yorktown.	Treaty of Paris ends the war. ▼

Teach **Skill Building**

■ Read aloud the explanation of chronological order.

■ Model chronological order by using dates, signal words, and *had* to discuss events in the timeline: *In 1781, the British surrendered. At the beginning of the war, they had won most battles.*

Teach the Pictures

George Washington was elected the first president of the United States. He took his oath of office on April 30, 1789. Many people wanted him to be the king, but he thought the United States should not have one. Ask students, *Do you think it's better to have a king or a president?* Have students give reasons to support their opinions.

Activity: Timeline

Have students draw a timeline showing three to five major events in their lives. Encourage them to add pictures and captions. Then have students describe the events to their partners in two rounds.

First round: Students describe events in chronological order using dates and signal words, such as *first, then,* and *later.*

Second round: Students describe events out of order, using the word *had.*

Program Resources

Student Activity Journal
Use page 28 to build key vocabulary.

Use page 29 to practice using chronological order.

Overhead Transparencies
Use 28, Timeline, with page 69.

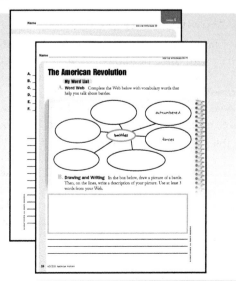

Introduce The American Revolution

■ Review the Key Concept *independence* from Lesson 4. Ask students to predict what this reading will be about.

■ In Lesson 4, students studied the events that caused the American Revolution. Have students discuss how Britain's actions made the colonists want to fight for their independence. Focus discussion on such previous vocabulary words as *Britain, representation, massacre, punished, force, Redcoats,* and *revolution.*

Key Connection: Geography

Develop understanding of these important geographical terms related to water or land bordering water: *peninsula, strait, island, coast, harbor.* Have volunteers point out examples of each form on a U.S. map. Waterways were important to the war, both as routes for navies and as barriers. Have students watch for this in the last big battle of the war.

▲ George III

The American Revolution

During the American Revolution, the colonists fought the British for their freedom. The colonists got help from overseas and won the war. The United States of America became a new country.

Two Very Different Armies

The start of the war was hard for the colonists. Britain already had an army. The colonists had to rush to put an army together. Also, not all the colonists were **Patriots** in favor of the war. Some were **Loyalists**—people still **loyal** to the British king, George III. Loyalists wouldn't fight for the Americans.

WASHINGTON'S DIFFICULTIES

General George Washington's army had many problems. His soldiers were mostly untrained farmers and **craftsmen.** The British army, on the other hand, was the world's best fighting force. The chart shows the differences between these armies. Who do you think had the better chance to win?

Comparing the Armies

	Patriot Army	British Army
NAME	The Continental Army	The British Army
LEADERS	Washington, Lafayette	Clinton, Cornwallis
SKILLS	Untrained, did not behave like soldiers	Well trained, followed orders well
SUPPLIES	Badly lacked guns, food, and uniforms	Had excellent weapons, supplies, and uniforms
LOCATION	Were fighting in their own land, which they knew well	Were fighting far from home
PURPOSE	To get freedom for themselves	To do their duty to their government

VOCABULARY
Patriots—colonists who wanted independence from Britain
Loyalists—colonists who stayed loyal to Britain
loyal—faithful, true
craftsmen—men who use skill to make things. A shipbuilder or printer is a craftsman.

Activity: Classify Vocabulary

Have pairs create a Three-column Chart with these headings: *About Any War, About the American Revolution,* and *Other Words.* Then have them classify the vocabulary words in one of the three categories. Ask why they chose to put the words where they did.

Differentiating Instruction

Beginning
Vocabulary Review Have students explain or demonstrate these previously learned vocabulary words: *American Revolution, colonists, freedom, independence, British, war.* Then reread the introduction, having students read aloud each sentence after you. Next, read the first sentence of each paragraph. Explain to students that the first sentence often gives a clue to what the entire paragraph is about.

Intermediate
Identifying the Ideas Have students read one paragraph at a time, taking turns with their partners. Tell them to stop after each paragraph and identify the main idea.

Advanced
Finding Out Encourage students to write down questions they have about unfamiliar words or ideas. In small groups, ask students to work together to answer their questions. Provide assistance if necessary.

BATTLE OF SARATOGA—A TURNING POINT

At first the war went very badly for the **Continental Army.** They lost major **battles** to the British in New York and in Pennsylvania. Thomas Paine said, "These are the times that try men's souls."

Meanwhile, the British were making a plan to end the war quickly. The plan called for the British to bring large **forces** together in New York. They wanted to **defeat** the Americans by **cutting off** New England from the other colonies.

▲ Fighting at Saratoga

A large British army started marching through New York. The Patriot forces met up with it in the summer of 1777. The British soldiers were marching in straight lines. The American soldiers, on the other hand, used ways of fighting they learned from the Indians. They hid behind trees and earth forts they had made. When the British came by, the Americans ran out, attacked, and ran back into hiding again.

After several such surprise attacks, the British were forced to go to a camp near Saratoga, New York. In October 1777, the Continental Army overpowered them there. The Battle of Saratoga stopped British plans to end the war quickly.

▲ British General Burgoyne (left) surrenders to American General Gates (right) at Saratoga.

(TALK AND SHARE) **Talk with a partner about how the Patriot army was different from the British army.**

VOCABULARY

Continental Army—the American army in the American Revolution
battles—large fights between armed forces

forces—groups of people organized to fight; armies, navies
defeat—beat; win against the enemy
cutting off—separating

Teach Battle of Saratoga—A Turning Point

■ Ask students to describe what they see in the pictures on page 71.

■ Tell students to focus on the meaning of the sentences they read, not just the individual words.

■ Explain that they should often stop and ask themselves, *Am I getting this?* If they lose the meaning, they should try these strategies:

- **Reread** Go back and read the piece again—slowly.
- **Read Ahead** Sometimes the meaning becomes clear when they read further.
- **Ask for Help** A teacher or partner can help if they get stuck.

(TALK AND SHARE)

Have partners take turns talking about the two armies. One partner describes the Continental Army while the other partner talks about the British Army. Ask them to tell how the armies were similar and different.

 Activity: Comparative Sentences

Divide the class into three groups and assign each group two rows of the chart on page 70. Have students create a sentence for each row that compares the two armies. Afterward, have them share their sentences with the class. Remind them to use comparison words such as *but, however,* and *although.*

Example: *George Washington led the Patriot army, but George Cornwallis led the British army.*

 Program Resources
Student Activity Journal
Assign page 30:

- To create study notes for students to review
- To provide reinforcement of key vocabulary

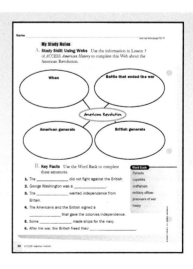

Discuss Help from Overseas

- Emphasize the hardships that the Continental Army suffered at Valley Forge.

- Help students use a U.S. map to locate the vicinity of the camp (*northwest of Philadelphia, Pennsylvania*).

- Explain that there were no buildings at Valley Forge for about 10,000 American soldiers who stayed there in the winter of 1777–1778. With only rags to wear in the cold, many died. Hundreds more died of starvation and disease.

- Say, *Most soldiers stayed at Valley Forge instead of deserting. Why do you think they stayed loyal?*

Teach the Pictures

Washington camped with his soldiers at Valley Forge, Pennsylvania, during the winter of 1777–1778. During that difficult time, more than 2,000 American soldiers died of starvation, cold, or disease. Today, Valley Forge has many historic sites and a national park. Students can learn more about this historic area online at the website: http://www.nps.gov/vafo.

Look and Read

Help from Overseas

The fight for freedom in America **excited** many people in Europe. France and Spain sent supplies. European **military officers** came to help General Washington. One was 19-year-old Marquis de Lafayette from France. Washington was his **idol**. Soon, Lafayette won Washington's trust, and Lafayette joined him in leading American troops.

WINTER AT VALLEY FORGE

In the winter of 1777–1778, Washington's army camped at **Valley Forge**. It was cold, and there was little money for supplies. Soldiers were barefoot. Many had no shelter, no warm clothes, and little food. Soon many became sick, and many others died. Still, few soldiers left the army. The soldiers believed in their fight and wanted to win.

▲ Marquis de Lafayette

▲ Washington and Lafayette at Valley Forge

VOCABULARY

excited—stirred up people's feelings
military officers—people of high rank in the armed forces, such as captains, admirals, and generals
idol—a hero; someone admired
Valley Forge—Washington's army camp in Pennsylvania

72 UNIT 2 • BUILDING A NEW NATION

 Activity: Tic-Tac-Toe Vocabulary

Have pairs create a tic-tac-toe grid with nine of the vocabulary words from the bottom of pages 70–73. Have players take turns using each word in a sentence. If the partner agrees the sentence is correct, the player can fill in the square with his or her mark—an *X* or an *O*.

X	O	O
	X	
		X

 Differentiating Instruction

Beginning
Role-Play Focus students on the picture of Valley Forge above. Have them identify the place and who is in the picture (*George Washington, General Lafayette, Continental soldiers*).

Then have them point to one of the men in the picture and role-play what he might be saying. Provide vocabulary, such as *cold, winter, snow,* and *hungry.*

Intermediate/Advanced
Role-Play Have students work in small groups to role-play the men shown in the picture on page 72, including George Washington, General Lafayette, and the soldiers.

First, have them discuss what the men may be thinking and feeling. Then have them take roles and act out their parts. If time allows, have groups act out their role-plays for the class.

FRANCE

For a long time, France and Britain had been enemies. So Americans believed that France would help them. At first, France gave some help, but it was not **official**. The Battle of Saratoga in the fall of 1777 changed that. After the American victory at Saratoga, the French signed an **alliance** with the Americans. Then, France sent more money and supplies.

OTHER HELP

During the winter at Valley Forge, another kind of help came. A general from the European country of Prussia joined Washington. Baron von Steuben

▲ Baron von Steuben

wrote a training **manual** and began quickly to train the troops. Also, General Washington got Congress to see how bad things were for his soldiers, and Congress voted more money for supplies. Now Washington had an army he could count on!

(TALK AND SHARE) With your partner, talk about why Europeans helped the Americans fight the British.

▲ Lafayette, on the right, with his idol, General George Washington

VOCABULARY

official—from the government
alliance—an agreement between countries to help each other fight a common enemy
manual—a small book of instructions; a handbook

Benjamin Franklin ▶

People in History

Benjamin Franklin

Benjamin Franklin had many talents. He was a writer, publisher, and inventor. He was a member of the Second Continental Congress, and he helped write the Declaration of Independence. During the American Revolution, he went to France to get that government's help. After the Treaty of Paris, he wrote, "I hope [the peace] will be lasting.... In my opinion, there never was a good war or a bad peace."

Talk About France and Other Help

- Emphasize that European help was very important. Baron von Steuben trained the troops to fight, and France sent money and supplies.

- Have students read the definition of *alliance*. Invite volunteers to act out the definition. Ask volunteers to introduce themselves as leaders from different countries. Then role-play asking for their help in a war. Student volunteers say *yes* and shake hands in agreement.

(**TALK AND SHARE**)

As a discussion prompt, write the word *enemy* on the board and act out its meaning for students. Students will use the word as they discuss how France and America shared a common enemy—Britain.

People in History

Benjamin Franklin

Read aloud the profile of Benjamin Franklin with students. Encourage interested students to find out more about him at this website: http://bensguide.gpo.gov/benfranklin. Have them share their findings with the class.

 Activity: Internet Resources

Students can learn more about the American Revolution at this PBS website: http://www.pbs.org/ktca/liberty. Features include an illustrated timeline and a quiz. Encourage students to discuss their findings with partners.

Activity: Use Chronological Order

On the board, write these events out of order (as shown):

- France sends America money.
- France signs an alliance with America.
- The Americans win at Saratoga.

Help students practice chronological order by working in groups to put the events in the order they occurred. Afterward, have volunteers write the sentences on the board in the right order.

Discuss Winning Independence

- Direct students' attention to a map of the thirteen colonies, such as that on page 50 of their books.
- Point to New York and review that the Americans won the Battle of Saratoga in New York.
- Then trace your finger down to Georgia and South Carolina.
- Tell students that the defeat at Saratoga caused the British to leave the North and go to these southern colonies where more people were loyal to Britain.

Language Notes

- Read aloud the Language Notes with students. To model the meaning of the time-order words, do a simple series of actions, such as sharpening a pencil.
- Then describe what you did using the red words. (*First,* I got a pencil. *Then,* I went to the sharpener. *Next,* I. . . .)
- Afterward, have students read aloud each sentence on pages 74–75 that contains a red word. Ask them time-order questions about the events.

Look and Read

Language Notes

Signal Words: Time Order
These words are clues to the order in which things happened.

- ☐ after
- ☐ then
- ☐ next
- ☐ first
- ☐ meanwhile
- ☐ soon

Winning Independence

After Saratoga, the British made a new plan. They knew that fewer Patriots and more Loyalists lived in the southern colonies than in the northern ones. As a result, the British moved the war south.

BRITISH VICTORIES

The British brought a huge force of 3,500 to Georgia. In December 1778, they took back control of that colony.

Then, in 1780, British General Henry Clinton sailed south with 8,500 men. His forces took over Charleston, South Carolina. They took 4,650 **prisoners of war!** It was the worst American **defeat** in the Revolution. After Charleston, Clinton was sure he could win the war. He went north to fight in New York and left General Charles Cornwallis in charge in the south.

▲ The revolution was fought at sea as well as on land.

VOCABULARY

prisoners of war—soldiers captured by the enemy and held until the war is over

defeat—a lost battle. *Defeat can also be a verb: In this battle, Cornwallis defeated the Americans.*

74 Unit 2 • Building a New Nation

 Activity: Sequence Organizers

Have students add important events to a Sequence Organizer. Suggest that they color-code the battles in their organizers so they can see at a glance who was winning the war. They can use one color for a British victory and a second color for an American victory.

Differentiating Instruction

Beginning
Visualizing Vocabulary Have partners copy each vocabulary word from Lesson 5 on a sticky note. Then have them place as many notes as they can on the corresponding pictures. Ask students to say the words as they place them on the pictures.

Intermediate
Making a Glossary Have students make an illustrated glossary of war terms, using *army, battle, defeat, military officer, alliance, manual, prisoner of war,* *defeat, outnumber, surrender,* and *treaty.* They should begin by alphabetizing the list.

Advanced
Conveying Meaning Ask students to list different ways to show what a word means. Their list might include *examples, similar words, drawings, opposites, using in a sentence,* and *defining.* Then have them choose methods for the words in the list above and show what each means.

THE END OF THE WAR

In 1780, the French sent an army of 6,000 men and ships from their navy. They were fighting in the north. Then Lafayette suggested the winning plan. He said French and American forces should join and go south to beat Cornwallis.

Cornwallis and his force were on a **peninsula** at Yorktown, Virginia. The American and French forces trapped him there. Off the coast, British and French warships **went at** each other. After 4 days, the French **fleet** won. Then French and American armies attacked the British at Yorktown. Cornwallis was cut off from sea and **outnumbered** on land. He **surrendered** to General Washington on October 19, 1781. The war was over.

Next, the Americans met with the British in Paris, France. They signed the **Treaty** of Paris. It gave the colonies independence. America was finally a free nation.

TALK AND SHARE With your partner, talk about how the Americans defeated Cornwallis. Draw a map about it and share your map with your class.

The Peninsula at Yorktown

Virginia

James River

Yorktown

N

ATLANTIC OCEAN

KEY

Peninsula

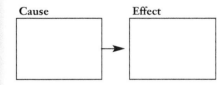

▲ Cornwallis surrenders at Yorktown.

VOCABULARY

peninsula—a point of land that sticks out into the sea
went at—attacked; fought
fleet—a group of ships
outnumbered—had fewer people
surrendered—declared that an enemy had won and that fighting could stop
treaty—a signed agreement between countries

Summary

The colonists fought the American Revolution to be free of British rule. The Americans won the war with help from Europe. This is how the United States of America became a new country.

Teach The End of the War

■ Emphasize that both geography and brilliant planning helped the Americans win at Yorktown.

■ Focus students on the map on page 75. Circle Yorktown with your finger.

■ Explain that the British were trapped on the peninsula by American soldiers, who greatly outnumbered them.

■ Then point to the Atlantic and explain that the British could not escape by sea because the French navy had control there.

TALK AND SHARE

Suggest that students draw a map with pictures to illustrate the Battle of Yorktown. Have them color-code the French, American, and British troops.

Discuss the Summary

Focus students on the Summary at the end of the lesson. Have them chart the key points of the Summary in a Cause-effect Organizer. Provide this visual prompt:

Cause		Effect
	→	

Assessment

Assess students' comprehension by asking the following questions:

History

• How were the Patriot and British armies different?

• Why did other countries help the colonists?

• How did American forces finally beat the British?

Language

Which term does not belong?

• Patriots, Loyalists, Valley Forge, Continental Army

• Defeated, surrendered, outnumbered, excited

• Leader, military officers, Washington, Paris

Assessment Book

Use page 23 to assess students' comprehension.

Teach Interpreting

Tell students that in their study of history they will need to interpret, or understand, events. This page will teach them strategies for interpreting why certain events are important.

Model the Organizer

- Have students perform a choral reading of the chart, with half the class reading the *Before* column and the other half reading the *After* column.

- Afterward, guide the class in drawing a conclusion about how important the Battle of Saratoga was to the Americans. Write their conclusion on the board.

Give Practice Interpreting

Have students work in pairs to complete one activity.

- **Draw** Have beginning learners complete the Draw activity.

- **Write** Suggest that students work in pairs to brainstorm ideas for a Before-and-After Chart about the Battle of Yorktown. They should conclude that the battle was extremely important because it convinced France's government to help the Continental Army.

Develop Language

Interpreting

Interpreting the Importance of Events

When you interpret an event in history, you tell what it means. You explain how the event affected later events. You tell in what way it was important. Follow these steps.

1. Look at what happened before the event.

2. Look at what happened after it.

3. Make a conclusion about how the event changed things.

A Before-and-After Chart can help you. This one organizes information for interpreting the importance of the Battle of Saratoga.

Before-and-After Chart

Before the Battle of Saratoga	After the Battle of Saratoga
The British won the major battles.	France signed an alliance with the Americans.
The Continental Army looked weak to Europeans.	Spain joined the American fight.
Europeans held back their support.	Generals from Europe helped America win the war.
My Interpretation:	The Battle of Saratoga was important because it changed people's minds in Europe. After it, Europeans helped Americans fight the British.

Practice Interpreting

1. Draw Make a Before-and-After Chart. In it, draw what happened before and after von Steuben joined Washington. Use your chart to tell your partner how he affected the revolution.

2. Write How would you interpret the Battle of Yorktown? First, make a Before-and-After Chart about the battle. Then, use your chart to write a paragraph of 3 or 4 sentences. Exchange paragraphs with a partner and check each other's writing.

Check Your Writing

Make sure you
- [ ] Use complete sentences.
- [ ] Use a period at the end of each sentence.
- [ ] Spell all the words correctly.

Activity: Internet Resources

Students can see pictures of the people and places of the Revolutionary War at the National Park Service Museum Collection website: http://www.cr.nps.gov/museum/exhibits/revwar/index1.html.

Differentiating Instruction

Beginning

Before and After Help students find details for their Before-and-After Chart. What does the chart on page 70 tell about the skills of the Patriot army? What do they learn on page 73 about von Steuben? Have them use their own background knowledge to tell what it meant to have a trained army.

Intermediate

Making a Conclusion Student paragraphs for the Write activity should include a sentence that tells their conclusion. It can be either the first or last sentence in the paragraph. Have students exchange paragraphs and identify each other's conclusion sentence.

Advanced

Peer Editing Have partners exchange papers and proofread for errors and suggest revisions. Ask them to look for the use of signal words showing time order in each other's paragraphs.

Grammar Spotlight

Plurals The word *plural* means "more than one." To make most words plural, just add *s* or *es*. When you write some plurals, you need to make spelling changes. Look at these examples.

One	Spelling Changes	Plural—More Than One
a *soldier*	Add s.	two *soldiers*
the *battle*	Add s.	several *battles*
a *march*	Add es.	many *marches*
an *army*	Change *y* to *i*. Add es.	both *armies*

Use plurals to complete these sentences: The_____ marched to fight the enemy. Generals lead their_____ into_____.

Partner Practice

Wrong Word Which word doesn't belong? Explain why to your partner.

1. island   peninsula   partner
2. hero   prisoner   idol
3. army   alliance   treaty
4. Patriots   Loyalists   Continental Army

Hands On

Make a Poster In a small group, make a poster about a series of events. It can be about something you learned from the lesson or something that happened in school. Put the events in chronological order. Write one sentence for each picture. Make sure to use dates or signal words like *first, next, finally,* and *last.* Then share your poster with the class.

Oral Language

Defeat at Yorktown With a partner, tell how the Americans beat Cornwallis. Get details from page 75. Put them in a Before-and-After Chart to help you.

Activities

Grammar Spotlight

Explain to students that the word *plural* means *more than one.* To make most words plural, just add *-s* or *-es.* Some plurals require spelling changes.

Read aloud the Grammar Spotlight and chart examples with students. Then call on volunteers to write plural nouns on the chalkboard that can fit in the sample sentences.

Partner Practice

Encourage students to state the relationship of the two words that belong in each row. For example, *island* and *peninsula* are both landforms.

Hands On

Some students may choose to make their posters about a series of events in the news.

Oral Language

Provide these key words as prompts: *peninsula, trapped, escape by sea.*

 Activity: Extend the Lesson

For additional reading, recommend the following books:

- *The Fighting Ground* by Avi (HarperTrophy, 1987). A boy sees the hardships of the American Revolution.
- *My Brother Sam Is Dead* by James Lincoln Collier and Christopher Collier (Scholastic, 1999). A family is split by loyalty to the British crown and patriotism for a new country.

 Program Resources

Student Activity Journal
Use page 31 to practice *interpreting.*

Overhead Transparencies
Use 2, Before-and-After Chart, with page 76.

Getting a Constitution

STANDARDS CONTENT

History
- Evaluate Internet sources
- Recognize events that showed the weaknesses of the Articles of Confederation
- Describe the debate that led to the Great Compromise
- Explain the events that led to the ratification of the Constitution

Language
- Identify the following Key Concepts: *delegate*, *debate*, and *compromise*
- Recognize multiple-meaning words
- Practice synthesizing details

Begin Building Background

- Have students describe the scene on page 78. As a class, answer the questions under the picture.

- Encourage students to share personal experiences they've had in class discussions or club/team meetings, especially those where different opinions were debated. How were issues resolved? Were tempers sometimes high?

- Focus students on:
  - Why lawmakers need to meet
  - How people at a meeting may feel about differing opinions
  - How meetings can resolve issues

Talk and Explore

Getting a
Constitution

Here you'll learn how the United States Constitution was created and became law. You'll also learn how to evaluate Internet sources and practice synthesizing information.

Building Background

▲ Japan's constitution is only 60 years old. The U.S. Constitution is about 220!

- **What's happening in this picture?**
- **How do you think the men feel?**
- **Tell about a meeting of people that was important to you.**

78 UNIT 2 • BUILDING A NEW NATION

 Activity: Role-Play

Tell students, *You won a free trip to any place in the world. Write down where you want to go.* Then tell them the second part of the scenario has one catch: *You have a traveling partner. You both must agree to go to the same place. Try to find a* compromise, *or an agreement reached by each person giving up some demands.* Call on volunteers with different destinations to role-play the scenario. Have them defend their choices in a free debate and try to compromise.

 Differentiating Instruction

Beginning
Using Picture Clues Focus students on using picture clues to increase understanding of major themes. Begin by reviewing these words and people that students have encountered in earlier chapters: *leaders, government, laws, George Washington, Benjamin Franklin.* Then have them work in small groups to list or point out who is in the picture and what is going on, based on picture clues.

Intermediate
Writing a Caption Have students work in pairs to write a caption for the picture. Ask some pairs to share their captions with the class. Encourage students to write in complete sentences.

Advanced
Dictionary Use Have students research dictionary definitions for *constitution.* Then have partners work to put together their own explanation and share it with the class.

Big Idea

At first, the new government was weak. A meeting was called to plan a stronger government. After a long debate, the Constitution was written. Then the states voted it into law.

1. **A Weak Government**

2. **Planning a New Government**

3. **Debate**

4. **The Constitution**

LESSON 6 • GETTING A CONSTITUTION **79**

Introduce the Big Idea

- Read aloud the title of the lesson and the Big Idea on page 79.

- Explain that a constitution is a plan for government. It is the law of the land.

- Walk through the four steps with students. Tap into their background knowledge of the Declaration of Independence to help them recognize that Step 4 shows an official government document.

- Explain that the large picture shows the meeting to plan the Constitution at Independence Hall, Philadelphia, Pennsylvania. Students can see a photograph of Independence Hall at this website: http://www.cr.nps.gov/worldheritage/ind.htm.

Review

In Lesson 4, students learned how Thomas Jefferson drafted the Declaration of Independence. Ask:

- What were some important ideas that Jefferson included in the Declaration of Independence?

- How might those ideas have influenced leaders of the new U.S. government?

Activity: Role-Play

Using a volunteer, role-play a debate between two people in charge of school cafeteria menus. Each person wants a different type of food served. In addition, ask a third student to play the part of a meeting chairperson. Have a script ready like the one below.

Debater A: *Our cafeteria should serve Mexican food. It's delicious!*

Debater B: *No! Chinese food—that's what we should have!*

Debater A: *Mexican food!*

Debater B: *Chinese food!*

Chairperson: *Order! Order! Maybe we can have both.*

Debater B: *We could have Chinese food on Mondays.*

Debater A: *And we could have Mexican food on Tuesdays.*

Debaters A and B: *Great!*

Tell students that government leaders at the Constitutional Convention often disagreed with each other, just as the debaters in the role-play did. Likewise, the government leaders had to find ways to meet in the middle.

Resource Library

Reader's Handbook (red)
Reading a Website 514–535

Reader's Handbook (yellow)
Reading a Website 390–409

All Write
Using the Internet 227–232

Teach [Key Concepts]

- Model correct pronunciation by saying each Key Concept slowly.
- Write the word *delegate* on the board and tell students that one of the word's meanings is *someone who acts for somebody else.*
- Provide a real-life example of *delegate* by identifying a student who recently served as spokesperson for his or her group.

Teach the Visual Aid

The Constitutional Convention

Focus students on the visual aid and read each label aloud. Ask students to describe what they see in each illustration. Ask, *What story is the visual aid telling?* Help them see that it shows the story of how the U.S. Constitution was created.

- Government leaders came to a meeting in Philadelphia.
- They debated, compromised, and wrote up the Constitution.
- People in the states discussed the Constitution.
- The United States Constitution became the law of the land.
- The states voted to add a new part called the Bill of Rights.

Key Concepts

Delegates speak for the people who send them to a meeting. At the meeting they **debate**, or discuss, ways to solve problems. Often, there are two sides, and they do not agree.

Then someone will suggest a **compromise**, a way to solve the problem that gives each side part of what it wants.

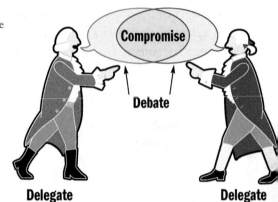

Compromise

Debate

Delegate   Delegate

The Constitutional Convention

Delegates traveled to Philadelphia in 1787.   There delegates debated the problems.   They agreed on the Great Compromise.

80 UNIT 2 • BUILDING A NEW NATION

 Activity: Culture Connection

Have students connect the Key Concepts to a debate or conflict currently in the news. Ask them to work in pairs to write a short description of the conflict using the Key Concepts. Ask, *Can you think of a compromise that could solve this problem?*

 Differentiating Instruction

Beginning

Answering the Questions Present *yes/no* questions about the pictures in the Key Concepts and visual aid. Have students answer in complete sentences, inverting the words in your question.

Teacher: *Is he a delegate?*

Student: *Yes, he is a delegate.*

Intermediate

Speaking Chain Have students form a speaking chain to explain the pictured events in the visual aid. One student tells what happened first and then

passes the story to the next person. Encourage students to use time-order signal words, such as *first, next, then,* and *after that.*

Advanced

In Their Own Words Have students write a paragraph telling what they understand from the visual aid. Ask them to use time-order signal words to connect the events.

Evaluating Internet Sources

The Internet connects you to information all over the world. You can find pictures, music, and documents about how we got the Constitution. However, nothing stops people from putting false information on the Internet. So you must decide whether something you read is true. Ask yourself these questions.

1. Who is giving the information?
2. What do I know about that organization or person?
3. Could the source be wrong or be telling only one side?

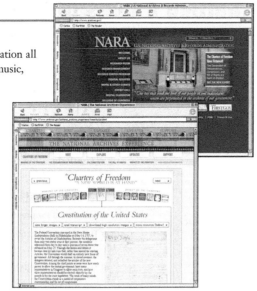

People in the states debated.

The *Federalist Papers* persuaded people.

The Constitution became law in 1789.

The Bill of Rights became law in 1791.

Teach Skill Building

■ Read aloud with students the explanation of evaluating Internet sources.

■ Demonstrate the meaning of bias by recalling the role-play enacted for the Big Idea (page 79):

- Tell the class to imagine that the person who wanted Mexican food wrote an Internet review of the cafeteria food.
- What would she or he most likely say about the Mexican meals? About the Chinese meals?
- How might her or his writing mislead Internet readers?

■ Connect the discussion to the skill by asking volunteers to describe what kinds of Internet sites may have biases.

■ Help them see that commercial sites (dot-coms) will be biased toward their products, whereas news and government sites (dot-govs) may give more even reporting.

Teach the Skill

Search engines such as http://www.google.com help find information on nearly any subject in just seconds. However, Google doesn't say if the information on a website is right or not. Ask, *What might make you think a website's information is right? How could you tell if it was wrong?*

 Activity: Good Surfing

Ask students to work in pairs to check out an Internet site about Liberty Hall in Philadelphia. Have them evaluate their site by answering the three questions provided in Skill Building. Ask them to summarize their findings by drawing a "thumbs-up" or a "thumbs-down." Afterward, ask pairs to compare their findings with other pairs.

Program Resources

Student Activity Journal

Use page 32 to build key vocabulary.

Use page 33 to practice evaluating Internet sources.

Overhead Transparencies

Use 34, Website Profiler, with page 81.

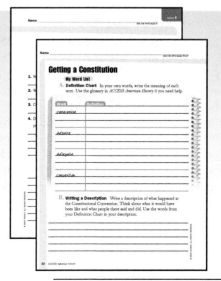

Introduce Getting a Constitution

- Explain that the reading tells the story of how and why the United States Constitution was created.

- Reinforce the key points by having students complete these sentences:
  - The thirteen colonies became the thirteen (*states*).
  - Before the American Revolution, the colonies were ruled by (*Britain*).
  - Afterward, they were ruled by (*themselves*).
  - A written law of a government is called a (*constitution*).

Key Connection: Government

Teach students the concept of federal and state governments using a U.S. map as a visual aid.

- Point to various states and explain that each state has its own government, called a *state government*.

- Circle the entire map with your finger. Explain that the country also has its own government, called the *federal government*.

- Explain that the colonies (states) were used to governing themselves.

Getting a Constitution

The revolution was won. A new nation began. The 13 "united" states agreed to a central government. In it, the state governments were strong, but the national government was weak.

A Weak Federal Government

The first government was set up in 1781 in the **Articles of Confederation.** But there were many problems.

Problems with the Articles of Confederation

- There was no president.
- There were no courts to solve problems among the different states.
- There was a **legislature,** but it didn't have the power to tax people. It couldn't raise money.
- Each state had its own money.

▲ Each state had its own money.

VOCABULARY

Articles of Confederation—the law that described the first government of the United States

legislature—the part of government that makes laws. In the federal government, it is called *Congress.*

 Activity: Vocabulary Race

Have students write each vocabulary word on a separate 3" x 5" card. Divide the class into groups of students at similar proficiency levels to play Vocabulary Race. Read aloud the definition for each word, one at a time. The first player in each group to find the corresponding vocabulary card throws it into a center pile and earns three points. Each subsequent player who finds and plays the correct card earns one point.

 Differentiating Instruction

Beginning

Word-Picture Association Throughout pages 82–87, read aloud the headings and have beginning English learners repeat them after you. Then ask them to match them to corresponding pictures, when available. Then read aloud the paragraphs to students, or have them listen to advanced readers. Afterward, encourage them to talk about the topic.

Intermediate

Identifying Main Ideas Have students read one paragraph at a time with partners or in small groups. After each paragraph, have them identify the main topic or idea.

Advanced

Internet Resources Partners can explore Internet resources by keyboarding *Shays's Rebellion* into a search engine such as Google. They can share pictures or quotations they find with the class.

SHAYS'S REBELLION

Times were hard for farmers in western Massachusetts. Many of them owed money. When farmers couldn't pay their **debts,** the courts took away their farms.

One day in 1786, a group of angry farmers, led by Daniel Shays, marched with guns to a courthouse. They closed the court. The governor asked the **federal government** for help, but the government didn't have any money to pay troops. It couldn't answer the call for help. This was a **crisis!** People were very upset. They didn't feel safe. In the end, Shays's Rebellion was stopped. However, the **rebellion** showed Americans they needed a stronger government.

A MEETING IN PHILADELPHIA

Leaders called for a meeting to deal with the government's problems. The states agreed and chose their **delegates.** On May 25, 1787, the **Constitutional Convention** opened in Philadelphia, Pennsylvania. All of the great leaders of the time came. Among them were George Washington, Benjamin Franklin, James Madison, and Alexander Hamilton. Together the delegates who founded the U.S. government are known as the Founding Fathers.

(**TALK AND SHARE**) **Talk with a partner about why Shays's Rebellion made leaders feel they needed a stronger government.**

VOCABULARY

debts—money owed
federal government—the central government that unites the states. Today it is the government in Washington, D.C.
crisis—a time of great difficulty when change must come
rebellion—a violent challenge to an authority. A rebellion is a smaller fight than a revolution.
delegates—people sent to a meeting to represent others
Constitutional Convention—the meeting that decided what should be in the Constitution

▲ Shays's Rebellion

Language Notes

Multiple Meanings
These words have more than one meaning.

□ call
1. demand or request
2. a shout
3. a use of a telephone

□ state
1. one of 50 parts of the United States
2. to say

□ found
1. to build something for the future
2. discovered something that was lost

LESSON 6 • GETTING A CONSTITUTION **83**

Teach Shays's Rebellion and A Meeting in Philadelphia

Reinforce the concepts on pages 82–83 by working with students to create a Cause-effect Organizer for the Constitutional Convention.

Language Notes

■ Read aloud the Language Notes with students. Call on volunteers to act out or draw one of the sets of meanings for each red word. Have the rest of the class guess what meaning is being shown.

■ Then divide the class into three groups. Give each group a red multiple-meaning word. Have the groups create a sentence for each meaning of the word. (Students assigned to the word *call* can choose two of the three definitions.)

■ Afterward, have groups share their sentences with the class.

TALK AND SHARE

During their discussions with their partners, encourage students to use these new vocabulary terms: *federal government, crisis, rebellion.*

 Activity: Take Notes

Help students begin taking notes about the Constitutional Convention and have them continue throughout Lesson 6. Suggest that they begin their notes by putting the causes for the Constitutional Convention in a graphic organizer. Encourage them to make simple drawings as visual aids.

 Program Resources

Student Activity Journal
Assign page 34:
• To create study notes for students to review
• To provide reinforcement of key vocabulary

Overhead Transparencies
Use 3, Cause-effect Organizer, with page 83.

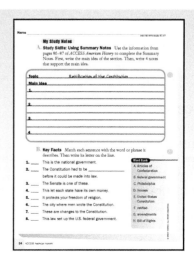

Discuss Debate and Compromise

■ Emphasize that the Virginia Plan based the number of representatives from each state on population.

■ Demonstrate this concept by dividing the class into two unequal sections. The larger section can send four representatives to a meeting while the smaller section can send only one. All the representatives will vote on an issue. Ask students if they find this system fair. Discuss its advantages and disadvantages.

People in History

James Madison:
Father of the Constitution

Read the profile of James Madison on page 84 aloud with students. Ask volunteers to identify important details about Madison in the profile and tell which ones made him a good leader for our country (*knew the law, knew history, was careful, took good notes*).

Debate and Compromise

The men who came to the **convention** had ideas. Some of them came from states in the South. Some came from states in the North. Some came from large states with many people. Others came from states with fewer people and different interests. The **debate** was exciting. The delegates agreed to keep their discussion private until they had finished their work.

▲ Benjamin Franklin speaks at the Constitutional Convention.

TWO PLANS

One big question the delegates had was, How many **representatives** should each state have in the legislature? James Madison, from Virginia, gave one answer. William Paterson, from New Jersey, had another. Delegates from the larger states wanted the Virginia Plan because it gave them more representatives. Colonists from smaller states wanted the New Jersey Plan because it gave each state the same number of delegates.

VOCABULARY
convention—a meeting
debate—a formal talk between people who have different opinions
representatives—lawmakers; people in government elected by the voters in a state to speak and vote for them

▲ William Paterson

People in History

James Madison: Father of the Constitution

James Madison was small and thin. As a young man, he did not believe in himself very much. Thomas Jefferson saw how smart he was. He pulled Madison into the group of leaders. Madison became one of its stars. He knew the law, and he knew history. He was a careful man. He took very good notes during the Constitutional Convention, and they tell us what happened. Madison later was elected the fourth president. He is best known, however, as the Father of the Constitution.

84 UNIT 2 • BUILDING A NEW NATION

🏃 Activity: Internet Resources

Ask students to work in pairs to create a James Madison poster. Suggest that they draw a Web that shows key facts about the man, his life, and his work. Encourage them to search the Internet for more information about Madison and to illustrate their posters. Following is one suggested website: http://www.americanpresident.org.

📘 Differentiating Instruction

Beginning
Matching Pictures and Terms Have students connect the terms below to as many pictures on pages 82–87 as they can:

- James Madison
- Philadelphia
- Constitution
- Representatives
- Rebellion
- Debate
- Constitutional Convention

Intermediate
Summarizing In pairs, students should read aloud the headings from pages 82–85. Then ask them to give a summary of the content, using the words in the headings.

Advanced
Group Talk In small groups, have students discuss these questions:

- Why was the Constitutional Convention called?
- How did the needs of small and big states differ?
- What was the Great Compromise?

THE GREAT COMPROMISE

Finally, Roger Sherman from Connecticut suggested a **compromise.** His plan had something for both sides. It is called the Great Compromise. The diagram below shows how it worked.

Virginia Plan
- The legislature has two **houses.**
- The number of representatives is based on the number of people in a state.

New Jersey Plan
- The legislature has one house.
- Each state has the same number of representatives.

The Great Compromise
- The legislature has two houses.
- In one house, the number of representatives is based on state population.
- In the other house, each state has the same number of representatives.

▲ Roger Sherman

To learn more about the Constitution, see pages 270–279.

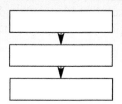 **TALK AND SHARE** To your partner, explain how the Great Compromise solved the debate between the smaller and larger states. Together, draw a chart and share it with your group.

VOCABULARY

compromise—a way of settling a disagreement in which each side gets part of what it wants

houses—parts of the legislature. The two houses are the House of Representatives and the Senate.

Talk About The Great Compromise

- Explain that graphics—such as diagrams, charts, and tables—are useful reading aids.
- Model using graphics by focusing attention on the diagram on page 85.
- Point to the state outlines. Ask, *What do these pictures represent?* Then point to the arrows. Ask students what they think the arrows mean. Have them connect the diagram to the concept of compromise.
- Then ask one or more students to retell what the graphic shows.

TALK AND SHARE

Encourage pairs to look at the graphic on page 85 to locate details from both plans that were used in the Great Compromise. Allow time for pairs to share what they found.

Activity: Sequence Notes

Have students make Sequence Notes using the events of the Constitutional Convention. They should start with the events that caused leaders to call for the meeting. Use Overhead Transparency 24, Sequence Notes.

Activity: History Notebook

Help students build a notebook for this lesson. The notebook should include items from the Student Activity Journal, pictures, lists, and drawings they've made about the events. Have them share their notebook with a partner.

Discuss Ratification of the Constitution

■ Emphasize that after the Founding Fathers were finished with their work in Philadelphia, the Constitution still was not the law of the land. The states had to vote for it first.

■ Ask students:
  • What is one good thing about a strong federal government?
  • What is one bad thing?

Building VOCABULARY

Say aloud each vocabulary term. Ask volunteers to explain the meaning in their own words. Then work with changing word forms. Supply this table and have students use the words in sentences:

Verb	Noun
ratify	ratification
amend	amendment
represent	representative
convene	convention
rebel	rebellion

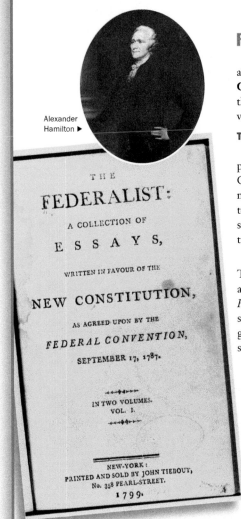

◄ Alexander Hamilton

▲ The *Federalist Papers*

Ratification of the Constitution

On September 17, 1787, the delegates finished, and most of them signed the **United States Constitution.** Still, the Constitution was not yet the law of the land. First, it had to be **ratified**— voted in—by at least 9 states.

THE STATES DEBATE

Now the debate about the Constitution became public. One group, called the Federalists, liked the Constitution. However, the Anti-federalists did not. They thought it made the central government too powerful. They wanted power to stay with the states. They wanted a government that couldn't take away the rights of the people.

A bitter fight took place between the two sides. Three Federalists, including Alexander Hamilton and James Madison, wrote articles known as the *Federalist Papers.* Their writings pointed out the strengths of the Constitution. They wrote that the government it described was not dangerous. It shared power with the states.

Throughout the states, people read the *Federalist Papers.* They debated with their friends and in their state legislatures. Then voting began. Delaware was the first state to ratify, in December 1787. By June 1788, more than 9 states had voted for the Constitution.

On March 4, 1789, the Constitution became law. In the next month, George Washington became president. The new nation now had a strong national government and its first president.

VOCABULARY
United States Constitution—the law that sets up the U.S. federal government and gives power to the states and rights to the people
ratified—made into law; approved formally. The states had to ratify the Constitution before it became official. *Ratification* means the act of approving a major law.

 Activity: Paired Writing

Have students work in small groups to summarize the viewpoints, key leaders, and actions of the Federalists and Anti-federalists. Have them chart their findings in a chart organizer. Have them label the left side *Federalists* and the right side *Anti-federalists.*

 Differentiating Instruction

Beginning
Concept Diagram Help students see that the Bill of Rights is a part of the United States Constitution, and ten amendments make up the Bill of Rights. Ask students to draw a diagram with labels that show these relationships.

Intermediate
Role-Play Assign sides: Federalists and Anti-federalists. Provide a sample script.

F: *Vote for the Constitution. It's great!*

A: *No! Vote no! The Constitution is dangerous. It takes too much power away from our state.*

F: *We need a strong government. The Constitution gives us what we need.*

Advanced
Free Script Let advanced students free-script their role-play debate.

THE BILL OF RIGHTS

However, the Constitution was not complete. Anti-federalists had asked, What would protect people's rights? They wanted the Constitution to include a bill of rights. A bill of rights protects people with a set of rules that leaders must obey.

James Madison agreed such a bill was needed. He asked for **amendments**—changes—to the Constitution. Ten of the amendments he suggested became known as the **Bill of Rights.** It was ratified by the states in 1791. The Bill of Rights protects the right to follow your own religion. It protects against the government hurting you for anything you say or write. It promises that people accused of crimes will get a fair trial in court. To learn more about the Bill of Rights, see pages 282–291.

▲ Your right to meet and ask for changes is protected by the Bill of Rights.

TALK AND SHARE Talk to your partner about why the Bill of Rights was important. Make a list of 3 reasons and share your list with your group.

VOCABULARY

amendments—changes. The amendments are part of the Constitution.
Bill of Rights—the first 10 amendments to the Constitution. It protects the basic rights of people.

▲ You can see the Bill of Rights in Washington, D.C.

Summary

At first, the government was too weak. Delegates from the states met to fix it. They created the Constitution. Then people in the states debated it. The states ratified the Constitution and on March 4, 1789, it became law. Then the Bill of Rights was added in 1791.

Teach The Bill of Rights

Provide this "pocket summary" of important rights included in the Bill of Rights:

- Freedom of Speech
- Freedom of Religion
- Freedom of the Press
- Protection of People Accused of Crimes

Give one example of each. Tell students they can find more about these rights on pages 282–293.

TALK AND SHARE

Have partners complete the Talk and Share activity. Then have students combine their answers by creating a large Bill of Rights poster that lists all of the reasons it is important.

Discuss the Summary

Direct students to read the Summary at the end of the lesson. Then return them to the Big Idea on page 79. Have them summarize each of the four points.

✔ Assessment

Assess students' comprehension by asking the following questions:

History

- Why did the Articles of Confederation cause problems for the new nation?
- What was the Great Compromise?
- What were the views of the Federalists and the Anti-federalists?
- What is the Bill of Rights?

Language

Write or say sentences to show how the paired words are related:

- U.S. Constitution
- Ratified
- Legislature
- Houses
- Debate
- Compromise
- Bill of Rights
- Amendments

Assessment Book

Use page 24 to assess students' comprehension.

Teach Synthesizing

Tell students that when they read many pieces of information, they have to *synthesize*, or make a general statement that covers the details. This section will give them practice fitting details together.

Model the Organizer

- Read aloud the three details in the Web. Ask students to stop and think about how all these details add up.

- Then read aloud the general statement.

- Encourage students to follow these steps when completing a Web:
  - Write the details first.
  - Pause. Think how the details fit together.
  - Write a general statement that fits all the details.

Give Practice Synthesizing

- **Draw** Some students may need this prompt to compose a general statement: *The federal government was weak under the Articles of Confederation.*

- **Write** Suggest that students work in pairs to brainstorm ideas for a Web. Then have them work individually to write their paragraphs.

Develop Language

Synthesizing

Fitting Details Together

To synthesize, you fit details together to make a general statement. When you synthesize, look for details about a subject. Then figure out how the details add up. A Web can help organize your ideas. This Web shows 3 details about James Madison.

Web

Detail
James Madison gave speeches at the Constitutional Convention.

Detail
He helped write the Federalist Papers.

Detail
He pushed for and wrote the Bill of Rights.

General Statement
James Madison played a key role in the Constitution.

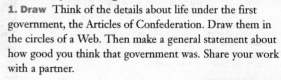
▲ James Madison

Practice Synthesizing

1. Draw Think of the details about life under the first government, the Articles of Confederation. Draw them in the circles of a Web. Then make a general statement about how good you think that government was. Share your work with a partner.

2. Write Reread the details about the Anti-federalists. Why were they against the Constitution? Put the details you find into a Web. Use the ideas in your organizer to write a paragraph of 3 to 4 sentences. Exchange paragraphs with a partner and check each other's work.

Check Your Writing

Make sure you
- ☐ Use complete sentences.
- ☐ Use a period at the end of each sentence.
- ☐ Spell all the words correctly.

Activity: Internet Resources

Students can learn more about the workings of the federal government by viewing these websites:

- The original "Charters of Freedom" from the National Archives: http://archives.gov/national_archives_experience/charters.html

- Ben's (Franklin's) Guide: http://bensguide.gpo.gov/3-5/government/index.html

Differentiating Instruction

Beginning
Writing a Phrase Help students write in simple phrases, such as *no taxes, no presidents, no courts, couldn't raise money.*

Intermediate
Grammar Review Reinforce the Grammar Spotlight as students revise their writing. Have them work with a peer editor to check their use of *a, an,* and *the.*

Advanced
Writing in Detail Suggest that students begin their paragraphs by writing the general statement from their Webs. Then have them complete the paragraph by adding the details from their Webs. Have students check their writing to make sure they used complete sentences. Additionally, have them check their use of articles.

Activities

Grammar Spotlight

Articles The words *a*, *an*, and *the* are called *articles*. The chart shows how to use these words.

When to Use *a*, *an*, or *the*	Examples
Use *a* or *an* to tell about any member of a group.	*Pennsylvania was a large state.* *Madison was an important leader.*
Use *the* to tell about a particular group member.	*Washington was the first president.* *Fifty states make up the United States.*

Write these sentences. Choose *a* or *the* to fill in the blanks.

James Madison wrote_____Bill of Rights. He was_____delegate.

Hands On

Class Bill of Rights In small groups, decide what rights students have in your class. Make posters showing your ideas. Choose a person in each group to be your delegate. Delegates take posters to a "convention." Posters go on the wall. Delegates debate. Delegates vote. Then the class votes to ratify.

Oral Language

What's a Crisis? Think of a time when things got so bad you knew they had to change. It could be about sports or anything that needs rules. That's your crisis. Tell a partner about it and talk about ways to solve it.

Tell how your crisis was like or different from the crisis that led to the Constitution.

Partner Practice

Use the Internet With a partner, find a reliable website about the U.S. Constitution. Write the name and address of the website on a sheet of paper.

- Tell who or what group created the site.

- Explain how you know the website is reliable.

Activities

Grammar Spotlight

- Explain to students that the words *a*, *an*, and *the* are called articles.

- Demonstrate the grammar skill by requesting simple classroom objects from student volunteers. For example, place three books of different colors on your desk and tell volunteers:
  - Please give me a book.
  - Please give me the red book.
  - Please give me an English book.

Hands On

Provide prompts for the debate, such as *What right is the most important? Why?* Allow ten to fifteen minutes for debate and voting. Limit each debating team to two minutes.

Oral Language

Suggest that students describe the crisis, the turning point, and the solution or outcome.

Partner Practice

Have partners write the address of the website they find in their history notebooks so they can return to it at a future date.

 Activity: Extend the Lesson

For additional reading on Lesson 6 topics, recommend these books to students. Have them rate the books for the class:

- *Shh! We're Writing the Constitution* by Jean Fritz (Putnam Publishing Group, 1998)

- *The Constitution* by Marilyn Prolman (Childrens Press, 1995)

- *The U.S. Constitution: And Fascinating Facts About It* by Terry L. Jordan (Oak Hill Publishers, 1999)

Program Resources

Student Activity Journal
Use page 35 to practice *synthesizing*.

Overhead Transparencies
Use 33, Web, with page 88.

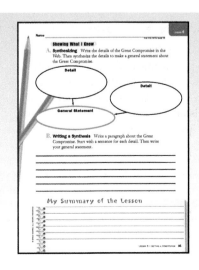

The New Nation

STANDARDS CONTENT

History
- Distinguish facts from opinions
- Explain the beginnings of the presidential cabinet and political parties in the U.S. government
- Recognize the importance of the Louisiana Purchase and its exploration
- Recognize how U.S. territorial expansion affected relations with other countries

Language
- Identify the following Key Concepts: *wilderness, frontier,* and *expedition*
- Recognize and use verb phrases
- Practice supporting an opinion

Begin [Building Background]

- Use the picture and questions underneath to elicit conversation about exploring new lands and meeting new people.

- Encourage students to share any experiences they have had exploring new places. Provide students with words as needed (*explore, discover, exciting, scary, unknown, dangers*). Lead students to discuss these ideas:

  - The original thirteen states were small. The United States grew by exploring and moving to new lands.

  - Exploring a wilderness involves facing unknown animals, people, plants, weather, and landforms.

Talk and Explore

The New Nation

Here you'll learn about the first years of the United States. You'll also learn how to sort facts from opinions and practice supporting your own ideas.

Building Background

▲ I'd love to explore a wilderness!

- **What do you see in this picture?**
- **What are the people doing?**
- **What would it feel like to be there?**

▲ Sacajawea coin

90 UNIT 2 • BUILDING A NEW NATION

 Activity: New Nation Web

Ask students to create a large Web poster entitled *The New Nation.* Provide them with these categories and ask them to fill in the Web with details and drawings during the lesson:

- First president
- First large land purchase
- First major land exploration
- First cabinet members
- First political parties

Differentiating Instruction

Beginning
Word Web Write each heading of the Big Idea in the center of a Web. Invite learners to brainstorm ideas associated with each one. They can pantomime, draw, or state their ideas. Fill in the details on the Web.

Intermediate
Interpreting Ideas Have student pairs explain the three ideas of this lesson using the sentence starter *The new nation. . . .* Examples: *The new nation*

had a cabinet of advisers and political parties. The new nation got new land.

Advanced
Answering Questions Have students work in groups of three to discuss and write an answer to one of the questions below the picture. Encourage students to point out details in the picture that support their answers.

Big Idea

The first presidents gave the United States government a new shape, much more land, and a way of working with other countries.

1 Cabinet and Political Parties

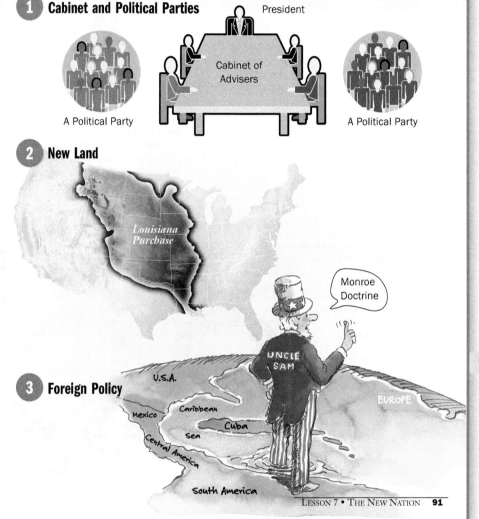

President

A Political Party

Cabinet of Advisers

A Political Party

2 New Land

Louisiana Purchase

Monroe Doctrine

UNCLE SAM

U.S.A.

EUROPE

Mexico

Caribbean

Cuba

Sea

Central America

South America

3 Foreign Policy

LESSON 7 • THE NEW NATION **91**

Introduce the Big Idea

- Read aloud the Big Idea and the label for each picture.

- Identify the first pictures as two groups with different ideas about running the government. These groups are called *political parties*. People from both groups are shown as members of the president's group of advisers, or *cabinet*.

- Point to the highlighted portion of the map (*Louisiana Purchase*) on page 91 and then to the picture on page 90 to show correspondence between the two.

- Tell students that Uncle Sam, whose initials are *U.S.*, is a symbol for the United States.

- Refer again to the lesson title *The New Nation*. Emphasize that the new nation had to do many things for the first time: set up a working government (picture 1), explore new land (picture 2), and establish its role in the world (picture 3).

Review

Thomas Jefferson, the third president, wanted government power to be shared with the states. However, he used the power of the strong federal government to make the Louisiana Purchase. Ask, *Why do governments need power?*

Activity: Predictions

Have students work in small groups to make predictions about the three parts of the Big Idea: *cabinet and political parties, new land,* and *foreign policy.*

Encourage them to base their predictions on these factors:

- Picture clues
- Prior knowledge
- Their own experience

Each group should list or draw their predictions. Afterward, have each group share its predictions with the class.

Then post them on a class bulletin board to refer to at the end of the lesson.

Resource Library

***Reader's Handbook* (red)**
Fact and Opinion 281

***Reader's Handbook* (yellow)**
Fact and Opinion 203

All Write
Using Facts and Opinions 253

Teach · Key Concepts

- Model correct pronunciation by saying each Key Concept slowly. Have students repeat each word after you.

- Then read aloud the text, calling on volunteers to point to corresponding pictures.

- Elicit or provide the following structural cues to help students recall the terms:

  - The root word of *wilderness* is *wild*.

  - The root word of *frontier* is *front*.

  - The root word of *expedition* is *ped*, also found in other words related to feet and walking (*pedal*, *pedestrian*).

Teach the Visual Aid

The First Five Presidents

Read aloud the title and the name of each president and his dates in office. Then ask students:

- Who was the first president? (*George Washington*)

- When was Madison president? (*1809–1817*)

- Which man served only four years? (*John Adams*)

- Who was president in 1819? (*James Monroe*)

Talk and Explore

Key Concepts

Wilderness is land in its wild, natural state where few or no people live.

The **frontier** is the place where settled land ends and the wilderness begins.

An **expedition** is a trip people take for a purpose. People can take an expedition beyond the frontier to explore a wilderness.

The First Five Presidents

These leaders helped a young nation become stronger and stronger.

1789–1797
George Washington

1797–1801
John Adams

92 · Unit 2 • Building a New Nation

Activity: Classify Vocabulary

Divide the class into small groups. Have each group copy the classification grid below.

Have the groups write each vocabulary word in the lesson on a sticky note and distribute the notes among their group. Have students take turns placing their sticky notes in the appropriate column of the chart. They should explain their reasons to the group.

People	Ideas	Places	Other

Differentiating Instruction

Beginning
Pantomime Have students take turns pantomiming or drawing one of the Key Concepts while the other students guess the word that is being enacted.

Intermediate
Making Sentences Present the rows of words opposite and have students choose the word in each horizontal row that doesn't belong. Then have them choose a word that belongs and use it in a phrase or sentence:

- Expedition Trip Row
- Journey Border Edge
- Frontier Wilderness City
- Rivers Lands People

Advanced
Exploring Meanings Have students use a dictionary to find other meanings of *frontier*. With a partner, students should write a sentence using a different meaning from that given here. Example: *Astronauts explore frontiers in space.*

Facts and Opinions

When you read history, you need to tell facts from opinions. Facts are ideas that can be proved. Opinions are ideas that people *believe* are true. Everyone agrees on facts. However, different people may have different opinions.

This chart gives a fact and an opinion about the founding of the government of the United States.

Ideas About the U.S. Government

FACT	OPINION
It can be proved.	What some people believed
EXAMPLE	**EXAMPLE**
Washington became president in 1789.	*The government should be led by upper-class people.*

1801–1809	1809–1817	1817–1825
Thomas Jefferson	**James Madison**	**James Monroe**

Teach Skill Building

- Read with students the explanation of facts and opinions.

- Then demonstrate the meaning of each term by stating a fact and opinion about today's weather, such as the following example:

  Fact: *It's raining.*

  Opinion: *The weather today is awful.*

- Invite a student to share a different opinion about the weather.

- Then walk through the examples of fact and opinion about the U.S. government that are listed in the chart.

- Ask a volunteer to state a different opinion from the one listed.

Teach the Pictures

Ask volunteers to tally the number of years each president pictured in the gallery was in office. Explain that since 1951, every U.S. president is elected for a four-year term and cannot serve more than two terms.

Activity: What's That You Say?

Have student pairs locate facts and opinions in a newspaper or magazine ad. You can also have them search for and print out ads on the Internet. Provide students with two different-colored markers. Have them highlight all the facts in one color and all the opinions in the second color.

Program Resources

Student Activity Journal

Use page 36 to build key vocabulary.

Use page 37 to practice identifying facts and opinions.

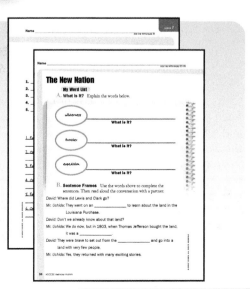

Introduce The New Nation

- Ask students to look for ways the lesson on pages 94–99 tells the story of the new nation after the Revolutionary War.

- Invite students to preview the lesson by looking at the pictures and reading the headings. Have them describe the pictures.

Language Notes

- Read aloud the Language Notes with students. Model using each of the phrases in a sentence that easily conveys its meaning.

- Then direct students' attention to the use of the phrase *took shape* at the top of page 94. Have a volunteer read aloud the sentence and paraphrase its meaning.

Key Connection: Government

Help students understand the focus of each cabinet department:

- State—maintaining relations with other countries
- Treasury—budgeting, taxing, and spending
- War—keeping armed forces ready if they are needed
- Attorney General—enforcing federal laws

Look and Read

The New Nation

Under the leadership of the first presidents, the government took shape, and the nation grew.

▲ George Washington with his cabinet

The Shape of the New Government

During George Washington's **presidency,** the form of American government began to take shape. **Departments** of state and a **cabinet** helped the president run the country. Also, political parties began.

DEPARTMENTS IN WASHINGTON'S GOVERNMENT

Washington set up his government. He made 3 departments. The men President Washington chose to **head** these departments became his cabinet. The department heads are called *secretaries.* His cabinet also included a lawyer called the *attorney general.* All presidents since then have had **advisers** in their cabinet. Together, the president and his cabinet make decisions about how to govern the country.

Washington's Cabinet

Department	Secretary
Department of State	Thomas Jefferson
Department of the Treasury	Alexander Hamilton
Department of War	Henry Knox
Attorney General	Edmund Randolph

Language Notes

Verb Phrases
These phrases have a special meaning.

- ☐ take shape: develop; grow into what it will become
- ☐ take over: take control away from someone else
- ☐ take time: do something slowly and carefully

VOCABULARY
presidency—the time a person serves as president
departments—parts of the government that report to the president
cabinet—the group of people a president names to act as official advisers and head the departments of government
head—lead; be the top person
advisers—people who give advice, or opinions, about how to solve problems

---

Activity: Vocabulary Password

In groups, have students copy each vocabulary word from pages 94–95 on 3" x 5" cards. Then invite them to play Vocabulary Password. Each player reads the word aloud and tells *one* of these things about the word:

- What it means
- A similar word
- An opposite word
- The word used in a sentence
- An example

Differentiating Instruction

Beginning

Word Focus Focus students on the introductory sentence and its key words: *first, presidents, government, nation, grew.*

Have students convey the meaning of each word by pantomiming, drawing, or pointing to a picture in their books.

Then help them preview pages 94–99 by reading aloud all the headings and demonstrating the meanings of the key words.

Intermediate

Previewing Have students preview the headings and pictures on pages 94–95. Then have them close their books and recall the ideas they previewed. Encourage partners to prompt each other. Then have them read together to learn more.

Advanced

Cabinet Poster Invite a small group to design a poster showing the main activities of each of Washington's cabinet members.

TWO POLITICAL PARTIES

Hamilton and Jefferson were strong men who gave President Washington good advice. However, they did not always agree with each other. They often had different **points of view**.

Two Points of View

Hamilton
- Most government power should be in Washington, D.C.
- Shipping and **manufacturing** are the most important businesses.
- People can turn into a **mob** and bring **violence**.

Jefferson
- Government power should be shared with the states.
- Farming is the most important business.
- Government leaders can turn into **tyrants** and take away rights. The people should be trusted.

Over time, two **political parties** developed. Hamilton's party believed the country needed a strong central government led by educated upper-class citizens. Most of his support came from the North, especially New England.

Jefferson's party wanted power to stay with the "citizen farmers" and the states. Most of his support came from the South and the West. In time, Jefferson's party became the Democratic Party. The Republican Party began later.

TALK AND SHARE With a partner, talk about the things that began when Washington was president.

VOCABULARY

points of view—opinions
manufacturing—the business of making goods by hand or by machine
mob—a large crowd that is out of control
violence—damage and harm
tyrants—rulers who are cruel to their people
political parties—groups of people who share ideas about government and who work to get their members elected

Teach About Two Political Parties

■ Alexander Hamilton was a lawyer from New York, and Thomas Jefferson was a planter from the South. The opposing views of Hamilton and Jefferson were not surprising.
- Hamilton wanted the nation to grow big businesses and cities.
- Jefferson saw the strength of the United States in its farms and small towns.

■ Ask students what they know about differences of opinion. Ask when they have defended an argument to someone who thought they were wrong. Have volunteers explain their point of view.

TALK AND SHARE

If students created New Nation Webs, have partners use them during their discussion. Encourage partners to use their Webs as visual props, just as they would in a formal presentation.

 Activity: Facts and Opinions

Focus students on the *Two Points of View* chart on page 95. Ask pairs to write one of the opinions they agree with on an index card. Then have them work together to write or discuss a fact to support the opinion. Afterward, invite partners to defend their opinions in a group circle.

 Program Resources

Student Activity Journal
Assign page 38:
- To create study notes for students to review
- To provide reinforcement of key vocabulary

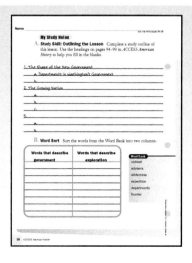

Discuss The Growing Nation

■ Explain that before the Louisiana Purchase, the Mississippi River was the western border of the country.

■ Ask a volunteer to point out the Mississippi River on the map.

■ Emphasize the importance of the Louisiana Purchase in doubling the size of the new nation.

■ Demonstrate the concept of *doubling* by filling a glass of water half full and then doubling its contents by filling it to the top.

Teach the Map

The map on page 96 shows the United States and the Louisiana Purchase. Ask students:

• What other nations owned land in North America? (*Spain and Britain*) Point to their lands.

• Do you think the Louisiana Purchase was a good idea? Why or why not?

• Would you have stayed in one of the original states or gone to the new land to explore? Why?

Look and Read

The Growing Nation

At first, only the land east of the Mississippi River belonged to the United States. Soon, the country grew.

Louisiana Purchase

KEY
☐ United States
☐ Louisiana Purchase, 1803
← Route of Lewis and Clark, 1804–1805

THE LOUISIANA PURCHASE

Before 1803, France owned much of the land west of the Mississippi River. The French called this land Louisiana after Louis, their king. Louisiana went west to the Rocky Mountains— and maybe farther. Few Europeans had visited Louisiana, so no one knew how far it stretched.

In 1803, French leaders offered to sell Louisiana to the United States. Thomas Jefferson was president by this time. He agreed to buy it for $15 million. That was a lot of money! Some Americans thought Jefferson was spending too much for a piece of **wilderness.**

Still, Louisiana was big. It was so big that each acre of land cost the government only about 3 cents! The **Louisiana Purchase** doubled the size of the United States. Jefferson thought that the new land was worth the price.

Jefferson wanted to learn about the land he had just bought. He asked Meriwether Lewis and William Clark to explore it. Both men were soldiers who loved the outdoors. Lewis knew about science, and Clark knew about maps. Lewis was quiet, and Clark loved to talk. Together, they made a good team.

VOCABULARY
wilderness—a land in its wild, natural state where few or no people live
Louisiana Purchase—the 1803 sale by France of much of western North America to the United States

 Activity: Internet Resources

Encourage students to explore the Lewis and Clark website developed by the National Park Service: http://www.cr.nps.gov/nr/travel/lewisandclark.

Students can view an animated map that follows the trails of the explorers. They also can click on a wealth of links that show the landscapes, people, and places that Lewis and Clark encountered.

☐ Differentiating Instruction

Beginning
Telling What You Know Have pairs take turns using the vocabulary words from pages 94–97 to tell about the new nation. Encourage students to point to relevant pictures as they speak.

Intermediate
Using Headings Ask pairs to select headings from pages 94–97. Then have students take turns giving a summary to their partners using the words in the headings. Encourage

listening partners to add a detail that was not previously mentioned.

Advanced
Partner Quiz Have students quiz their partners on the key ideas from pages 94–97. Ask them to form questions that use the headings. Partners can scan the text to find the answers, if they wish.

THE LEWIS AND CLARK EXPEDITION

In 1804, Lewis and Clark began their **expedition.** They set out from the **frontier** city of St. Louis, Missouri. They traveled all the way to the Pacific Ocean by boat, on foot, and on horseback. Their trip took them across plains, through rivers, and over the Rocky Mountains.

SACAJAWEA

For a while, a Native–American woman named Sacajawea traveled with Lewis and Clark. She helped the men talk to Indians they met. One time, she helped them buy horses from Indians when they badly needed more.

Two years after they left, Lewis and Clark returned to St. Louis. Lewis had scientific notes. Clark had maps. They were able to tell Jefferson and other Americans about the new land included in the Louisiana Purchase.

(TALK AND SHARE) **Look at the map on page 96. Find the route Lewis and Clark took. Talk with your partner about where they traveled.**

VOCABULARY

expedition—a trip made by a group of people for a definite purpose; also the group that makes such a trip
frontier—the area on the edge of a settled region

Primary Source

The Journals of Lewis and Clark

Lewis and Clark kept journals during their trip. They wrote about the people and things they saw—the Native Americans, the animals, the land. They described waterfalls as "jets of sparkling foam." They wrote about "immense herds of buffalo." They even wrote about bear attacks and not having food to eat.

Lewis and Clark were not good spellers. They sometimes spelled *beautiful* as "beatifull" and *break* as "brake." But they were very good at describing what they saw and felt. Today people still read their journals. They can feel as if they are traveling with Lewis and Clark!

Sacajawea ▶

▲ Pages from the journals of Lewis and Clark

Talk About The Lewis and Clark Expedition and Sacajawea

■ Tell students that Lewis and Clark traveled more than 8,000 miles on their famous expedition between 1804 and 1806.

■ Ask students, *Why was it important to President Jefferson for someone to explore the western United States?*

(TALK AND SHARE)

Encourage students to refer to the map on pages 16–17. Have them trace the route with their fingers to see which states Lewis and Clark explored.

Primary Source

The Journals of Lewis and Clark

Read and discuss The Journals of Lewis and Clark on page 97 with students. Interested students can listen to and read journal entries of the famous expedition on this website: http://www.lewis-clark.org.

 Activity: Role-Play

Have each student role-play either Meriwether Lewis, William Clark, or Sacajawea. Have students sit in circles of five or six and tell about their exploration of the Louisiana Purchase. Each student should relate one detail and then pass the story to the person on the right. Provide these prompts:

- We saw __.
- We met __.
- We did __.
- We felt __.
- We traveled by __.
- We went to __.

 Activity: Lewis and Clark Theater

Invite small groups to brainstorm a short scene on the Lewis and Clark expedition. They should decide on a setting (on land, in a canoe) and any props or backdrops they will need, and then they should take parts. In addition to Lewis, Clark, and Sacajawea, students can take on the roles of other men who went on the expedition. Have students improvise scripts and practice before performing for the class.

Discuss Foreign Policy

- Discuss with students the cartoon on the bottom of page 98.
- Ask how it represents the policy of isolationism.
- Ask volunteers to role-play people practicing isolationism.
- Tie the concept to the lesson by asking students to give George Washington's reasons for recommending the policy.
- Have students create a Two-column Chart that compares America's foreign policy between Washington's and Monroe's terms. Use Overhead Transparency 29, Two-Column Chart.

America's Foreign Policy

Under Washington	Under Monroe

Foreign Policy

At first, American leaders just wanted the rest of the world to leave them alone. Over time, they changed that **policy**.

ISOLATIONISM

In 1796, George Washington gave his Farewell Address. It was his last speech as president. In it, he warned Americans: Don't get too friendly with other nations. He didn't want America to get into European wars. It was "unnecessary and unwise," he said, to get involved.

Washington's policy was **isolationism.** The name comes from the word *isolate*, which means "alone." The next 3 presidents agreed with Washington. What happened in Europe was up to Europe, they said. Americans would mind their own business, and they did. Except for one small war—the War of 1812—the United States and Europe left each other alone.

This cartoon is about U.S. isolationism. It shows the United States with a big fence and a locked door. What is this cartoon saying? ▼

VOCABULARY
policy—a plan of action that a government makes
isolationism—a policy of not getting involved in other countries' wars

---

Activity: "Firsts" Poster

Have students make posters with some of the "firsts" they've learned so far (*first president, cabinet members, political parties*). Encourage them to work with a partner to brainstorm details to add to the poster for each item. In addition, have them illustrate their poster by drawing pictures or copying them from the Internet.

Differentiating Instruction

Beginning
Pantomime Demonstrate these examples of vocabulary words:

- *Isolationism:* a person slamming the door and saying, *Stay out!*
- *Aggression:* a lion attacking prey
- *Policy:* a school policy

Invite students to give other examples of these words.

Intermediate
Cartoons Have students draw cartoons to illustrate the meanings of three vocabulary words in the lesson. As an example, direct their attention to the cartoon above.

Advanced
Charades Have students copy each vocabulary word on an index card. Ask them to take turns drawing a card and acting out its meaning. Group members guess the vocabulary word.

THE MONROE DOCTRINE

Then the fifth president, James Monroe, changed the **foreign policy.** He decided that isolationism didn't make sense anymore. Monroe said it was time for the United States to take a stronger role in the world.

Monroe was especially thinking about South America and the Caribbean Sea. Some European nations were fighting to set up new colonies in these places. Monroe said, "No!"

In 1823, Monroe told the European countries to stay out of the New World. Monroe's opinion became known as the **Monroe Doctrine.** The Monroe Doctrine changed the way the United States acted toward other countries. The Monroe Doctrine was a way of saying that the United States will control what happens in the western **hemisphere.** Monroe thought that the United States might want more land one day.

(TALK AND SHARE) **With a partner, talk about how the foreign policy of Washington was different from that of Monroe.**

VOCABULARY

foreign policy—the plans a country makes for how it will act toward other countries

Monroe Doctrine—the idea that Europe should not set up new colonies in the Americas and the United States would stay out of European problems

hemisphere—one half of the earth's surface. North and South America are in the western hemisphere, and Europe, Africa, and Asia are in the eastern hemisphere.

▲ The ideas of James Monroe helped America grow into a strong nation.

Summary

In its first years, the United States government took shape. The country grew because of the Louisiana Purchase. In time, the United States grew strong enough to say no to European rulers.

Teach About The Monroe Doctrine

■ Provide this background information:

- Several countries in Latin America had gained independence from Spain and Portugal.

- The United States worried that some European countries planned to help Spain and Portugal get their colonies back.

- In the Monroe Doctrine, President Monroe told Europe not to make or retake any colonies in the Americas.

■ Connect to students' lives by asking what they think about one nation trying to control another.

(TALK AND SHARE)

Encourage intermediate and advanced students to draw a Venn Diagram to show their comparisons. Use Overhead Transparency 31, Venn Diagram.

Discuss the Summary

Direct students to read the Summary at the end of the lesson. Have students match each sentence in the Summary to one of the pictures of the Big Idea on page 91. Then have volunteers add details to each sentence.

✓ Assessment

Assess students' comprehension by asking the following questions:

History

- What were the departments in Washington's government?

- How did Hamilton's and Jefferson's views differ?

- Why was the Louisiana Purchase important?

- What did the Monroe Doctrine say?

Language

Match the word to its definition:

Words	Definitions
1. Cabinet	A. The area on the edge of a settled region
2. Isolationism	B. A policy of not getting involved in other countries' wars
3. Frontier	C. The president's official advisers

Assessment Book

Use page 25 to assess students' comprehension.

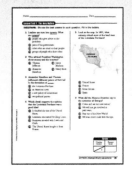

Teach Persuading

- Model the skill of supporting an opinion by suggesting an opinion about a topic of interest to students and then backing it up with two or three reasons.

- Ask volunteers to suggest another opinion and give reasons for or against it. Then read Supporting an Opinion.

Model the Organizer

- Ask volunteers to read aloud the opinion in the Opinion and Reasons Organizer and the three reasons that support it.

- Tell students that an organizer like this will help them develop strong ways to back up their opinions.

- Emphasize that reasons based on *facts* are the most convincing.

Give Practice Persuading

- **Discuss** Direct less fluent language learners to work in pairs to complete the Discuss activity. Emphasize that they can include an opinion and reasons. Encourage them to write single words or phrases.

- **Write** Suggest that students work in pairs to brainstorm reasons for their opinions. Have them work individually to write their paragraphs.

Persuading

Supporting an Opinion

Sometimes you need to persuade another person that your opinion is right. To do this, you give reasons that support your idea. The reasons can be facts or opinions. Use an Opinion and Reasons Organizer to help you persuade others. This organizer shows 3 reasons that support an opinion about the Monroe Doctrine. Using it, you could say, "The Monroe Doctrine made sense. I have 3 reasons for believing that." Then you would go on to state your reasons.

Opinion and Reasons Organizer

> **Reason**
> By 1823, the United States was bigger and stronger than before.

> **Reason**
> It was wrong for Europe to set up colonies in the Caribbean Sea and South America.

> **Reason**
> The United States might someday want more land for itself.

> **Opinion**
> In 1823, the Monroe Doctrine made sense for the United States.

Practice Persuading

1. Discuss What is your opinion? Should the United States get involved in events in other countries? Make an Opinion and Reasons Organizer to show what you think. Use it to persuade your partner to agree with you.

2. Write Was Jefferson right to buy the Louisiana Territory? Make an Opinion and Reasons Organizer. Then use the ideas in your organizer to write a persuasive paragraph. Begin by saying, "I believe Jefferson was . . . ." The Word Bank may help you.

> **Word Bank**
> right
> wrong
>
> Louisiana Purchase
>
> Rocky Mountains
> Mississippi River
> Pacific Ocean
>
> cost
>
> doubled

Activity: Presentation

Review the importance of Lewis and Clark's travel journals. Students should write two to three journal entries from the point of view of a person described in Lesson 7. Entries should mention at least one event or opinion from the lesson.

Differentiating Instruction

Beginning

Using Sentences Give students sentence structures to use in talking to a partner about U.S. involvement in other countries.

- I think the United States should . . . because. . . .

- In [*name of country*], the United States should . . . because. . . .

- It is [*good/bad*] for the United States to . . . because. . . .

Intermediate

Grammar Have partners exchange papers from the Write activity and identify sentences that use subject pronouns. If there are none, students should suggest to their partner what pronouns could substitute for the subject nouns.

Advanced

Powerful Persuasion Have students coach each other on making their arguments for the Write activity more powerful.

Activities

Grammar Spotlight

Subject Pronouns Pronouns stand for the names of people, places, and things. Subject pronouns are used for the subjects of sentences. A subject does the action of the sentence.

Example: *He agreed to buy the land for $15 million.*

	Subject Pronouns	Examples
First Person	I	*I think...*
	we	*We stayed out...*
Second Person	you	*You can't...*
Third Person	he	*He agreed...*
	she	*She might...*
	it	*It could make...*
	they	*They didn't...*

Write 3 sentences. Begin each one with a pronoun.

Oral Language

What Do You Need? This game is for groups of two people. Pretend you are on the Lewis and Clark expedition. What do you need? Each person makes a list. Then read from your lists to ask questions. Take turns. Ask, "Would you need a ___?" If it is on your list, say, "Yes, I would need a ___." If it is not on your list, say, "No, I would not need a ___." Score one point for every *yes* either one of you says. The group with the most points wins.

Partner Practice

Facts and Opinions With a partner, take a class survey. Find out what the class knows about a famous person or event. Separate what your classmates say into facts and opinions. Make a chart like the one on page 93. Share your chart with the class.

Activities

Grammar Spotlight

Explain to students that pronouns are used as replacement words for people, places, and things.

Read aloud the Grammar Spotlight with students. Provide classroom practice by asking students questions about class members that they can answer using subject pronouns. Use the following examples:

- Look at (name of student). What color is ___ wearing today?
- Are ___ and ___ holding pencils?

Oral Language

To guide students in making their lists, suggest that they consider what the expedition party will need in these categories: food, shelter, transportation, protection from wild animals, meeting Native Americans, mapping, keeping a journal.

Partner Practice

Suggest that students ask about famous people in history as well as famous people in the news.

Activity: Extend the Lesson

How America Grew (Stories in History series: McDougal Littell, 2003) gives high-interest narratives about the years from 1775 to 1914. In particular, "Lewis and Clark Meet the Shoshone," by Judith Lloyd Yero, includes shortened versions of some entries the men of the expedition wrote in their journals.

Program Resources

Student Activity Journal
Use page 39 to practice *persuading*.

Overhead Transparencies
Use 19, Opinions and Reasons Organizer, with page 100.

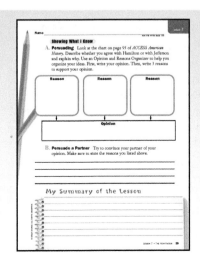

Moving West

STANDARDS CONTENT

History
- Read a map key
- Recognize causes and effects of westward expansion from 1787 to 1840
- Recognize major new technologies of the period
- Explain the conflicts between slave and free states

Language
- Identify the following Key Concepts: *technology, pioneers,* and *territory*
- Recognize idioms
- Practice evaluating events in history

Begin Building Background

- Ask students the questions under the picture. Encourage them to answer the questions using vocabulary from previous chapters, such as *wilderness, expedition,* and *frontier.* Provide students with words as needed (*transportation, horses, covered wagon, traveling, west*).

- Encourage students to share their knowledge or experience about why families risk going to an unknown land. Draw out these key ideas:
  - Sometimes moves can be dangerous and difficult.
  - People take such risks in hopes of having a better life.

Moving West

Here you'll learn about Americans moving to the West. You'll also learn more about reading maps and practice evaluating events in history.

Building Background

▲ When we left Haiti, we traveled by plane.

- **What things do you see in this picture?**
- **Why do you think the family is moving?**
- **What would be hard about traveling this way?**

102 UNIT 3 • GROWING DIFFERENCES

 Activity: Pioneer Breakfast

Have pairs write or draw what they ate for breakfast today. Then have them brainstorm what the family in the picture would have to do in order to have the same breakfast. Ask them to write or draw their answers. Provide these ideas as starter prompts:
- Milk a cow.
- Chop wood.

 Differentiating Instruction

Beginning
Studying Vocabulary Write these words from previous lessons on the board and have students copy them on sticky notes: *settlers, regions, continent, dangerous, slaves, property, wilderness, frontier.*

Ask volunteers the meanings of the words. Then have volunteers place the sticky notes where they see the words in their textbooks.

Intermediate
Captions Divide the class into three groups and give each a sticky note. Assign each group to write a caption for one of the pictures above.

Advanced
Technology Trip Ask students to consider how technology has affected a trip they or someone they know took. They should discuss in small groups and present what they know to the class.

Around 1800, many Americans began moving to the West. New technology made travel easier. Settlers formed new states. Some new states allowed slavery; others did not.

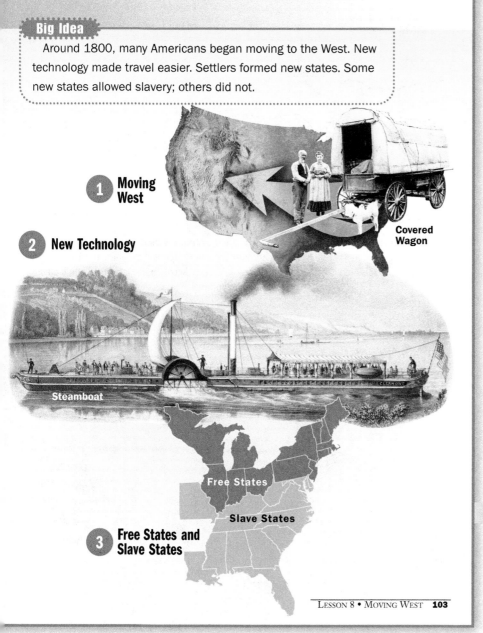

1 Moving West

2 New Technology

Covered Wagon

Steamboat

Free States

Slave States

3 Free States and Slave States

LESSON 8 • MOVING WEST **103**

Introduce the Big Idea

- Use a familiar map to review the cardinal directions (*east, west, south, north*).
- Ask students to identify what they see using picture clues, such as forms of transportation.
- Use the pictures to describe the changes in the United States during this time:
  - Explain that the story of westward movement started around 1800.
  - Not only was there new land to settle, there was new technology to help settlers move.
  - As the nation grew, new states started. Some allowed slavery; others were free.

Teach the Pictures

Pioneers had to cross mountains with no roads as a guide. They crossed rivers without bridges, too. Pioneers carried all their belongings with them when they traveled. Ask, *What would you take on such a hard trip?*

Review

In the last lesson, students learned how to persuade people by giving an opinion and supporting it with facts. Remind them to use facts in their role-play to convince the other person whether to stay or to move west.

Activity: Role-Play

Prepare by making two large signs. They should read:

- Yes, we should go!
- No, we should stay!

Present this scenario to students. The year is 1830. A couple lives in New York City with their two children. The couple both work as servants for a wealthy family. They hear about people moving to the West who are able to build their own homes.

However, the trip west is hard and dangerous. There are no roads or bridges. There are no stores and no towns. One person in the couple wants to go. The other wants to stay.

Ask students to think about reasons the two people might give each other for going or staying. Have volunteers take turns holding up the sign of their choice and giving a reason for going or staying.

Later, they may change their minds. Record the reasons on the board in a Two-column Chart.

Resource Library

Reader's Handbook (red)
Maps 163–164, 555–556

Reader's Handbook (yellow)
Maps 121, 431

All Write
Using Maps 465–480

Teach ~~Key Concepts~~

- Say each Key Concept slowly and have students repeat it. Point to the illustration for each Key Concept and ask the class to say the word together. Then read aloud the text, pointing to corresponding pictures.

- Ask students to name new technologies they own or have used, such as computers, cell phones, and calculators.

- Have students return to the map on page 96. Circle a state on the map with your finger, saying *state*. Then circle a territory, saying *territory*. Call on volunteers to demonstrate other states and territories on the map.

Teach the Visual Aid
~~Pioneer Life~~

Ask a volunteer to read aloud the title of the visual aid. Then read the captions aloud, providing definitions as needed, such as *sod* means *earth*. Emphasize that pioneers made everything they needed for themselves.

Key Concepts

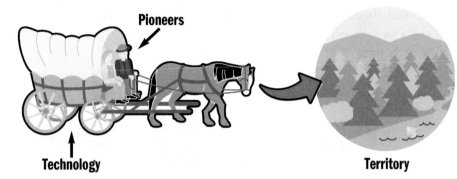

Pioneers

Technology

Territory

Technology is the use of new knowledge to make new machines.

In the early 1800s, **pioneers** used new technology (covered wagons called *prairie schooners*) to settle in new parts of the country.

They moved into new **territory**, or new parts of the land.

Pioneer Life

Farms in the Wilderness   **Simple Houses Made of Logs or Sod**

104 UNIT 3 • GROWING DIFFERENCES

👥 Activity: Pioneer Web

Create a sample Concept Web on the board with the heading *Things That Pioneers Made and Did.*

Divide the class into small groups. Have them study the pictures in the visual aid to find things that pioneers made (*soap, clothes, houses*) and tasks they did (*chop wood, cook over fire, grow food*). Ask groups to complete the Web by listing things they find. Then gather as a class. Have each group contribute details to finish the sample Web.

📄 Differentiating Instruction

Beginning
Pioneer Circle Ask a student to act out or draw something pioneers made or did for themselves. Supply words as necessary. Then ask the next student to tell what the first student suggested and to act out or draw another response.

Intermediate
Pioneer Chain Have each player complete this sentence: *Pioneers made their own. . . .* Have each player in turn repeat what previous players said in

order, adding his or her own item at the end.

Advanced
Pair Practice Have pairs write the headings of the visual aid on index cards and place them facedown. Then have them take turns drawing a card and explaining the actions to each other.

Reading a Map

Some maps show something special about a region. The map key and the symbols in it give you information. Here's what you do.

1. Read the map title. The title tells you what the map shows.

2. Find the map key.

3. Study the symbols and colors in the key. What does a star mean on this map?

4. Find the symbols on the map. Point to the places where a star appears. What else does this map show you?

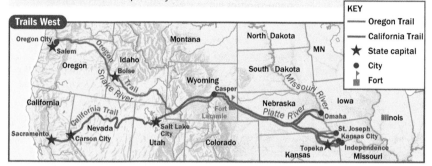

Trails West

KEY
— Oregon Trail
— California Trail
★ State capital
● City
▟ Fort

Boys and Girls Working   **Cooking over Fire**   **Making Soap and Clothes**

LESSON 8 • MOVING WEST **105**

Teach Skill Building

■ Read aloud with students the explanation and steps for reading a map.

■ Walk through each step with students, first demonstrating the step yourself and then calling on volunteers to give another demonstration. Provide this additional practice:

• Point to symbols on the map key. Have volunteers find the symbols on the map and tell what they stand for.

• Find symbols on the map. Ask volunteers to use the map key to explain what they mean.

Teach the Pictures

Sometimes pioneers could go to a general store in a town to buy what they needed. However, most of the time, pioneers had to use what they found in nature to make clothes, build shelter, and eat. For example, they used lye, made from steeping water in wood ashes, and grease from animal fat to make soap. They cooked over open fires and sewed their own clothes. Ask students, *What else do you think pioneers had to do for themselves?*

Activity: Student Map Quiz

Have each student in a pair create a quiz of two to four questions about the Oregon Trail. Ask them to use information shown on the map. Then have pairs give their quizzes to each other. The answering partner uses the map and map key to find the answers. You might provide this sample prompt: *What river did pioneers cross on the way to Boise?*

Program Resources

Student Activity Journal

Use page 40 to build key vocabulary.

Use page 41 to practice reading a map.

Overhead Transparencies

Use 33, Web, with page 104.

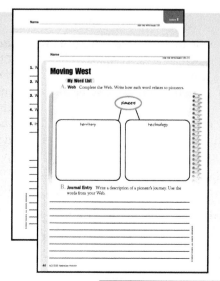

Introduce Moving West

- Begin by reviewing the Louisiana Purchase made by President Jefferson in 1803 (Lesson 7).

- Direct students' attention again to the map on page 96. Ask them to point out where most Americans lived at the beginning of the 1800s.

- Emphasize that early pioneers began to settle land in the Louisiana Purchase and beyond.

Key Connection: Geography

Gradually, students are becoming familiar with the fifty states in the Union. Provide practice in identifying the states by referring them to the U.S. map on pages 16–17.

Moving West

Americans slowly began to move west. When they wanted to make new states, problems between slave states and free states grew.

The Nation Grows West

In the early 1800s, many Americans began to move west. Land there was **cheap.** A person who was a servant in the East could own land in the West. People felt they had great **opportunities** in the West.

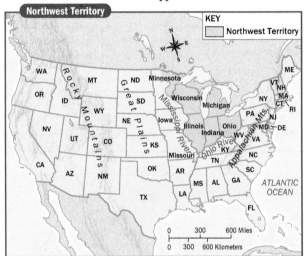

Northwest Territory

KEY
Northwest Territory

THE NORTHWEST ORDINANCE

The first American states were on or near the Atlantic Ocean. The land west of the Appalachian Mountains was **wilderness.** Little by little, Americans moved into it.

The first movement was into the rich farmland north of the Ohio River. This area today includes the states of Ohio, Michigan, Indiana, Illinois, and Wisconsin. **Congress** had divided this land into **territories.** It also had passed a law in 1787 called the Northwest Ordinance. The law set up a plan for government in the territories. The law said that when a territory got 60,000 people (not counting slaves), it could ask to become a state. Then Congress would vote to decide if it would be a state.

VOCABULARY

cheap—not expensive; costs very little
opportunities—chances to live a better life
wilderness—a land in its wild, natural state where few or no people live

Congress—the lawmaking part of government. The Senate and the House of Representatives together are Congress.
territories—parts of U.S. land that aren't states

Activity: Prior Knowledge

Divide the class into three groups. Assign each an area: 1. Appalachians to the Mississippi River; 2. Great Plains; 3. Far West. Have students in each group brainstorm what they know about these areas, recording the information in a chart like the one below.

Have groups share their charts.

Native Americans	Animals	Plants	Weather

Differentiating Instruction

Beginning

Choral Reading Ask students to do a choral reading with you of the title, introduction, and headings. Reinforce their understanding of the words *moving west* by having students demonstrate on the map above where pioneers traveled. Point to *govern*, the root word of *government*, and explain that the Northwest Ordinance set up a plan for governing the territories.

Intermediate

Using the Map Have reading pairs stop after each paragraph and discuss what they read. Encourage them to use the map on page 106 to locate all the places in the text.

Advanced

Active Learning Ask students to stop at the end of each section and paraphrase what they just read to their partner. Encourage them to record key words and phrases in their history notebooks.

BEYOND THE MISSISSIPPI RIVER

By the 1820s, **pioneers** had settled west to the Mississippi River. By the 1830s, they had moved farther west into such midwestern lands as Iowa and Missouri. **Beyond** that lay the **Great Plains**. These lands were dry and without trees. Pioneers moved to these open lands too.

The Far West lay beyond the Rocky Mountains. Pioneers heard that the land there was good for farming. In the 1840s, many pioneers went all the way to the Far West.

TALK AND SHARE With a partner, talk about the reasons why many people moved west.

Language Notes

Idioms
These sayings don't mean what they seem.

☐ **little by little:** slowly moving, as if by little steps

☐ **piece of cake:** something easy to do

VOCABULARY
pioneers—the first people who settle an area and get it ready for others who come later
beyond—on the far side; past
Great Plains—a region in the middle of the United States, from the Missouri River to the Rocky Mountains. See the map on page 106.

LESSON 8 • MOVING WEST **107**

Teach Beyond the Mississippi River

■ Talk to students about the regions mentioned in the text: the Great Plains and the Far West.

■ Ask students what region the picture reminds them of.

■ Elicit responses on why people would want to move to a place with mountains and few trees. Ask students if they remember from Lesson 1 what resources are in these regions.

Language Notes

■ Explain that an idiom is a group of words that has a meaning different from the meanings of the words by themselves.

■ Discuss the idioms listed in the Language Notes. Have volunteers read them in context on pages 106 and 108.

■ Start an Idiom Corner in your classroom where students can contribute idioms they find in books or hear in conversation.

TALK AND SHARE

Have students discuss why pioneers moved west. Ask students why people would take such a difficult trip.

Activity: Sentence Patterns

Practice sentence patterns for describing cause-effect relationships.

Beginners: *Why did _____ do it?*

Intermediate: *They did it because _____.*

Advanced: *_____ happened as a result of _____.*

Use sentences directly related to classroom events to make the practice relevant.

Program Resources

Student Activity Journal

Assign page 42:

• To create study notes for students to review

• To provide reinforcement of key vocabulary

Discuss New Technology Speeds Travel

- Help students understand that the Erie Canal was dug through 363 miles of wilderness.

- Explain that it helped trade by creating a trade route between two cities in New York: Buffalo and Albany.

- Ask volunteers to trace this transportation route on a U.S. map.

Teach the Pictures

Although Robert Fulton is credited with introducing the steamboat as a successful means of travel, the steamboat originally was invented by John Fitch. Fitch built three working steamboats between 1785 and 1796, but he died before his invention became widely used.

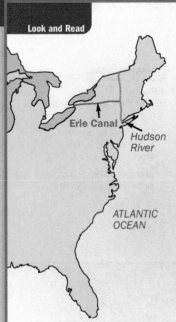

Look and Read

New Technology Speeds Travel

Getting to the West was no piece of cake in the early 1800s. Still, it was much easier than it had been before. New **technology** helped people travel more quickly.

STEAMBOATS

The new **steamboats** made river travel much faster and safer. In 1807, Robert Fulton showed his boat, the *Clermont*. He made his ship with an engine that got its power from steam. People were excited. Before the steamboat, people moved on rivers by sailboat or canoe. The steamboat could carry many more people and all their things. Thousands of pioneers moved west on steamboats.

▲ The Clermont

THE ERIE CANAL

In 1825, the Erie Canal opened. It joined the Great Lakes with the Atlantic Ocean. Now ships could travel from the sea into **ports** along the Great Lakes. Boats were tied to **mules.**

Then the mules pulled the ships by walking on the banks of the **canal.** The Erie Canal was important for both travel and **trade.** **Goods** could move back and forth by ship from the East to the West.

▲ Mules pulled boats through the canal.

VOCABULARY

technology—the use of new knowledge to make new machines

steamboats—ships powered by steam engines

ports—places where ships stop to load and unload goods

mules—animals like horses that can be trained and used to pull or carry things

canal—a waterway that is dug between bodies of water

trade—the business of buying and selling goods

goods—things for sale

 Activity: Word Connect

Have students write word cards for lesson vocabulary words and look for relationships among them. Ask them to rearrange their words in columns that make sense. Afterward, have pairs play Word Connect. The first player places a vocabulary word on the table and uses it in a sentence. The next player places a word beside the first and uses both words in a sentence. Play continues until a player cannot create a new logical sentence.

 Differentiating Instruction

Beginning

Caption Writing Read aloud the headings on pages 108–109 with students. Have them use key words from the headings to write simple captions for the pictures.

Intermediate

Word Web Have students create a Web Mural of the word *technology*. In each circle, have them write one or two sentences that describe a form of technology from this time period. Use Overhead Transparency 33, Web.

Advanced

Pioneer Postcards Have students write a postcard about traveling on one of the means of transportation described on pages 108–109. The postcard should be written from the point of view of a nineteenth-century person.

Encourage students to add details that describe the technology, where they are going, and what the experience is like.

RAILROADS

The new steam engine also changed railroad travel. Before the steam engine, horses pulled wagons on tracks. In 1830, a steam-powered train made its first run on American tracks. After that, workers laid railroad tracks across the wilderness. Some lucky pioneers rode trains into the West.

▲ Train pulled by a steam engine

PRAIRIE SCHOONERS

The greatest number of pioneers moved west on land trails. The **Oregon Trail** and the **California Trail** both led west from the new territory of Missouri. **Prairie schooners** helped pioneers carry their things through the mountains. This new kind of wagon was built for travel. Its sides were slanted to keep things from falling out. Plus, it was easy to repair if anything broke on the rough trails.

(TALK AND SHARE) **Talk with your partner about which new technology in the 1800s is your favorite. Tell the reasons why you like it best.**

▲ Prairie schooner

VOCABULARY

Oregon Trail—a pioneer trail leading northwest from Missouri to Oregon. See the map on page 105.
California Trail—a pioneer trail leading southwest from Missouri to California
prairie schooners—strong wagons covered to keep out wind and rain and pulled by animals

Talk About Railroads

■ Tell students that, in the 1840s, America had 3,000 miles of railroad track. By 1860, however, trains rode more than 30,000 miles of track.

■ Explain that the canals, steamboats, and railroads made it cheaper, quicker, and easier to transport goods.

■ Ask students to give reasons that both farmers and manufacturers benefited from transporting their goods cross-country.

(TALK AND SHARE)

Encourage students to refer to the vocabulary terms on page 108 to find how these technologies improved the state of life. Guide them in using these facts to support their opinions.

Activity: Internet Resources

■ **Tour a Steamboat:**
http://www.steamboats.com/engineroom1.html

■ **Early Railroad Photos:**
http://www.transitpeople.org/lesson/train.htm

■ **Inside a Prairie Schooner:**
http://library.thinkquest.org/6400/wagon.htm

Activity: Pioneer Billboards

Assign each of four groups a technology described on pages 108–109: *steamboat, Erie Canal, railroad steam engine, prairie schooner.* Have groups create an illustrated ad for their technology that could be posted on a billboard in the early 1800s to attract pioneers to the West. Then post the ads in the classroom. Arrange for a viewing and Q & A time in which groups can exchange information.

Discuss Free States and Slave States

■ Read aloud the headings on page 110 with students.

■ Ask students to review the differences they learned between the colonies of the North and South. Look for these details:

- The New England colonies had many cities and factories.

- The Southern colonies had farms and plantations. Their crops required large amounts of labor for which many Southerners used slaves.

■ Ask students how they would react if their country were divided over an issue. Have them suggest steps for bringing the country together.

People in History

Henry Clay

Refer students to page 80 to review the Key Concept *compromise*. Then read aloud the feature on Henry Clay with them. Discuss the importance of Clay's Missouri Compromise in keeping peace between the North and South.

Tell students that Clay will appear again later to solve another problem with a compromise.

Look and Read

▲ Slaves Picking Cotton

▲ Cotton

Free States and Slave States

Many people in the North freed their slaves soon after the American Revolution. Northern states passed laws making slavery **illegal**. However, slavery was still common in the South. Plantation owners used slave **labor** to grow their crops. By 1800, slavery divided the North and the South.

THE NORTH AND SOUTH DIFFER

Over time, differences between the North and South grew in many ways. People in the South and North wanted different things. This led to **sectionalism**. People in each section, or part, of the country wanted to protect their way of life. Their section was more important to them than the nation. In Congress, leaders from the two sections of the country did not agree on many things.

Differences Between the South and the North

	The South	The North
SLAVERY	Legal	Illegal
FACTORIES	Very few	Many
FARMS	Many large plantations	Many small farms
CROPS	Cotton, rice, sugar, tobacco	Corn, wheat
CITIES	Very few	Many

▲ Factory

VOCABULARY
illegal—not allowed by law
labor—workers. *Labor* also means the work people do.
sectionalism—caring more about your own part of the country than about the country as a whole

People in History

Henry Clay

Henry Clay had not gone to school much, but he loved books. He read a lot. Clay became a great American leader. Many times, Clay had ideas that helped solve problems. One problem he solved was about slavery in new states. When it seemed impossible for Congress to reach agreement, Clay would find a way. People called him the "Great Compromiser." Henry Clay was very popular. But, although he ran for president 3 times, he never won.

110 UNIT 3 • GROWING DIFFERENCES

Activity: Compare Pair

Have students work in pairs to copy the chart headings (page 110) on separate index cards: *slavery, factories, farms, crops, cities*. Have them place the cards facedown and take turns drawing them. On each draw, partners describe the South, the North, or both in relation to the word.

Differentiating Instruction

Beginning
Concept Poster Help students complete a poster to illustrate the key points on these two pages. Review the vocabulary term *outnumber*.

Intermediate
Exploring Sectionalism Invite small groups to talk about what in their lives is like the divisiveness and the sectionalism of 1820. They should share their ideas with the class.

Advanced
Explaining the Missouri Compromise In a paragraph, have students tell first that the Missouri Compromise solved a problem. Supporting sentences should tell what the problem was and how the Compromise solved it.

WOULD NEW STATES BE SLAVE OR FREE?

Some of the new states were free states. Slavery was not allowed in them. Others were slave states. People could own slaves in these states. Each time a territory asked Congress to become a state, the **debate** about slavery began again.

In 1819, there were 11 free states and 11 slave states. The **balance** in the Senate was even. Then, in 1820, Missouri wanted to join the **Union.** That was a problem. The South wanted Missouri to be a slave state. The North wanted it to be free.

Then Senator Henry Clay came up with a plan called the Missouri **Compromise.** It solved the problem of slavery in new states for more than 20 years.

(**TALK AND SHARE**) **Draw a poster to show Clay's plan. Explain to a partner how it solved the debate over new states.**

VOCABULARY

debate—a formal talk between people who have different opinions

balance—a division of power. *To balance* something is to make both sides equal.

Union—the United States. *To join the Union* means to become a state.

compromise—a way of settling a disagreement in which each side gets part of what it wants

KEY
- ☐ Free state
- ▨ Admitted as a free state, 1820
- ☐ Slave state
- ▨ Admitted as a slave state, 1821
- ☐ U.S. territory

Missouri Compromise

Canada

Vermont · Maine

Michigan Territory · New York · New Hampshire · Massachusetts · Rhode Island · Connecticut

Unorganized Territory · Illinois · Indiana · Ohio · Pennsylvania · New Jersey · Delaware · Maryland

Missouri Compromise line · Missouri · Virginia · Kentucky · North Carolina · Tennessee · South Carolina

New Spain (Mexico) · Arkansas Territory · Mississippi · Alabama · Georgia

0   200   400 Miles
0   200   400 Kilometers

Louisiana · Florida Territory · ATLANTIC OCEAN

The Missouri Compromise

Missouri will be a slave state.

Maine can join the Union too. It will be a free state.

Congress will draw a line on the map of the United States. South of the line, slavery will be allowed. North of the line, slavery will be illegal.

Summary

New technology helped people move west. People in some territories asked to become states. Congress had to decide if they would be slave states or free states. The Missouri Compromise balanced both sides.

Teach Would New States Be Slave or Free?

- ■ Explain why it was important to the North and South to keep a balance of power in the Senate.
- ■ Review with students that every state in the Union elects two senators to Congress.
- ■ Ask students what could happen if states in the South had more senators than the North. (*The South could pass laws to extend slavery to other territories.*)

(**TALK AND SHARE**)

Suggest to students that they copy a map of the states onto their posters and visually demonstrate Clay's plan.

Discuss the Summary

Read aloud the Summary at the end of the lesson with students. Then have students return to the Big Idea on page 103. Ask them to recap key information about each part of the Big Idea.

✔ Assessment

Assess students' comprehension by asking the following questions:

History
- • Why did people want to move west in the early 1800s?
- • What forms of technology helped people travel?
- • What did the Missouri Compromise do?

Language
Try to figure out the meanings of these idioms:
- • Lend me a hand.
- • Broken heart
- • Keep an eye out.
- • Make up your mind.
- • Let loose
- • Hard feelings
- • Changed my mind

Assessment Book
Use page 26 to assess students' comprehension.

Teach Evaluating

Preview the skill by asking students if they think the Missouri Compromise was important and why. Afterward, explain that they just made an evaluation. This page will give students strategies for evaluating events.

Model the Organizer

- Call on volunteers to read aloud separate parts of the Evaluation Chart.
- Point out that a good evaluation is supported by facts.
- An Evaluation Chart can help students sort out facts that support their ideas.

Give Practice Evaluating

Have students work in pairs to complete one activity.

- **Draw** As students complete the Draw activity, have them use the map and key words on page 106.
- **Write** Guide students in using their evaluation as the beginning, or topic, sentence of their paragraphs. Tell them that the remaining sentences in the paragraph should give facts that support their evaluation.

Evaluating

Evaluating Events in History

When you evaluate an event, you decide what value it has. You answer the question: How important or fair or wise is it? First, you gather and present the facts. It helps to list them in an Evaluation Chart. Then, decide what the facts show and draw a conclusion.

Evaluation Chart

Subject		
Evaluating the Missouri Compromise		
Fact	**Fact**	**Fact**
It allowed Missouri, a slave territory, to become a state.	It allowed Maine, a free territory, to become a state.	It drew a line on the map that settled the question of slavery in new states for 20 years.
My Evaluation		
The Missouri Compromise was very important. It solved the problem about Missouri becoming a state by balancing it with Maine. It also solved the problem of slavery in new states for the next 20 years.		

Practice Evaluating

1. Draw With a partner, draw an Evaluation Chart to evaluate the Northwest Ordinance. Draw what things were like before it. Draw what it did. Use the chart to tell your partner if the Northwest Ordinance was a successful plan.

2. Write Evaluate how important technology was in the 1800s. First, put the new technology and what came from it in an Evaluation Chart. Then make your evaluation. Use information from your chart to write a paragraph. Exchange paragraphs with a partner and check each other's work.

Check Your Writing

Make sure you
- Use complete sentences.
- Use a period at the end of each sentence.
- Spell all the words correctly.

 Activity: Summary Chart

Write the three parts of the Big Idea as heads in a chart on the chalkboard (*Moving West, New Technology, Free States and Slave States*). Invite students to contribute information they learned in the lesson. Add it to the chart.

 Differentiating Instruction

Beginning
Encouraging Language Provide encouragement to students as they try to communicate. Limited English writers benefit from practice in writing key words and phrases, not in extensive rewriting or revising.

Intermediate
Communicating Work with students in making their meanings clear. When meanings are unclear, ask students to say aloud what they mean. Help them rephrase questionable sentences in ways that make sense.

Advanced
Editing Encourage students to check their writing for mistakes. Have them make corrections in a separate color. Their corrections will enable you to see which mistakes they are catching and help them identify mistakes of which they may not be aware.

Grammar Spotlight

Object Pronouns Pronouns stand for the names of people, places, and things. You use object pronouns when the person, place, or thing receives the action of the sentence.

	Object Pronouns	Examples
FIRST PERSON	me	*Give me the book.*
	us	*Tell us about pioneers.*
SECOND PERSON	you	*Does it make sense to you?*
THIRD PERSON	him	*Clay was a leader. Americans liked him.*
	her	*A pioneer girl sewed. Her mother taught her.*
	it	*The Oregon Trail went west. Pioneers took it.*
	them	*States were added. Regions fought over them.*

Write a sentence telling a friend to pass something to someone. Use an object pronoun in your sentence.

Partner Practice

Becoming Pioneers Read this script with a partner. Practice your lines. Then perform for your group or class.

Young Man: I work hard for my boss, but I don't get any respect. If I went to the West, I could have my own farm.

Young Woman: You're a good man. I respect you. All day long I sew and cook. I clean someone's house. I take care of her babies.

Young Man: If we moved to the West, we could work for ourselves.

Young Woman: Wouldn't that be wonderful?

Young Man: Pack up your things. We're going west!

Hands On

Make a Map Make a map of your neighborhood. Put in places like your home, your friend's home, your school, and your library. Then make a map key for it. Put things like parks or trails on your map and map key.

Grammar Spotlight

Using students and objects in the classroom, demonstrate how pronouns represent nouns: *(name of a girl)/she; (name of a boy)/he; blackboard/it.*

Partner Practice

Allow students to modify the script to their tastes or ability levels.

Hands On

With students, brainstorm places that they may include on their maps. Draw a map icon for one of the places as a prompt for them.

Activity: Extend the Lesson

For additional reading, recommend these books to students:

- *Little House in the Big Woods* by Laura Ingalls Wilder (HarperTrophy, 1953)
- *Children of the Wild West* by Russell Freedman (Clarion Books, 1990)
- *The Amazing Impossible Erie Canal* by Cheryl Harness (Aladdin Library, 1999)

Program Resources

Student Activity Journal
Use page 43 to practice *evaluating.*

Overhead Transparencies
Use 11, Evaluation Chart, with page 112.

The Age of Jackson

STANDARDS CONTENT

History

- Read a timeline
- Understand the factors that led to Jackson's popularity
- Evaluate the role of tariffs in the growing problems between North and South
- Explain the relationship between western expansion and relations with the Native Americans

Language

- Identify the following Key Concepts: *exports, imports,* and *tariffs*
- Identify words that signal time order
- Practice summarizing events in history

Begin

- Focus students on the picture. Ask them the questions below the image.

- Invite volunteers to point out and name details they see. Direct their attention to the clues that show that many people in the crowd are ordinary citizens and not wealthy.

- Explain that the crowd came to see Andrew Jackson become president. Tell them he was popular because he represented the "common man." Ask students to name popular people they know, including TV, movie, and music stars. Encourage them to describe what qualities in each person they admire.

The Age of Jackson

Here you'll learn about the time Andrew Jackson was president. You'll also learn more about timelines and practice summarizing.

Building Background

▲ It would be fun to see a new president.

- **What do you think is happening in this picture?**
- **Who would a crowd today go to see?**
- **What kind of person would you like for president?**

 Activity: Campaign Posters

Ask students to choose a personal hero who they think would make a good president. Have them create a campaign poster for their hero that convinces others he or she is a great candidate. Afterward, tape students' posters to the wall and allow time for the class to view them.

 Differentiating Instruction

Beginning

Describing Details Write down the details that students note in the pictures for Lesson 9. Review the words *president, the North, the South, Indians, homeland, settlers.*

In addition, introduce the name *President Andrew Jackson.* Have students copy all the words on sticky notes. Invite them to preview the pictures in Lesson 9 and attach the words to pictures the words describe.

Intermediate

Role-Play Have students create a dialogue between two of the people shown above. Encourage students to communicate the people's enthusiasm for their new president.

Advanced

Historical Comics Have students make a small comic book about President Jackson's inauguration day. Introduce the term *inauguration.* Students should use speech balloons for their dialogues.

Andrew Jackson became president in 1829. Troubles between the North and South grew stronger. More settlers moved to the Far West, and the government forced Native Americans to leave their homelands.

1 President for the Common Man

2 Fight over Tariffs

3 Removal of the Native Americans

Introduce the Big Idea

- Identify Andrew Jackson as the president whose inauguration is celebrated in the opening picture. Read aloud key phrases on the election poster (*The Man of the People! Jackson Forever!*).

- Ask students to describe Jackson based on the poster and his picture.

- Ask students to describe what they see in the tariff illustration.

- Ask students to predict what is happening to the Native Americans in the third picture.

Teach the Pictures

- Andrew Jackson is pictured in his military uniform. Explain that many people regarded him as a hero for fighting in the Revolutionary War and the War of 1812.

- Explain that serving in the U.S. military has helped many presidents get elected.

Review

Remind students about the movement west. The reasons the Native Americans moved west were very different.

Focus discussion on such previous vocabulary words as *territories*, *pioneers*, *Great Plains*, and *trail*.

Activity: Mock Election

Hold a mock election based on candidates chosen by students. They may select personal heroes or celebrities. Give each student a ballot and ask them to vote for two candidates—their own and one other person. Tally the votes. Then hold another election between the two candidates who had the most votes.

Before the final voting, invite students to give their opinions about why—or why not—a candidate would make a good president.

Resource Library

Reader's Handbook (red)
Timeline 276, 561, 681

Reader's Handbook (yellow)
Timeline 51, 64, 434–435, 557

All Write
Timeline 273, 489–500

Teach [Key Concepts]

■ Pronounce each Key Concept for students and read aloud the text that describes it.

■ Call on volunteers to point to the illustration for each Key Concept and explain in their own words what it means.

■ Emphasize that *imports* come *in* to the country; *exports* go *out*.

■ Suggest the words *in* and *exit* as memory cues.

Teach the Visual Aid
[The Cherokee]

Focus students on the pictures on the bottom of pages 116–117 and read aloud the captions. Supply meanings of these words, if needed: *Cherokee, alphabet, bilingual, newspaper, removal, one-fourth.*

By the early 1800s, the Cherokee had developed a culture similar in many ways to that of Americans who lived nearby.

Encourage students to tell what they infer about the Cherokee nation's culture.

[Key Concepts]

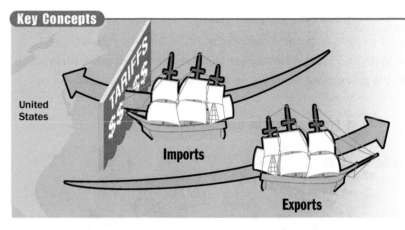

Exports are goods we sell to other countries. **Imports** are goods we buy from other countries. **Tariffs** are taxes put on imports so as to raise the price people must pay to buy them.

[The Cherokee]

Georgia
In the early 1800s, the Cherokee people lived in peace with the citizens of Georgia.

Government
The Cherokee had a legislature, courts, and a constitution.

Sequoya
He invented an alphabet for the Cherokee language.

116 Unit 3 • Growing Differences

Activity: Internet Resources

Encourage students to find out more about the Cherokee at the following sites and to report back to the class:

- http://www.cherokeehistory.com
- http://www.historychannel.com

Differentiating Instruction

Beginning
Answering Questions Pose *yes/no* questions that students can answer by repeating your key words. Use the following example:

Teacher: *Do imports come into the country?*

Student: *Yes, imports come into the country.*

Intermediate
Jackson Profile Direct students to work in pairs to give a profile of Andrew Jackson's life from 1795 to

1835 (years covered on the timeline). Encourage them to take turns telling events.

Advanced
Slide Show Ask students to present a "slide show" presentation of the Cherokee to their partners. Pointing to each picture, they should describe it in as much detail as they can.

Reading a Timeline

A timeline shows events in chronological order. Some timelines are divided into periods of time. The timeline below is divided into 10-year periods. Here's how to read this kind of timeline.

1. First, look at the dates at both ends of the timeline. They show all the time covered in the timeline.

2. Then, read the dates and events in the timeline.

3. Notice how the events relate to each other in time. Which ones came first? How close or far apart did they happen?

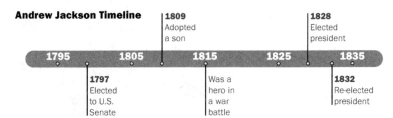

Andrew Jackson Timeline

1809 Adopted a son		1828 Elected president

1795	1805	1815	1825	1835

1797 Elected to U.S. Senate	Was a hero in a war battle	1832 Re-elected president

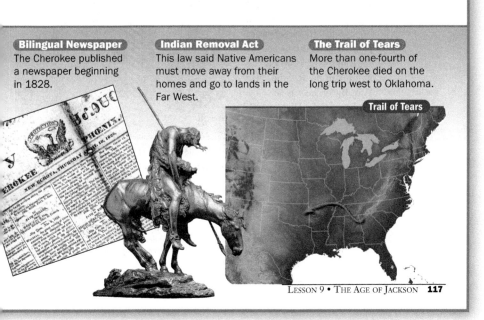

Bilingual Newspaper
The Cherokee published a newspaper beginning in 1828.

Indian Removal Act
This law said Native Americans must move away from their homes and go to lands in the Far West.

The Trail of Tears
More than one-fourth of the Cherokee died on the long trip west to Oklahoma.

Trail of Tears

Teach Skill Building

■ Remind students that they learned about *chronological order* in Lesson 5, page 69.

■ Ask a volunteer to give a definition of what it means.

■ Then read aloud with students the explanation and steps for reading a timeline.

■ Ask volunteers to point to part(s) in the timeline where they found answers to the following questions:

• What years of Jackson's life does this timeline cover? *(1795–1835)*

• When was Jackson first elected president? *(1828)*

• What did he do in 1809? *(adopted a son)*

• Did Jackson become a senator before or after he adopted a son? *(before)*

• In 1796, Jackson was elected to the House of Representatives. Where would you add that to the timeline?

Activity: Today's Timeline

Ask students to create a timeline of their day so far today. Have them divide the timeline into one-hour segments. Guide them in placing mid-hour events in the places between the hour markers.

Program Resources

Student Activity Journal
Use page 44 to build key vocabulary.

Use page 45 to practice reading a timeline.

Overhead Transparencies
Use 28, Timeline, with page 117.

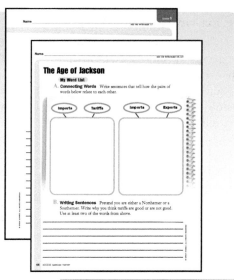

Introduce The Age of Jackson

- Read aloud the title, introduction, and headings.
- Then have students continue the reading in pairs, switching turns every few sentences.
- Ask students how being popular can make someone powerful.
- Ask students if they think being common makes someone a better leader. Have them give examples. Lead discussion with such words as *popular*, *stood for*, and *common*.

Key Connection: Government

Explain or elicit that today the United States has two main political parties:

- Democrats (started by Jackson)
- Republicans (started in 1854)

Tell students that other political parties, such as the Green Party and the Libertarian Party, exist, too. However, almost all political power is split between the two main parties.

Look and Read

The Age of Jackson

▲ Log cabin

Andrew Jackson was elected president in 1828. Events in the next 40 years were important to the future of the country. Problems between the North and South continued, people moved and settled the land, and Native Americans were forced from their homelands.

A President for the Common Man

Andrew Jackson began a new age in government. He pushed for the rights of **common** people. At the same time, he made the **presidency** very powerful.

JACKSON'S EARLY LIFE

The first 6 presidents all were born to rich parents. But Andrew Jackson was born in a **log cabin.** His parents were poor farmers. By the age of 13, Andrew Jackson was fighting in the Revolutionary War. By 14, he was an **orphan.** In the **War of 1812,** Jackson was a general. He became a hero when he led his troops to beat the British at a battle in New Orleans. Later, these facts made Jackson **popular** with voters.

▲ General Andrew Jackson

VOCABULARY

common—like most people, not rich and powerful
presidency—the job of the president and all its duties and functions
log cabin—a simple house made from logs
orphan—a person whose parents are dead
War of 1812—the last war the Americans fought against the British
popular—liked by many people

118 UNIT 3 • GROWING DIFFERENCES

 Activity: Flow Chart

Have students create a flow chart of events in Andrew Jackson's life that they will add to throughout the lesson. Provide the graphic organizer below and this prompt to get students started.

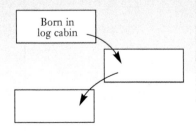

Born in log cabin

Differentiating Instruction

Beginning

Choral Reading Direct students' attention to the headings and the first two paragraphs of the reading. Work with them to understand these key words and phrases: *Andrew Jackson, common people, new age in government,* and *powerful presidency.* Then lead students in repeated choral readings of the first two paragraphs, stopping to let them fill in the key words on their own.

Intermediate

Identifying Ideas Have students read one paragraph at a time with a partner. Ask them to stop after each paragraph and identify four or five key words or phrases.

Advanced

Paraphrasing Concepts Encourage students to read through to the end of each section with a blue heading. Then have them talk to a partner, paraphrasing the main idea of what they just read.

DEMOCRATIC PARTY BEGINS

Jackson lived on the Tennessee **frontier.** He studied law and entered **politics.** At first, Jackson was part of the **political party** that Thomas Jefferson started. Then, he helped split that party in two. Jackson disagreed strongly with many people in his party. Jackson's side became the Democratic Party. It **stood for** the rights of the states and for taking government control away from the rich. The Democrats said they stood for the common people.

In 1828, Jackson was elected president. Thousands of Americans came to Washington to celebrate. By this time, Jackson was a rich man with a plantation and slaves. Still, to the voters, Jackson was a "man of the people."

TALK AND SHARE With your partner, make a list of the things about Jackson that made him popular. Tell your group.

Language Notes

Signal Words: Time Order
These words are clues to the order in which things happened.

- later
- at first
- then
- while
- during
- meanwhile
- right away

◄ When Jackson ran for president, he traveled around the country giving speeches.

VOCABULARY

frontier—the area on the edge of a settled region
politics—government; also the activities of government. *Political* means having to do with government.
political party—a group of people who share ideas about government and who work to get their members elected
stood for—was on the side of; represented

Teach Democratic Party Begins

Invite students to read this page to answer the following questions:

- How did the Democratic Party begin?
- What did Jackson have to do with it?

Language Notes

- ■ With students, read aloud the Language Notes at the top of page 119.
- ■ Have volunteers locate the red words in context on pages 118 and 119 and read those sentences aloud.
- ■ To reinforce students' understanding of words that signal time order, ask:
  - Did Jackson become popular before the Revolutionary War? (*no*)
  - What political party did Jackson join first? (*the party started by Jefferson*)

TALK AND SHARE

During discussion, have students use the sentence stem *Jackson was popular because* _____.

Activity: Election Poster

Have students design election posters for Andrew Jackson. With partners or in small groups, let them brainstorm the message they want their posters to carry. Students should work together, sharing their talents as they develop their posters. Then display them in the classroom and invite discussion about how effective they are.

Program Resources

Student Activity Journal
Assign page 46:

- To create study notes for students to review
- To provide reinforcement of key vocabulary

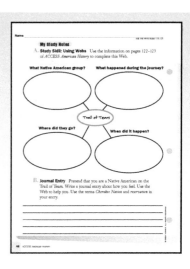

Discuss The Fight over Tariffs

- Review with students the differences between the North and South that caused friction over tariffs.

- Emphasize that tariffs aided U.S. factories in the North by taxing foreign competition.

- Ask students what they think about tariffs. What would they do if they had to pay a tariff on items they often buy?

Economics

How Tariffs Work

- To reinforce their understanding of tariffs, walk students through the diagram to the right.

- Then ask questions such as the following:

  • How much did the British teacup cost before the tariff?

  • Before the tariff, how much more did an American pay for a cup made at home? How much afterward?

The Fight over Tariffs

While Jackson was president, a big debate started over **tariffs.** Tariffs were taxes on **imported** goods. Tariffs raised the price of goods coming in from other countries.

NORTH AGAINST SOUTH

Northerners wanted tariffs. **Foreign** imports were cheaper than the goods made in Northern factories. Tariffs could give Northern businesses a better chance to **compete.**

Southerners did not want tariffs. Many cotton farmers lived in the South. Foreign countries bought their cotton. Southerners didn't want to make those countries mad. Also, they liked to buy the cheaper foreign goods. To Southerners, tariffs just made everything cost more.

Congress passed a tariff in 1816, raised it in 1824, and raised it again in 1828. This upset a lot of people in the South.

▲ Cotton

VOCABULARY

tariffs—taxes on goods from other countries
imported—brought into the country for sale. The goods we buy from other countries are called *imports.*
foreign—from another country
compete—take part in a contest. Sellers compete with each other for buyers like people in a race compete for a prize.

Economics

How Tariffs Work

Tariffs are taxes that raise the cost of foreign goods. Often that means American-made goods are cheaper to buy. Here's how tariffs might have worked on the sale of goods in 1830.

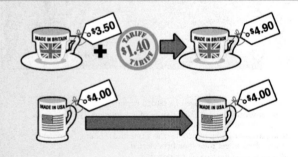

Activity: Role-Play

Divide the class into two groups to create a skit about tariffs using information in the diagram. Have each group find a prop to serve as a teacup (such as a paper cup). Then have them create price tags and tariff signs on sticky notes. Ask students to create a two-act skit that shows the points of view of important people before and after the teacup tariff. After students practice their skits, have them role-play for the class.

Differentiating Instruction

Beginning
Viewpoints Provide less fluent English speakers with the key phrases below. Have them match these phrases to groups who held these viewpoints:

- No tariffs!
- Yea for tariffs!
- States can leave the Union.
- States can disobey federal laws!
- States must obey federal laws!

Intermediate
Tariff Skits Have students use the Key Concept terms for their role-plays of

Calhoun and Webster. Provide these prompts: *obey, disobey, tariffs, secede, Union.*

Advanced
Matching Have students write each name or term on a separate index card: *John Calhoun, Daniel Webster, President Jackson, Northerners, Southerners.* In groups, have them take turns drawing a card and stating a viewpoint to match each name or term they draw.

JOHN CALHOUN AND DANIEL WEBSTER

The debate about tariffs almost tore the country apart. John C. Calhoun, a handsome man, was vice president. He came from South Carolina. Cotton farmers there were having a very hard time. Calhoun came up with an idea called **nullification.** He said the states had joined the Union freely. So a state could decide if a **federal** law had to be **obeyed.**

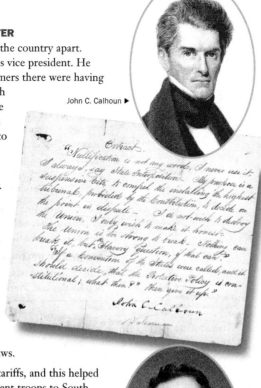
John C. Calhoun ▶

Daniel Webster, a senator from Massachusetts, was a wonderful speaker. Northerners loved him. He said it wasn't states that had made the Union. It was "made for the people, by the people, and **answerable** to the people."

In 1832, the tariff was raised once again. South Carolina said the law was no good and warned it would **secede.** Calhoun didn't want this to happen. He said his state should stay in the Union but just not obey the tariff law. Webster said states *must* obey federal laws.

Jackson did two things. He lowered tariffs, and this helped to please the South. However, he also sent troops to South Carolina to make sure that the laws were obeyed. This angered people in the South.

(TALK AND SHARE) **With a partner, role-play Calhoun and Webster having a debate about tariffs. Tell how you feel about tariffs.**

VOCABULARY

nullification—the idea that a state could decide not to obey a national law
federal—a kind of government in which power is shared between state governments and a central government. The government in Washington, D.C., makes federal laws.
obeyed—followed as an order
answerable—responsible; must explain itself
secede—leave, not be part of the United States

▲ Daniel Webster

LESSON 9 • THE AGE OF JACKSON **121**

Talk About John Calhoun and Daniel Webster

- Help students recall the debate about state and federal powers that took place during the ratification of the United States Constitution (page 86).

- Remind students that Federalists favored a strong national government, and Anti-federalists favored the states keeping their own, separate governments.

- Relate that John C. Calhoun favored the South. He said a state didn't have to obey a federal law if it didn't believe the law was right. Ask, *Would he have agreed with the Federalists or the Anti-federalists?*

- Daniel Webster, from the North, disagreed. He said states must follow all laws. Ask, *Would he have agreed with the Federalists or the Anti-federalists?*

- Ask students, *How do you think this debate affected relations between the North and the South?*

(**TALK AND SHARE**)

Have beginning students work with their partners to write scripts before performing the role-play. Advanced students can list major points before starting the debate.

⚑ Activity: Peer Teaching

Assign each of the vocabulary words for Lesson 9 to a pair of students. Have partners create a Web for their words. Encourage them to include drawings, synonyms, opposites, definitions, and word parts. Then have each pair teach their word to the rest of the class.

⚑ Activity: Speech Balloons

Divide the class into three groups. Ask each group to create a Point-of-View poster that shows the opinions of John Calhoun, Daniel Webster, or President Jackson over the issues of tariffs and a state's right to leave the Union. Ask students to state the opinions of each person in speech balloons.

Discuss Moving the Native Americans

- Explain to students that Native Americans signed several different treaties with the U.S. government during the late 1700s. The treaties gave settlers the rights to more and more Native American lands. Many of the treaties were unfair; many others were not honored.

- In the early 1800s, some Native Americans started to fight for their disappearing land. However, the more powerful U.S. Army crushed their forces. The Native Americans were forced to move to lands even farther west, where no one wanted to live.

- Elicit how students would feel if they were forced to leave their homelands and move to new lands.

- Ask whether they would go or stay and fight. Tell them to give reasons.

Look and Read

Moving the Native Americans

During the Age of Jackson, **settlers** continued to move west. Americans believed they had a right to the land. Meanwhile, Native Americans were pushed out of their homelands.

MANIFEST DESTINY

A new idea spread through America during the Age of Jackson. This idea was known as **Manifest Destiny.** *Manifest* means "clear." Americans believed their **destiny** was clear. They would settle the continent all the way to the Pacific Ocean. To Americans, it was a dream that would come true.

But Native Americans had homelands throughout the continent. They did not see things the same way. However, they did not have the power to protect themselves.

THE INDIAN REMOVAL ACT

In 1830, Congress passed a law called the Indian Removal Act. By this law, President Jackson could pay all the Native Americans in the East to move. The East was **prime** land, and Americans wanted it for themselves. The law said the Native Americans would be moved to land in the western areas where few settlers wanted to live.

VOCABULARY

settlers—people who move into a new area and make their homes there

Manifest Destiny—the idea that the United States had the right to own and settle lands from the Atlantic to the Pacific Oceans

destiny—what *will* happen; fate

prime—the very best

 Activity: Role-Play

Invite volunteers to help you role-play a scenario about a rich company that is buying up all the property in your city or town very cheaply. Provide these prompts: 1) *I'll pay you $25 for your house.* 2) *You must sell to me. The government says so.* 3) *I'll take it by force if you don't sell.*

Tie the role-play back to the lesson by reminding students that President Andrew Jackson acted very similarly to the Native Americans.

 # Differentiating Instruction

Beginning

Charades Ask students to write each vocabulary word from Lesson 9 on an index card. Have them place the cards facedown to play charades. Each player picks up the top card from the deck and draws a picture of the term. The other players guess what the vocabulary word is.

Intermediate

Vocabulary Guess Invite students to take turns drawing a 3" x 5" vocabulary card and paraphrasing its meaning. Other players guess the word.

Advanced

Sentence Sense Have students draw two vocabulary cards at a time. If a player can use both words in one sentence that makes sense, he or she gets two points. If the player can use only one of the words, he or she earns one point.

THE TRAIL OF TEARS

Some Native American groups left right away—but not all. The **Cherokee Nation** refused to go. It was the largest Indian group in the East. By the 1830s, the Cherokee lived much as other people in Georgia did. They had schools, farms, and a written language. Some Cherokee even owned slaves.

▲ About 1 out of every 4 Cherokee died on the Trail of Tears.

The Cherokee sued the state government to let them stay. Later, they wrote a letter to President Jackson. Nothing helped. Jackson said they must give up their land.

Then, in 1838, the next president, Martin Van Buren, ordered troops to remove the Cherokee. The soldiers forced the Cherokee to move west. They left behind their homes and businesses, the lands they had farmed, and all they had worked for. It was heartbreaking. Most of the Cherokee had to walk the hundreds of miles to Oklahoma. More than one-quarter of them died on the way. Their journey became known as the **Trail of Tears.**

(TALK AND SHARE) Tell your partner how you feel about what happened to the Cherokee.

Cherokee Nation—a Native American group
Trail of Tears—the trip on which the Cherokee people were forced to go west

Summary

Andrew Jackson got the vote of the "common man." He started the Democratic Party. When he was president, the North and South argued over tariffs and whether states had to obey federal laws. At the same time, Americans had a dream of settling the continent. They forced Indians to move from their homelands.

Teach About The Trail of Tears

■ Refer students back to the visual aid about the Cherokee across pages 116–117.

■ Ask volunteers to put into their own words the accomplishments and history of the Cherokee Nation.

■ Explain to students that the Trail of Tears is considered a terrible time in America's history.

■ Ask students if they think the government had the right to move the Cherokee people.

■ Elicit whether the government should have sent the soldiers to move the Cherokee. Have students tell why or why not.

(TALK AND SHARE)

Have partners complete the Talk and Share activity. Then gather the class and ask students to share their responses.

Discuss the Summary

Do a choral reading with students of the Summary at the end of the lesson. Have students return to the Big Idea on page 115. Ask them to recap key information about each part of the Big Idea.

✓ Assessment

Assess students' comprehension by asking the following questions:

History
• Why was Andrew Jackson a popular president?
• Why did the North and the South disagree about tariffs?
• What happened during the Trail of Tears?

Language
Write or say sentences using the following time order words:
• Later
• At first
• Then
• While
• During
• Meanwhile
• Right away

Assessment Book
Use page 27 to assess students' comprehension.

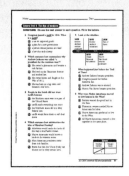

Teach Summarizing

- Tell students that summarizing is an important skill for studying history.

- Model the skill by inviting the class to create a summary of a recent school event or of a favorite TV show.

- Help them see that not every detail can be listed. Summaries include only the most important highlights.

Model the Organizer

- Help students navigate the Tariff Problem Web by asking volunteers to name ways in which tariffs almost tore the country apart.

- Tell students that a Web like this can help organize important ideas about cause and effect.

Give Practice Summarizing

Have students work with partners to complete one activity.

- **Draw** Encourage students with limited English proficiency to complete this activity by listing information about Jackson and putting a star next to the most important items. They should use only the starred events in their summary.

- **Write** Remind students to use the time-order signal words listed in the Language Notes on page 119.

Develop Language

Summarizing

Summarizing Events in History

When you summarize events, you tell the events again in fewer words. You tell only the main people and events and leave out small details. As you read, take notes about important people and things that happened. A Web can help you. Put the most important idea in the middle of the Web. Next, put related events and people in the circles around it. Then, tell how those ideas fit in.

Tariff Problem Web

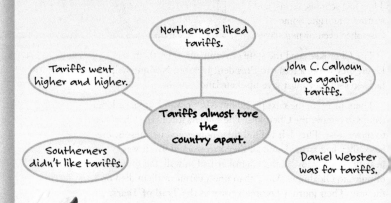

- Northerners liked tariffs.
- Tariffs went higher and higher.
- John C. Calhoun was against tariffs.
- Tariffs almost tore the country apart.
- Southerners didn't like tariffs.
- Daniel Webster was for tariffs.

Practice Summarizing

1. Draw Summarize the events that made Andrew Jackson popular with voters. Read page 118 again if you need to. Take notes and then draw the people and events in a Web. Use your Web to tell your partner about Jackson.

2. Write Summarize the events that led to the Trail of Tears. Read again the part called "Moving the Native Americans." Take notes and write the main events in a Web. Then use your Web to write a paragraph summarizing what happened. The Word Bank may help you.

Word Bank

President Jackson
Indian Removal Act
Cherokee Nation

way of life
army

protest

west

124 Unit 3 • Growing Differences

Activity: Flow Chart

Have students create a new flow chart that shows major events of the Cherokee Nation. Ask them to include events from the visual aid on pages 116–117, as well as events listed on page 123. Suggest that they keep their flow charts in their history notebooks.

Differentiating Instruction

Beginning

Vocabulary Words Encourage students to use the vocabulary words from page 118 in their Webs: *common, presidency, log cabin, orphan, War of 1812, popular.*

Intermediate

Identifying Main Points Have partners read the paragraphs on page 123 together and talk about which are the main events and people. They should make notes on such things as

Cherokee refusal, a letter to President Jackson, a terrible long walk, many deaths.

Advanced

Using Adjectives Encourage students to use adjectives in their writing, following the tips in the Grammar Spotlight. You could provide an additional Word Bank of adjectives, including *similar, angry, forceful, terrible, long,* and *deadly.*

Activities

Grammar Spotlight

Placement of Adjectives Adjectives describe nouns. Place adjectives in one of these places:

- *before* the noun it describes
- *after* the noun if a form of the verb *be* is used. *Was* and *were* are forms of *be*.

Adjective **Before the** <u>Noun</u>	Adjective **After the** <u>Noun</u> **and Form of** *be*
A *new* <u>age</u> arrived.	<u>Jackson</u> was *popular*.
A *log* <u>cabin</u> sat on the hill.	His <u>childhood</u> was *hard*.
Poor <u>farmers</u> struggled.	<u>Tariffs</u> were *high*.
Tax <u>laws</u> were passed.	<u>Homelands</u> were *lost*.

Write a sentence about Jackson's parents. Use the adjective *poor*.

Hands On

Moving Think of a time when you or someone you know moved. Make a timeline showing at least 4 things that happened. Then tell your partner how your story is like that of the settlers or the Native Americans. Also tell how it is different.

Oral Language

When Did It Happen? With a partner, look at the timeline on page 117. Take turns telling the things that happened in Jackson's life. Use the words *first, next, then,* and *last*.

Partner Practice

Working with Tariffs With a partner, draw 3 things you would like to buy. Put a price tag on each one, and write how much it should cost. Now imagine a tariff of $2 has passed. Cross out the old price and write in the new price. Discuss with your partner how you feel about the new price.

Activities

Grammar Spotlight

- Read aloud the Grammar Spotlight instruction. Then demonstrate the skill:
  - Hold up a pencil. Engage students in brainstorming adjectives that describe it.
  - Model the correct placement of adjectives with these sentences:
    This is a _____ (sharp) pencil.
    This pencil is _____ (sharp).
- Invite volunteers to describe the pencil with other adjectives (*yellow, long, short, broken*).

Hands On

Students can mark the periods of time in their timelines by either years or their ages. Encourage students to draw pictures and write labels for their events.

Oral Language

Form groups. Supply students with a ball that they can toss to the next person, who then adds to the story.

Partner Practice

Encourage students to use the Key Concepts in their discussion.

Activity: Extend the Lesson

For additional reading on Lesson 9 topics, recommend these books to students. Ask a volunteer to give a book review on one of these to the class:

- *Andrew Jackson: Getting to Know the U.S. Presidents* by Mike Venezia (Childrens Press, 2004)
- *The Journal of Jesse Smoke: A Cherokee Boy, Trail of Tears, 1838* by Joseph Bruchac (Scholastic, 2001)

Program Resources

Student Activity Journal
Use page 47 to practice *summarizing*.

Overhead Transparencies
Use 33, Web, with page 124.

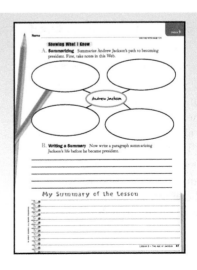

A Time of Change

STANDARDS CONTENT

History
- Read a bar graph
- Identify effects of industrialization in mid-nineteenth-century America
- Recognize how increasing immigration changed the lives of Americans
- Explain the reform movements of the suffragists and abolitionists

Language
- Identify the following Key Concepts: *reformer, abolitionists, movement,* and *goal*
- Recognize idioms
- Practice responding to history

Begin Building Background

- Ask students to study the picture and brainstorm details about it. Draw out literal details, as well as students' emotional impressions.

- Record their responses on the board in a Web entitled *A Time of Change.* Provide vocabulary prompts as needed, such as *dangerous, hard, machinery, factory,* and *workers.*

- Invite students to speculate who the workers are and where the factory is. Prompt their prior knowledge by asking if the North or South had more cities and factories.

Talk and Explore

A Time of Change

Here you'll learn about changes in the middle of the 1800s. You'll also learn how to read a bar graph and practice responding to events in history.

Building Background

▲ It's really hot in a kitchen too. My dad works in a kitchen.

- ■ What words would you use to describe this picture?
- ■ What would it be like to work there?
- ■ What changes have you lived through in your life?

126 UNIT 3 • GROWING DIFFERENCES

 Activity: Three-column Chart

In pairs, have students create a Three-column Chart for Lesson 10 titled *Questions, Predictions,* and *Answers.*

In the Question column, ask partners to write a list of questions they have about the four parts of the Big Idea. In the middle column, have them predict—or guess—answers to their questions. Tell students to fill in the third column as they find the answers while working through the lesson.

 Differentiating Instruction

Beginning
Word Work Have students write each label for the Big Idea on a separate index card. Then review with students these words from previous lessons: *slavery, rights, foreign.* Teach *industry* by circling the first picture of the Big Idea and saying, *all the factories.* Teach *immigrants* by saying, *people who come to America from a foreign land.*

Ask volunteers to draw a card, match it to the appropriate picture,

and use the word in a phrase or sentence that describes the picture.

Intermediate
Big Idea Web Have students create a Web for a picture in the Big Idea. Their Webs should present their ideas, knowledge, and feelings about the picture.

Advanced
Work Songs Have students explore the Internet for songs about work they can share with the class. Some students may want to write one.

Big Idea

After 1830, more Americans began to work in factories. Northern cities grew as people from other countries moved in. Reformers worked to free slaves and gain more rights for women.

1 Industry

2 Immigrants

3 Slavery

4 Women's Rights

Introduce the Big Idea

- Read the Big Idea on page 127 and the title for each picture.
- Refer to the Lesson title, *A Time of Change*.
- Invite students to study each picture and note changes they see in American society, economy, population, and customs.
- Add their responses to the Web started at the beginning of the lesson. The following questions can help spark discussion.

  What changes do you see in:
  - Buildings?
  - Ways of dress?
  - Cities?
  - Transportation?
- Recap the discussion by explaining that the mid-1800s was a time of change in America. Industry grew, immigrants moved to America, and reformers worked to fix social problems.

Review

In previous lessons, students have learned about *explorers*, *colonists*, *settlers*, and *pioneers*. Review descriptions of each past vocabulary term. Then define *immigrants*. Help students understand the differences among these terms.

 Activity: Brainstorm

Invite small groups of students to brainstorm reasons people leave their home country and immigrate to the United States. Encourage them to use personal experience and knowledge of the experiences of others and to be specific. Then have the groups take turns contributing to a master list that a volunteer records on the chalkboard or on chart paper. Keep the list to refer to as the class studies nineteenth-century immigration.

 Activity: Priorities for Reform

Tell students they will read about a time when many people worked to fix wrongs in society, such as slavery and lack of women's rights. Have partners talk about wrongs in society today that they feel should be made right. Introduce the terms *priority* and *issue*. Then hold a class discussion and vote to choose the issue that should have the highest priority.

 Resource Library

Reader's Handbook (red)
Reading Charts and Graphs 157, 159, 538–547

Reader's Handbook (yellow)
Reading Tables and Graphs 412–435

All Write
Reading Symbols and Charts 277–284

Teach   Key Concepts

- Slowly say each Key Concept and ask students to repeat it.
- Elicit or provide these root words: *reform, abolish, move.*
- Then read aloud the descriptions of the Key Concepts.
- Call on volunteers to walk through the connections in the word diagram.
- Emphasize these points:
  - One kind of *reformer* is an *abolitionist.*
  - Many abolitionists working together can form a *movement.*
  - Reformers in a movement work toward a *goal.*
- Ask students to identify the goal of abolitionists. (*end slavery*)

Teach the Visual Aid

Key People in the Mid-1800s

With students, read aloud the title and captions for the visual aid on pages 128–129. Provide these definitions for its key words:

- *Immigrants:* People who come from a foreign land to live in America
- *Suffragists:* Reformers who worked for women's right to vote
- *Abolitionists:* Reformers who worked to end slavery

Talk and Explore

Key Concepts

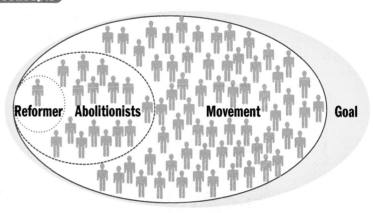

A **reformer** is someone who works to change things for the better. **Abolitionists** were reformers who worked to abolish, or end, slavery. A **movement** is a group of people working together to reach a **goal** they all share. Reformers can start a movement.

Key People in the Mid-1800s

Immigrants
Many people came to America from Europe. Some of them found jobs in Northern cities. Other immigrants moved to the Midwest.

Suffragists
Some people worked to get women the right to vote.

128 UNIT 3 • GROWING DIFFERENCES

Activity: News Reporters

Ask students to imagine they are news reporters. Have them write headlines about a reform movement for their papers. Advanced students can write the first paragraph of an article. All students should use at least three of the Key Concepts.

Differentiating Instruction

Beginning
Charade Game Have each student pick three words from page 128. Any word that appears on the page is appropriate. Then, in small groups, have students act out their words for the group to guess.

Intermediate
Diagram It Have students create a different diagram or drawing to demonstrate they understand the relationships among the four Key Concept words.

Advanced
Dialogue Review the use of commas and punctuation marks in dialogue. Then invite students to select one of the groups shown in the visual aid—immigrants, suffragists, or abolitionists—and write a short dialogue for two people in their group.

Reading a Bar Graph

A bar graph uses bars to show quantities. You can look at the bars to compare amounts. The taller the bar is, the greater the amount is.

1. Read the title. It tells you what the graph is about.

2. Read the line that goes up and down. It's called the *vertical axis*. The numbers on this line are percents.

3. Read the line that goes across from left to right. It's called the *horizontal axis*. It shows different dates.

Try this. Put your finger on 1790. Move it up the bar to the top. Look at the number on the vertical axis on the left. What percent of Americans lived in cities in 1790? Now find the percent of Americans living in cities in 1850. What was happening in cities between 1790 and 1850?

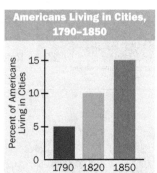

Americans Living in Cities, 1790–1850

Percent of Americans Living in Cities: 0, 5, 10, 15

1790 1820 1850

Teach Skill Building

- Read with students the instruction for reading a bar graph.

- Then read through the three steps.

- Use the sample chart to demonstrate how to do each step.

- Finally, work through the example and questions with students.

- Invite several volunteers to trace their fingers on the bar graph to show how to get the correct answers.

Teach the Pictures

As a young man in slavery, Frederick Douglass was taught how to read and write by his mistress. When his master forbade his education, he continued on his own. After Douglass escaped from slavery in 1838 at the age of twenty, he continued to learn and used his writing and speaking skills to protest slavery. He became such a powerful, persuasive speaker that in time he became an adviser to the president.

Suffrage Leaders

Susan B. Anthony was a great speaker who talked about women's rights. **Elizabeth Cady Stanton** helped set up a convention for women's rights.

Anthony ▶

Stanton ▼

Abolitionists

Some people worked to end slavery. **William Lloyd Garrison** published a newspaper against slavery. **Frederick Douglass** was a great speaker who spoke against slavery. **Harriet Tubman** led about 300 slaves to freedom.

▲ Garrison

▲ Douglass

▲ Tubman

LESSON 10 • A TIME OF CHANGE **129**

Activity: Culture Connection

Lead a discussion about reform efforts going on today. Ask students to tell what they know and to talk about how they could find out more.

Record their responses in a Web. Provide these categories as prompts:

- Tax Reform
- Civil Rights
- Environment
- Crime Victims
- School Reform
- Workers' Rights

Program Resources

Student Activity Journal

Use page 48 to build key vocabulary.

Use page 49 to practice reading a bar graph.

Overhead Transparencies

Use 33, Web, with page 129.

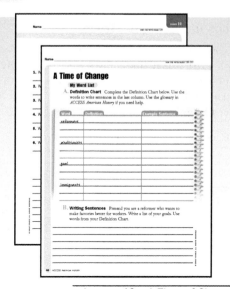

A Time of Change

My Word List

A. **Definition Chart** Complete the Definition Chart below. Use the words to write sentences in the last column. Use the glossary in *ACCESS American History* if you need help.

Word	Definition	Example Sentence
reformer		
abolitionists		
goal		
immigrants		

B. **Writing Sentences** Pretend you are a reformer who wants to make factories better for workers. Write a list of your goals. Use words from your Definition Chart.

Introduce **A Time of Change**

- With students, read aloud the introduction.
- Help them pull out these events in the mid-century *time of change:*
  - Factories began making most goods.
  - People came from Europe.
  - New industry brought new problems.
  - Reformers improved people's working conditions and lives.
- Have the class preview the lesson by looking at the pictures and reading the headings. Then have students continue reading in pairs.

Key Connection: Economics

- Teach students that *capitalism* is the economic system of the United States. Develop understanding of the following chief qualities of capitalism:
  - *Private Ownership:* People are free to buy and sell what they want.
  - *Free Competition:* Businesses try to outsell each other.
  - *Profit Motive:* Business owners try to make money on their goods.
- Call on volunteers to give examples of *competition* and *profit*.

▲ Many young women worked in factories for little pay.

▲ Cloth could be made faster in textile mills than by hand.

A Time of Change

Changes swept through America in the 1830s and 1840s. Factories made the goods people needed and helped businesses grow. They gave people jobs but caused problems too. Many people came from Europe. They had a hard time at first. Reformers worked to make lives better.

The Growth of Industry

In the 1830s, the United States was growing by leaps and bounds. At one time, small shops made the goods that people needed. As the country grew, business people looked for ways to make more things faster. They built large **factories.** A factory brought many workers together in one place. It made jobs for people who sold the **products.** Factories led to the growth of **industry.**

Some of these factories were **textile mills.** They made cloth. Others made boxes, steel, or paper. The factories were mainly in Northern states, such as Massachusetts and Pennsylvania. Most factories were in cities. Many farmers moved to the cities to get factory jobs. Industry changed the work people did and the way people lived.

VOCABULARY
factories—the buildings where things are made with machines
products—things made to be sold
industry—the whole business that involves making, shipping, and selling goods made in factories. The textile industry makes, sells, and ships cloth.
textile mills—the factories where cloth is made

Activity: Multiple Effects

Have students create a Multiple-Effects Organizer that shows what happened when industry grew. Use Overhead Transparency 3, Cause-effect Organizer.

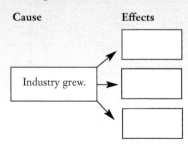

Differentiating Instruction

Beginning
Key Terms Cards Have students copy these key words on 3" x 5" cards:

- Factory
- Jobs
- Hard work
- On strike
- Industry
- Unions
- Products
- Small shops

Work with students to use two or three of the terms to tell about changes in industry during the mid-1800s.

Intermediate
Extracting Information Ask pairs to stop after reading a paragraph and discuss the main ideas. Encourage them to point out and say aloud important terms, names, or dates in each paragraph.

Advanced
Main Ideas and Details In pairs, have students record in a chart the main ideas and supporting details after reading each paragraph.

THE FACTORY SYSTEM

The factories used a new idea called the **factory system.** In the factory system, each worker made only one part of a product. Each worker did one job again and again. The factory system made products quickly. It also made them all the same. Factory products were cheaper than products made by hand. More and more people could buy things.

Unfortunately, factories were nasty places. People worked long hours for little pay. The work was boring, the air was **filthy,** and the rooms were dark. Factories were dangerous places too. Hot fires burned some workers. Dust from cotton choked them. Machines sometimes cut off fingers and arms.

UNIONS

Some workers joined together in **unions** to make their work life better. Sometimes union workers **went on strike.** Factory owners fought back. Even police would attack the strikers. At first, the court said it was illegal to go on strike. Then, in 1842, the Massachusetts Supreme Court said that workers had the right to strike. **Gradually,** the unions got better pay and safer jobs for workers.

(TALK AND SHARE) **Tell your partner what you think was good about factories. Then tell what was bad.**

▲ Sometimes strikes could become violent. A bomb exploded during the Haymarket Riot in Chicago on May 4, 1886.

VOCABULARY

factory system—a way of making products in which each worker does only a part of the work
unfortunately—sadly
filthy—very dirty
unions—groups of workers who join together to make business owners change things
went on strike—stopped working. A *strike* is a group action taken to make a business owner change things.
gradually—over a long time

LESSON 10 • A TIME OF CHANGE **131**

Language Notes

Idioms
These sayings don't mean what they seem.

☐ **by leaps and bounds:** very fast

☐ **the fabric of life:** all the parts of a way of life

☐ **paved the way:** made ready; prepared

Teach About The Factory System and Unions

■ Help students visualize factory conditions by describing work life in the textile mills.

• Most workers in the Lowell, Massachusetts, mill were young women.

• They worked from sunrise to sunset.

• The clanging machinery in the mills was deafening.

■ People united to protest the bad working conditions. They formed *unions* to voice their protests. Ask students what they think about unions. Have them give reasons they think unions are good or bad.

Language Notes

Read the meanings of the idioms in the Language Notes. Then ask students to find the idioms in context within the reading and to paraphrase the meaning of the sentences.

(TALK AND SHARE)

Encourage students to discuss their answers from the following viewpoints:

• Economic health of the nation

• Factory workers

• People who buy and use goods

 Activity: Problem-Solution Charts

Have students work in pairs to create a Problem-Solution Chart. In the Problem column, they should list problems in the early factory system. In the Solution column, they should list how workers tried to solve the problems.

 Program Resources

Student Activity Journal

Assign page 50:

• To create study notes for students to review

• To provide reinforcement of key vocabulary

Lesson 10 • A Time of Change **131**

Discuss European Immigration

- Explain that potatoes were the main part of the Irish diet.

- In the 1840s, potato crops in Ireland were destroyed. In the resulting famine, more than one million Irish died.

- Many Irish farmers immigrated to America. Too poor to buy land, they worked in factories.

- Have students pretend they are Irish immigrants. Elicit descriptions on how they would feel about leaving home to find work in a new country.

Teach a Reading Strategy

- Develop the skill of identifying by asking students to recall reasons that the Pilgrims and Puritans immigrated to America.

- Help them connect to their own experience by identifying reasons that their family or friends came to America.

- Then have students compare all these reasons to the causes for immigration in the mid-1800s.

Look and Read

European Immigration

Between 1830 and 1860, millions of **immigrants** came to the United States. Most of the new immigrants were poor. Many were hungry. They came in search of jobs and freedom.

Sources of Immigration, 1820–1860

ESCAPING PROBLEMS

Most immigrants came from Europe. At this time, most of them came from Ireland and Germany. Others came from Britain, Sweden, Norway, Switzerland, and Holland.

The immigrants left their home countries to **escape** huge problems. Some people left because of wars. Farmers left because of bad harvests. Townspeople left because new technology took away their jobs. Immigrants came to America for jobs, religious freedom, and a chance to live the way they wanted to live.

Many immigrants from Ireland came because of a terrible **famine** there. People in Ireland were **starving**. More than one million Irish people came to America between 1845 and 1854.

▲ An Irish family says goodbye to a daughter going to America.

VOCABULARY

immigrants—people who come to a new country to live. *Immigration* is the act of moving to a country.

escape—get free from

famine—a serious lack of food in a place

starving—dying from not having enough to eat

132 UNIT 3 • GROWING DIFFERENCES

Activity: Multiple Causes

Have students work in pairs to list reasons for immigrants coming to the United States during the mid-1800s. Ask them to organize their ideas in a Multiple-Causes Organizer.

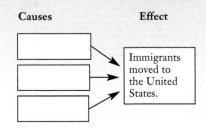

Differentiating Instruction

Beginning

Visual Art Ask students to draw or pantomime reasons for immigrants coming to America in the mid-1800s and what their life was like after their arrival.

Ask them to explain their drawings and encourage them to use words to describe their actions, especially the vocabulary words *immigrants*, *prejudice*, and *customs*. Supply words for students as needed and ask them to repeat after you.

Intermediate

Role-Play Have pairs role-play an immigrant in America today and an immigrant in the mid-1800s. Each should describe a hardship he or she faces. The other should suggest a way of solving the first person's problem.

Advanced

Skit In a group, ask students to create a short skit that shows a *Day in the Life of an Immigrant*. Provide an opportunity for the group to perform their skit for the class.

LIFE IN AMERICA

A great number of the immigrants settled in Northern cities. Irish immigrants settled in the cities of the Northeast, like Boston. German immigrants mostly moved into the Midwest, where they could farm and live as they had in Germany.

In the cities, immigrants worked for low wages in the new factories. Usually, they got the worst jobs and the worst places to live.

Some Americans were **prejudiced** against immigrants. They didn't trust them because their **customs** were different. Many immigrants were Catholics, while most Americans were Protestants. Americans made fun of the clothes immigrants wore. They made fun of the way their food smelled. Mostly, they worried that immigrants would take their jobs.

However, as time went on, immigrants became part of the fabric of life. Words from their languages came into English. Immigrant foods, like spaghetti, became popular. America had become a land of immigrants.

(TALK AND SHARE) **Tell your partner why immigrants came to America. Tell also what life in America was like for them. Talk about how it is today.**

VOCABULARY

prejudiced—had a bad opinion of people because of the group they belonged to

customs—ways of doing things, such as eating, following family traditions, and worshipping God

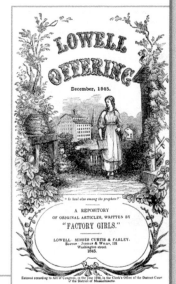

Primary Source

Lowell Offering

Many immigrant women worked in the textile mills in Lowell, Massachusetts. Most immigrants were teens, and some were even younger. They worked more than 12 hours a day. Girls at the Lowell mills published a magazine called the *Lowell Offering*. The magazine printed this letter from a young worker named Sarah: "At first the hours seemed very long . . . when I went out at night the sound of the mill was [still] in my ears. . . . You wonder that we do not have to hold our breath in such a noise."

Talk About Life in America

- Emphasize to students that immigrants faced a variety of hardships when they came to America.

- These hardships included low wages, poor homes, and prejudice.

- Nonetheless, as a group, they overcame the difficulties over time.

(TALK AND SHARE)

Ask pairs to write their responses in a list. Afterward, reconvene the class. Start a Web entitled *Immigrant Life in America* on the board and ask volunteers to contribute details from their lists.

Primary Source

Lowell Offering

With students, discuss the *Lowell Offering*. To read Sarah's entire original letter published in 1844—as well as other writings from the New England mill women—students can refer to the following website: http://www. berwickacademy.org/millgirls/ offering.htm.

Activity: Immigration Hardship Posters

Tap into students' knowledge and experience of immigration today to help them better understand the hardships that immigrants faced in the mid-1800s.

Provide this sentence starter as a prompt: *Coming to America was hard because.* . . . Arrange students in groups of four or five and have them take turns completing the sentence.

To spur more ideas, post the following categories:

- Making Friends
- Getting a Job
- Buying Things
- Finding a Home
- Getting Food
- Talking to People

Ask students to create a collage poster that shows their responses.

Finally, have them circle experiences that they think immigrants also had in the mid-1800s.

Discuss The Reformers

■ Explain that by 1807 the United States had banned importing African slaves. By then, most Northern states had outlawed slavery. Abolitionists in the North demanded that slavery be outlawed in the South, too.

■ Many slaves in the South tried to escape to the North to be free. They used the Underground Railroad, a series of secret stops on the trip north.

■ Some slaves made it. Others were caught and returned to their masters. They often faced severe punishments for trying to get away.

Teach the Pictures

Harriet Tubman rescued many relatives from slavery, including her sister, her sister's two children, her brother, and her parents. She also rescued many slaves she didn't know who wanted their freedom. Ask students to describe the scene of Tubman helping people through the woods.

▲ William Lloyd Garrison told about slavery in his newspaper, *The Liberator.*

▲ Slaves crossed dangerous rivers and forests using the Underground Railroad.

The Reformers

People saw the good things that changes brought. They also saw the bad things. Between 1830 and 1860, people called **reformers** worked to make life better.

ABOLITIONISTS

Some people strongly believed that slavery was a terrible evil. It had to end. These people were called **abolitionists.** They worked against slavery any way they could. Some abolitionists made speeches. A Massachusetts man named William Lloyd Garrison started a newspaper. In it, he told the country about how wrong slavery was.

Other people worked together in secret to help slaves escape from the South. They let runaway slaves hide in their houses, barns, and basements. At night, the slaves would travel from one safe house to another. **Eventually,** they reached the North—and freedom. This way of escaping to freedom was called the **Underground Railroad.**

Thousands of runaway slaves escaped to freedom on the Underground Railroad. Some of these runaway slaves became abolitionists themselves. Harriet Tubman was a slave who escaped slavery. Then she went back to the South 19 times and led about 300 people to freedom. Frederick Douglass, another escaped slave, became an important speaker and writer who **persuaded** many people to want to end slavery.

> **VOCABULARY**
>
> **reformers**—people who work to improve life and get rid of things that cause people harm
> **abolitionists**—the people who worked to end slavery
> **eventually**—in the end; finally
> **Underground Railroad**—a system that helped slaves escape. It was not a real railroad.
> **persuaded**—caused people to do something by giving strong reasons

134 UNIT 3 • GROWING DIFFERENCES

 Activity: Word Connect

Have pairs write vocabulary words on sticky notes to play Word Connect. The first player places a vocabulary word on the table and uses it in a sentence. The next player places a word beside the first and uses both words in a sentence.

Play continues until a player cannot find a word to create a logical sentence with all the words previously played. Pairs can play several rounds.

 Differentiating Instruction

Beginning

Sticky Notes Have students copy the following vocabulary words on sticky notes:

- Reformer • Abolitionist
- Suffragist • Famine
- Factory • Immigrants
- Union • On strike
- Underground Railroad

Ask them to attach each sticky note to a picture while saying the word or a short descriptive phrase.

Intermediate

Word Guess Have partners take turns reading aloud a definition for a Lesson 10 vocabulary word while the other partner supplies the word.

Advanced

Partner Quiz Ask students to copy the words in the Beginning Sticky Notes exercise, along with four others of their choice from Lesson 10. Have them develop a quiz for the words and give it to their partners.

SUFFRAGISTS

In the 1800s, women could not vote. Most women could not own property, go to college, or hold important jobs.

A few women began working to fight these problems. They were called **suffragists,** because *suffrage* means the right to vote. In 1848, Elizabeth Cady Stanton helped **organize** a women's rights **convention** in Seneca Falls, New York. Women at the convention wrote a document like the Declaration of Independence. It said, "All men *and women* are created equal."

The convention at Seneca Falls paved the way for the women's rights **movement.** During the rest of the 1800s, reformers worked hard to bring changes. Reform leader Susan B. Anthony gave many speeches. Slowly, over time, people's ideas about women began to change. However, it took until 1920 before women could vote in all the states.

(TALK AND SHARE) **Talk with your partner about how reformers worked to make life better. Together, make a list.**

VOCABULARY
suffragists—the people who worked to get the right to vote for women
organize—put together; arrange
convention—a meeting
movement—a group of people working together to reach a goal they all share

▲ Women marched to gain support for the right to vote.

▲ Susan B. Anthony dollar

Summary

Important changes happened during the mid-1800s. Cities grew. Factories made products quickly and cheaply. Immigrants from Europe came in large numbers. Many immigrants went to work in factories and faced problems. Reformers worked to solve them, to end slavery, and to help women get the right to vote.

Teach About Suffragists

■ Emphasize that getting the right to vote was the chief goal of the women's rights movement.

■ Ask students to figure out how many years after the Seneca Falls Convention women got the right to vote. (*seventy-two years*)

■ Ask students why they think women wanted the right to vote.

(TALK AND SHARE)

Suggest that pairs make a two-column list using the blue headings on pages 134–135: *Abolitionists, Suffragists.*

Have them include details describing what each group worked to reform and what its goals were.

Discuss the Summary

■ Read the Summary at the end of the lesson aloud with students.

■ Then have them review their Three-column Charts and the Talk and Share lists they made with their partners.

■ Encourage them to highlight the most important facts they learned in Lesson 10 and to keep these in their history notebooks.

✔ Assessment

Assess students' comprehension by asking the following questions:

History
- How did the factory system help the growth of industry?
- What were some reasons for European immigration between 1830 and 1860?
- What did abolitionists believe?
- What did suffragists believe?

Language
Write or say sentences using the paired words and phrases:
- Factories
- Industry
- Unions
- On strike
- Famine
- Starving
- Reformers
- Movement

Assessment Book
Use page 28 to assess students' comprehension.

Teach **Responding**

- Model the skill of giving a personal response by asking a volunteer to briefly describe a good TV show or movie he or she saw.

- Respond by summarizing personal reactions, such as *That sounds exciting*. Invite class members to give personal responses.

Model the Organizer

- Call on four volunteers to read aloud a fact about Harriet Tubman in the left column of the Response Chart and the corresponding personal response to her in the right column.

- After each response is read, ask volunteers if they can add responses of their own.

Give Practice **Responding**

Have students work with partners to complete one activity.

- **Draw** Ask beginning learners to complete the Draw activity. If necessary, help them find words for their drawings.

- **Write** Encourage students to support their personal responses with sound reasoning or facts.

Develop Language

Responding

Responding to History

When you respond to history, you give your own feelings and ideas about it. The first step in responding is to think about the subject. Decide what it means to you. Make a Response Chart. Show what you know about the subject on one side. On the other, use words that describe your response.

Response Chart

Subject	
Harriet Tubman	
What I know about her	**What that means to me**
She was a slave.	I feel sorry for her difficult, hard life.
She escaped to the North.	I would have been scared. She did a dangerous thing to get her freedom.
She went back to the South 19 times.	I admire her courage.
She led other slaves to freedom.	I think she was saintly because she risked her life to help others.

Harriet Tubman ▼

Practice Responding

1. Draw Think about factory workers in the mid-1800s. What was it like to work in a factory then? Draw a picture of it. Then find descriptive words for the things you drew. Use the chart to tell your feelings about factory workers and their lives.

2. Write Think about the immigrants who came to America in the mid-1800s. Make a Response Chart. Then write a paragraph that tells your feelings about the lives of immigrants in the mid-1800s. Begin with the words, "I feel that . . . ." Exchange paragraphs with a partner and check each other's writing.

Check Your Writing

Make sure you
- ☐ Use complete sentences.
- ☐ Use a period at the end of each sentence.
- ☐ Spell all the words correctly.

136 Unit 3 • GROWING DIFFERENCES

Activity: Internet Resources

Have students search the Internet for information on key events from the lesson. Have students work in pairs to find one of the types of items below and present a summary about it to the class:

- Pictures
- First-person accounts
- Short stories
- Video reenactments
- Timelines
- Music

Differentiating Instruction

Beginning
Word Help Read *The Factory System* on page 131 aloud with students and ask them to listen for words that they can use in a personal response (for example, *nasty, boring*). Have them snap their fingers each time they find a word. Then supply this sentence starter for them: *Factory work was _____*.

Intermediate
Word Bank Provide students with these words to spur their ideas for responding to the Write activity:

- Prejudice
- Hard work
- Escape famine
- Low pay
- New start

Advanced
A Way to Organize Suggest to students that they can organize their paragraphs for the Write activity this way:

- My first personal response
- My reason for it
- My second personal response
- My reason for it

Activities

Grammar Spotlight

Adverbs   Adverbs describe verbs and adjectives or other adverbs. Many adverbs are made from adjectives by adding *ly*.

Adjective	Adverb	Examples
quick	quick<u>ly</u>	America was growing quickly.
slow	slow<u>ly</u>	Slowly, workers got more rights.
usual	usual<u>ly</u>	Immigrants usually held the worst jobs.

Find 3 adverbs in the Vocabulary in this lesson. Look for words that end in *ly*. Write a sentence using each one.

Hands On

The Best and the Worst   With a partner or in a small group, make a poster about the mid-1800s. Draw a line down the middle. On one side, show what you think were the best things about life in America between 1830 and 1860. On the other side, show the worst things.

Oral Language

The Power of Speech   Frederick Douglass made people change their minds about slavery. With a partner, talk about Douglass. What do you think he said against slavery? What would you say to persuade people to end slavery? Take turns. Then give your group a speech about slavery as Douglass might have done.

Partner Practice

Make a Bar Graph   Ask your classmates what countries their families come from. Then use the information to make a bar graph. Label the countries on the horizontal axis. Label the vertical axis with numbers regularly spaced up to the number of students in your class. Then show in the bars how many students come from each country.

LESSON 10 • A TIME OF CHANGE   **137**

Activities

Grammar Spotlight

- Point out the placement of adverbs in the sample sentences.
- Explain the following simple rules for adverbs:
  - An adverb always can be correctly placed right before the word it describes.
  - If there is a helping verb, the adverb comes between the helping verb and main verb.

Hands On

Tell students to include the four groups of people shown in the visual aid on pages 128–129: *immigrants, suffragists, suffrage leaders,* and *abolitionists.*

Oral Language

Remind students that to persuade others, speakers must give strong reasons for their ideas. Can they back up their ideas with words from the U.S. Constitution?

Partner Practice

As models, refer students to the bar graphs on pages 129 and 132.

 Activity: Extend the Lesson

Recommend the following books to deepen students' understanding of Lesson 10 topics:

- *Steal Away Home* by Lois Ruby (Simon & Schuster, 1994)
- *So Far from Home: The Diary of Mary Driscoll, an Irish Mill Girl, Lowell, Massachusetts, 1847* by Barry Denenberg (Scholastic, 1997)

Program Resources

Student Activity Journal
Use page 51 to practice *responding.*

Overhead Transparencies
Use 23, Response Chart, with page 136.

Two New States

STANDARDS CONTENT

History
- Recognize causes and effects
- Explain the Texas fight for independence and statehood
- Recognize causes and effects of the War with Mexico
- Explore the Gold Rush and struggle for statehood in California

Language
- Identify the following Key Concepts: *territory, population,* and *statehood*
- Recognize idioms
- Practice analyzing historical events

Begin   Building Background

- Elicit that the "two new states" in the title refer to California and Texas.

- Focus students on the opening picture and tell them the scene takes place in California.

- Ask for students' responses.

- Then ask the questions under the picture. If needed, provide this background information:
  - The men are looking for gold.
  - The search for gold caused many settlers to rush to California.

- Call out students' ideas about searching for treasure. What feelings does it inspire?

Two New States

Here you'll learn how Texas and California became states. You'll recognize causes and their effects and practice analyzing events in history.

Building Background

▲ If I heard of a place where it was easy to find gold, I'd go there fast!

- **What are the people in this painting doing?**
- **Why would people move to a place where gold was found?**
- **Why would people want their area to become a state?**

 Activity: Role-Play

Ask students to role-play a scenario about finding gold. Prepare a script like the one below.

Eager: *I found gold! You should try too!*

Unsure: *Well, I don't know. What if I don't find anything?*

Invite students to give ideas about what the role-players should do. Tie discussion back to the lesson by telling them a few miners took a risk and got rich, but most did not.

 Differentiating Instruction

Beginning
Concept Review Review these words and concepts introduced in previous lessons: *immigrants, territory, war, moving west, slave states, free states, fights between North and South.* Have students use the words and terms to discuss the ideas shown in the pictures on pages 138 and 139.

Intermediate
Picture Clues Ask students to use picture clues to predict four or five things they will learn in Lesson 11. Have them save their lists and check later to see if they were right.

Advanced
Question-Response Divide the class into three small groups and assign each to write an answer to one of the questions on page 138. Afterward, have them discuss their responses together and point out picture clues they used.

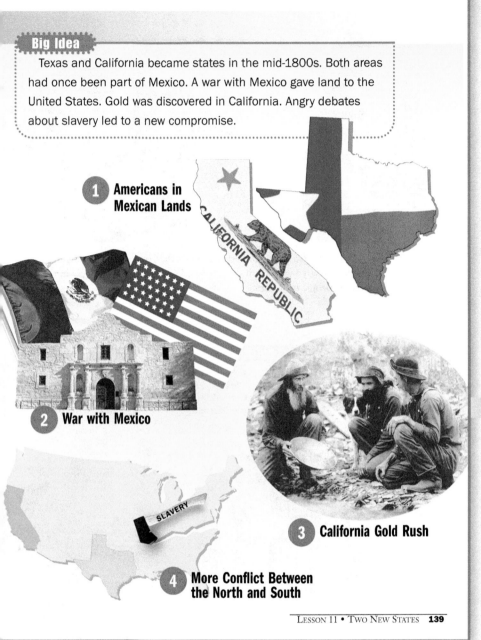

1 **Americans in Mexican Lands**

2 **War with Mexico**

3 **California Gold Rush**

4 **More Conflict Between the North and South**

LESSON 11 • TWO NEW STATES **139**

Introduce the Big Idea

- Introduce students to the Big Idea of Lesson 11 by reading the paragraph and the labels for the four pictures.
- Invite them to share their ideas and background knowledge. Elicit previous vocabulary and Key Concept words in their responses.

Teach the Pictures

Provide or elicit the following information:

- The flags of California and Texas are pictured within their state outlines.
- The second picture shows the Alamo, where a fierce battle took place in the war between Texas and Mexico.

Review

In past lessons, students have studied compromises that were supposed to help end debate over slavery between the North and South.

In Lesson 11, students will learn about a new compromise over slavery. Ask students to give details on the compromises they already have studied. Ask students to predict what they think this compromise will include. Do they think it will be successful?

Activity: Big Idea Map

Have students draw or trace a map of North America. They can trace onto a piece of paper the map on page 139 if they wish.

Have students label the map where they think California and Texas belong. Have them label where Mexico is. Ask them to make a map to show where slavery and the Gold Rush were.

When they are finished, ask students to explain how they labeled their maps.

Activity: Culture Connection

Point out that major economic and political events in a country can cause people to move. For example, the Great Irish Famine in Ireland and political unrest in Cuba caused many people in these countries to emigrate to America.

Invite students to talk about economic or political events in their homelands or other countries that have caused people to leave.

Resource Library

Reader's Handbook (red)
Cause and Effect 59, 644–645, 667

Reader's Handbook (yellow)
Cause and Effect 54, 72, 524–525, 545

All Write
Cause and Effect 270–271

Teach (Key Concepts)

- Pronounce each of the Key Concepts while pointing to the corresponding pictures.

- Ask students to repeat each word.

- Call on a volunteer to identify the map outline as the state of California.

- To reinforce students' understanding of *population*, ask what the population of your class is.

- Emphasize the idea that when a territory had enough people, it could ask Congress to become a state.

Teach the Visual Aid

Statehood for Texas and California

Talk through the timeline with students. Reinforce the information by asking:

- When did the California Gold Rush begin? (*1849*)

- What happened in 1845? (*Texas became a state.*)

- What country won its independence in 1821? (*Mexico*)

Talk and Explore

Key Concepts

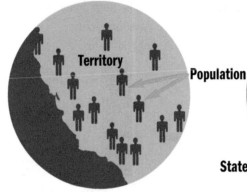
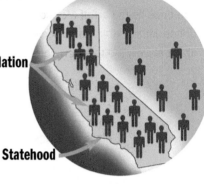

A **territory** was a large area of the United States that didn't have many settlers in it. **Population** is all the people in an area.

When the population in a territory reached 60,000, then the people in the territory could ask to become a state. The process of becoming a state is called **statehood**.

Statehood for Texas and California

1821	1836	1845
Mexico wins independence from Spain.	Texas wins independence from Mexico.	Texas becomes a U.S. state.

140 UNIT 4 • NEW STATES AND CIVIL WAR

Activity: Timeline Shuffle

Ask students to write the date for each timeline event on one side of an index card and to write the timeline caption on the other side. Have them work in pairs and shuffle their decks. With the caption side facing up, challenge students to take turns placing the cards in the correct order.

Next, have partners take turns giving each other the dates on the cards while the other player guesses the event that took place then.

Differentiating Instruction

Beginning

Choral Reading Invite students to do a choral reading of the timeline. Have them find the names of these states and countries in the timeline:

- Texas
- California
- Mexico
- United States

Ask students to write each place name on a sticky note and attach it to the appropriate place on a map. Then have students attach these group names to the matching country:

- Californian
- Mexican
- Texan
- American

Intermediate

Partner Talk Have students take turns telling each other what a territory was and how it could become a state.

Advanced

Writing History Using the information from the history chain in the Skill Building section, have students write a short story about how Texas became independent.

Recognizing Cause and Effect

In history, one important event can lead to others. Study the chain of causes and effects below. Notice that one cause starts a chain of other events.

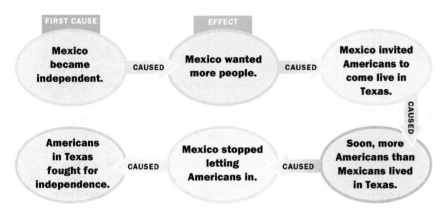

FIRST CAUSE — **Mexico became independent.** — CAUSED — EFFECT — **Mexico wanted more people.** — CAUSED — **Mexico invited Americans to come live in Texas.**

CAUSED

Americans in Texas fought for independence. — CAUSED — **Mexico stopped letting Americans in.** — CAUSED — **Soon, more Americans than Mexicans lived in Texas.**

1846–1848
United States and Mexico fight a war.

1849
The California Gold Rush begins.

1850
California becomes a U.S. state.

CALIFORNIA REPUBLIC

LESSON 11 • TWO NEW STATES **141**

Teach [Skill Building]

■ Read Skill Building aloud with students. Build their understanding of the connections in a Cause-effect Chain by asking questions, such as the following:

- What was an effect of Mexico becoming independent?
- What caused Mexico to stop letting Americans in?

■ Invite students to sit in a circle. Ask them to help model a Cause-effect Chain by adding events to a story. Present this starter: *One day _____ woke up late. That caused. . . .*

■ Ask volunteers to add events in turn. After each one, supply the link *That caused. . . .*

Teach the Pictures

Gold Rush miners "panned" for gold by filling a pan with dirt and water and swirling the mix. Gold, being heavier, would settle to the bottom.

Miners also poured dirt into a *sluice*—a channel with ridges for a flow of water. The ridges trapped the gold while the dirt ran off the sluice.

Activity: History Chains

Have students work in pairs to create a Cause-effect Chain about one of the following historical events they have studied:

- Boston Tea Party (Review page 59.)
- Constitutional Convention (Review pages 82–87.)
- Louisiana Purchase (Review pages 96–97.)

Program Resources

Student Activity Journal

Use page 52 to build key vocabulary.

Use page 53 to practice recognizing cause and effect.

Overhead Transparencies

Use 28, Timeline, with page 140.

Use 24, Sequence Notes, with page 141.

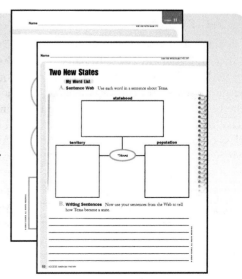

Two New States

Introduce TWO New States

■ Write the headings *California* and *Texas* on the board. Ask students what they know about these two states. Have them write words and descriptions that relate to either heading. Focus students on:

- Location
- Geography
- Resources
- Culture

■ Brainstorm with students a list of topics they expect to learn.

■ Tell them they will learn how Texas and California became states. Both were once part of Mexico, which once was part of Spain.

Teach the Pictures

The Alamo was a Catholic mission. Construction on the building began in 1724.

More than 100 years later, the Alamo served as the defense post for the Americans. The first assault by Santa Anna's army came on February 23, 1836. The Mexican army overtook the Alamo on March 6, killing all the American men there.

Look and Read

Two New States

Problems arose before Texas and California became new states. One set of problems led to a war with Mexico. Another set of problems involved slavery. Once again, the North and South clashed over the question of slavery.

Texas

The story of Texas **statehood** begins with the Spanish. They were the first settlers in the area.

Spain's Empire in the Americas

NORTH AMERICA

ATLANTIC OCEAN

Gulf of Mexico

PACIFIC OCEAN

SOUTH AMERICA

KEY

☐ Spain's empire

AMERICANS IN MEXICAN LANDS

In 1820, Texas was part of Mexico. Mexico itself was part of the huge Spanish **empire.** Then, in 1821, Mexico won its **independence** from Spain. As a free nation, Mexico wanted to build its **population.** Few people lived in Texas. So the Mexican government invited Americans to settle there. The settlers could buy land for 12½ cents an acre.

Thousands of Americans went to Texas—whites, free blacks, and Southerners with slaves. In time, many more Americans than Mexicans lived in Texas. The **imbalance** upset the Mexican government. In 1830, it passed a law saying no more Americans could settle in Texas.

VOCABULARY

statehood—being a state
empire—a group of lands or countries under one government
independence—freedom from the control of a government
population—all the people in a place
imbalance—not being equal

Activity: Role-Play

Have students prepare to role-play Mexican leaders in 1822. In pairs, have them discuss letting Americans settle in Texas. Put this organizer on the board. Then gather the pairs and have them contribute ideas to the class organizer. Have them role-play Mexican leaders debating the issue.

Should Mexico Let Americans Settle in Texas?

Pros (+)	Cons (–)

Differentiating Instruction

Beginning

Key Words Focus students on drawing out key ideas in the pictures, headings, and introductions. Read aloud all the introductions and headings for Lesson 11 and have them do an echo reading. Afterward, have them draw out key words and ideas in each section with a partner.

Intermediate

Paired Reading Divide the class into reading pairs and have them take turns reading paragraphs. Ask them to pause

after reading each paragraph to discuss its key ideas. Encourage them to take notes by jotting down key dates, names, words, and phrases.

Advanced

Revising As students read, have them record details they will use to revise their stories about Texas independence. They should continue this note-taking through page 144.

FIGHTING SANTA ANNA

Mexico was ruled by a **dictator** named Antonio López de Santa Anna. Stephen Austin, a leader of the Americans in Texas, tried to get Santa Anna to let more Americans come. However, Santa Anna would not. So the Americans in Texas **rebelled.** In 1835, they set up their own government. Santa Anna sent troops in to stop them.

In 1836, a fierce battle was fought at the Alamo, an old fort in San Antonio. One of the Americans **defending** the Alamo was Davy Crockett, a frontier hero. The leader was William Travis. He wrote, "I shall never **surrender** or **retreat**." The Alamo defenders died as heroes. It was a **slaughter.**

Just two months later the Americans got **revenge.** Sam Houston and 800 men beat Santa Anna's army in a 15-minute battle near the San Jacinto River. During the battle, they captured Santa Anna.

▲ Antonio López de Santa Anna

Defending the Alamo ▼

VOCABULARY

dictator—a ruler who has complete control
rebelled—fought against the one who rules
defending—fighting to protect
surrender—end the battle by saying the enemy won
retreat—go away from the fighting
slaughter—the killing of large numbers of people; a massacre
revenge—the act of getting even, of hurting people because they hurt you

▲ Davy Crockett

Teach About Fighting Santa Anna

■ Help students understand that Mexico's successful fight for independence from Spain was like America's Revolution against British rule.

■ The Mexican government invited Americans to settle in Mexico after winning independence. Later, the government decided it wanted the Americans out.

■ The Americans fought Mexico to become a free nation.

Review

Santa Anna fought against the *population* of U.S. citizens living in Mexico. They had *settled* there after the Mexican government invited them to move onto the lands.

Remind students of other vocabulary words used to describe these events, such as *settlers, explore,* and *territories.* Have them use each word in a sentence or draw what they think it means.

Activity: Concept Wheels

Work with the class to create a Concept Wheel for *imbalance.* Then divide the rest of the vocabulary words on pages 142–143 between two groups of students.

Have each group create Concept Wheels for their words. Provide the following category prompts:

- Opposite
- Example
- Sentence
- Picture
- Meaning
- Similar word

Program Resources

Student Activity Journal

Assign page 54:

- To create study notes for students to review
- To provide reinforcement of key vocabulary

Discuss The Republic of Texas and Texas Statehood

- Review the debate in Congress over admitting free states and slave states.
- Jog students' memories by returning them to page 111.
- Discuss the terms of the Missouri Compromise that settled the issue in 1820.

Teach a Reading Strategy

- Explain that good readers look for the main ideas in a text. While they read, they should ask themselves, *What information is important?*
- Give students these clues for deciding upon main ideas:
  - Study the headings. They often summarize the main ideas.
  - Look at the pictures. They usually show the key points.
  - Notice what most of the sentences in a paragraph are about.
- Model the skill by asking students, *What is the main idea of* Texas Statehood? (*It took ten years for Texas to become a state because of the debate in Congress between slave and free states.*)

(**TALK AND SHARE**)

Return students to the chain of events on page 141 as a model.

Look and Read

▲ Sam Houston

THE REPUBLIC OF TEXAS

The Texans didn't let Santa Anna go until he signed a **treaty** saying Texas was free. The new nation called itself the Republic of Texas. Sam Houston became its president.

TEXAS STATEHOOD

Most Texans hoped the United States would give them statehood. But, at first, Congress said no. Texas was a slave state. Northerners **feared** that adding Texas would make the South much stronger.

Ten years later, in 1844, it was a **presidential election year.** The **candidates** were James Polk and Henry Clay. Polk, a slave owner from Tennessee, wanted the nation to grow all the way to the Pacific Ocean. Clay, from Kentucky, did not want to **extend** slavery. Polk won the election, in part because he favored Texas statehood. In December 1845, Texas became a state.

(**TALK AND SHARE**) Explain to your partner how Texas became a state. Make a chain of events on a poster.

▲ James Polk was for slavery.

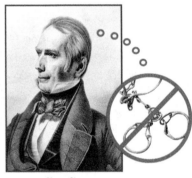

▲ Henry Clay was against slavery.

VOCABULARY

treaty—a formal agreement among countries
feared—felt afraid
presidential election year—the year that Americans vote for a new president
candidates—people who are trying to get elected
extend—make something larger in area or longer in time

144 Unit 4 • New States and Civil War

Activity: Texas Flags

Have students draw a small poster that shows the three different flags of the Texan national government.

Supply the tip that they can find pictures of these flags on pages 139 and 140 (Mexican flag, p. 139; Nation of Texas flag, 140; U.S. flag, p. 139). Ask students to write call-outs that explain each flag.

Differentiating Instruction

Beginning
Slavery and Politics Help students locate the words on page 144 that link slavery and politics: *Congress, Texas statehood, slave state, Northerners, South, presidential election year, candidates, slave owner, grow the nation, extend slavery.* Then have them direct you in drawing a Web or diagram on the chalkboard to show the relationships.

Intermediate
Political Posters Have student partners work together on posters for Polk and Clay. They should focus on the message each tried to convey to voters.

Advanced
Presenting History Have students use their notes to revise their stories about how Texas became a state. Ask volunteers to practice telling their story to a partner before presenting it to the class. Other students may wish to publish their stories in a class book.

War with Mexico

By this time, **conflicts** were strong between Mexico and the United States.

REASONS FOR THE WAR

Americans believed in **Manifest Destiny.** They wanted to expand the country all the way to the Pacific. The two nations disagreed over the **border** of Texas, each nation **claiming** the same land. Also, the United States wanted the areas shown in green on the map below. These lands were at the time part of Mexico. America offered to buy the lands. Mexico, however, refused to sell.

In 1846, the War with Mexico broke out between the United States and Mexico. With Zachary Taylor leading the army, the Americans soon won. By September 1847, most of the fighting was over, and a year later, Taylor was elected president of the United States.

▲ Zachary Taylor

THE UNITED STATES WON LAND FROM MEXICO

Mexico paid a high price for defeat. In 1848, Santa Anna signed a peace agreement called the Treaty of Guadalupe Hidalgo. Mexico gave half of its territory to America. In return, America paid $15 million to Mexico. Within 5 years, America's **mainland** reached its present size. The American dream of Manifest Destiny came true.

(TALK AND SHARE) Tell your partner the events that led to the war with Mexico.

Land Won from Mexico

KEY
- Land gained when Texas became a state (1845)
- Land gained by the Treaty of Guadalupe Hidalgo (1848)

VOCABULARY

conflicts—long struggles
Manifest Destiny—a future in which the United States extended all the way west to the Pacific Ocean
border—the official line that separates two lands

claiming—saying something belongs to you
mainland—a country's biggest piece of land. The U.S. mainland does not include the states of Alaska and Hawaii.

Talk About War with Mexico

■ Review with students the belief in Manifest Destiny, which led the United States to fight against Mexico to gain western lands.

■ Emphasize that Americans believed it was their right and fate to settle the land from the Atlantic to the Pacific Oceans.

■ Refer students to page 122 for more review.

Key Connection: Government

■ Tap into students' knowledge of treaties by helping them recall the Treaty of Paris that ended the American Revolution (page 75).

■ Extend their understanding by emphasizing that a treaty is a formal agreement among nations. The sides that sign the document agree to keep its terms.

■ Ask students to identify a term of the Treaty of Guadalupe Hidalgo.

■ Treaties are like contracts (such as rental leases) that private citizens sign. Some treaties end wars, but many are formed for economic or political reasons.

(TALK AND SHARE)

Suggest that partners record the events in a Sequence Organizer.

Activity: Texas Leaders

Divide the class into pairs. Assign each pair two of these leaders important to Texas history:

- Santa Anna
- Sam Houston
- James Polk
- Zachary Taylor

Have pairs review information about their two leaders on pages 143–145. Ask them to create a collage for each person to show why he is important. Afterward, have pairs attach their collages to those of partners who depicted other leaders.

Activity: Review Quiz

Provide the following two questions. Have pairs discuss and write the answers. Afterward, have pairs share their answers in a group:

- What group of people wanted slave states, and why? (*The South wanted them because its economy depended on large cash crops that were farmed with slave labor.*)

- Why was the balance of free states and slave states important? (*It kept equal votes in the Senate between the North and South.*)

Discuss California

- Emphasize that the prospect of finding gold in California attracted thousands of people.

- Gold seekers came from America, Mexico, China, Germany, France, and Turkey.

- They flooded the area so quickly that the event became known as the California Gold Rush.

- Ask students if they have seen many people move into an area all at once. Tell them to describe what it looked like. Ask, *Why were the people moving?*

People in History

The First Asians in America

- Read and discuss this feature with students.

- Then compare the reasons the first Asians came to America to the reasons of immigrants discussed in the previous lesson (page 132).

▲ Panning for gold

California

Next, the North and the South were at odds over California becoming a state. Once again, the issue was slavery.

Gold nuggets ▶

THE CALIFORNIA GOLD RUSH

In 1848, when America got California from Mexico, few people lived there. Soon all that changed. That year, gold was discovered in California. Word spread like wildfire.

What happened next became known as the California Gold Rush. Thousands of people rushed into California in search of gold. In one year alone, more than 80,000 people moved there. Since that year was 1849, these people were called **forty-niners.** Most of the forty-niners were Americans. The rest came from other countries, including Mexico and China.

The population of California quickly **soared.** By 1850, California asked Congress for statehood. That again sparked a **crisis** between the North and South. California was a free state. Adding it to the Union would give the North more power in Congress than the South.

VOCABULARY
forty-niners—people who moved to California in 1849 in search of gold
soared—rose, grew higher
crisis—a time of great difficulty

People in History

The First Asians in America

"Gold in America!" Crops were failing in China when this news raced around the globe. So, in 1849, 300 Chinese men sailed to California. They were called Gam Saan Haak—Travelers to Gold Mountain. They were the first large group of people from Asia who came to America. Most of them were farmers. Soon more Chinese followed them. By 1852, more than 20,000 Chinese lived in the state.

146 UNIT 4 • NEW STATES AND CIVIL WAR

Activity: Before-and-After Charts

Ask students to create a Before-and-After Chart that shows California before and after the Gold Rush. Have them illustrate their organizers with maps and pictures that show important details, such as gold nuggets and pans.

California

Before 1848	After 1848

Differentiating Instruction

Beginning

Choral Reading Read aloud to students each paragraph on pages 146–147. Read slowly and pronounce words clearly. Pause after each paragraph to clarify difficult words and phrases. Then reread the paragraph aloud together with students before going on.

Intermediate

Role-Play Focus students on the pictures and story of the two gold miners. Have them imagine what these miners might say about their experiences in California. Encourage students to role-play their responses. Supply words and phrases for them as needed.

Advanced

Creating a Dialogue Have students create a dialogue for what the family members pictured on page 147 might say about the Fugitive Slave Act.

CONFLICT BETWEEN NORTH AND SOUTH

Debate over California statehood **raged** in Congress. The North said yes. The South said no. **Tensions** rose to the boiling point. Some states in the South began to talk about **seceding.**

Once again, Henry Clay came up with a **compromise**—the Compromise of 1850. This plan let California join the Union as a free state. That pleased the North.

Another part of the compromise pleased the South. It was called the Fugitive Slave Act. This terrible law made it easier for slave owners to get their slaves back if they ran away. It said anyone who helped runaway slaves would have to pay a fine and go to jail. Anyone who caught a runaway slave got a reward. The law gave no protection to African Americans, not even to those who were *not* slaves!

The Compromise of 1850 held the country together for a while. Still, the North and the South did not agree on slavery. Soon tensions would break out again.

(TALK AND SHARE) With your partner, make a list of everything you know about the Compromise of 1850.

VOCABULARY
raged—was very angry
tensions—feelings of fear or nervousness
seceding—leaving; not being part of the United States
compromise—a way of settling a disagreement in which each side gets part of what it wants

Language Notes

Idioms
These sayings don't mean what they seem.

☐ **were at odds:** disagreed

☐ **rose to the boiling point:** got very strong, as when water gets so hot that it boils

Summary

Texas and California were part of Mexico. Americans in Texas fought for freedom from Mexico and then became a state. The United States fought a war with Mexico and got land that included California. When Californians asked for statehood, the North and the South could not agree. The problem was solved by the Compromise of 1850, and California became a state.

Teach About Conflict Between North and South

■ Emphasize that tensions between the North and South over slavery were growing strong.

■ The Compromise of 1850 would only hold the peace for a while.

■ Ask students if they've been in a situation with a lot of tension. Ask how the situation was resolved.

Language Notes

With students, read aloud the meanings of the idioms in Language Notes. Then guide them in finding the idioms in context on pages 146 and 147. Have them substitute other words for the idioms in the sentences.

(TALK AND SHARE)

Suggest these categories:
• Causes of the Compromise
• What it gave the North
• What it gave the South
• Effect of the Compromise

Discuss the (Summary)

Have students read the Summary. Then refer them to the Big Idea on page 139. Divide the class into four groups. Have each group summarize one part of the Big Idea and then tell their summaries to the class.

✓ Assessment

Assess students' comprehension by asking the following questions:

History
• Why did Americans move to Texas?
• What were the causes of the War with Mexico?
• How did the Gold Rush change California?
• What was the Compromise of 1850?

Language
Match the word to its definition:

Words	Definitions
1. Manifest Destiny	A. A formal agreement among countries
2. Treaty	B. Long struggles
3. Conflicts	C. A policy of the United States

Assessment Book
Use page 29 to assess students' comprehension.

Teach Analyzing

Explain that analyzing events involves finding out how the events are connected. This page will show students how to develop this skill.

Model the Organizer

■ Call on different volunteers to read each segment of the chain.

■ Point out that a visual organizer helps students clearly see and make connections among events.

Give Practice Analyzing

Have students work with partners to complete one activity.

■ **Draw** Ask students with limited English to complete the Draw activity and encourage them to add words where they can. If necessary, help students call out the following key ideas:

- Americans in Texas rebel against Mexico.
- Texas wins independence and becomes a state.
- Americans want to expand their country.
- The U.S. and Mexico disagree over the Texas border.

■ **Write** Refer students to pages 142–144 to refresh their memories about Texas statehood.

Develop Language

Analyzing

Analyzing Historical Events

When you analyze something, you separate it into its parts to see what it is made of. Then you look at the parts to see how they are related. In history, one event can cause other events like links in a chain. You can make a Chain to help you analyze historical events. This Chain shows the causes and effects of the Compromise of 1850.

Compromise of 1850 Chain

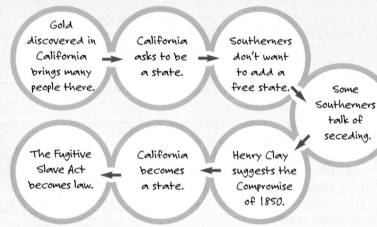

Practice Analyzing

1. Draw Analyze the events that led to the war with Mexico. Draw a War with Mexico Chain. Then use your chain to explain to your partner or group why the United States and Mexico fought a war in the 1840s.

2. Write Analyze how Texas became a state. Make a Texas Statehood Chain showing the events after Texas became independent that led to statehood. Then write your ideas in a paragraph of 3 or 4 sentences. Exchange paragraphs with a partner and check each other's writing.

Check Your Writing

Make sure you
- ☐ Use complete sentences.
- ☐ Use a period at the end of each sentence.
- ☐ Spell all the words correctly.

🔲 Activity: Internet Resources

Have students research one of the following sites and report back to the class:

- **The Alamo**
  http://www.pbs.org/wgbh/amex/alamo
- **The Gold Rush**
  http://www.isu.edu/~trinmich/home.html
- **War with Mexico**
  http://www.pbs.org/kera/usmexicanwar

🔲 Differentiating Instruction

Beginning
Writing Sentences Dictate these sentences:

- People rushed to California.
- The first Asians came to America.

Ask students to listen to the sentences and write them correctly. Suggest that they use the headings on page 146 for help in spelling.

Intermediate
Texas Statehood Direct students to begin their chain with the events of

1835 discussed on page 143. How long was it from that time until Texas became a state? Students can use that fact in the first sentence of their paragraphs.

Advanced
Using Idioms Encourage students to use idioms from page 147 in their paragraphs for the Write activity. Example: *After the Alamo, Texan anger at Santa Anna and his troops rose to the boiling point.*

Activities

Grammar Spotlight

Questions with *Where, When,* and *Why* The chart shows you how to ask and answer questions with *where, when,* and *why.*

Questions	Answers
Question with *Where*	**Answer tells a place.**
Where was the Gold Rush?	It was in <u>California</u>.
Question with *When*	**Answer tells a time.**
When did the Gold Rush start?	It started in <u>1849</u>.
Question with *Why*	**Answer tells a reason.**
Why did the Gold Rush start?	It started <u>because gold was discovered</u>.

Write 3 questions about Mexico. Then write the answers to your questions.

Oral Language

Using Idioms In a small group, talk about times when you could say "rose to a boiling point" or "were at odds." Take turns using these idioms in a sentence.

Partner Practice

Where, When, Why Take turns asking and answering questions about the battle at the Alamo. Be sure to ask where it happened, when it happened, and why it happened.

Hands On

Map Practice
1. Draw a map of the United States.
2. Put a ★ for Washington, D.C.
3. Show Texas and California.
4. Show the border with Mexico.
5. Draw an arrow in the Pacific Ocean pointing to California and label it "From China." It shows where some Gold Rush immigrants came from.
6. Put a ■ where the Alamo is. You can find San Antonio on a modern map of Texas. That is where the Alamo is.
7. Share your map with your group.

LESSON 11 • TWO NEW STATES **149**

Activities

Grammar Spotlight

- Divide the class into two groups. Have one group read the questions in the chart and the other group read the answers.
- Provide extra practice by writing the questions *Where? When?* and *Why?* on separate file cards.
- Invite students to take turns drawing the cards and asking a classmate questions about their favorite things: songs, TV shows, colors, and the like.

Oral Language

If students have trouble interpreting the idioms, have them draw pictures of the phrases' literal meanings. Then have them guess how the picture could relate to other ideas.

Partner Practice

Students can write their questions before asking them. Have them draw a Three-column Chart, labeled *Where, When,* and *Why.* They can place their questions in the correct columns.

Hands On

Ask students to compare their finished maps with one found in an atlas.

 Activity: Extend the Lesson

In a group, ask students to create a newspaper that could have been published during the California Gold Rush. Sample writing prompts are:

- News about Chinese miners
- Story about a broke miner
- Feature on how to pan for gold
- Advice column

Program Resources

Student Activity Journal
Use page 55 to practice *analyzing.*

Overhead Transparencies
Use 24, Sequence Notes, with page 148.

Seven Years to Civil War

STANDARDS CONTENT

History

■ Utilize note-taking strategies

■ Identify the steps that led to the Civil War

■ Recognize key people and events in the years from 1854 to 1861

■ Identify why Southern states seceded from the Union

Language

■ Identify the following Key Concepts: *representation*, *compromise*, and *balance*

■ Recognize words with multiple meanings

■ Practice interpreting events in history

Begin Building Background

■ Explain that a *civil war* is a war between citizens of the same country.

■ Discuss details from the pictures. Elicit or supply this information:

 • The man (John Brown) is holding a Bible and a rifle.

 • At his sides are fighting pro-slavery and anti-slavery forces.

 • Dead Civil War soldiers are in front.

 • In the background are a tornado, a raging prairie fire, and pioneers.

■ Explore the emotional content of the picture. Ask students the questions under the picture.

Seven Years to Civil War

Here you'll learn about some events that led to the Civil War. You'll also learn how to take notes and practice interpreting events in history.

Building Background

▲ Once I heard a very angry man. It was scary!

■ **What do you think is happening in this picture?**

■ **What could make you feel like this man?**

■ **When was a time you got angry and left a group?**

 Activity: Art Critics

In pairs, students should share their impressions of the painting on page 150. Then have them give a short response to the piece of art. Students with limited English proficiency can use words to describe how they feel about it, while more advanced students should write a paragraph stating their opinion and providing reasons to support it.

Differentiating Instruction

Beginning

Describing Pictures To help students build word-picture associations for pages 150–151, write words on the board they can use to identify pictured items: *tornado, John Brown, flag, settlers, fighting, slave, newspaper, Abraham Lincoln, free states, slave states.* Point to each word and pronounce it. Have students repeat after you. Then have them take turns using the words as they point to a picture.

Intermediate

Using Pictures Invite students in small groups to talk about the picture of John Brown. What do they see? What does it mean? What story is the picture telling?

Advanced

K-W-L Chart With a partner or small group, have students complete a K-W-L Chart for the steps that led to the Civil War. Encourage partners to share what they know and to make predictions.

Laws about slavery made problems between the North and the South grow worse and worse. People began killing each other. Then Abraham Lincoln was elected president, and the South left the Union.

1 Laws About Slavery

2 A Supreme Court Decision

3 Abraham Lincoln Elected

4 Secession

Introduce the Big Idea

- Read the Big Idea titles with students. Invite them to share their background knowledge, ideas, and impressions about each picture.

- Review previous conflicts between the North and South, including:
  - Economic and social differences (p. 110)
  - Conflict that led to the Missouri Compromise (p. 111)
  - Fight over tariffs (pp. 120–121)
  - Fight over abolition (p. 134)
  - Fight over Texas (p. 144)
  - Fight over California (pp. 146–147)
  - Fugitive Slave Act (p. 147)

- Help students see that the call for civil war had been growing louder for years. Explain that in this lesson, they will learn the final events that led to secession and war.

Review

Remind students of the many arguments that the North and South had tried to compromise on before. Ask students to give details on these compromises, such as the Missouri Compromise and the Compromise of 1850.

Activity: Role-Play

Present the following scenario to students.

Two classmates often go to each other's homes. They are friends, but they like completely different pastimes. One likes to watch TV after school. The other likes to play outdoors. They try to make compromises. After awhile, they grow more and more frustrated about their differences.

In pairs, have students discuss what will happen between the two people. Will they get angrier or will they work out their differences? Have each pair of students role-play the situation. Afterward, invite partners to do their role-plays for the class.

Tie the theme of conflict in the role-plays to the conflict between the North and South. Explain that each side felt differently about slavery. Neither side wanted to compromise on the issue any longer.

Resource Library

Reader's Handbook (red)
Note-taking 74–76, 646–647, 677

Reader's Handbook (yellow)
Note-taking 526–527, 553, 556

All Write
Note-taking 262–275, 316–317

Teach [Key Concepts]

- ■ Model correct pronunciation of each Key Concept term and have students repeat after you.

- ■ Then read aloud the explanation below the diagram.

- ■ Call on volunteers to explain each Key Concept to the class in their own words, using the diagram as an aid.

Teach the Visual Aid

[Seven Years to Civil War]

- ■ Draw students' attention to the visual aid.

- ■ Explain that each event in the timeline shows a conflict between the North and South.

- ■ Tell students that they will learn more about each event as they read the lesson.

- ■ For now, they should become familiar with the names and dates.

[Key Concepts]

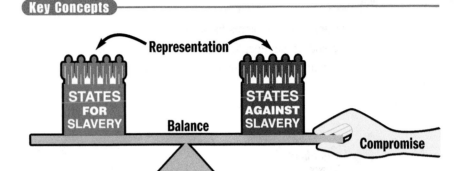

Representation is having a voice in government. The slave states and the free states were equal in number, so they had equal representation in the Senate. A **compromise**, in which each side got part of what it wanted, kept this **balance**.

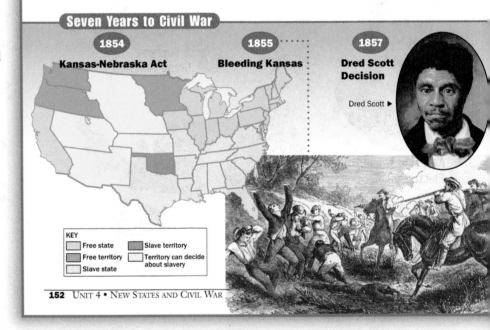

Seven Years to Civil War

1854 Kansas-Nebraska Act

1855 Bleeding Kansas

1857 Dred Scott Decision

Dred Scott ▶

KEY
☐ Free state   ☐ Slave territory
☐ Free territory ☐ Territory can decide about slavery
☐ Slave state

152 UNIT 4 • NEW STATES AND CIVIL WAR

Activity: Internet Resources

Have students research:

- • Your state's *representation* in Congress. Have them name your state representatives and senators.

- • The *balance* in today's Senate between Democrats and Republicans.

Provide the following Internet sites as a resource:

- • http://www.senate.gov
- • http://www.house.gov

Differentiating Instruction

Beginning

Key Concept Focus Assign partners one of the three Key Concept terms: *representation, balance, compromise.* Have partners discuss the best way of explaining what their term means. They can choose to demonstrate with props, draw, or act out the meaning. Give time for practice and then invite volunteers to explain their terms to the class.

Intermediate

Interpreting a Map Have partners study the map on page 152 and interpret the map key to each other. Ask a volunteer to identify Kansas. Ask, *How does the map help explain why fighting between proslavery and antislavery people broke out in Kansas?*

Advanced

Gathering Facts Have students study the pictures and text here to prepare for the reading. Have them list the people and events they expect to read about.

Taking Notes

Notes help you understand and remember history. Here's how to take good notes.

1. Use your own words.

2. Keep your notes short.

3. Write down the main ideas, or key words, on the left.

4. Group notes about these key words together on the right.

Study the notes about the Kansas-Nebraska Act shown here.

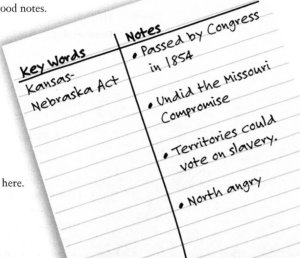

Key Words	Notes
Kansas-Nebraska Act	• Passed by Congress in 1854
	• Undid the Missouri Compromise
	• Territories could vote on slavery.
	• North angry

1859

John Brown's Raid at Harpers Ferry

1860

Abraham Lincoln is elected president.

1861

The South secedes.

▲ John Brown

LESSON 12 • SEVEN YEARS TO CIVIL WAR **153**

Teach Skill Building

■ Model how to take notes. Ask a student volunteer to recall information about the Missouri Compromise (page 111).

- Ask the rest of the class to listen carefully.

- Have students brainstorm key points of the Compromise, and write their responses on the board.

- If students suggest minor or unimportant details, suggest that the final list is too long.

- Ask students which notes they would cut.

■ Then read aloud Skill Building with students. Walk through the example of notes.

Teach the Pictures

■ The map on the bottom of the page shows how much of the South seceded from the Union.

■ Ask students to tell how they think the North felt about the secession. Elicit words such as *angry, worried, afraid, nervous, scared,* and *upset.*

■ Have students support their opinions with examples.

Activity: Note-taking Practice

Have students tell their partners about the plot of a TV show or book they recently enjoyed. The listening partner should take notes about the key ideas. Afterward, the listener retells the plot, using their notes.

Program Resources

Student Activity Journal

Use page 56 to build key vocabulary.

Use page 57 to practice taking notes.

Overhead Transparencies

Use 17, Key Word or Topic Notes, with page 153.

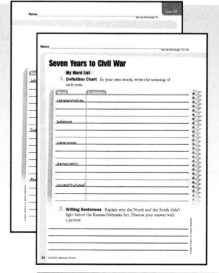

Introduce Seven Years to Civil War

- Explain that this lesson describes several events that caused trouble between the North and South.

- The North and South had different opinions about issues. Review characteristics of both regions by dividing the class in half to represent them. Have each group of students state one quality of its assigned region. Then discuss the differences.

Key Connection: Government

Elicit what students know about the Supreme Court and record all their ideas in a Web. Then explain any of the following points that were not mentioned. Add them to the Web.

- The U.S. Supreme Court is the highest court in the land.

- It has nine judges appointed by the president and approved by the Senate.

- Justices can serve for life.

- One important job is ruling on whether laws and their interpretation by judges are in keeping with the rules of the United States Constitution.

Seven Years to Civil War

Laws about slavery were passed—and broken. Trouble between the North and South became violent. Then in 1861, after Abraham Lincoln was elected president, the South left the Union.

▲ The Fugitive Slave Act required people to capture and return slaves to their owners.

The Fight over Slavery

For many years, the North and South argued **bitterly** over slavery. Then in the mid-1850s, the fight became violent.

THE FUGITIVE SLAVE ACT

The **Fugitive Slave Act** was very **harsh.** If an African-American person was caught, there was no proper trial. All that was needed was a description of the missing slave written by the owner. Nothing the person said mattered. Slaves could not **testify** in courts. Frederick Douglass was a famous **abolitionist** who had escaped from slavery. He said that in the United States, "There is more protection for a horse, for a donkey, or anything, rather than a **colored** man."

The Fugitive Slave Act made some people in the North angrier than ever. In the beginning, many people thought abolitionists were strange and foolish. Now, more and more Northerners agreed with the abolitionists that slavery should end.

VOCABULARY
bitterly—with anger and disappointment
Fugitive Slave Act—an 1850 law that made people return runaway slaves to their owners
harsh—cruel and severe
testify—tell under oath what happened; tell or show proof
abolitionist—a person who worked to end slavery
colored—black; African American

154 UNIT 4 • NEW STATES AND CIVIL WAR

Activity: Two-column Charts

Ask students to take notes in a Two-column Chart on the main ideas of page 154.

Then provide additional modeling on note-taking. Work with students to create a class set of notes in the format below.

Fugitive Slave Act

South	North

Differentiating Instruction

Beginning

Key Ideas Focus learners on getting the key ideas of the reading. As they work through pages 154–159, have them read aloud the headings and match them to corresponding pictures when available. Then read aloud the paragraphs with students, or have them listen to advanced readers. After each paragraph, ask students to tell its topic.

Intermediate

Note-taking Ask students to use the skill they learned on page 153. As they read together, partners should take notes. For each paragraph, pairs should decide together on the key words and record details in a Two-column Chart.

Advanced

Summarizing Have partners read silently, stopping at the end of each paragraph to give each other an oral summary of the paragraph.

THE KANSAS-NEBRASKA ACT

Back in 1820, in the Missouri Compromise, Congress had drawn a line on a map of the United States. Slavery was not allowed in **territories** above the line. Kansas and Nebraska were above the line, so slavery was **illegal** there. Then, in 1854, Congress agreed it was more **democratic** to let people who lived in the territories vote on slavery. The members of Congress thought the balance would not be broken. They believed Nebraska would choose to be a free state, and Kansas would choose to be a slave state. So they passed the Kansas-Nebraska Act and undid the old law.

The South liked the Kansas-Nebraska Act. It opened up new territory to slavery. Some Northerners liked it because they thought the new law would help settle the West.

Other Northerners were **outraged.** Lands that had not allowed slavery for 30 years could now vote it in. Slavery would **expand.** "No slavery in the territories!" they cried. They would stop Kansas from becoming a slave state.

(TALK AND SHARE) With a partner, look at the map. Find 3 states that allowed slavery. Find 3 states that did not allow slavery.

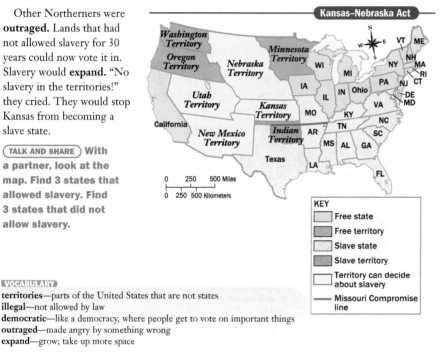

Kansas–Nebraska Act

KEY
- Free state
- Free territory
- Slave state
- Slave territory
- Territory can decide about slavery
- — Missouri Compromise line

VOCABULARY

territories—parts of the United States that are not states
illegal—not allowed by law
democratic—like a democracy, where people get to vote on important things
outraged—made angry by something wrong
expand—grow; take up more space

LESSON 12 • SEVEN YEARS TO CIVIL WAR **155**

Teach The Kansas-Nebraska Act

- ■ Underscore that the conflict created by the Kansas-Nebraska Act once again was about two states becoming either free or slave states.

- ■ Explain that the act was meant to please both the North and South by taking the federal government out of the decision.

- ■ Ask students, *Why did the Kansas-Nebraska Act anger the North?*

(TALK AND SHARE)

Point out the Missouri Compromise line on the map to students. Ask a volunteer to locate the Kansas and Nebraska territories. Ask them to show why the two would have been free states rather than slave states under the old law.

Review

Have students describe what they think *compromise* means. Ask them what an example of compromise in everyday life would be. Have them draw an example, such as doing an extra chore in return for a privilege.

Activity: Vocabulary Charades

Write the eleven vocabulary words from pages 154–155 on the board. Then divide the class into small teams. Have each team write the words on index cards and place them facedown. On their turns, players should pick a card and pantomime a clue to its meaning. The rest of the team should guess the word.

Program Resources

Student Activity Journal
Assign page 58:
- To create study notes for students to review
- To provide reinforcement of key vocabulary

Overhead Transparencies
Use 29, Two-column Chart, with page 154.

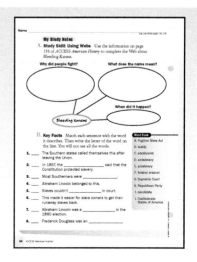

Discuss Troubles Grow

■ Tell students that soon after the Kansas-Nebraska Act was passed, Kansas had an election.

■ People both for and against slavery swarmed into Kansas.

■ When the new legislature took office, it voted in slavery.

■ After that, armed conflict between the two sides began.

Teach a Reading Strategy

■ Tell students that readers sometimes come upon a word they don't understand.

■ Before taking time to look up the word in the dictionary, they should ask themselves:

  • Is this word important?

  • Can I easily understand the meaning of the sentence without knowing the word? (*If so, they should read on.*)

■ Provide this example for students to test out the strategy: *The inflammatory events led to civil war.*

  • Explain that the events must be in some way bad, if they led to civil war, so the context gives you a clue as to the meaning of *inflammatory.*

Look and Read

▲ Fighting in Kansas

▲ Brown was hanged on December 2, 1859.

Troubles Grow

Immediately, Kansas became a **hotbed** of conflict. Both abolitionists and slave owners rushed into the state. One group in New England sent guns to Kansas for the fight against slave owners. In 1855, slavery was voted into Kansas. **Antislavery** people refused to obey the new laws. Both sides armed themselves. Newspapers named the land "Bleeding Kansas."

JOHN BROWN

John Brown was a Northerner who was deeply against slavery. He was a **fanatic** who believed he was doing God's work. In 1856, he turned to murder. Brown and his sons pulled 5 **proslavery** men out of bed in the middle of the night and killed them.

Brown's actions were **brutal,** and the South was outraged. More trouble was to come. In 1859, John Brown led a **raid** on the **federal arsenal** in the town of Harpers Ferry, Virginia. His goal was to free slaves and arm them to fight their masters.

Brown and his men were caught. The court sentenced Brown to be hanged. John Brown's death made him a hero to many in the North. People rang bells, fired guns, and listened to great speeches. All this **offended** people in the South. They felt it was an insult to honor John Brown. Brown's raid helped drive the North and the South further apart.

VOCABULARY

hotbed—a place where anything grows and develops quickly
antislavery—against slavery. The word part *anti* means "against."
fanatic—someone whose support for a belief is taken to an extreme; unbalanced, crazy
proslavery—supporters of slavery. The word part *pro* means "for."
brutal—cruel like an animal, not human
raid—a sudden attack
federal arsenal—a building where the national government keeps weapons
offended—caused hurt feelings and anger

156 UNIT 4 • NEW STATES AND CIVIL WAR

Activity: Events Chain

Ask students to work in pairs to create a chain showing a series of events caused by the Kansas-Nebraska Act.

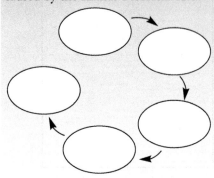

Differentiating Instruction

Beginning
Summaries Tell students they will learn two stories. Teach the blue heads and the vocabulary words and summarize the stories of John Brown and the Dred Scott decision using key words.

Intermediate
Brainstorming In a group, have students brainstorm what opposing lawyers on the Dred Scott case might have said to the Supreme Court. Have them write their ideas in a Web. Then ask pairs of students to role-play the lawyers in court.

Advanced
Role-Play Divide the class into pairs. Have pairs role-play a Northerner and Southerner arguing about the events listed below. Ask them to switch sides after each event they role-play.

  • The Fugitive Slave Act

  • The Kansas-Nebraska Act

  • John Brown's raids

  • The Dred Scott case

THE DRED SCOTT DECISION

Meanwhile, Southerners won a famous case in the **Supreme Court.** Abolitionists helped a slave named Dred Scott bring his case to court. Scott had been taken from a slave state (Missouri) into a free state (Illinois) to live. Then his master took him back into a slave state. Scott **sued** to be free. He said that because slavery was against the law in Illinois, he became free when he went there.

In 1857, the Supreme Court ruled against Scott. It said a slave was not a citizen and had "no rights which the white man was bound to respect." The Court went even further. In the Dred Scott **decision,** it said that the Constitution protected slavery. This meant the Missouri Compromise was **unconstitutional.** Slave owners could take their property anywhere. This decision by the Supreme Court made Northerners furious!

▲ Dred Scott and his wife, Harriet, sued for their freedom in 1846 in the St. Louis Circuit Court in Missouri.

(TALK AND SHARE) **Tell your partner one reason why problems between the North and the South grew worse. Ask your partner to tell you a different reason.**

VOCABULARY

Supreme Court—the highest court in the United States
sued—asked a court to rule about the law
decision—a ruling by the Supreme Court
unconstitutional—going against the Constitution, and therefore not the law of the land

Language Notes

Multiple Meanings
These words have more than one meaning.

☐ arm	☐ sentence	☐ case
1. give weapons to	1. a judgment by a court	1. a matter for a court of law to decide
2. a body part	2. one or more words that expresses a complete thought	2. an example
		3. a convincing argument
		4. a box

LESSON 12 • SEVEN YEARS TO CIVIL WAR **157**

Talk About The Dred Scott Decision

Explain that Supreme Court justices can make mistakes. The Dred Scott decision was particularly terrible because it drove the nation closer to war.

Explain to students that sometimes a later court will undo the bad results of an earlier one. In 1954 *Brown v. the Board of Education of Topeka, Kansas* overturned the 1896 "separate but equal" idea in *Plessy v. Ferguson.*

(**TALK AND SHARE**)

Encourage students to refer to their notes as they share their ideas. Elicit vocabulary words such as *compromise, proslavery, antislavery, offended.*

Language Notes

■ Call students' attention to the following multiple-meaning words in context:
  • *4 men* ran *for president*
  • *the* party *was founded*
  • *would not let slavery* spread
  • *joined together to* found *a new nation*

■ Have students identify what each word means in context.

■ Then help them find another meaning for each word. If they have trouble, invite them to use the dictionary.

 Activity: Two-column Organizer

Remind students to update their organizers with information from pages 156–157. Ask them to tell about the North and South's differing viewpoints on these topics: *Bleeding Kansas, John Brown, the Dred Scott decision.*

 Activity: Oral Story String

In small group circles, have students retell the story of the Dred Scott case. Start the story yourself with a piece similar to the following.

Dred Scott was a slave. At first, he lived in the slave state of Missouri. Then. . . . (Pass the story to the first student.)

Discuss The South Leaves the Union

- Emphasize that the election of President Lincoln in 1860 was important because the nation was in crisis.

- Then tell students that electing Lincoln did not solve the crisis, and have them read to find out why.

Teach the Pictures

Abraham Lincoln was born in Kentucky. His family moved first to Indiana and then to Illinois.

Lincoln loved to learn and studied law. He spent years as a lawyer and ran for senator in 1858. He lost the race but gained national prominence as a promising candidate. Two years later, Lincoln was the Republican Party's nominee for president.

▲ Abraham Lincoln

The South Leaves the Union

By the time of the **presidential election campaign** of 1860, people in both the North and South were very angry.

ELECTION OF ABRAHAM LINCOLN

In 1860, 4 men ran for president. One was an Illinois lawyer named Abraham Lincoln. Lincoln belonged to the new **Republican Party,** and he was the Republican **candidate** for president. The Republicans were against slavery. The party was started in 1854 to work against slavery spreading in the territories.

Lincoln himself was against slavery. "If slavery is not wrong," he said once, "nothing is wrong." However, Lincoln was willing to let the South keep slavery where it already **existed.** He wanted to hold the country together.

Still, many Southerners didn't trust Lincoln. They knew he would not let slavery spread. Almost no Southerners voted for Lincoln in the 1860 election. Many Northerners voted for him, and Abraham Lincoln won the election. Because there were 4 candidates, however, he won with less than half the votes. The **majority** of the country was not behind him.

▲ Lincoln becomes president.

> **VOCABULARY**
> **presidential election campaign**—the series of activities to get a person elected to be president
> **Republican Party**—one of the two main political parties in the United States
> **candidate**—a person who is working to get elected
> **existed**—was present, was there
> **majority**—an amount greater than half

 Activity: Newspaper Reports

Have students create a newspaper report that announces Lincoln winning the presidency in 1860.

Encourage students to illustrate the article with a diagram that shows what percentage of people voted for him. Then tell students that electing Lincoln did not solve the crisis, and have them read to find out why.

Students can find a map of the 1860 election results at http://fisher. lib.Virginia.edu/collections/stats/ elections/maps/1860.gif.

Differentiating Instruction

Beginning
Clarify Meanings To help students understand *majority*, take a poll, such as *How many ride the bus to school?* Have students identify the majority answer. Engage them in finding the root words *president* and *elect* in *presidential election* campaign. Explain that the goal of such a campaign is to become president.

Intermediate
Odd One Out Have students choose the word that doesn't fit in each list:

• Happiness	• Secede	• Allow
• Election	• Join	• Refuse
• Cheer	• Exit	• Permit

Advanced
Create a Glossary Ask students to create a Personal Glossary of the lesson's vocabulary words in their history notebooks.

▲ Here *dissolved* means "ended."

▲ Flag of the Confederate States of America

THE SOUTH SECEDES

Now the Southern states had to decide what to do. Some Southerners wanted to stay in the Union and work with the new president, but others **refused.**

In early 1861, just before Lincoln took office, 7 Southern states voted to **secede.** They were South Carolina, Mississippi, Florida, Alabama, Georgia, Louisiana, and Texas. These states joined together to found a new nation called the **Confederate States of America.** Soon 4 more states—Virginia, North Carolina, Tennessee, and Arkansas—joined them. America had split in two.

(**TALK AND SHARE**) **Tell your partner why the election of Abraham Lincoln was a problem for the South.**

VOCABULARY
refused—said no
secede—leave the United States and form a separate country
Confederate States of America—the nation founded in 1861 by Southern states that left the Union

Summary

For many years, slavery divided the North and South. Conflicts became bitter—then violent. When Abraham Lincoln was elected president, the South left the Union. The United States was split into two countries.

Primary Source

Uncle Tom's Cabin

In 1851, a story about slaves began to appear in a magazine. It was published one chapter at a time. People couldn't wait to read the next part. Would Mr. Shelby sell Uncle Tom to a slave trader? Would Eliza and her little boy get across the icy river before the slave catchers get them? Readers cried at the end, when a cruel owner had Uncle Tom whipped to death. The author of *Uncle Tom's Cabin* was Harriet Beecher Stowe. Her book did so much to change people's minds that when Abraham Lincoln met her, he said, "So you're the little woman who wrote the book that started this great war."

LESSON 12 • SEVEN YEARS TO CIVIL WAR **159**

Teach The South Secedes

■ Tell students the Southerners who seceded were known as Confederates.

■ Direct students to the map of the United States on pages 16–17.

■ Have students find the states that formed the Confederacy.

Primary Source

Uncle Tom's Cabin

■ Read aloud the feature about *Uncle Tom's Cabin.*

■ Emphasize that Stowe's book had an enormous impact. Prior to it, many Northerners thought slavery did not concern them.

■ Ask students:
• What effect do you think the book had on Northerners?
• Why did some Southerners resent the book?

(**TALK AND SHARE**)

Encourage students to use the new vocabulary word *secede* in their discussion.

Discuss the Summary

Read the Summary aloud with students. Then direct them to the timeline on pages 152 and 153 to create their own summaries of each event.

✓ Assessment

Assess students' comprehension by asking the following questions:

History
• Why did the Fugitive Slave Act and Kansas-Nebraska Act anger Northerners?
• What was the Dred Scott decision?
• Why did the South secede when Lincoln was elected president?

Language
Write or say sentences to show how the paired words are related:
• Balance
• Compromise
• Secede
• Confederate States of America
• Supreme Court
• Unconstitutional

Assessment Book
Use page 30 to assess students' comprehension.

Teach Interpreting

Tell students that interpreting is a useful skill for taking history tests. This page will teach them interpreting skills.

Model the Organizer

■ Elicit how details in the *after* column were not problems before. Ask students what changed.

■ Use these prompts to initiate discussion:

• Why did the North not have slavery before the Kansas-Nebraska Act?

• What happened in Kansas?

Give Practice Interpreting

Have students work in pairs to complete one activity.

■ **Draw** Refer students to the map on page 155 that shows the Missouri Compromise line. Suggest that students show in their drawings how the Missouri Compromise line was taken away in the Dred Scott decision.

■ **Write** In their paragraphs, students completing the Write activity should include effects of the Harpers Ferry raid on both the North and South.

Develop Language

Interpreting

Interpreting Events in History

When you interpret something, you explain what it means. How can you interpret an event in history? Look at the way things were *before* and *after* the event. What did the event mean in the history of the period? A Before-and-After Chart can help you see what the event might have caused.

Before-and-After Chart

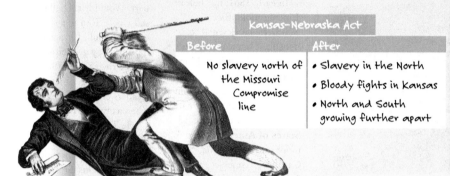

Kansas-Nebraska Act	
Before	**After**
No slavery north of the Missouri Compromise line	• Slavery in the North • Bloody fights in Kansas • North and South growing further apart

▲ Even Congress could be brutal. A Southern congressman beat a Northern senator with his cane after the senator made an angry speech about Kansas.

Practice Interpreting

1. Draw Write notes in a Before-and-After Chart for the Dred Scott decision. Make a drawing to show what the decision meant. Use it to explain this Supreme Court decision to your partner or group.

2. Write Interpret the importance of John Brown's raid on Harpers Ferry. First, list the important information in a Before-and-After Chart. Then use those details to write a paragraph of 3 or 4 sentences. Use words from the Word Bank in your paragraph.

Word Bank

slaves
masters
hero
dead
violence
insult
bad
worse

 Activity: Internet Resources

Students can do additional research on Lesson 12 topics at the following Internet sites on Lincoln and John Brown. Ask them to create a poster of their findings. Encourage them to draw or use illustrations and photos. Display their posters.

• http://www.pbs.org/wgbh/amex/lincolns

• http://www.pbs.org/wgbh/amex/brown

Differentiating Instruction

Beginning

Word Bank Provide this Word Bank of sentence starters for students to use as labels in their drawing. Have volunteers read the phrases aloud first:

• The Supreme Court said _____.

• The Missouri Compromise was _____.

• Northerners felt _____.

• Southerners felt _____.

• Slavery was illegal in _____.

• Slavery was legal in _____.

Intermediate

Arranging Ideas Suggest that students begin by describing who did what at Harpers Ferry. Next have them tell how the North and South reacted. Have them end by telling what the raid meant in the story of the country splitting apart.

Advanced

Using Vivid Language Encourage students to use words that help people feel and see events (for example, *wild, murderous, fanatic, heroic*).

Activities

Grammar Spotlight

Using Same and Different *Same* means "alike." *Different* means "not alike." These words are used when you make comparisons.

Using . . .	Examples	Focus
the same	*The South liked the Kansas-Nebraska Act. Some Northerners felt* the same.	Use *the same* when it stands alone.
the same as	*A few Northerners felt* the same as *Southerners about the Kansas-Nebraska Act.*	Use *the same as* when two things are compared in a sentence.
different from	*The Northern view of slavery was* different from *the Southern view.*	*Different from* is the opposite of *same as.*

Write two sentences comparing the Missouri Compromise and the Kansas-Nebraska Act. Use *the same as* and *different from* in your sentences.

Partner Practice

Taking Notes Together with your partner, read the information about taking notes on page 153. Then, as you read pages 154–159 together, decide what is important to write down. Share your notes with other groups or partners. Talk about what you chose to write. Tell each other why.

Hands On

Growing Problems Between North and South Make a poster for the classroom wall. Show the events that made problems between the North and the South grow worse. Use your imagination. Arrange the events on a staircase, or draw them in firecrackers that lead to a large explosion. Use a picture that shows how serious you believe these events were.

Activities

Grammar Spotlight

- Read the definitions of *same* and *different.*
- Read through the Focus column with students. Call on a volunteer to read the example sentences. Elicit how the sentences show what the Focus column describes.
- Ask volunteers to share their sentences with the class and write them on the board.

Partner Practice

Some students may have been taking notes as they read pages 154–159. Group these students together to share their notes.

Encourage all students to share their shortcuts and personal note-taking tips with their classmates.

Hands On

If possible, display the posters on the classroom wall so you can refer to them as students read Lesson 13 on the Civil War.

Activity: Extend the Lesson

To study the role of conflict and compromise in the world around them, tell students to notice conflicts outside school for a day.

Have them take notes on how the conflicts end. Is there compromise or growing unease? Gather students in a group to discuss their findings.

Program Resources

Student Activity Journal

Use page 59 to practice *interpreting.*

Overhead Transparencies

Use 2, Before-and-After Chart, with page 160.

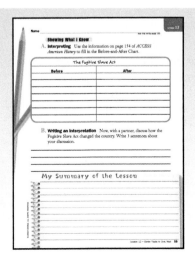

The Civil War

STANDARDS CONTENT

History
- Recognize how to read primary sources
- Recognize factors that influenced the outcome of the Civil War
- Explore major events of the Civil War
- Identify how the Union was saved

Language
- Identify the following Key Concepts: *liberty, freedom,* and *emancipation*
- Recognize idioms
- Practice making comparisons

Begin Building Background

- Read the lesson title to establish the subject (*civil war*).
- Ask students the question below the boy's picture. Encourage discussion.
- Point to the large picture and ask students to point out details such as the ages of the soldiers, the battlefield, and weaponry.
- Focus students on who the enemies are in a civil war, how soldiers might feel fighting their countrymen, and the difficult tolls of war.

Talk and Explore

The Civil War

Here you'll learn about the Civil War. You'll also learn how to read primary sources and practice making comparisons.

Building Background

▲ Some people think there should never be wars. But I think sometimes you have to fight. What do you think?

- **What do you see in the pictures?**
- **How do they make you feel?**
- **In your opinion, how could the war have been avoided?**

Before: A slave   After: A drummer in the Union Army

162 UNIT 4 • NEW STATES AND CIVIL WAR

 ### Activity: Postcards

Have student pairs compose a postcard to President Lincoln from a former slave who escaped to the North. Ask them to tell what this freed man or woman experienced and what Lincoln should do.

 ## Differentiating Instruction

Beginning
Picture Discussion Begin by reviewing these words from previous lessons: *forces, battles, defeat, military officers, crisis, Union, outnumbered, seceded, Confederate States of America.* In a circle discussion, have students take turns sharing their knowledge, ideas, thoughts, and questions about the pictures on pages 162 and 163.

Intermediate
Role-Play Have students choose one of the soldiers pictured on page 162

and role-play what he might have told his family when he left to serve in the Union army. What reasons would he give for serving? How would he feel?

Advanced
Photos: Primary Sources Tell students that photos also are primary sources. The photos on this page were shot during the Civil War. Have partners discuss what the two photos of the drummer boy tell them about history.

1 The Union

2 The Confederacy

3 Battle Losses

4 The Union Saved

Introduce the Big Idea

■ Review with students some of the major events leading to the Civil War.

- The Kansas-Nebraska Act (page 155)
- John Brown's raids (page 156)
- The Dred Scott decision (page 157)
- The South seceding from the Union (page 159)

■ Ask students what options the U.S. government had when the South seceded. Help them explore:

- Finding more compromises between the North and South
- Allowing the South to become a separate nation
- Going to war to keep the Union together

■ Then read aloud the Big Idea. Call on volunteers to point out details in the pictures and tell what they represent.

Review

In the previous lesson, students learned the events that led to the Civil War, as well as the differences between the North and the South.

Remind students of the differences between the colonists and the British during the American Revolution. Ask students, *How are the two events similar? How are they different? Give examples.*

 Activity: K-W-L Organizer

Guide students in creating a K-W-L Organizer to preview and track information throughout the lesson. Draw a K-W-L Organizer with the headings *What I Know, What I Want to Know*, and *What I Learned.*

Before reading the lesson, have students fill out the first two columns by listing things they already know about the Civil War (first column) and questions they have about it (second column).

 Activity: Real-World Connection

Invite students to compare the methods of warfare in the Civil War with those of today. Encourage them to use the pictures in this lesson as clues.

Emphasize that Civil War soldiers engaged in face-to-face combat with swords and rifles. Today's combat includes suicide bombing attacks by terrorists.

 Resource Library

Reader's Handbook (red)
Reading History 66–83

Reader's Handbook (yellow)
Reading Social Studies 58–73

All Write
Reading Primary Sources 224–226

Teach Key Concepts

- Say each Key Concept slowly while pointing to the corresponding picture.
- Ask students to repeat the words. Have students read aloud the descriptions of the words.
- Then call on volunteers to use the words in other sentences.

Teach the Visual Aid

The Civil War 1861–1865

- Focus students on the visual aid.
- Read through the charts with students. To reinforce the information, read aloud headings.
- Have students find the matching information and read it aloud.

Key Concepts

Liberty

Liberty is what the colonists wanted.

Freedom

Freedom is what the slaves did <u>not</u> have. It is another word for *liberty*.

Emancipation

Emancipation is the act of freeing slaves.

The Civil War 1861–1865

NORTH

The nation	United States of America
The army	Union Army
The capital	Washington, D.C.
The president	Abraham Lincoln
Its general	Ulysses S. Grant
What soldiers were called	Yankees, Yanks
Goals	■ Saving the Union ■ Ending slavery
Color	Blue

164 Unit 4 • New States and Civil War

Activity: Game Quiz

Divide the class into teams of four or five students each. Have the groups copy the headings for each row of the visual aid (*The nation, The army*) on a separate index card. Then have them create two cards labeled *North* and two labeled *South*.

Students can then play Game Quiz. The first player draws a card from both decks. The player can name or paraphrase the corresponding fact on the chart. If he or she cannot, anyone else on the team can give the answer.

Differentiating Instruction

Beginning

Verbal Response Ask students about the visual aid. Have them answer in complete sentences, using the words in your questions as guides.

Question: *Who was the general of the South?*

Answer: *The general of the South was Robert E. Lee.*

Intermediate

Partner Quiz Have partners quiz each other on the information in the visual aid charts. They can ask questions based on either the headings or the details. For example, *What was the capital of the South?*

Advanced

Memory Game Ask students to study the chart and then, with books closed, play I Remember. Have each player tell a fact listed in the visual aid. The next player must repeat what the other players said and add a new fact.

Reading Primary Sources

Primary sources are the documents written by people in history. They can be hard to read because they were written long ago and use hard words. Follow these steps when you read primary sources.

1. Look up unknown words in a dictionary.

2. Carefully watch the punctuation to see where ideas start and stop.

3. Study key words and phrases.

"The Gettysburg Address" is a primary source. It is a famous speech made by President Lincoln during the Civil War. His words gave strength and hope to the Union.

Lincoln's Words	Meaning
Four score and seven years	87 years
conceived	born
dedicated	set apart for a special purpose
proposition	idea

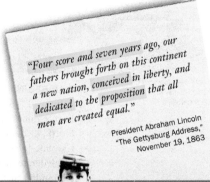

"Four score and seven years ago, our fathers brought forth on this continent a new nation, conceived in liberty, and dedicated to the proposition that all men are created equal."

President Abraham Lincoln
"The Gettysburg Address,"
November 19, 1863

SOUTH

The nation	Confederate States of America
The army	Confederate Army
The capital	Richmond, Virginia
The president	Jefferson Davis
Its general	Robert E. Lee
What soldiers were called	Rebels, Rebs, Johnny Reb
Goals	■ Keeping a way of life ■ Protecting states' rights
Color	Gray

LESSON 13 • THE CIVIL WAR **165**

Teach Skill Building

■ Read aloud Skill Building with students. Work through the three steps in reading primary sources by using Lincoln's quotation.

■ Ask a volunteer to suggest an unknown word in the quotation and demonstrate looking it up in the dictionary.

■ Model using the commas to "chunk" the quotation into readable parts. Then divide the class into three groups and have each of them read a "chunk" of the quote in turn.

■ Call on students to identify key words and phrases, such as *all men are created equal*.

■ Discuss Lincoln's quotation from "The Gettysburg Address." Ask students to paraphrase its meaning. (Sample response: *America was founded on the idea that all people are equal.*)

Activity: Quoting the Gettysburg Address

Divide the class into three groups. Assign each a part:

- *"That we here highly resolve that these dead shall not have died in vain,*

- *That this nation under God shall have a new birth of freedom,*

- *And that government of the people, by the people, for the people shall not perish from the earth."*

Have students paraphrase their part.

Program Resources

Student Activity Journal

Use page 60 to build key vocabulary.

Use page 61 to practice reading primary sources.

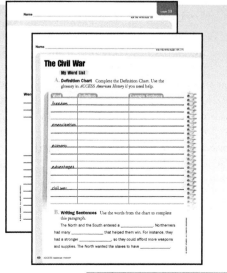

Introduce The Civil War

- Ask students to describe what they see in the upper left-hand corner. Elicit words such as *war, smoke, women,* and *soldiers.*

- Invite students to preview the lesson by reading the headings and studying the pictures. Ask, *What do you think you will learn about in this lesson?*

Key Connection: Government

- Discuss the meaning of national flags with students.

- Ask them what the symbols on the U.S. flag stand for. (*Fifty stars stand for the fifty states; thirteen stripes stand for the original thirteen colonies.*)

- Focus students on the Union flag on page 164.

- Ask what the thirty-four stars stand for. (*thirty-four states in 1861*)

- Explain that President Lincoln refused to remove the stars of the Southern states that had seceded.

Look and Read

▲ People went to watch the battle at Fort Sumter in Charleston, South Carolina.

The Confederate States of America

Virginia

North Carolina

South Carolina

Georgia

Florida

Alabama

Mississippi

Tennessee

Arkansas

Louisiana

Texas

The Civil War

The North and South had argued bitterly for years. In 1861, the two parts of America went to war against each other. After 4 years, the Union won. Many people died on both sides, and the South suffered terribly.

The North and South at War

No one expected the Civil War to be long. It became one of the worst wars in American history.

WAR BEGINS

In April 1861, the Civil War began at Fort Sumter. The fort belonged to the North, or the Union, but it was in South Carolina—deep in the South. The Confederate president, Jefferson Davis, **demanded** that Union forces leave the fort. President Lincoln **refused,** so the Confederate Army fired on Fort Sumter.

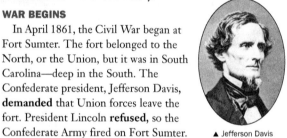

▲ Jefferson Davis

Immediately, more Southern states joined the **Confederacy.** In all, 11 states left the Union.

Border states weren't sure what to do. These states stayed in the Union. Slavery was legal in the border states, and many people sided with the South. Some people fought in the Confederate Army. Other people in the border states were **spies.** Some spies worked for the Union side and some for the Confederate side.

VOCABULARY

demanded—said firmly; called for
refused—said no to. Lincoln refused to let the South split off.
Confederacy—the states that left the Union. See the chart on the left.
border states—Union states on the border with the Confederacy: Delaware, Maryland, West Virginia, Kentucky, and Missouri
spies—people who find out or carry secret information in wartime

166 UNIT 4 • NEW STATES AND CIVIL WAR

 Activity: Civil War Maps

Working in pairs, have students draw a U.S. map or copy one from the Internet (http://abcteach.com/Maps/usa.htm). Ask them to shade the Confederate states gray, the Union states blue, and put stripes in the border states. Then have them mark where the first shot of the Civil War was fired.

 Differentiating Instruction

Beginning

Choral Reading Have students read aloud together with you. Begin with the title and headings. Then have students follow along as either you or more fluent students read the lesson aloud. Next, put students in pairs to read the lesson again, switching turns after each sentence.

Intermediate

Finding Key Ideas Divide the class into pairs to read through the lesson. Suggest that students pause after each paragraph to identify key words or ideas. Ask them to jot down any questions they may have.

Advanced

Reading Aloud Form a circle and have students take turns reading two sentences at a time. At the end of each page, have the group briefly discuss the main ideas.

DIFFERENCES BETWEEN THE STATES

In fighting the war, the main aim of the North was to save the Union. Ending slavery became an important goal later. The main goal of the South was to keep its way of life—including slavery. The South also believed strongly in **states' rights,** including a state's right to leave the nation.

Both sides had certain **advantages.** The North had a stronger **economy.** Its army and navy were bigger and better **equipped.** Also, it had a wise and strong leader in President Abraham Lincoln.

The South had a smaller population. It also had less money, food, and supplies. But it had some advantages too. Excellent **military** leaders came from the South. Most of the fighting was located in the South, so the land was **familiar** to Southern soldiers. They fought hard for their land and homes.

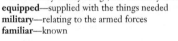 **TALK AND SHARE** With a partner, talk about how the Civil War began and how the North and South were different.

VOCABULARY

states' rights—the idea that states had joined together freely and had power in government
advantages—strengths someone else doesn't have
economy—the state, or condition, of business activities. When people have money to buy things, the economy is strong.
equipped—supplied with the things needed
military—relating to the armed forces
familiar—known

> *"A house divided against itself cannot stand."*
>
> President Abraham Lincoln
> The "House Divided Speech"
> June 16, 1858

▲ Lincoln quoted these lines from the Bible to say he believed the United States could not stay half slave and half free.

▲ Soldiers rest at Petersburg, Virginia

Teach About Differences Between the States

- The states that made up the Confederacy deeply believed in their cause and their right to form a separate country in order to keep their way of life.

- Ask students, *Does the Confederacy's determination remind you of another group in American history?*

TALK AND SHARE

Provide vocabulary prompts to students who have trouble finding this information in the text. Encourage them to look for the boldfaced words to help them reply.

Review

Ask students if they would be willing to fight for their or someone else's freedom. Why or why not? Ask them to support their answer.

 Activity: Role-Play

Create an equal number of index cards labeled *North* and *South*. There should be enough cards for the entire class. Shuffle the cards. Then write these roles on the board: *soldier, parent of a soldier, army nurse, African American, politician.*

Have students take turns drawing a North or South card. Then ask them to choose one of the roles listed on the board and role-play how that person feels about the Civil War.

 Program Resources

Student Activity Journal

Assign page 62:

- To create study notes for students to review
- To provide reinforcement of key vocabulary

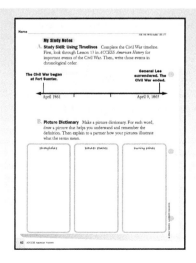

Discuss **The Battlefield**

- Have students locate Vicksburg, Virginia, on a U.S. map.

- Then have a volunteer trace the path of the Mississippi River to the Gulf of Mexico.

- Ask which Southern states west of the river were cut off from the Confederacy. (*Texas, Louisiana, Arkansas*)

Primary Source

"The Gettysburg Address"

Discuss with students the ideas in "The Gettysburg Address." Ask the following questions:

- How do you think it made listeners feel during the war?

- What happened at the battlefield?

- Why was that a powerful place to give the speech?

▲ Fierce fighting at Gettysburg

The Battlefield

For the first two years of the Civil War, the fight was mostly even. Then, slowly, the Union Army began to win.

MAJOR BATTLES

At first, the two armies were almost equal. Battles were **ferocious** and deadly. On September 17, 1862, for instance, more than 23,000 soldiers died or were **wounded** at the Battle of Antietam, in Maryland. It was the bloodiest day of fighting in the Civil War.

Then, in July 1863, the Union won two important battles. At the Battle of Vicksburg in Mississippi, Union General Ulysses S. Grant got control of the Mississippi River. His victory cut the Confederacy in half.

At the same time, Confederate General Robert E. Lee **invaded** the North. His army had reached Pennsylvania. But, at the Battle of Gettysburg, Pennsylvania, Union leaders **defeated** Lee. They drove his troops back toward the South.

Gettysburg and Vicksburg were **turning points** of the war. After those battles, the Union Army slowly began to win. Still, the fighting would last almost two more terrible years.

VOCABULARY

ferocious—fierce, like an animal
wounded—injured or hurt
invaded—led an army into a land to take it over

defeated—beat
turning points—events that change the way things are going

Primary Source

"The Gettysburg Address"

In July 1863, more than 50,000 soldiers were killed or wounded in the Battle of Gettysburg. A few months later, President Lincoln gave a speech on that sad battleground. "These dead [men] shall not have died in vain," said the president. He vowed that their deaths would help save the Union and freedom itself. "We here highly resolve," he said, "that government of the people, by the people, for the people, shall not perish from the earth."

 Activity: Sequence Organizer

Ask students to work in pairs to create a Sequence Organizer that shows key events on Civil War battlefields. Use Overhead Transparency 24, Sequence Notes.

Civil War Battles

Differentiating Instruction

Beginning
Describing the Pictures Provide the following terms to students. In pairs, ask them to take turns using the words to identify pictures in the lesson:

- Union flag
- Union soldier
- Confederate soldier
- Civil War
- President Lincoln
- "The Gettysburg Address"

Intermediate/Advanced
Practicing the Speech Assign half the students the opening quotation from "The Gettysburg Address" on page 165 and the other half the ending quotation of "The Gettysburg Address" in the Primary Source box.

Have students practice the parts until they can say them fluently. Then group students in a circle. Have them take turns standing and delivering the beginning and ending lines of "The Gettysburg Address."

FIGHTING THE WAR

Soldiers suffered terrible **hardships** during the Civil War. **Losses**—hundreds of thousands of them—were felt on both sides. In addition, Confederate soldiers lacked food and supplies. Because the war was a **civil war,** it **pitted** American against American. Sometimes brother battled brother. Neighbor battled neighbor. Father battled son.

MEMORIAL DAY

This holiday, celebrated on the last Monday in May, honors those who have died in war. It began as a day to remember the soldiers who died in the Civil War. The first Memorial Day was May 30, 1868. On that day, at Arlington National Cemetery, flowers were put on the graves of both Union and Confederate soldiers.

TALK AND SHARE **Look at the map with your partner. Talk about the battles shown on it. Where were they?**

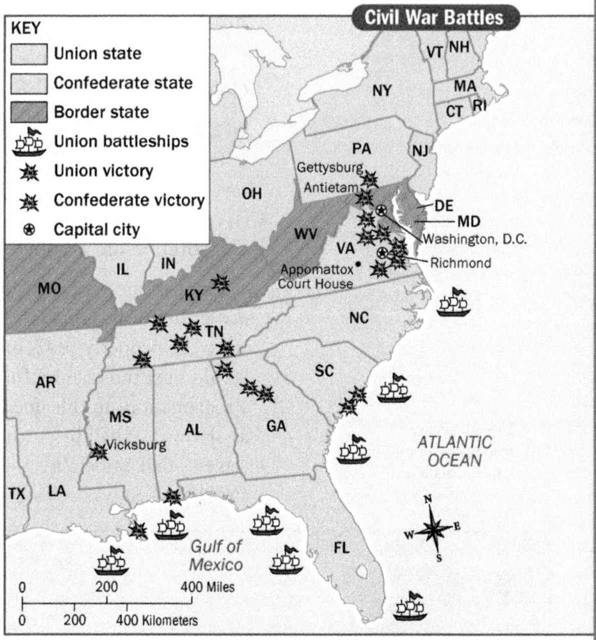

Civil War Battles
KEY
Union state
Confederate state
Border state
Union battleships
Union victory
Confederate victory
Capital city
VT
NH
NY
MA
CT
RI
PA
NJ
Gettysburg
Antietam
OH
DE
MD
Washington, D.C.
WV
VA
Richmond
Appomattox Court House
IL
IN
MO
KY
TN
NC
AR
SC
MS
AL
GA
Vicksburg
ATLANTIC OCEAN
TX
LA
N
W
E
S
Gulf of Mexico
FL
0
200
400 Miles
0
200
400 Kilometers

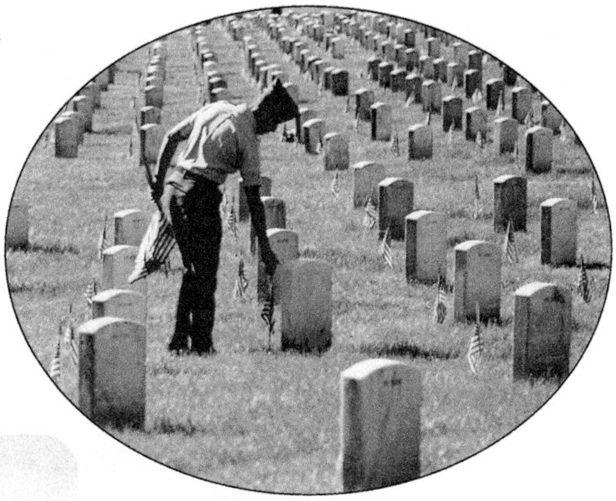

▲ Arlington National Cemetery

VOCABULARY

hardships—difficulties, problems
losses—deaths
civil war—a war between parts of the same country
pitted—set to fight

Talk About Fighting the War

- Help students understand the critical toll of the Civil War by working with the map on page 169.
- Ask volunteers to identify facts such as:
  - Names of important battlefields
  - Locations of battlefields
- Ask students what they think about the war so far. Have them use vocabulary words such as *suffered, defeated, ferocious, refused,* and *states' rights.*

TALK AND SHARE

To reinforce their discussion, suggest that students mark the major Civil War battles on their own map outlines.

Activity: Costs of War

In small groups, have students create posters that show the costs of war. Have them discuss the losses that war brings about. In addition, have them discuss what costs a civil war brings about.

Encourage students to draw on their prior knowledge from wars they have studied in this book, as well as wars they know about from TV, the newspaper, or their own experience.

Present the following category prompts on the board:

- Human Life and Health
- Economic Loss
- The Land
- Bond Among Citizens

Afterward, reassemble the class. Ask spokespersons from the groups to present their posters.

Then display them in the classroom as students work through the lesson.

Discuss The Union Saved

- Explain that the Emancipation Proclamation freed all slaves in the Confederacy.

- The United States Constitution did not permit President Lincoln to free slaves throughout the nation.

- However, as commander-in-chief, Lincoln could free Southern slaves in order to weaken enemy forces in time of war.

- The Emancipation Proclamation had a huge impact on the country. Have students study the scene on page 170. Ask:
  - What do you think the people in the picture will do now?
  - How do you think they feel?

The Union Saved

In 1863, President Lincoln freed the slaves in the Confederacy. By 1865, the Civil War was over.

THE EMANCIPATION PROCLAMATION

Early in the war, President Lincoln's main goal was to save the Union, not to end slavery. Lincoln himself believed slavery was wrong. However, being a lawyer, he knew the Constitution did not give him the power to end slavery.

Later in the war, Lincoln had an idea. The Constitution *did* let him take property away from an enemy. The slaves were the property of Confederates. If he freed them, it would hurt the enemy! In 1863, he wrote the Emancipation Proclamation. In this document, he said that "persons held as slaves . . . shall be . . . forever free." He didn't free all the slaves—that came after the war—but the Emancipation Proclamation was an important first step.

A Union soldier reads news of the Emancipation Proclamation to a family of slaves. ▼

 Activity: Response Web

In pairs, have students create a Response Web that gives the responses of various people to the Emancipation Proclamation.

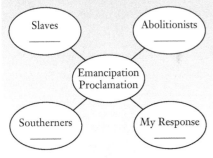

 Differentiating Instruction

Beginning

Vocabulary Review Work with students to identify the roots of emancipation and proclamation (*emancipate, proclaim*). Point out that *-(t)ion* words are nouns.

Review the following vocabulary words with students and have them create word wheels for each: *emancipation proclamation, population, representation, plantation, revolution, rebellion*.

Intermediate

Pantomime In groups, have students take turns acting out the meanings of the vocabulary words for Lesson 13. The rest of the group should guess which word is being enacted.

Advanced

Word Grid Ask students to create a Word Grid with these five headings: *Vocabulary Word, Similar Word, Opposite, Another Form of,* and *Sentence*. They should fill in the boxes using the vocabulary words in this lesson.

THE CONFEDERACY SURRENDERS

During 1864 and 1865, the Confederate Army lost its **strongholds.** On April 2, 1865, Southern troops **fled** their capital of Richmond, Virginia. General Lee knew the time had come to **surrender.** "There is nothing left for me to do but go and see General Grant, and I would rather die a thousand deaths," he said. On April 9, 1865, Lee surrendered to Grant at a small town in Virginia called Appomattox Court House. The bloodiest war in American history was over.

The Civil War had taken a terrible toll on America. In it, 620,000 soldiers died. The cities and fields of the South lay in **ruins.** But the Union was saved, and the evil of slavery was gone forever from America. Now the country, whole once more, turned to heal its wounds.

(**TALK AND SHARE**) **Tell your partner why the Emancipation Proclamation was important.**

Language Notes
Idioms
These sayings don't mean what they seem.

☐ **die a thousand deaths:** nothing could be worse

☐ **taken a terrible toll:** been "paid for" with many, many lives

☐ **heal its wounds:** do the things needed to make it well again

General Grant, seated on the right, watches while General Lee signs the surrender document. ▼

VOCABULARY
strongholds—the strongest places
fled—ran away from
surrender—declare that the enemy has won and the fighting can stop
ruins—what is left after buildings fall to pieces or are blasted

Summary

In 1865, the South surrendered. The long and brutal Civil War was over. Hundreds of thousands of people had died, and the South was in ruins. But now the country was whole again, and slavery was soon gone forever.

Teach The Confederacy Surrenders

Explain that General Grant was somber at Lee's surrender. Grant wrote this in his memoirs of that time:

"I felt like anything rather than rejoicing at the downfall of a foe who had fought so long and valiantly, and had suffered so much for a cause, though the cause was, I believe, one of the worst for which a people ever fought."

Language Notes

Read through the Language Notes with students and guide them in finding the sample idioms in context. Then call on volunteers to use the idioms in a sentence of their own.

TALK AND SHARE

Have partners complete the Talk and Share activity. Then gather as a class and ask students to share their responses.

Discuss the **Summary**

■ Call on volunteers to read aloud the Summary.

■ Then have students work in a group to create their own summaries using the headings in Lesson 13.

✔ **Assessment**

Assess students' comprehension by asking the following questions:

History

• What advantages did the Union Army have?

• What advantages did the Confederate Army have?

• What happened at Gettysburg?

• How did the Civil War end?

Language
Which word does not belong?

• Advantages, liberty, freedom, emancipation

• Flee, surrender, retreat, pit

• Hardships, strongholds, ruins, losses

Assessment Book
Use page 31 to assess students' comprehension.

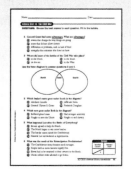

Teach Comparing

Students need to compare and contrast different things in their study of history. Venn Diagrams will help them visualize differences and similarities between things.

Model the Organizer

- Have students read aloud the three parts of the Venn Diagram.
- Reinforce their understanding by asking, *What was an outcome of the Civil War for the South? For the North? For both?*

Give Practice Comparing

Have students work in pairs to complete one activity.

- **Draw** Show students how to make a Venn Diagram for this exercise by drawing two overlapping ovals.

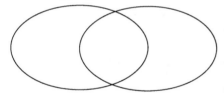

- **Write** To refresh their memories about the advantages of each army, refer students to page 167.

Develop Language

Comparing

Making Comparisons

When you compare and contrast, you tell how things are alike and different. It helps to put your ideas in a Venn Diagram like the one below. This diagram shows the outcome of the Civil War for the North and for the South.

Venn Diagram

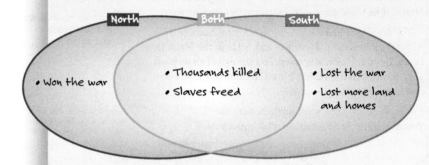

North / Both / South
- Won the war
- Thousands killed
- Slaves freed
- Lost the war
- Lost more land and homes

Practice Comparing

1. Draw Make a Venn Diagram to compare the goals each side had in fighting the war. Draw pictures or write words in the circles. Then use the Venn Diagram to tell your partner or group how the goals of the North were alike and different from the goals of the South.

2. Write Make a Venn Diagram to compare the advantages each army had at the start of the war. Write a paragraph of 3 to 4 sentences comparing the advantages of the Union Army and the Confederate Army. Use such words as *both, however, like,* and *but.* You also may want to use words from the Word Bank.

Word Bank

money
population
supplies
leaders
familiar land
soldiers
army
president

🏃 Activity: Internet Resources

Students can do additional research on Lesson 13 topics at the following Internet sites. Ask them to create a poster of their findings.

- http://memory.loc.gov/ammem/ cwphtml/cwphome.html
- http://www.cr.nps.gov/museum/ exhibits/gettex
- http://www2.lhric.org/ pocantico/civilwar/cwar.htm

📶 Differentiating Instruction

Beginning

Key Words Write the following key words and phrases on the board to provide support for the Draw activity:

- Confederacy
- Union
- Way of life
- Stop slavery
- Save the Union
- States' rights

Intermediate

Improving Writing Focus students on using linking words, such as *and, but,* neither/nor, either/or, both, and however, to make their writing smoother.

Advanced

Revising Paragraphs Help students organize their paragraphs. Suggest that one good way to arrange their information is by telling the advantages of one army at a time. For example, they could tell the advantages of the Union army and then compare these to the Confederates' advantages.

Activities

Grammar Spotlight

Using _and, or,_ and _but_ The words _and, or,_ and _but_ join ideas.

Rule	Examples
■ Use _and_ to add an idea.	Slavery was legal, and Southerners fought to keep it.
■ Use _but_ to show that one idea goes _against_ another idea.	The Rebels lacked supplies, but they had excellent generals.
■ Use _or_ to show a choice.	Lincoln had to give up Fort Sumter or fight for it.

Write 3 sentences about the Civil War. Use _and_ in one sentence. Use _or_ in another sentence, and use _but_ in the last sentence.

Hands On

Draw What It Means To You Lincoln's "House Divided Speech" is a primary source. Read the sentence from it on page 167. Talk with your partner about the sentence. Share your ideas. Then show that you understand what it means by drawing a picture. Show your picture to the class and explain how you understand Lincoln's words.

Oral Language

In Their Own Words Make cards for each of these sentences from primary sources. You may want to illustrate them. Then read them out loud with a partner or small group.

"My shoes are gone; my clothes are almost gone. I'm weary; I'm sick; I'm hungry."
— _Confederate soldier, 1863_

"The Emancipation Proclamation is the greatest event of our nation's history."
—_Frederick Douglass, 1864_

"If my name ever goes into history, it will be for this act."
—_Abraham Lincoln, 1863, referring to the_ Emancipation Proclamation

Activities

Grammar Spotlight

■ Read aloud the Grammar Spotlight with students.

■ Ask a volunteer to share his/her sentences about the Civil War. Have him/her read the sentences aloud.

Hands On

Discuss the sentence with students. Students with limited English proficiency might need a lesson about metaphors, such as Lincoln's comparison of the country to a physical house.

Oral Language

Encourage students to practice their lines until they can say them fluently and with expression. Ask them to imagine their facial expressions before acting out their parts.

Activity: Extend the Lesson

To learn more about Lesson 13 topics, suggest these books:

• _If You Lived at the Time of the Civil War_ by Kay Moore and Anni Matsick (Scholastic, 1994)

• _War, Terrible War (History of Us)_ by Joy Hakim (Oxford University Press, 2000)

• _Behind Rebel Lines: The Incredible Story of Emma Edmonds, Civil War Spy_ by Seymour Reit (Gulliver Books, 2001)

Program Resources

Student Activity Journal
Use page 63 to practice _comparing._

Overhead Transparencies
Use 31, Venn Diagram, with page 172.

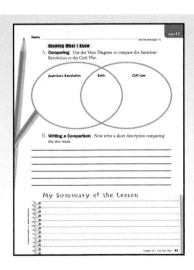

After the Civil War

STANDARDS CONTENT

History

- Recognize the message in political cartoons
- Identify the Thirteenth, Fourteenth, and Fifteenth Amendments
- Recognize the effects of Reconstruction on the South and on African Americans
- Recognize the effects of the Homestead Act and the transcontinental railroad on the settlement of the continent

Language

- Identify the following Key Concepts: *reconstruction, reaction,* and *bitterness*
- Distinguish words that form confusing word pairs
- Practice explaining an event

Begin Building Background

- Draw students' attention to the photo on page 174. Have students describe the scene.
- Ask students the questions below the photo. Provide them with words as needed, such as *building, destroy, attack,* and *bricks.*
- Draw out key ideas about what happens when a war ends:
  - The fighting stops.
  - People may still be angry with one another.
  - Some people may want to make a new life for themselves somewhere else.

Talk and Explore

After the Civil War

Here you'll learn how America changed after the Civil War. You'll also study political cartoons and practice explaining events in history.

Building Background

▲ Some people leave a country after a war.

- **What do you think happened here?**
- **How would you feel if this was your city?**
- **What can people do after a war is over?**

174 UNIT 5 • A CHANGING AMERICA

 Activity: Word Category

Have students work in pairs or small groups. Ask them to name words they think of when they look at the picture on page 174. Encourage them to come up with two kinds of words: words that describe feelings, such as *sad, angry,* and *scared,* and words that tell about the picture, such as *destroyed* and *broken.* Have students write their words on index cards. Then have students sort the cards according to whether the word tells about the picture or about feelings.

Differentiating Instruction

Beginning
Describing the Picture Write the sentence *I see ____.* on the board. Have students use the sentence to tell the things they see in the picture, such as windows or bricks.

Intermediate
Caption Writing Have students work in pairs to write two different captions for the picture. Encourage them to use what they know about the Civil War from the previous lesson. Then have students share their captions with the class.

Advanced
War Stories Encourage students to think about a war they know about and how it felt or would feel once the war was over. Have them write three sentences on this topic. Then have them share their sentences with a partner.

After the Civil War, slavery ended. Former slaves became citizens. At first, African Americans in the South gained power in government. In time, they lost many of their early gains. Many Americans moved west to the Great Plains to start new lives.

1 Changes After the War

2 African Americans After the War

3 Settling the Great Plains

Introduce the Big Idea

■ Read aloud the Big Idea and the three headings on page 175.

■ Point in succession to the pictures marked 1, 2, and 3. Ask volunteers to describe what is happening in each picture.

■ Explain that many changes took place after the Civil War ended:
  • Many peoples' lives became very different.
  • African Americans were no longer slaves.
  • Some people moved to new parts of the country.

Teach the Pictures

The middle picture, an illustration titled "The First Vote," appeared on the front cover of *Harper's Weekly* magazine in 1867. Three African-American men—an older man, a man in fine clothes, and a soldier—stand in line to cast ballots in the first election that allowed them to vote.

Review

Connect to the key content of Lessons 11–13. Reinforce the reasons that the United States went to war. Ask students to predict how the country changed after the Union's victory.

Activity: Role-Play

With a volunteer, role-play a discussion between two soldiers who have just learned that the war is over. One soldier is grateful that there will be no more fighting. The other soldier is angry that their side lost.

Prepare a script such as this.

First Soldier: *At last! This horrible war has ended!*

Second Soldier: *Why are you so happy about it? We lost!*

First Soldier: *Yes, but now I can go home to my family. I've missed them a lot. Don't you miss your own family?*

Second Soldier: *Yes, but I would rather stay and fight. I'm still very angry with the enemy!*

Then discuss the role-play with students. Which students sympathized more with the angry soldier? Which students sympathized more with the happy one? Why? Tie the discussion back to the lesson by asking students what they think the soldiers should do now that the war is over.

Resource Library

Reader's Handbook (red)
Cartoon 550–551

Reader's Handbook (yellow)
Elements of Graphics 425–435

All Write
Reading Symbols and Charts 277–284

Teach [Key Concepts]

- To model correct pronunciation, say each term slowly. Ask students to repeat after you. Then read aloud the Key Concept sentences and talk about what they mean.

- Have students connect *reaction* and *bitterness* to a different historical event or to a current event.

- Have them write a short description about the event using the terms.

Teach the Visual Aid

People Moved to the Great Plains

- Have students look carefully at the pictures and the text.

- Tell students this graphic is not a timeline. It does not reflect chronological order. These events characterized the period from 1865 to 1880.

- Ask students to describe each picture.

- Then explain each change briefly.

- Invite students to show which changes tell about homes, farms, transportation, and conflict.

Talk and Explore

Key Concepts

Reconstruction   **Reaction**   **Bitterness**

Reconstruction was the series of steps that Congress took to bring the Southern states back into the country.

Some of the steps were hard on Southern white people. One **reaction** they had was **bitterness.** Bitterness is a feeling people have when something is painful and hard to accept.

People Moved to the Great Plains

Homesteaders settled the land.   **Trains carried people and goods.**   **Native Americans fought back and lost.**

176 UNIT 5 • A CHANGING AMERICA

 Activity: Life on the Plains

Have students use the pictures to make guesses about what life was like for settlers of the Great Plains. Students should choose a pictured person and write some phrases or sentences describing his or her life. Have students share their ideas.

 Differentiating Instruction

Beginning

Guessing the Picture Have students work with a partner. One student thinks of one of the pictures and gives brief verbal clues to its identity. Possible clues include *It shows a way to travel* or *It shows how people farmed.* The partner then guesses the picture. Then ask partners to switch roles.

Intermediate

Alike and Different Have students find what makes the pictures alike and what makes them different. Students can then draw or tell their ideas to one another in small groups.

Advanced

Telling Ideas Have students imagine what it would be like to be a person in one of the pictures. Students should write down a few key words to help them remember their ideas. Then they can tell their ideas aloud to a partner or a small group.

Reading Political Cartoons

Political cartoons express opinions about political figures, issues, or government. Newspapers have cartoons on the editorial page. On that page, editors and other writers give their opinions about people and events in the news. Here's how to read a cartoon.

1. Read all the words.

2. Figure out who the people are.

3. Ask yourself, "What is the subject?"

4. Look carefully at each thing in the picture. Ask yourself, "Why did the artist put it in?"

5. Study the overall tone. How are people feeling? What are they doing?

6. Think and decide, "What opinion does this cartoon give?"

1850—Driven by the Negro

PLANTERS HOTEL

1870—Still driven by the Negro

▲ The lives of African Americans, called *Negroes* in the 1800s, changed from 1850 to 1870. This cartoon comments on how the change affected white Southerners.

Cowboys drove cattle to markets.

Stronger plows and machines helped farmers.

Teach Skill Building

■ Read the first paragraph on page 177 with students.

■ Point out that most cartoons students know are meant to be funny. A political cartoon, in contrast, may or may not be funny but always uses drawings to say something about the news.

■ Read through the numbered steps on page 177 with students.

■ Remind students that the people and objects in the picture may also be symbols that stand for something else.

■ Discuss the political cartoon on page 177 with students. Point out what the men are doing in the two panels. Call students' attention to the way that both parts of the cartoon have similar captions.

■ If students don't understand the cartoon, explain: *In 1850, the closest African Americans got to voting was when they drove a rich Southerner to the polls to vote. But in 1870, African Americans got the right to vote, and then they could "drive" white Southerners away from power by electing black representatives.*

⚒ Activity: Draw Political Cartoons

Have students identify important issues or controversies in their school or communities. Then have them draw political cartoons expressing a point of view on these topics. Remind them that the cartoon should express an opinion and encourage others to agree. Invite volunteers to draw cartoons on the board.

📖 Program Resources

Student Activity Journal

Use page 64 to build key vocabulary.

Use page 65 to practice reading a political cartoon.

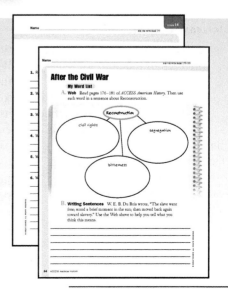

Introduce After the Civil War

- Ask students what they think they will learn from these two pages. Have students read the headings and look at the pictures and make predictions about what they will read about.

- Work with students to begin creating a K-W-L Chart about the headings in the Big Idea. Label the chart *After the Civil War*. Have students tell what they know and what they want to know about new settlements and the status of African Americans after the war. Save the chart for future use.

Language Notes

- Draw students' attention to the Language Notes. Point out to students how the paired words can easily be confused with one another. Help students understand the differences between these and other confusing word pairs.

- Students can work in pairs to write sentences for the paired words.

- Each partner should pick one of the words in the pair and write a sentence for it.

- Partners should read their sentences to each other.

Look and Read

After the Civil War

The Civil War tore the nation apart. Now Americans needed to put it back together again.

▲ John Wilkes Booth shot President Lincoln on April 14, 1865, while Lincoln and his wife were watching a play.

Language Notes

Confusing Word Pairs
These words are easily mixed up.

- [ ] want: feel a need
- [ ] went: left

- [ ] chance: an opportunity
- [ ] change: a difference

- [ ] former: earlier; used to be
- [ ] farmer: a worker who grows food

Changes After the War

When the Civil War ended in 1865, much of the South lay in ruins. About 260,000 of its soldiers were dead. Southern business was badly hurt. **Bitterness** was strong on both sides.

DEATH OF LINCOLN

President Lincoln did not want to **punish** the South. His goal was to bring the war-torn nation back together. However, Lincoln had no chance to work out his peace plan. Just 5 days after General Lee surrendered, Lincoln was **assassinated.** The nation's great leader was gone.

RECONSTRUCTION

After Lincoln's death, a **radical** Congress took charge and began **Reconstruction.** It voted to give former slaves and poor whites food and clothing. It set up hospitals and schools in the South.

Congress was harsh in other ways. It passed laws making it very hard for Confederate leaders to be elected to Congress or to state government jobs. It sent federal troops into the South to make sure the new laws were followed. White Southerners became bitter over these changes.

VOCABULARY

bitterness—a deep, painful feeling of anger
punish—make someone suffer for doing wrong
assassinated—killed. This word is used for the murder of a public leader.
radical—extreme, or far to one side
Reconstruction—the series of steps that Congress took to bring the Southern states back into the country

---

 Activity: Concentration

Have students work in pairs. Have them write each of the nine vocabulary words for pages 178–179 on an index card. Have them make nine more cards with brief words or pictures that define the words. Working in pairs, students shuffle the eighteen cards, lay them out facedown, and take turns turning over two at once. They may keep any cards in which the word and definition match.

Differentiating Instruction

Beginning
Working with Headings Emphasize the idea of change. Ask volunteers to show or tell about something that has changed in their own lives. Then explain that each of the headings on pages 178–179 tells about a change that took place soon after the Civil War.

Intermediate
Paired Reading Have one student read a paragraph aloud while the other follows along. For the next paragraph,

have them switch roles. After each section, have partners discuss it.

Advanced
Small Group Discussion When discussing the Talk and Share activity on page 179, students should point to the parts of the text that support their ideas.

CHANGES TO THE CONSTITUTION

Congress wrote 3 new **amendments** to the Constitution. It passed laws saying that the Southern states had to vote for the amendments. The new amendments gave **civil rights** to all African Americans. For the first time, the former slaves could vote and use the courts.

Reconstruction Amendments

13th Amendment	1865	Ended slavery
14th Amendment	1868	Made all people born in the United States full citizens
15th Amendment	1870	Protected the right to vote for all male citizens, including former slaves

▲ What opinion about carpetbaggers does this cartoon show?

BITTERNESS IN THE SOUTH

Many white Southerners hated the new laws. They were angry at Northerners who moved to the South to get rich off Southern pain. They called them **carpetbaggers**. They were angry at the **scalawags** who worked with the new state governments. Most of all, white Southerners were bitter that their former slaves suddenly had new rights.

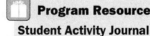 **TALK AND SHARE**) Talk with your partner about the changes that came after the war. Tell what people thought of them.

VOCABULARY
amendments—changes to a document
civil rights—the rights of citizens
carpetbaggers—Northerners who moved South after the war for financial gain. The name came from the idea that they carried all their things in a bag made from carpets.
scalawags—white Southerners who worked with the new state governments

Government

Amending the Constitution

Passing an amendment to the U.S. Constitution is hard. Many more than half the people in the country must want it. Two steps are needed to make an amendment.

Step 1. Proposing the Amendment
The amendment must be called for by 2/3 of both houses of Congress or by 2/3 of the states.

Step 2. Ratifying the Amendment
The amendment must be voted for by 3/4 of the state legislatures or by conventions in 3/4 of the states.

Teach Changes to the Constitution

- Explain that these amendments were especially important in the process of expanding the Constitution to include all people.

- Explore the idea of bitterness in the South over the new amendments. Ask students why some people might have been angry at the government.

- Explain that the terms *carpetbagger* and *scalawag* are not used today. These were insulting names that white Southerners gave to people who they felt had betrayed or abused them.

- Talk about the opinion expressed by the political cartoons on pages 177 and 179.

TALK AND SHARE

Encourage students to record their ideas in words or pictures.

Government

Amending the Constitution

- Sketch a simple flow chart on the board and help students draw the process by which an amendment becomes part of the Constitution.

- Point out that the process is designed to be difficult. Amendments are more powerful than ordinary laws, so they must reflect the will of the people.

Activity: Reconstruction Amendment Cartoons

To help students remember the big ideas of the Thirteenth, Fourteenth, and Fifteenth Amendments, have them draw a four-panel cartoon with captions showing the new rights won by African Americans.

Sample captions:

- I am a slave.
- Now I am free.
- Now I am a citizen.
- Now I can vote.

Program Resources

Student Activity Journal

Assign page 66:

- To create study notes for students to review
- To provide reinforcement of key vocabulary

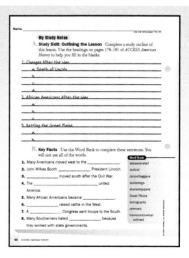

Discuss African Americans After the War

■ Emphasize to students that the legal condition of African Americans changed sharply during Reconstruction. Before the war, they were property; now, they were free. For the first time, slaves had choices.

■ Ask students to imagine themselves as newly freed former slaves. Ask:
  • How would you feel about gaining your freedom?
  • What would you do next?
  • How would your life change?

■ Remind students that African Americans still were very poor and not well educated, so life continued to be very difficult for the freed slaves.

■ Ask students to think about which of their answers in the discussion above were realistic for people with little money or schooling.

■ Explain to students that new laws may not change the way people are treated or the amount of money they have.

African Americans After the War

The war won freedom for millions of African Americans. However, making a new life was often hard.

Sharecropper family ▼

SHARECROPPERS

Most African Americans in the South had nothing. To make a living, many former slaves became **sharecroppers.** Now they could sell part of the crops they grew. Even so, sharecroppers were poor no matter how hard they worked.

GAINS

In many ways, life was better for blacks. For the first time, former slaves went to schools. A part of the federal government called the Freedmen's Bureau helped former slaves. It set up more than 40 hospitals, 4,000 schools for children, and 74 schools to train teachers. People set up colleges for African Americans.

Reconstruction laws helped African Americans enter **politics.** Sixteen African Americans were elected to Congress during these years after the war. Many other African Americans were elected to jobs in the new state governments.

▲ Some of the first African-American congressmen. Hiram Revels, seated on the left, was the first African American elected to the U.S. Senate.

VOCABULARY
sharecroppers—people who live on someone else's land and farm it for them
politics—government

Activity: Compound Words

Draw students' attention to the word *sharecropper.* Point out the two roots *share* and *crop.* Explain that words made up of two or more other words are called *compound* words.

Have students generate other compound words for a list to display on the wall. Challenge students to find other vocabulary terms in this lesson that are compound words (*carpetbagger, cowman, railroad*).

Differentiating Instruction

Beginning
Reading Aloud Read the introductory paragraph aloud. Then read the headings on pages 180–181 aloud. Use simple words and phrases, such as *Things get better/Things get worse,* to illustrate the concepts of *gains* and *reversals.* Have students use words or simple sentences to tell one another some gains and reversals from their own lives.

Intermediate
Summarizing Have students work in pairs. Have one student read each

paragraph aloud. Have the other summarize what has just been read. Then students should switch roles.

Advanced
Group Work Have students work in small groups to discuss these questions:
  • What were some of the gains for African Americans during Reconstruction?
  • Why do you think those gains did not last?

REVERSAL

In the 1870s, new leaders took over Congress. The people who wanted to punish the South were voted out. By 1877, African Americans had a **reversal** of fortune.

The new leaders pulled government troops out of the South. Soon former Confederates took back power in state governments, and African Americans were forced out.

Then some Southern states passed laws against blacks. The laws enforced **segregation**—keeping the races apart. Black children had to go to all-black schools. African Americans had to pass unfair tests in order to vote.

The most deadly attacks came from the Ku Klux Klan. This hate group began after the war. Its members hurt and murdered African Americans. As Klan members did **crimes** of **terror**, they hid their faces behind hoods.

By 1877, Reconstruction was over. With it went many gains of African Americans. As the black writer W. E. B. Du Bois wrote, "The slave went free; stood a brief moment in the sun; then moved back again toward slavery."

(TALK AND SHARE) **With your partner, draw a cartoon to show how the lives of African Americans changed after the war. Show one good change and one bad change.**

▲ In segregation, even drinking fountains were different for whites and blacks.

◀ Ku Klux Klan members

▲ W. E. B. Du Bois

VOCABULARY

reversal—a turning backward; a change to the opposite
segregation—the separation of people of different races
crimes—acts against the law
terror—great fear. Groups use terror to punish people or to try to force changes.

Talk About Reversal

■ Point out to students that the gains of Reconstruction did not last. White prejudice, bitterness, and greed created hard feelings against African Americans. When Congress no longer had a commitment to the rights of former slaves, many civil rights disappeared.

■ Point out to students that the word *reversal* comes from the word *reverse*, which is the opposite of *forward*. Mention the *reverse* gear of a car or what happens when an athlete *reverses* direction.

■ Ask students to imagine that certain rights they enjoy—such as going to school with one another—were suddenly reversed. Discuss how they would feel.

(TALK AND SHARE)

Have students complete the Talk and Share activity. This activity can be used as a comprehension check. Have students write a short sentence describing the gains and reversals shown in their cartoon.

 Activity: K-W-L Charts

Have students refer to the K-W-L Charts they made earlier in the lesson. They should work in pairs to fill in what they have learned about Reconstruction and the experiences of African Americans during that time.

If further questions remain, suggest that students use library materials or the Internet to see if they can find answers. Suggest these key words to help their search: *Reconstruction, Freedman's Bureau.*

Activity: Scrambled Words

Have each student select three vocabulary words from pages 180–181. Students should rearrange the letters of their words; for instance, *crimes* could become *remsci*. Students can then trade lists with a partner. Have them unscramble the letters of each word, write the word, and give its definition.

Discuss Settling the Great Plains

- Before they read these two pages, have students review their observations about the pictures in the visual aid on pages 176–177. Then refer them to their K-W-L Charts to see what they wanted to learn about westward movement.

- Invite students to look for information about the Homestead Act as they read. This act made it easy for people to own land.

- Have students use the pictures on these two pages to make guesses about what life was like for the settlers of the Great Plains. Students should share their ideas and explain why they hold that opinion.

- Invite students to talk about farms in their country of origin. Are these farms large or small? What kinds of crops do farmers grow? What tools do they use?

- Explain to students that farms and farming methods have changed over time. As farms get bigger and more productive, fewer people are farmers. This has been happening for years in the United States and some other countries, and it is starting to happen in many more.

Look and Read

Settling the Great Plains

After the Civil War, many Americans wanted a fresh start. They got their chance by moving west to the **Great Plains.**

▲ Families traveled to the Great Plains in covered wagons.

THE HOMESTEAD ACT

Congress had passed the Homestead Act in 1862. It gave 160 acres of land free to any settler who farmed it for 5 years. This new act drew large numbers of people to the Great Plains. (See the map on page 14.) Some of these people were **immigrants.** Thousands of them were African Americans leaving the South.

About 10 percent of the settlers were single women. Women just **lately** had won the right to own land.

VOCABULARY

Great Plains—a dry, treeless region in the middle of America. All or parts of the states of Montana, Wyoming, Colorado, New Mexico, North Dakota, South Dakota, Nebraska, Kansas, Oklahoma, and Texas are in the Great Plains.

immigrants—people who come into a country to live

lately—recently; not long ago

▲ *Pioneer Woman* by artist Harvey Dunn

182 UNIT 5 • A CHANGING AMERICA

 Activity: Oral Story String

Divide the class into small groups. Have students use the vocabulary on pages 182–183 to create an Oral Story String about the Great Plains settlers or the coming of the railroads. Have one student start the story with a sentence of his or her choosing. Then have the remaining students add new sentences in turn, continuing the story.

 Differentiating Instruction

Beginning

Drawing It Out To help students understand *transcontinental* and *transport*, call attention to the shared prefix *trans-*, or *across*. To *transport* is literally to *carry across*. *Transcontinental* means *across the continent*. Have students look for other words with this prefix. Ask them to choose one of the new words and draw its meaning. Have volunteers talk about their drawings with the class.

Intermediate

Strong Verbs Call students' attention to strong action words like *blasted*, *shivered*, and *sweated*, all of which appear on page 183. Have students find or generate a list of strong action words to use in their speaking and writing.

Advanced

Using Vocabulary Have students generate new sentences with the vocabulary words on pages 182–183, then share sentences with a partner.

RAILROADS FROM EAST TO WEST

Trains were very important to settlers in the West. Farmers and miners needed to **transport** their products to cities in the East. Factories in the East needed to transport their goods to the settlers in the West. **Cowmen** shipped their cattle to markets by train.

During the Civil War, work began on the first **transcontinental railroad.** Thousands of Chinese workers began building the railroad in the West. Thousands of Irish and African-American workers began building it in the East. Railmen worked long hours for low wages. They blasted tunnels through mountains and forests. They laid down miles of track. They shivered in snow and sweated in the desert heat.

On May 10, 1869, the two train **crews** met in Utah. A golden **spike** was driven into the last rail. Now the railroad reached across the nation. America was united like never before.

▲ More than 10,000 railroad workers were Chinese.

Workers laid the final 10 miles of track in 12 hours. This famous photograph shows the trains meeting. ▼

(TALK AND SHARE) **Talk with your partner about each picture on these two pages. Tell what it shows about settling the Great Plains.**

VOCABULARY

transport—move goods or people by a vehicle, such as a train
cowmen—farmers who raise cattle (cows, bulls, and steers)
transcontinental railroad—a rail line reaching across the nation
crews—groups of workers
spike—a large, strong nail

Summary

After the Civil War, Congress rebuilt the South. African Americans gained new freedom, but later they lost much of it. At the same time, millions of people in America moved to the Great Plains.

LESSON 14 • AFTER THE CIVIL WAR **183**

Teach Railroads from East to West

■ As a class, study the western United States on the physical map on page 14. Ask, *Why might it be hard to build a railroad in this area of the country?*

■ Reinforce that the railroad had to be built across deserts and mountains. Point out that trains cannot go up steep hills or around sharp curves easily, so workers had to build tunnels and bridges as well.

■ Discuss how a transcontinental railroad would have affected the United States.

(TALK AND SHARE)

Ask individual students to share their responses.

Discuss the Summary

■ Direct students to read the Summary at the end of the lesson.

■ Then return to the Big Idea on page 175.

■ Help students see the connection between the Summary and the Big Idea.

■ Then ask volunteers to put into their own words what they learned from this lesson.

✔ Assessment

Assess students' comprehension by asking the following questions:

History
• How did Reconstruction affect the South?

• In what ways did African Americans gain and then lose rights during Reconstruction?

• Why did large numbers of people move to the Great Plains after the Civil War?

Language
Match the word to its definition.

Words
1. Radical
2. Segregation
3. Transport

Definitions
A. Move goods or people
B. Extreme
C. The separation of people of different races

Assessment Book
Use page 32 to assess students' comprehension.

Teach Explaining

Tell students that when one is asked a question beginning with *why*, the answer usually begins with the word *because*. This word tells the listener or reader that the answer will give a reason.

Model the Organizer

- Tell students that a Web like this one can help them organize their reasons for an event.

- Each of the four circles connected to the statement gives a reason that Southerners became bitter.

- Help students express the reasons in a form such as Why *did Southerners become bitter?* Because *they did not like some of the new laws passed by Congress.*

Give Practice Explaining

- Invite students with limited proficiency in English to draw their reasons and give them one or two words to use as labels.

- From students at intermediate language levels accept a list of phrases and help them build sentences from their phrases.

- Advanced students should be helped to write a main idea sentence as either the first or last sentence in their paragraphs.

Develop Language

Explaining

Explaining Events in History

"Why did people act a certain way?" "Why did an event in history happen?" To answer questions like these, you need to find reasons. In your explanation, you give the reasons. You use the word *because*. A Web can help you keep track of reasons. For example, this Web shows the reasons why people in the South were bitter during Reconstruction.

Reconstruction Web

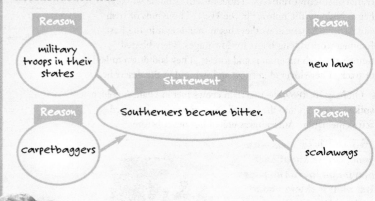

Reason — military troops in their states

Reason — new laws

Statement — Southerners became bitter.

Reason — carpetbaggers

Reason — scalawags

◄ From the painting *His First Vote* by Thomas Waterman Wood

Practice Explaining

1. Draw Make a Web with pictures showing the reasons that people settled in the Great Plains. Use your Web to explain the reasons to your partner.

2. Write Think of the ways that life changed for African Americans after the Civil War. List the reasons for those changes in a Web. Then write a paragraph that explains the changes. Use your Web and the Word Bank for help.

Word Bank

better
bitter
harder

sharecroppers
farmed

schools
politics

segregation
Ku Klux Klan

Activity: Internet Resources

Have students carry out research on the Internet to find further information about the people, places, and events in this lesson. Students can work in pairs to find information and present it to the class. Useful websites include:

- http://www.pbs.org/wgbh/amex/reconstruction

- http://cprr.org

Differentiating Instruction

Beginning

Asking Questions Focus on the words *why* and *because*. Have students generate three to five examples of questions that begin with *why* and answers that begin with *because*. Students may create small booklets of these questions and answers and illustrate them, putting one question-answer set on each page.

Intermediate/Advanced

Constructing a Web Have students preview the words listed in the Word Bank before starting to gather their ideas. Encourage them to use some of these words as they construct their Web.

After they have finished writing their paragraphs, remind students to read over their work and check for missing words or misspellings.

Activities

Grammar Spotlight

Possessive Nouns Possessive nouns show ownership. Possessive nouns have apostrophes ('). The chart shows where to put the apostrophe.

If a noun is singular, add an apostrophe (') + s.	If a noun is plural and ends in s, just add an apostrophe (').
Example	**Example**
The nation had a leader.	African Americans have rights.
The <u>nation's</u> great leader was gone.	<u>African-Americans'</u> rights were backed by law.

Write these sentences. Make the words on the left possessive.

immigrants   1. The_____new home was in the West.

Lincoln   2. _____ goal was to unite the country.

Oral Language

Role-Play Role-play a talk between two people after the Civil War. One person is a freed slave. The other is a former Union soldier. Explain to your partner how you feel. Begin this way.

Freed slave: I'm free now!

Union soldier: I'm glad you are free.

Freed slave: You fought hard to help free slaves. Thank you!

Union soldier: You're welcome! What will you do with your freedom?

Freed slave: I'm moving west! I want to own land.

Hands On

Political Cartoon In a small group, draw a political cartoon. First, pick your subject. Your subject could be from history or something going on today. Decide together how you feel about your subject. Then draw a cartoon that shows the subject and how you feel. You can use speech balloons, labels, or a caption to make your meaning clear.

Activities

Grammar Spotlight

- Explain to students that nouns can show possession, as in *the child's toy* or *the monkey's face*.
- Tell them that possession is indicated by an *apostrophe*. Explain that the apostrophe can go in one of two places, depending upon whether the noun is singular or plural.
- Then ask students to look back in the reading selection and find examples of possessive nouns in the reading.

Oral Language

Students also may role-play a talk between two other people after the Civil War. A sample dialogue might begin like this:

Freed slave: *I'm so glad I'm free!*

Former owner: *Well, it makes me mad.*

Slave: *I am finally learning to read!*

Owner: *I liked it better the old way. I miss being in charge.*

Hands On

Explain that the cartoons need not show examples from history. They may show examples of fair and unfair treatment from students' own lives and observations of the world around them.

 Activity: Extend the Lesson

Sarah, Plain and Tall by Patricia MacLachlan (HarperTrophy, 2004) is a short historical novel that tells the story of a young woman who comes from the East Coast to help a widower on the Great Plains raise his children. This moving story is written in spare, simple language that students with intermediate and advanced language skills can manage and enjoy.

Program Resources

Student Activity Journal
Use page 67 to practice *explaining*.

Overhead Transparencies
Use 9, Details and Statement Organizer, with page 184.

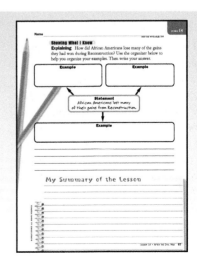

Immigrants, Cities, and Reform

STANDARDS CONTENT

History

- Read a circle graph
- Recognize the effects of immigration
- Identify ways new inventions transformed American life
- Recognize how the rise of corporations, the labor movement, and social reform changed U.S. society

Language

- Identify the following Key Concepts: *inventions, communication,* and *American culture*
- Recognize and understand idioms
- Practice synthesizing

Begin [Building Background]

- Ask students the questions on page 186. Explain that this photo shows an ordinary day in New York City, 1900. Focus students on:
  - The people's clothing, belongings, and activities
  - Differences and similarities with life today
- Encourage students to share their experiences of cities. Provide students with words as needed (*streets, homes, buildings, busy, marketplace*). Draw out key ideas:
  - Cities often are home to new immigrants.
  - Cities are places where people of different backgrounds can meet.

Immigrants, Cities, and Reform

Here you'll learn how American life changed in the years before and after 1900. You'll also learn how to read a circle graph and practice synthesizing information.

Building Background

▲ Many immigrants live in cities when they first come to America.

- **What do you see in this photo?**
- **How are cities different today?**
- **What do you know about visiting or living in a city?**

186 Unit 5 • A Changing America

 Activity: City Mural

Have students use markers, paints, or cutout photographs to create a mural showing an American city scene today. Students should decide together where to place buildings, people, and streets. Then have students use sticky notes or index cards to label important parts of the mural. Encourage them to use words and phrases such as *sidewalk, office building, driver, streetlight,* and *store.* Compare the mural to the picture on page 186.

Differentiating Instruction

Beginning
Object Search Focus on building word-picture associations. Have students work in pairs. One student names an object or color in the picture. The second student locates it. Then the two switch roles.

Intermediate
Sentences Have students work in pairs to create three sentences that tell about the picture. They may describe the people or objects they see or tell what the picture makes them think about. Then have students share their sentences with the class.

Advanced
Describe and Guess Have students work in pairs. One student uses three to five sentences to describe an object in the picture to his or her partner without actually naming it. The partner guesses the object, using the form *Is it a _____?* Then the two switch roles.

1 New Immigrants

2 Important Inventions

3 Business and Reform

LESSON 15 • IMMIGRANTS, CITIES, AND REFORM **187**

Introduce the Big Idea

- Read aloud the Big Idea on page 187.
- Then call students' attention to the three headings listed on the page. Explain that the years around the turn of the century were full of big changes. Immigrants changed the population of the United States. Inventions changed the way people worked and lived. And reforms changed the ways that businesses could operate.
- Have students look carefully at the pictures on the page and form small groups to discuss what they see.

Review

In Lesson 14, students learned about life on farms. Have students compare the images of the Great Plains on pages 176–177 to the images in this lesson. Ask students how life might have been different at the time for children on a Kansas farm and in New York City.

 Activity: Changes Chart

Make a Two-column Chart on a bulletin board. Label the left-hand column *Once* and the right-hand column *Now*. Draw a very simple sketch of a baby in the *Once* column and a sketch of an adult in the *Now* column. Say, *Once I was a baby, and now I am a grown-up.*

Invite volunteers to add their own sketches to the chart. They should use a similar format to describe their drawings to the class. Possible sentences include:

- Once I lived in a town, and now I live in a city.
- Once I had a pet dog, and now I have two pet dogs.
- Once I hated to eat eggs, and now I love to eat them.

Write some of these sentences for everyone to see. Point out that these sentences show changes. The chart shows changes in students' own lives; the lesson discusses the changes in American life around 1900. Encourage students to add to the chart throughout the lesson.

 Resource Library

Reader's Handbook **(red)**
Pie Chart 558

Reader's Handbook **(yellow)**
Circle Graph 427

All Write
Pie Graph 282

Teach Key Concepts

- Read the three words aloud. Say each term slowly to help model correct pronunciation. Have students repeat the terms. Then read the definitions aloud.

- Ask for examples of inventions. Point out that many new inventions came along at the turn of the century.

- Ask students what forms of communication they use in their own lives.

- Review the meaning of *culture*, which was a Key Concept in Lesson 1.

Teach the Visual Aid
New York City, 1910

Focus students on the graphic. Help them see that the pictures refer to life in New York City in 1910. Have students discuss what they see in each picture. Where possible, emphasize the idea of change over time. For instance, streetcars and subways were new ways of getting around New York City in 1910, and baseball was a new sport growing in popularity.

Key Concepts

Communication

Inventions

American Culture

Inventions are new things created out of the imagination. The telephone was an invention that changed the way people exchanged news and ideas.

The telephone is one form of **communication.** Inventions in the late 1800s and early 1900s changed American **culture,** or way of life.

New York City, 1910

Statue of Liberty

Immigrants at Ellis Island

Streetcar

New Fashions

188 UNIT 5 • A CHANGING AMERICA

Activity: Pantomime

Pantomime two to three forms of communication, such as writing by hand, speaking with another person, or talking into a telephone. Have students guess what you are enacting. Then have volunteers act out other forms of communication, such as radios or the Internet. Help students compile a list of different forms of communication. Explain that several new forms of communication were invented around the turn of the century.

Differentiating Instruction

Beginning
Picture Talk Focus on the pictures in the visual aid. Divide the class into small groups. Encourage students to use words they know to talk to one another about each picture.

Intermediate
Cause-Effect Have students work in pairs. They should use the word *because* and form sentences about one of the pictures in the visual aid. Model examples such as *The people are waiting because they want to get onto the subway*

or *The woman is happy because she is wearing her new clothes.*

Advanced
Exploring Meaning Explore the phrase *turn of the century.* Have students generate phrases and sentences with *turn,* e.g., *turn left* and *it's my turn.* Draw a connection between *turn* and *change.* Introduce the idea that a century turned again in 2000.

Reading a Circle Graph

A circle graph lets you compare the amounts or importance of things. Circle graphs also are called *pie charts*, because their parts look like slices of a pie. Follow these steps to read a circle graph.

1. Read the title. It tells what the *whole circle* shows.

2. Study the key. This tells you what *each slice* shows.

3. Compare the *sizes* of the slices to each other.

This circle graph shows where immigrants came from between 1891 and 1900. A *homeland* is the land in which one is born. It is the country the immigrants called home. Did more people come from Germany or from Asia?

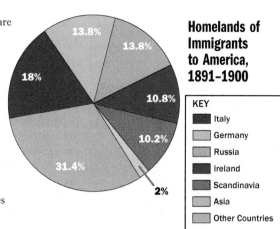

Homelands of Immigrants to America, 1891–1900

13.8%
13.8%
18%
10.8%
10.2%
31.4%
2%

KEY
- Italy
- Germany
- Russia
- Ireland
- Scandinavia
- Asia
- Other Countries

Workers on Strike

Baseball

City Slum

Subway

Teach Skill Building

- Invite students to look at the circle graph. Encourage them to guess how the graph works and what it shows. Then read aloud the explanation of the circle graph while students follow along.

- Be sure that students understand the following academic vocabulary: *immigrants, homeland, slice, size.*

- Ask students which slice of the pie is larger: the light blue slice or the yellow slice (*the light blue slice*). Call students' attention to the key at the right. Have students match the colors of the light blue and yellow slices with the homelands in the key (*Germany and Asia*).

- Then refer students to the numbers in the two slices. Explain that *2%* next to the yellow slice means that two out of every 100 immigrants during this time came from Asia, and *13.8%* on the light blue slice means that about fourteen out of every 100 came from Germany.

Activity: Create a Circle Graph

Draw a circle on the board. Label it *Do You Have a Sister?* Divide the circle into eight equal sections. Then ask eight students if they have sisters. Record the results in a tally chart. Write the following key on the board: *Yes = shaded space; No = empty space.*

Have students use the tally chart and key to help you determine how many pie slices should be shaded and how many should be left blank.

Program Resources

Student Activity Journal

Use page 68 to build key vocabulary.

Use page 69 to practice reading a circle graph.

Overhead Transparencies

Use 3, Cause-effect Organizer, with the Intermediate activity on page 188.

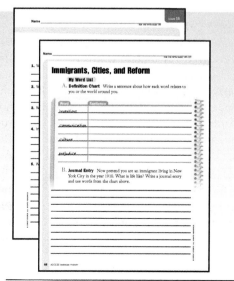

Introduce Immigrants, Cities, and Reform

- Students first read about immigrants to the United States in Lesson 10. Here they will read about new waves of people arriving from Southern and Eastern Europe as well as Asia. These immigrants often entered an urban environment during a time of great change.

- Remind students that the Big Idea and the Key Concepts mentioned new people (*immigrants*), new things (*inventions*), and new ways of life (*reforms*). Tell students to look for new ideas and changes as they read.

Language Notes

- Draw students' attention to the Language Notes box.

- Point out that the phrases connect with the usual meaning of the words. For instance, a *wave* on the ocean carries a lot of water all at once. A *wave* of immigrants means that a lot of people move to the country at once.

- Then point out to students how these idioms appear in red type in the reading.

Immigrants, Cities, and Reform

▲ These young Polish women carry all they have in cloth bags as they enter America.

Millions of new immigrants came to America between 1870 and 1920. Cities and industry grew. Inventions changed the American way of life. Problems and reforms came with the growth.

A New Wave of Immigration

At the turn of the century, a new **wave** of **immigrants** flooded into America. Earlier in the 19th **century,** most immigrants came from Western Europe. Now most immigrants came from Eastern Europe. They came from such countries as Italy, Russia, and Poland. Other immigrants came from Asia.

ENTERING THE COUNTRY

Immigrants from Europe most often entered the country at New York Harbor. The Statue of Liberty was their first view of America. It seemed to promise what they had come for—freedom and a better life. After landing, **newcomers registered** with the U.S. government at Ellis Island. Immigrants from Asia usually entered the country at Angel Island, in San Francisco Bay. At both these **inspection stations,** newcomers had to show their papers and pass certain tests before they could enter the United States.

Language Notes

Idioms
These sayings don't mean what they seem.

- **turn of the century:** the years near the end of one century and the beginning of the next

- **fit in:** become American; look and act like everyone else

VOCABULARY

wave—a movement of many people coming in, like an ocean
immigrants—people who come into a country to live. The coming in of people is called *immigration.*
century—100 years. The 1800s were the 19th century. We live in the 21st century.
newcomers—people who have just come into a place
registered—signed or filled out a record
inspection stations—places where people are inspected—looked over—to be sure they meet the rules

---

Activity: Word Quiz

Have students work in pairs to choose four vocabulary words of interest to them. Have them write the words on cards and add a small sketch or picture to help them recall the meaning of each word. Then have students shuffle their cards and quiz each other on the meanings.

Have students save their cards for future use. They may add new vocabulary terms to their card decks as they progress through the lesson.

Differentiating Instruction

Beginning
Recognize Sequence Remind students that the lesson discusses changes in American life. With their help, generate some signal words, such as *new, now, first,* and *earlier.* Read the first page with students. Ask them to tap on their desks when they hear these words.

Intermediate
Paired Reading Have students work in pairs. They should read one paragraph at a time and discuss what they read with a partner. Remind them that they can ask each other for help with unfamiliar words.

Advanced
Partner Talk Have students read the first two pages on their own, stopping at the Talk and Share activity on page 191. Have them look carefully for words that describe what it was like to be an immigrant in the early 1900s. Then have them discuss their ideas with a partner.

THE NEW LIFE IN AMERICAN CITIES

After immigrants passed the inspection, they tried to fit in with American life. It was not easy to be a newcomer. At first, immigrants lived near others from their **homeland.** Many lived in crowded buildings without light and fresh air. **Neighborhoods** full of these buildings were called **slums.**

Immigrants helped **industry** in America grow. In their homelands, many people had farmed. Here they worked in factories. Some Americans feared that immigrants would take their jobs. Fears led to **prejudice,** and in the 1920s, new laws were passed against immigration. The laws ended most immigration to America for many years.

TALK AND SHARE With your partner, talk about what it was like to come to America in the early 1900s.

VOCABULARY

homeland—land where a person is born; the country a people call home
neighborhoods—areas in a city
slums—the crowded, dirty parts of a city where buildings are old and need repairs and the people are poor
industry—the business of making and selling goods
prejudice—bad and unfair ideas about people based on a group they belong to
horrified—shocked

▲ Many immigrants live in poor homes when they first come to America.

◀ Jane Addams comforts immigrant children who come to Hull House.

People in History

Jane Addams

Jane Addams was an American hero. She grew up rich. As an adult, she visited the slums of Chicago. She saw broken-down buildings, crowded apartments, and sick and hungry children. Addams was **horrified!** She bought a house, called Hull House, and set it up to help poor people. Addams brought in nurses to care for the sick. She started classes in English, reading, and music. She set up playgrounds for children. Addams said, "We were asked to wash the newborn babies, and to prepare the dead for burial, to nurse the sick, and to mind the children."

LESSON 15 • IMMIGRANTS, CITIES, AND REFORM **191**

Teach The New Life in American Cities

■ Have students brainstorm reasons that immigrants come to a new place. Some are running from bad things at home (*poverty, war, prejudice*). Others are running to good things in another country (*jobs, freedom*). Some are doing both at once.

■ Ask students, *Is it better for a country to have a lot of immigration or a little?* As a class, come up with two advantages and two disadvantages of large numbers of immigrants entering a country. Emphasize that Americans and their leaders have argued about this issue throughout history—and still do.

TALK AND SHARE

Students can point to photographs in the lesson as they talk to their partners.

People in History

Jane Addams

Explain that Jane Addams lived in a time when the U.S. government did very little to help the poor and the sick. Point out that there were no day care centers, food stamps, or similar programs at this time. This made Addams's work especially important. Ask students to discuss what problems in their own communities they would like to solve.

 Activity: Immigration Stories

Encourage students to share immigration stories. Have students write down some of these stories, if they are willing, and compile them into a class book. Students can illustrate their work with drawings or photographs.

Use this lesson as an opportunity to connect with students' families. Perhaps a parent or other adult could be invited to talk about his or her experiences as an immigrant.

 Program Resources

Student Activity Journal

Assign page 70:

- To create study notes for students to review
- To provide reinforcement of key vocabulary

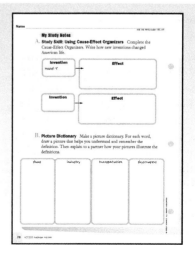

Discuss Inventions

■ Have students read the two paragraphs on page 192. Then have students study the photographs on pages 192–193. Ask them to form small groups and describe to one another what they see in the pictures. Next, ask them to tell how these early inventions are different from the same objects today.

■ Point out that the first paragraph of page 192 divides some inventions into two categories: *transportation* and *communication*. Tell students that making categories can be a useful way to organize and display information. Remind them that things that are alike in some way can go together in a category.

■ To extend the idea of categories, have four volunteers come to the front of the room. Ask the rest of the students to put them into categories. Have them use sentences such as the following:

• The category is _____ (*people with red shoes/girls*).

• All the people in this category have/are _____ (*red shoes/girls*).

Repeat with other combinations of volunteers.

▲ Alexander Graham Bell, inventor of the telephone, makes the first long distance phone call between New York and Chicago in 1892.

Inventions Changed the Way People Lived

The time between 1865 and 1920 was full of new **inventions** that caused huge changes in American life. **Electricity** brought light to America and opened the way to new products. The telephone changed **communications**. Cars and airplanes changed **transportation**. Elevators made tall buildings possible, and **skyscrapers** changed city skylines.

The new inventions made factories **boom** and cities grow. Millions of Americans moved to the cities to get jobs. Back when the Civil War ended in 1865, only 1 in 4 Americans lived in large cities. By 1910, nearly half of all Americans did.

Cable Cars, 1873
Run by electricity, they replaced horse-drawn streetcars.

Typewriter, 1867
It changed the work of clerks in all kinds of businesses.

Telephone, 1876
Americans had 2 million phones by 1900.

Electric Light, 1880
Thomas Edison turned night into day with this invention.

Activity: Timeline

Have students work in pairs to choose an invention not mentioned on these pages, such as computers. Direct students to library resources or the Internet to learn when the invention was created. Students should write the name of the invention and the year of its creation on a sheet of paper, add a drawing or photograph, and include the name of the inventor (if known). Assemble all the sheets into a timeline. Use Overhead Transparency 28, Timeline.

Differentiating Instruction

Beginning
Word Lists Focus students' attention on the vocabulary words *transportation* and *communication*. Have students generate words, such as *car* or *telephone*, that fit under each heading. Students may draw or pantomime objects. Make a list of the words they find.

Intermediate
It's Electric! Focus students' attention on the vocabulary word *electricity*. Direct them to find things in school that do and do not use electricity.

Have them tell a partner, _____ *uses electricity*, or _____ *does not use electricity*.

Advanced
My Invention Have students work with partners to describe an invention they would like to create. They should use complete sentences in their discussions and address such questions as *What would the invention do?* and *How would it change the way people live?*

TALK AND SHARE Talk with a partner about some of the inventions on these pages. Tell which *you* think are most important.

VOCABULARY

inventions—new things created by the imagination
electricity—a form of power, or energy. *Electricity* moves inside wires.
communications—the ways people exchange news and ideas
transportation—ways of getting from one place to another
skyscrapers—very tall buildings
boom—grow very large, like a loud explosion

Subway, 1904
People could get around
New York City underground.

Kodak Camera, 1895
It made taking
photographs easier.

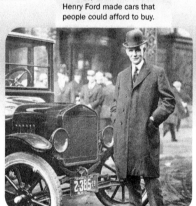
First Airplane Flight, 1903
Orville and Wilbur Wright
were the first to fly a plane.

Model T, 1908
Henry Ford made cars that
people could afford to buy.

Radio, 1895
It brought the world
into people's homes.

LESSON 15 • IMMIGRANTS, CITIES, AND REFORM **193**

Teach About the Way People Lived

■ Explain to students that these new inventions changed the way people lived and worked.

■ Ask, *Who has ever listened to a radio?* Draw out that many people use radios to hear music.

■ Then ask how people might have listened to music before the radio was invented. Encourage conversation about life without this invention.

■ Have students make two circle graphs to show the fraction of Americans living in large cities in 1865 and 1910. Have students divide the 1865 graph into four equal parts and the 1910 graph into two equal parts. Ask them to use red to show the fraction living in cities for each year ($\frac{1}{4}$ and $\frac{1}{2}$) and blue to show the fraction living outside of cities ($\frac{3}{4}$ and $\frac{1}{2}$). Discuss the differences.

TALK AND SHARE

Have students work with partners to discuss the topic. After the conversation, each student should name the invention he or she thinks was most important. Help students represent their choices in a tally chart or bar graph.

Activity: A World Without

Assign small groups one of the inventions pictured on pages 192–193. Students should discuss what the world would be like without this invention.

Group members should use a Web, like the one opposite, to organize their ideas. Have students write the name of the invention in the middle and then write a few words describing the changes the world would face without the invention.

Then group members should work together to write a paragraph of three to four sentences describing the world without the invention. Have student volunteers read their work aloud for the class. Use Overhead Transparency 33, Web.

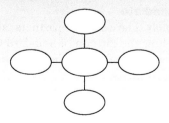

Lesson 15 • Immigrants, Cities, and Reform **193**

Discuss Problems and Reform

Focus students' attention on the cartoon at the upper left showing Standard Oil as a giant octopus. Have students describe the cartoon. Explain that the octopus stands for an oil company that was trying to put other oil companies out of business. Then have students read the page.

Key Connection: Economics

Develop understanding of the concepts of *competition* and *monopoly*.

■ Explain that companies *compete* with one another to sell their products to customers. They are in a contest to see who can get people to buy *their* goods. To sell goods, they have to convince people to buy from them. They do this by making a better product and by lowering prices.

■ When companies have no competition, they have a *monopoly*. They no longer have to make better products or worry about prices. This hurts customers. The activity below can help students grasp this concept.

Problems and Reform

By the turn of the century, American business began to boom. In time, however, some businesses got too big.

Standard Oil is a giant octopus crushing other businesses. What opinion about Standard Oil does the cartoon show? ▶

BIG BUSINESS

In the late 1800s, some businesses grew to become **monopolies.** John D. Rockefeller set up the Standard Oil Company. It controlled the whole oil **industry.** Smaller oil companies had to be part of Standard Oil or they were forced out of business. Andrew Carnegie did the same thing in the steel industry. These monopolies ended all **competition.** Buyers had to pay whatever the monopolies charged. There was no one else to buy from.

THE RISE OF UNIONS

As businesses became larger and larger, workers often suffered. The **unions** that began earlier in the century got stronger. Workers **went on strike** more and more often, and many strikes became violent.

▲ A union leader talks to striking workers.

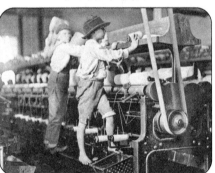

▲ Children work long hours in factories.

VOCABULARY

monopolies—businesses that completely control the making and selling of a product
industry—all the companies in a business
competition—the contest between businesses to "win" buyers for their goods
unions—groups of workers who join together to make owners change things
went on strike—stopped working. A strike is a group action taken to make a business owner change things

194 UNIT 5 • A CHANGING AMERICA

Activity: Monopolies

Post two simple signs, one that says *APPLES 25 cents* and one that reads *APPLES 20 cents*. Have students choose a "store" from which to buy an apple. Ask them to explain their choice. Now, change the 25-cent sign so it reads *APPLES 15 cents*. Have students choose a store now. Point out that when the stores are in competition, prices may get lower. Explain how monopolies can charge almost any price they like.

Differentiating Instruction

Beginning
Word-Picture Associations Using pantomime and gestures, help students associate *octopus*, *speaker*, and *children* with the pictures and blue heads. Summarize the content on these pages.

Intermediate
Monopoly Have student partners talk about how the cartoon of Standard Oil as an octopus helps explain the section on Big Business.

Advanced
Shop Talk Have students work in pairs and list the things they think a union leader might say to workers on strike. Then create a short four- to five-sentence speech based on their lists and the information in the text.

REFORMS FOR BIG BUSINESS

Big business caused big problems, but at first the government did nothing. Government leaders believed in a **policy** called **laissez-faire.** This term is French, meaning "let people do what they want."

Then, in 1901, Theodore Roosevelt became president. He started to **regulate** big business. Other presidents had supported owners against the strikers. But Roosevelt made business owners **negotiate** with striking workers. He also worked for new labor laws. Some of these laws made monopolies **illegal.** The big companies had to break up by selling off parts of their business. Other laws raised the pay of workers and lowered the number of hours they had to work. Slowly, **reforms** helped make the American workplace better.

▲ President Theodore Roosevelt

What opinion of Roosevelt does this cartoon show? ▼

(**TALK AND SHARE**) **With your partner, use the vocabulary words on these two pages to talk about big business and the reforms.**

VOCABULARY

big business—the group of large businesses that controlled their industries in the late 1800s and 1900s

policy—a plan that a government makes for the actions it takes

laissez-faire—an economic policy in which the government doesn't make rules about business

regulate—control by giving rules

negotiate—talk in order to settle a conflict

illegal—against the law. It was a crime to have a monopoly.

reforms—changes for the better

Summary

America went through many changes from 1870 to the start of the 1900s. Millions of new immigrants came. New inventions were made. Cities became big, and so did businesses. Then President Theodore Roosevelt brought reform.

LESSON 15 • IMMIGRANTS, CITIES, AND REFORM **195**

Teach About Reforms for Big Business

■ Have students preview the heading and pictures on this page. Ask them what they think will happen to big business.

■ After students finish reading, ask, *What did Roosevelt do to improve the country's business problems?*

(**TALK AND SHARE**)

Have students work in pairs to discuss the topic. You can use students' responses to check their comprehension of pages 194 and 195.

Discuss the Summary

Have a volunteer read the Summary at the end of the lesson while students follow along. Then return to the Big Idea on page 187. Have students state the connections between the Summary and the Big Idea.

✓ Assessment

Assess students' comprehension by asking the following questions:

History

• What were three big changes in the United States at the turn of the century?

• Why did immigrants come to the United States during this time?

• What were some important inventions from 1870–1920?

• What problems did big businesses create? What were Roosevelt's solutions?

Language

Which word does not belong?

• Immigrant, newcomer, homeland, monopoly

• Neighborhood, city, policy, slums

• Union, prejudice, strike, negotiate

Assessment Book

Use page 33 to assess students' comprehension.

Teach Synthesizing

Explain to students that when they synthesize information, they look for details that connect with a bigger idea. Synthesizing details will help students write paragraphs and answer test questions.

Model the Organizer

■ Ask a volunteer to read aloud the Broad Statement in the center of the organizer. Explain to students that *broad statement* is another way of saying *big idea.* Have volunteers read each of the supporting details.

■ Emphasize that these are not big ideas themselves, but single actions that Roosevelt took. Explain that each detail shows a way that Roosevelt worked to reform big business.

Give Practice Synthesizing

■ Tell students that they will now practice synthesizing information.

■ **Draw** Have students whose English is limited work on the Draw activity with a partner.

■ **Write** Have intermediate and advanced language learners complete the Write activity. Encourage students to share their assignments with the class.

Develop Language

Synthesizing

Synthesizing Information

When you synthesize information, you show how details are part of a big idea. Begin by looking for important details. Then figure out how the details add up. A Details and Statement Organizer can help you. The organizer below synthesizes 4 details about President Theodore Roosevelt.

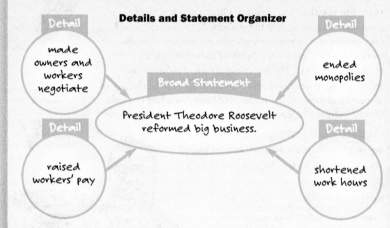

Details and Statement Organizer

Detail: made owners and workers negotiate

Detail: ended monopolies

Broad Statement: President Theodore Roosevelt reformed big business.

Detail: raised workers' pay

Detail: shortened work hours

Practice Synthesizing

1. Draw Make a Details and Statement Organizer about the new inventions around 1900. For details, draw pictures of inventions and what they changed. Use your organizer to tell a partner a broad statement about how inventions changed people's lives.

2. Write Tell about immigrants who came to America near 1900. Start by making a Details and Statement Organizer. Then use the broad statement in your organizer to start a paragraph. Finish the paragraph by filling in your details. Exchange paragraphs with a partner and check each other's work.

> **Check Your Writing**
> **Make sure you**
> ☐ Use complete sentences.
> ☐ Use a period at the end of each sentence.
> ☐ Spell all the words correctly.

Activity: Internet Resources

Have students use the Internet to help them research important topics that relate to the lesson. Students may work in pairs to find items like pictures, stories, and timelines. Useful websites include:

- http://www.mcny.org/ Exhibitions/riis/riis.htm
- http://kclibrary.nhmccd.edu/ decade00.html

Differentiating Instruction

Beginning
Generating a Broad Statement Focus on the words *details* and *statement.* Have students start with the details for their organizer. Help students generate names and uses of inventions from the turn of the century. Have them look back to the pictures on pages 192–193 if necessary. Then ask them how these inventions changed American lives. A model sentence may help, such as *They made it easier to ____* or *They let people ____.*

Intermediate
Prompting Students Focus students on starting with a broad statement, such as *Immigrants changed the country by . . .* or *Immigrants' lives were. . . .*

Advanced
Persuasive Paragraph Ask students to consider how they feel about the details they include in their organizer. Have them write a paragraph that persuades the reader to feel the same way.

Grammar Spotlight

Word Order Many English sentences put words in a certain order. The chart shows you examples.

Word Order

Subject ➝ Verb	Subject ➝ Verb ➝ Object
Immigrants came.	_Roosevelt_ made reforms.
Many _businesses_ grew.	_Rockefeller_ set up the Standard Oil Company.

Write a sentence using these words: _invented Bell telephone._

Partner Practice

On Strike! Imagine that you and your partner are workers on strike in 1900. Make signs. Tell the changes you need at work. List the demands you will make to the business owners.

Oral Language

Show You Know Make a card for each of these words: _immigrants, neighborhood, homeland, slums, prejudice, change._ Turn the cards face down and mix them up. Pick one. Take turns with a partner. Say a sentence using the word. Then your partner picks up a card and says a different sentence using your word _and_ the new word. Put those two cards away. Do it again for the next two cards. Then do it again for the last two cards.

Hands On

Graph It With a partner or in a small group, collect information about where the students in your class come from. Then show your data in a circle graph. Give your graph a title. Use a key to show what places the colors stand for. Put the actual percentages inside the parts of the graph.

Activities

Grammar Spotlight

Explain to students that the order of words is very important in English. The _subject_, the person or thing that does something, usually comes first in a simple statement. Next comes the _verb_, or the action word; and after that the _object_, or other noun.

Have volunteers read the words in sentence order. Then have students identify the subject, verb, and object in the word set _invented_, _Bell_, and _telephone_. Point out clues to each word's part of speech, such as the _-ed_ ending of _invented_ and the uppercase _B_ in _Bell_.

Partner Practice

Students should begin by generating a list of different complaints about how they imagine their companies treat them.

Oral Language

Remind students that they can use such words as _and_ or _but_ to join ideas in a sentence.

Hands On

Students may make a bar graph or a circle graph to display their information. For a circle graph, rough estimates of the size of each slice are acceptable.

 Activity: Extend the Lesson

A Changing America (from the Stories in History series, McDougal Littell, 2002) has an article and short stories, many of which deal with immigration, city life at the turn of the century, and business practices of the time. Stories include "The Man Who Exposed the Slums," "Cornelius Vanderbilt, Robber Baron," "A Day at Ellis Island," and "Breaker Boys," among others.

Program Resources

Student Activity Journal

Use page 71 to practice _synthesizing_.

Overhead Transparencies

Use 9, Details and Statement Organizer, with page 196.

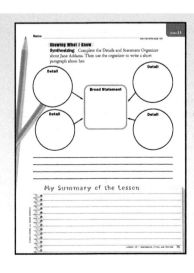

Becoming a World Power

STANDARDS CONTENT

History
- ■ Recognize chronological order
- ■ Identify ways America became a world power in the early 1900s
- ■ Recognize America's role in foreign trade
- ■ Describe the changing role of the United States in world affairs around 1900

Language
- ■ Identify the following Key Concepts: *imperialism, annexation,* and *foreign trade*
- ■ Recognize and use verb phrases
- ■ Practice identifying outcomes

Begin   Building Background

- ■ Have students use words and sentences to tell about the picture to the right. Provide students with words as needed (*flag, globe, eagle, fierce, symbol*). Point out that the eagle in the picture is a national symbol of the United States.

- ■ Read aloud the statement below the photo of the girl. Draw out key ideas about power:
  - • Countries grow powerful because of people, money, and resources.
  - • Countries may or may not use their power to do good.

Becoming a World Power

Here you'll learn how the United States became a world power. You'll also learn how to recognize chronological order and practice identifying outcomes of events in history.

Building Background

▲ It is good to be powerful *only* if you use the power to do good.

- ■ How would you describe this picture?
- ■ What do you think the bird stands for?
- ■ What is your opinion about the United States? What opinion does this picture show?

198 UNIT 5 • A CHANGING AMERICA

 Activity: Power Drawings

Have students fold a sheet of paper in fourths. Have them draw the following four pictures, one in each quarter of the paper: a powerful person; a person without much power; a city in a powerful country; and a city in a country without much power.

Explain that these should be pictures from students' imaginations. Have students share their work with a partner. Ask them to discuss how their drawings are alike and different.

Differentiating Instruction

Beginning
Using Vocabulary Have students work in pairs. One student names an object in the picture, using basic vocabulary such as *wing, bird,* and *map.* The second student points to the object. Then the two switch roles.

Intermediate
Guessing Objects Have a student think of an object in the picture and then give a clue to the object by using the form *I see something that begins with*

the letter ___. Other students then guess the object, using the form *Is it a* ___?

Advanced
Drawing Political Cartoons This picture is a political cartoon; it uses drawings that people understand to make a point about world affairs. Invite students to work in pairs or small groups to design their own cartoon about the world.

In the early 1900s, the United States became a world power. It got new lands and used its power to increase its trade.

1 Winning Land from Spain

2 Getting Hawaii

3 Increasing Trade

Introduce the Big Idea

■ Draw students' attention to the three labels for the pictures on page 199. Ask students what they see in the pictures. Ask them how they think the pictures relate to the lesson title.

■ Explain that the lands the United States took over around 1900 were different from the lands the United States annexed earlier.

■ Have volunteers find the following locations on a map: Hawaii, Guam, the Philippines, Puerto Rico, and Cuba. Ask students how they think the United States got these lands and how Americans kept control of them. Have students use the pictures on the page to help form their ideas. Then have them discuss their ideas in small groups.

Teach the Picture

Have students look at the picture of the ship on page 199. Tell students that *trade* means *business*. Ask students how they think a ship could help encourage and protect trade.

Review

Remind students that the United States had taken over new lands before, especially at the time of the Louisiana Purchase and the Mexican-American War. Ask students to describe what they remember about the United States acquiring new lands.

Activity: Role-Play

Ask students to imagine that they are living in an imaginary country. Tell them that the leaders of their country want to take over land that belongs to another imaginary country, Badland. Explain to students that Badland's government does not treat its people very well.

Ask three students to come to the front of the room and play the roles of government leaders. Ask other students to take turns approaching the leaders and arguing for or against taking land from Badland. Encourage students to provide reasons for their opinions.

After the government leaders have heard all the arguments, ask them to decide together whether to take Badland's territory. Have them explain which arguments most helped them make their decision.

Extend the discussion by asking how students would feel if their country was instead planning to take land from Goodland—a country that treats its people very well.

Resource Library

***Reader's Handbook* (red)**
Chronological Order 77, 276

***Reader's Handbook* (yellow)**
Chronological Order 198

All Write
Chronological Order 272–273

Teach Key Concepts

- Read the three concepts aloud. To model correct pronunciation, say each term slowly. Then have students repeat the terms after you. Next, read the definitions aloud. Remind students that *foreign trade* means *doing business with people in other countries.*

- Ask students if they have ever had a brother, sister, or friend move into their space on a couch, in a bus, or in a car. Have two volunteers act this out using chairs. Explain that this is a small everyday example of *annexation.*

- Have students draw connections to past lessons. Ask them to describe past events that relate to the three concepts. Possible answers include *Britain starting colonies; the United States buying the Louisiana territory;* and *the thirteen colonies participating in foreign trade with Britain.*

Teach the Visual Aid

The United States in the Pacific

Focus students on the maps. Have a volunteer use a globe to show the relative positions of these regions in the world. Point out that the green shadings all show places where U.S. influence increased around 1900. Ask students to predict why these regions attracted the United States.

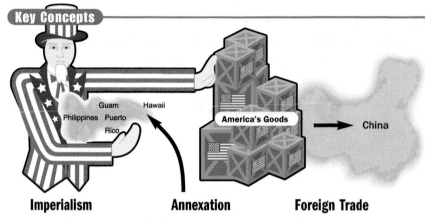

Talk and Explore

Key Concepts

Guam · Hawaii · Philippines · Puerto Rico · America's Goods → China

Imperialism

Imperialism is taking control over other countries.

Annexation

Annexation means adding land. That can be one part of imperialism.

Foreign Trade

Getting control over **foreign trade** is another part of imperialism.

The United States in the Pacific

Russia · Mongolia · China Open Door Policy in 1899 · North Korea · South Korea · Japan · PACIFIC OCEAN · Myanmar · Laos · Thailand · Vietnam · South China Sea · Cambodia · Malaysia · Philippines Became a U.S. territory in 1898 · Philippine Sea · *Guam* Became a U.S. territory in 1898 · Hawaii Annexed in 1898 · Indonesia · Papua New Guinea · Solomon Islands

KEY — U.S. involvement

0   500 Miles
0   500 Kilometers

200 UNIT 5 • A CHANGING AMERICA

Activity: Identify Terms

Ask students to define the terms *island* and *continent.* Tell how some islands, such as the Philippines, are close together in an *island chain,* while others are many miles from other lands. Have students identify islands on the map, such as Puerto Rico, Guam, and the Hawaiian island chain. Then have five students at a time stand up. Ask a volunteer to call out *islands, island chains,* or *continent.* Use distance between students to demonstrate each concept.

Differentiating Instruction

Beginning
Map Reading Focus students' attention on the map. Divide the group into pairs and have them work with the words *island, land,* and *ocean.* One student asks the other, *Where is the ___?* The other student responds by pointing to an example on the map and saying, *The ___ is here.*

Intermediate
Synonyms Focus students' attention on synonyms, or words with similar meanings, such as *trade* and *business.*

Generate a list of words and their synonyms. Have each student choose a favorite pair of synonyms and write them on a sheet of paper with a sketch that shows their meanings.

Advanced
Studying Time Order Have students look in the lesson to find sentences that use *first, finally, next, before,* and other signal words for sequence. Have students copy down one sentence each and tape it to a poster labeled *Time-Order Sentences.*

Skill Building

Recognizing Chronological Order

The order of events in history is important because an early event can cause later ones. *Chronological order* is time order, or the order in which things happen. To recognize chronological order when you read history, look for dates and words about time, such as these.

first second	then next	finally last
earlier later	before after	while soon

First

First, America helped Panama become free.

Then

Then, America started to build the Panama Canal.

Finally

After 10 years, the canal was *finally* done.

The United States in Latin America

KEY

☐ U.S. involvement

United States

ATLANTIC OCEAN

N W E S

Cuba
Became a U.S. protectorate in 1898

Bahamas

Puerto Rico
Became a U.S. territory in 1898

Mexico

Gulf of Mexico

Dominican Republic

PACIFIC OCEAN

Jamaica

Haiti

Caribbean Sea

Belize

Guatemala Honduras

Republic of Panama
Panama Canal built 1904–1914

El Salvador

Nicaragua

Costa Rica

Venezuela

Guyana

Colombia

0   200   400 Miles
0   200 400 Kilometers

LESSON 16 • BECOMING A WORLD POWER **201**

Teach Skill Building

- Toss a coin into the air and let it fall to the ground. Say to students, *First, I tossed the coin. Then, it fell to the ground.* Have students create and say similar sentences based on other actions, such as *First, I picked up the pencil. Then, I picked up the tape.*

- Explain to students that words such as *first* and *then* tell about chronological order. Read the paragraph aloud while students follow along. Have volunteers give examples of earlier events that caused later ones, such as the invention of the telephone changing the speed at which news travelled.

- Call students' attention to the example. Then go over the highlighted words. Ask volunteers to think of sentences that use the words or give examples yourself. Possibilities include *I went to bed after I brushed my teeth* and *I did my homework while I was at my aunt's house.*

Activity: First/Second/Last

To give students practice in ordering events, write the words *first, second,* and *last* on the board. Ask three students to stand up, one after the other. Point to the word *first* and ask students, *Who stood up first?* Continue with *second* and *last.* Then have the students sit down in a different order. Ask, *Who sat down first/second/last?*

Program Resources

Student Activity Journal

Use page 72 to build key vocabulary.

Use page 73 to practice recognizing chronological order.

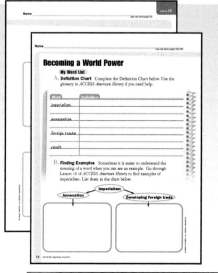

Introduce Becoming a World Power

- Talk about the pictures. Ask students, *Which of these pictures shows an example of power over others?* Have students explain their opinions.

- Tell students that Spain was one of the first European countries to explore and colonize other lands.

  • Show students a map of the Americas and point out some of the places taken over by the Spanish, such as Puerto Rico, Colombia, and Mexico. Ask volunteers to remind the class of what they have learned about Spain's empire in the Americas. (*It had once been great and powerful, but then it lost much of its power.*)

  • Ask students to give examples of Spain's continuing influence in the rest of the world.

Look and Read

Becoming a World Power

In the years around 1900, America reached overseas to get new lands and used its power to protect foreign trade.

Winning Land from Spain

It was an age of U.S. **imperialism.** In 1898, the United States declared war on Spain. When Spain lost the Spanish-American War, the United States got land from Spain.

CUBA LIBRE!

Spain ruled the small island country of Cuba. In the late 1800s, the people of Cuba were fighting **fiercely** to be free. "Cuba Libre!" was their battle cry. Many Americans **sided** with Cuba. They believed Cuba should be **independent.** But business people who had **invested** in Cuba thought the United States should help Spain.

Americans could not agree. Newspapers carried stories about suffering in Cuba. Then an American ship, the U.S.S. *Maine*, blew up. U.S. newspapers said Spain did it. That finally settled it. In April 1898, the U.S. Congress declared war on Spain.

▲ Theodore Roosevelt became a hero when he led his troops, called the Rough Riders, in the Battle of San Juan Hill in Cuba. Later, in 1901, he became president of the United States.

▲ More than 250 people died when the U.S.S. *Maine* blew up on February 15, 1898.

VOCABULARY
imperialism—the plan of a country for getting control of other countries
fiercely—very hard, with much anger and violence
sided—supported in a fight or quarrel; was on the same side
independent—free from outside control
invested—put money into business to make a profit

202 UNIT 5 • A CHANGING AMERICA

Activity: Vocabulary Charades

Have students work in small groups to work with the vocabulary words on pages 202–203. One student chooses a word and acts out its meaning for the rest of the group. For example, for *fiercely*, a student might put on an angry facial expression, and for *cavalry*, a student could pantomime a horseback rider. Have the other students guess the word. Then another student takes a turn.

Differentiating Instruction

Beginning
Learning Place Names Help students find and identify names of places as they read. Remind students that place names always begin with a capital letter. Write the words *Cuba, Spain, United States,* and *the Philippines* on the board and have students find these names in the text.

Intermediate
Paired Reading Have students work in pairs. They should read the text one paragraph at a time. After each paragraph, have partners stop and tell each other what they learned or what they found surprising.

Advanced
Partner Quiz Have students read pages 202–203 independently. Each student then creates one factual question about each page to ask his or her partner. Upon finishing the reading and answering each other's questions, partners should discuss the Talk and Share activity on page 203.

THE SPANISH-AMERICAN WAR

The first fighting of the war was in the *Philippines*, not in Cuba. The Philippines was a Spanish colony thousands of miles away in the Pacific. The people there also wanted to be free from Spain. American **victory** came quickly.

Then the fighting turned back to Cuba. The U.S. **cavalry** won important battles on the ground. Next, the U.S. Navy destroyed the Spanish **naval fleet.** On August 12, Spain surrendered. Just 4 months after it started, the Spanish-American War was over.

After the war, Spain signed a **treaty** that gave some of its lands to the United States. The **empire** of Spain—once huge—was now gone.

▲ Roosevelt liked the African proverb: "Speak softly and carry a big stick." His foreign policy was called the Big Stick Policy.

U.S. Lands Won in the Spanish-American War

	Where It Is	After the Spanish-American War
CUBA Capital: Havana	It is in the Caribbean Sea, 90 miles south of the United States.	It was a U.S. **protectorate** for a short time. It became independent in 1901.
PUERTO RICO Capital: San Juan	It is in the Caribbean Sea, 1,000 miles south of the United States.	It came under U.S. control. To this day, Puerto Ricans debate whether they want to be a state, become independent, or stay a territory.
PHILIPPINES Capital: Manila	It is in the Pacific Ocean near China.	It came under U.S. control. It fought the United States from 1899 to 1902 and lost. It became independent in 1946.

TALK AND SHARE On a map, find Cuba, Puerto Rico, the Philippines, and Spain. Tell a partner what happened in each place during the Spanish-American War.

VOCABULARY

victory—a success in a war; the defeat of an enemy
cavalry—the part of an army that fights on horseback
naval fleet—a group of ships used to fight on the ocean
treaty—a formal agreement between nations
empire—a group of nations or territories ruled by one country
protectorate—a weak country under the protection and control of a strong country

U.S. soldiers talk with a frightened woman in the Philippines. ▶

Teach The Spanish-American War

■ Draw students' attention to the picture of the *Maine* on page 202. Have students describe the picture and ask them if it reminds them of anything they have seen or heard about.

■ Explain that the *Maine* had been sent to Cuba to protect Americans there and was in a Cuban harbor when it blew up. Emphasize that most historians today believe that the explosion happened by accident and was not Spain's fault. Still, many Americans were angry at Spain, and the sinking of the *Maine* was blamed on the Spanish. It was the excuse many Americans needed to go to war.

TALK AND SHARE

Have students work with a partner to find the countries and discuss what happened. Remind students that Spain is in Europe, far from its island colonies. Use students' ideas to check their understanding of pages 202–203.

Activity: Role-Play

Have students work in pairs to act out a brief conversation about the war. One person is an American soldier who is helping to take over the Philippines. The other is a Filipino who wants independence. A sample discussion might go like this:

American: *I am here to save you from the Spanish!*

Filipino: *When you save us from the Spanish, then will you let us be free, as you are?*

American: *Hmm. Let's talk about that later.*

Filipino: *You will see, my friend. There is no time for later. We <u>will</u> be free!*

After students have completed their skits, have them form small groups and discuss what happened in the Philippines. They should use the chart as a reference.

Discuss Annexing Hawaii

- Ask if students know anything about Hawaii. On the board, write words and phrases students use to describe it. Ask the class to predict why the United States would show interest in Hawaii.

- Draw students' attention to the photograph on the left of page 204. Point out that the picture shows workers on a sugar cane plantation. Explain that sugar cane grows best in Hawaii and other places where the weather is warm year-round.

TALK AND SHARE

Encourage students to use time-order words as they talk with their partners.

People in History

Queen Liliuokalani

Use this feature to increase students' understanding of the role of power in history. Emphasize that Liliuokalani was a strong and popular leader, but her country was too small and too poor to fight off the much more powerful Americans. Ask students to state reasons why Liliuokalani was a strong leader.

Look and Read

▲ Hawaii has rich soil, and American business people found it an excellent place to grow sugar.

Annexing Hawaii

Hawaii is a beautiful chain of **islands** in the Pacific. Its ties to the United States started in the 1700s. First, American whaling ships stopped in the islands for supplies. Then, **missionaries** went to Hawaii, bringing American language and culture. Later, Americans started a huge sugar industry in Hawaii. The sugar planters grew rich and powerful.

In time, the Hawaiians disliked American control of their lands. In the name of Queen Liliuokalani, they revolted against the sugar planters in 1895. The powerful planters put down the revolt and set up their own government. Quickly, they asked the United States to **annex** Hawaii.

The people of Hawaii were against annexation. So, at first, America did not go along with the idea. However, when President McKinley took office, he supported the sugar planters. In 1898, the United States annexed Hawaii. Many years later, in 1959, Hawaii became America's 50th state.

TALK AND SHARE
With a partner, find Hawaii on a map. Then use the vocabulary words on this page to talk about how Hawaii became one of the United States.

VOCABULARY
islands—lands surrounded by water
missionaries—people who go to another country to spread their religion
annex—add territory to one's land

People in History

Queen Liliuokalani

Liliuokalani was the last queen of Hawaii. By the time she became queen in 1891, foreign powers had begun to take over Hawaii. Liliuokalani helped her people revolt. But when the lives of her people were in danger, the Queen stepped down.

Queen Liliuokalani was a strong leader. She helped set up schools for children. She believed in women's rights. Also, she was a superb musician. Liliuokalani wrote a song called "Aloha Oe [Farewell to Thee]," which Hawaiians still sing today.

 ### Activity: Hawaii Timeline

Have students in small groups look on page 204 to find important events in Hawaiian history. Then have them write a word, phrase, or short sentence about each event on a quarter-sheet of paper. Students should add a drawing and the date of the event when possible. Next, have students work together to put their sheets in chronological order. They may use dates and the time-order words in the text to help them.

Differentiating Instruction

Beginning
Connecting Ideas Copy this chart on the board and use it to help students see that American activities in Hawaii and Panama were aimed at helping American business grow.

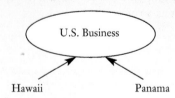

Intermediate
Dialogue Have students imagine they are workers building the Panama Canal. Have them create a short dialogue telling what it is like. Examples might include *This work is hard* and *I feel so sick, I think I may die.*

Advanced
Expressing Opinions Have students work with partners to summarize the building of the Panama Canal. Then ask them to tell what they think about U.S. actions in Panama and why.

Building and Protecting Foreign Trade

American businesses **expanded** throughout the world. To protect its businesses in other countries, the United States used its power.

THE PANAMA CANAL

Panama lies on a thin strip of land between the Atlantic and Pacific Oceans. The United States wanted to make a **canal** across Panama so ships could go easily from the Atlantic to the Pacific. Without a canal, ships had to sail all the way around the tip of South America.

Panama belonged to the country of Colombia. So, in 1903, U.S. President Theodore Roosevelt offered Colombia money to let the United States build a canal. Colombia turned down the offer. Roosevelt did not give up. He then urged Panama to fight for independence. With U.S. help, Panama fought Colombian troops and won. Then the new nation of Panama let the United States build the canal. The Panama Canal took 10 years to build, and the first ship sailed through it in 1914.

Building the Panama Canal was hard. More than 5,600 workers died from disease and accidents. ▶

Verb Phrases
These phrases have special meanings.

- **put down:** stop by using force
- **set up:** arranged, planned and began
- **go along:** be willing to accept
- **take over:** take control of
- **step down:** leave a position of power
- **turn down:** say no
- **give up:** stop trying

Talk About Foreign Trade

- Remind students that *foreign trade* means *doing business with other countries*.

- As a class, read through the captions on pages 205–207. Invite students to predict what the United States did.

Key Connection: Geography

Use a globe to show the locations of Panama, South America, and the United States. Have a volunteer sketch a line with his/her finger to show the route a ship would have to take from New York to San Francisco before the Panama Canal was built (around South America). Then sketch a second New York–San Francisco route across Panama. Ask students why a canal across Panama would make the following people happy: an officer in the navy, a business person in California with customers in Florida, the president of the United States.

Language Notes

Point out that the phrases in red are idioms with meanings that students may not expect. Discuss with students the differences between the following words and phrases:

- *Give* and *give up*
- *Turn* and *turn down*
- *Put down the pencil* and *put down the rebellion*

Activity: Use Maps

Show students a large map. Choose two points along coastlines. Describe a sea route between these two points. Trace the route with your finger and use time-order and direction words to explain the route to the class. For instance, *First, go south. Then, turn and go east. Finally, go north.* Have students work in small groups with maps of their own. Have students take turns choosing points and describing a sea route between them.

Program Resources

Student Activity Journal
Assign page 74:

- To create study notes for students to review
- To provide reinforcement of key vocabulary

Overhead Transparencies
Use 28, Timeline, with page 204.

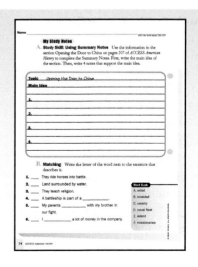

Discuss Protecting Trade in Latin America

- Focus students' attention on the photograph at the upper left of page 206. Have students describe what they see. Point out that the photo may look like a clip from a cowboy movie, but it is actually a real-life picture.

- Explain to students that the United States traded with several countries in Latin America. Then revolts in these countries during the early 1900s put this trade in danger. Have students use the picture and earlier information in the lesson to predict how the United States responded to the revolts. Finally, have students read page 206 to check their predictions.

Teach the Skill: Cause and Effect

Read aloud the following sentences:

- I was hungry, so I ate dinner.
- It was cold, so she put on a coat.
- The people of Nicaragua rebelled, so the United States sent troops.

Explain that the word *so* suggests that the first part of the sentence caused the second. Have students use this model to create sentences of their own. Encourage them to make up at least one sentence that involves the ideas presented in this lesson.

▲ U.S. troops fought against the Mexican revolutionary Pancho Villa. They never captured him.

American troops fought in Nicaragua in 1912. ▼

PROTECTING TRADE IN LATIN AMERICA

Around 1900, U.S. trade with Latin America grew. Businesses bought things cheaply there and sold them for higher prices at home. They also bought up lots of land in Latin America.

These business investments overseas needed **protection.** For that, the United States used its **military.** In 1906, American troops put down a **revolt** in Cuba. In 1912, they went to bring order in Nicaragua. In 1914, U.S. troops went into Mexico to put down the start of a revolution. The United States made itself the police of Latin America.

VOCABULARY

protection—a guard used to keep something safe
military—fighting forces. The army, navy, air force, and marines make up the U.S. military.
revolt—a fight against a government

Activity: Sequence Charts

Have students create a Three-column Sequence Chart labeled *first*, *then*, and *last*. Have them use information from the text on this page to fill in two rows of the chart. For instance:

- First: The people of Mexico started a revolution.
- Then: The United States sent its military.
- Last: The United States stopped the revolt.

Differentiating Instruction

Beginning

Pantomime Have students work in pairs. Ask one student to name an object in one of the pictures on pages 206–207, such as *wall*, *man*, or *horse*, and pantomime it if necessary. The other student finds the object. The two then switch roles.

Intermediate

Creating Sentences In pairs, have students choose one of the images on pages 206–207. Then have them create three sentences about the picture. They may tell about what is happening, who the people are, or what ideas the picture gives them.

Advanced

Picture Analysis Call students' attention to the picture of the Great Wall of China on page 207. Have students use time-order words to describe in a few sentences how they think the wall might have been built.

The United States helped to win World War I, and good times followed. Then the economy crashed. Life was very hard for most Americans, so the government began to help people.

1 **America in World War I**

2 **The Roaring Twenties**

3 **The Great Depression**

4 **The New Deal**

Introduce the Big Idea

- Call students' attention to the four headings on the page.
- Ask students to use the headings and the picture clues to guess which tell about good times and which tell about bad times. Have students explain their reasoning.

Review

In Lesson 15, students learned about reforms that bettered the lives of immigrants and city-dwellers. Review the work of reformers such as Jane Addams (page 191) and Theodore Roosevelt (page 195).

Activity: Boom and Bust

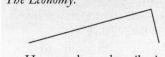

Sketch a line graph on the board like the one below. Label it *The Economy*.

Have students describe in words what the line graph shows about the economy. Emphasize that the economy usually does not stay the same year after year but can get better or worse for many reasons. Draw out that the economy got better for a long time and then crashed. Have students imitate the motion of the graph with their hands while you follow the line with a pointer.

Explain to students that when times are good, people sometimes say the economy is *booming;* this word means *big* or *loud.* Explain that people sometimes call a bad time a *bust,* from a slang term meaning *to break* or *explode.* Ask students to locate the part of the graph that shows a *boom* (*the peak*) and the part that shows a *bust* (*the end*).

Resource Library

Reader's Handbook (red)
Propaganda Techniques 287–288

Reader's Handbook (yellow)
Timeline 64, 434–435, 557

All Write
Timeline 273, 489–500

Teach [Key Concepts]

- Read the three concepts aloud, saying each term slowly to model correct pronunciation. Ask students to repeat the terms after you. Next, read the definitions aloud. Point out that students may know other meanings of the word *depression*. It also can mean *sad feelings* or *a low place in the ground*.

- Ask students how the three meanings connect. To clarify, refer students to the line graphs they drew to show boom and bust. Explain that an economic depression is like a *low place* in the graph of the economy.

Teach the Visual Aid
Good Times and Bad Times

- Focus students' attention on the timeline. Help students see that each event has a date and that the dates are arranged in chronological order. Summarize each event.

- After describing each of the six events, have students use their thumbs to indicate whether they think the event was good, bad, or neither. Ask students to put their thumbs up for good, down for bad, and to the side for neither. Ask volunteers to explain their reasoning.

Talk and Explore

Key Concepts

Economy

The **economy** is all the business activities of a country.

Unemployment

When many people are out of work, there is high **unemployment**.

Depression

When the economy is very bad, that's a **depression**.

Good Times and Bad Times

1914
World War I begins.

1917
The U.S. enters the war.

1918
The Treaty of Versailles ends the war.

212 Unit 6 • America in Two World Wars

Activity: *Un-* words

Draw students' attention to the word *unemployment*. Point out that the prefix *un-* means *not*. Explain that *unemployed* means *not employed*—that is, *not having a job*. Ask students to generate a list of other *un-* words, such as *unkind*, *unfair*, and *unhappy*. Write the root words on the board. Discuss the meaning of each root word with students. Then add the prefix and discuss how the meaning changes.

Differentiating Instruction

Beginning
Pantomime Focus on words that describe feelings. Have students use the pictures and talk about how the people in them are feeling. Have students use facial expressions and body stances to act out words such as *sad*, *happy*, and *angry*.

Intermediate
Writing Sentences Have students work in pairs to draw pictures of people showing different emotions. Have students write a short sentence

to describe each picture. Have volunteers share their work with the class.

Advanced
Small Group Discussion Have students work in small groups to generate a list of words about business and the economy, such as *jobs*, *money*, and *employment*. They may use words in the text as well as others they may know. Then have students take turns using each word in a sentence.

Analyzing Propaganda

Propaganda is information that tries to make people think a certain way. Often it does not use facts. Instead, propaganda uses words and pictures to affect people's feelings. In times of war, governments often use propaganda to make people angry at the enemy. Then they will want to fight and help win the war.

When you analyze propaganda, you look for the ways that the information makes you feel.

This propaganda poster was made during World War I. How does it make you feel about America's enemy? What in the picture makes you feel that way?

War Saving Stamps (W.S.S.) let American people loan the government money to fight the war. ▶

HELP
STOP
THIS

W.S.S.

BUY **W.S.S.**
& KEEP HIM OUT of AMERICA
NATIONAL WAR SAVINGS COMMITTEE

Teach Skill Building

■ Read with students the description of propaganda on page 213. Call their attention to the picture. Explain that the poster shows a German soldier during World War I. Ask students to think about what the poster is saying.

■ Ask students for words and phrases that describe the soldier on the poster and their feelings about him. Write their ideas on the board. Make sure that students understand that the poster was meant to make people feel scared and worried. The artist tried to draw the soldier in a way that would bring up these feelings. Ask students how their feelings might be different if the picture showed a friendly, smiling soldier who was protecting someone.

1927
The first solo flight is made across the Atlantic.

1929
The stock market crashes.

1933
The New Deal begins.

LESSON 17 • GOOD TIMES AND BAD TIMES **213**

Activity: Analyze Advertisements

Bring in several advertisements clipped from magazines or newspapers. Have students tell what the ads show.

Ask the class what they think the advertisers want people to believe. Have students analyze how these ads encourage certain kinds of thinking. Then tie them to the lesson by explaining that propaganda uses many of the same techniques and ideas.

Program Resources

Student Activity Journal

Use page 76 to build key vocabulary.

Use page 77 to practice analyzing propaganda.

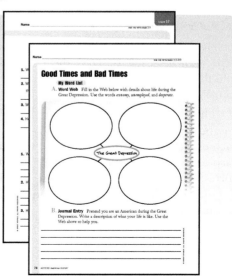

Good Times and Bad Times

A. **Word Web** Fill in the Web below with details about life during the Great Depression. Use the words *economy, unemployed,* and *desperate.*

The Great Depression

B. **Journal Entry** Pretend you are an American during the Great Depression. Write a description of what your life is like. Use the Web above to help you.

Introduce Good Times and Bad Times

- Tell students that the United States fought in two world wars in the last century. In this lesson, they will read about the first.

- Ask volunteers to tell what they know about World War I.

- Invite students to explain what is meant by *world war*.

- Ask the class to predict what the United States did during World War I. Revisit this discussion after students have read these two pages.

Good Times and Bad Times

Europe at War in World War I

ATLANTIC OCEAN

North Sea

Great Britain

Belgium

Germany

Russia

France

Austria-Hungary

Italy

Serbia

Ottoman Empire

Mediterranean Sea

0   250   500 Miles

0   500 Kilometers

KEY

Central Powers

Allied Powers

Neutral Countries

More than 20 million people were wounded in World War I. ▼

America became a bigger world power after it helped win World War I. For a while, the economy boomed, but hard times lay ahead. Then government programs, called the New Deal, helped Americans.

World War I

World War I began in Europe in 1914 and lasted 4 years. It was one of the biggest wars in history.

THE WAR BEGINS

World War I started because nations in Europe **competed** for power. They had many secret agreements. These agreements meant that if one of them got in a war, they all would help in the fight.

Two groups of nations, called *powers*, fought the war. Germany and Austria-Hungary, with their **allies,** were the Central Powers. Britain, France, Russia, and their allies were the Allied Powers. In 1914, a man from Serbia shot a member of the ruling family of Austria-Hungary. Austria-Hungary declared war on Serbia, and the secret agreements brought the other nations into war too.

FIGHTING THE WAR

Fighting in World War I was **brutal** and bloody. The worst fight was the Battle of the Somme. It lasted 4½ months, and more than one million soldiers died. New weapons made that possible. For the first time, airplanes were used in battle. Poison gas and powerful machine guns were used on the ground. At sea, submarines were used to sink ships. In all, 13 million people died.

VOCABULARY

competed—were in a contest with each other
allies—nations that joined together to fight an enemy
brutal—cruel

214 UNIT 6 • AMERICA IN TWO WORLD WARS

Activity: Word Squares

Have students cut a sheet of paper to make a square. Have them fold the four corners to the center to make a diamond.

Then have students choose four vocabulary words and write one on each of the folded corners. Under each corner, they should write the corresponding definition. Students can use multiple word squares to study vocabulary throughout the lesson.

Differentiating Instruction

Beginning
Prior Knowledge Ask students what they know about wars. Have them look for words such as *weapons*, *army*, and *soldiers* as they do paired reading or follow as you read aloud.

Intermediate
Wh- Questions Have students work in pairs to read the text a section at a time. After each section, students should think of a question such as *What countries were the Central Powers?* or *When did America join the war?*

Model appropriate sentence patterns for questions and help students generate a list of *wh-* words for asking questions.

Advanced
Research After students read pages 214–215, have them work in pairs to identify three questions about World War I. Have them write their questions in complete sentences and use family members, the library, or the Internet to find answers.

AMERICA ENTERS THE WAR

At first, the United States stayed **neutral** and out of the fighting. In time, however, it was pulled into the war. One reason was that many Americans felt close to the British. Another reason was that German submarines sank U.S. ships. So, in 1917, America joined the war on the side of Britain.

The government of Britain was more democratic than the government of Germany. President Woodrow Wilson told Americans that by entering the war, they could "make the world safe for democracy." Still, many Americans were not for the war. So the U.S. government used **propaganda** to help make fighting the war a more **popular** idea.

THE WAR ENDS

America helped to change the direction of the war. In 1918—one year after U.S. soldiers entered the fighting—Britain and its allies won.

Germany surrendered and signed the Treaty of Versailles. This harsh peace **treaty** took away Germany's air force and most of its navy and army. Germany also had to pay huge fines. The Germans felt angry and **humiliated.** Years later, German anger at what had been done led to another world war.

(TALK AND SHARE) Work with your group to make a chart on World War I. On your chart, explain *why* it happened, *what* sides were fighting, *where* and *when* it took place, and *who* won.

▲ How is this army poster propaganda?

Language Notes

Homophones
These words sound alike, but they have different spellings and meanings.

- one: the number 1
- won: came out on top; had a victory

- their: belonging to them
- there: that place

- sea: a very large body of water or an ocean
- see: look at; understand

- peace: having no war
- piece: a part

 VOCABULARY

neutral—not taking sides in a war
propaganda—booklets, movies, and posters put out by a government to push an idea onto society
popular—well-liked by many people
treaty—a signed agreement that ends a war
humiliated—lowered in pride and dignity and ashamed

Teach About World War I

Help students understand why the United States was slow to enter the war. The biggest reason was *isolationism*—the idea that a nation should avoid political or economic relationships with other countries. Most American leaders of the time believed that the United States should not get involved with European politics. Ask students to think of reasons the United States changed its mind.

Language Notes

Call students' attention to the Language Notes box. Point out that these words are very easy to confuse. Tell students that to tell which word is which, they have to memorize each word's meaning and spelling. For practice, copy the following sentences on the board. Include both answer choices. Have students determine which word belongs.

- We [*won, one*] the game.
- My baby brother is [*won, one*].
- I see a cat over [*there, their*].
- This is [*there, their*] house.

TALK AND SHARE

Have students work with a group to make the chart and discuss the topics. Remind students that they need to have a column for each of the five *wh-* words.

 Activity: Debate

Have students generate a list of reasons countries go to war. Then, divide the class into two groups. The members of one group give reasons why the United States *should* join World War I. The members of the other group give reasons why the United States *should not* be involved. Encourage students to use complete sentences.

Program Resources

Student Activity Journal
Assign page 78:

- To create study notes for students to review
- To provide reinforcement of key vocabulary

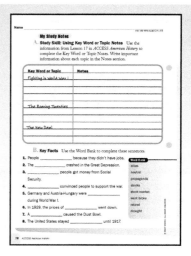

Discuss The Roaring Twenties

Use the pictures on page 216 to spark conversation among students. Have students compare the fashions and technologies of the 1920s to those of today. Sample discussion questions might include:

- What kinds of cars are popular in the United States today? How are modern cars different from the cars shown in the photograph?
- Who are the most famous U.S. athletes today? What do they play?

Teach the Pictures

- Write these three categories on the board: *culture*, *technology*, and *politics and government*. Remind students that *culture* includes arts and entertainment, and that *technology* involves machines, transportation, and methods of communication.

- Help students assign each of the pictures on the page to one of the three categories. Draw out that only one of the photos involves politics and government. Explain that the Roaring Twenties are best remembered today for their impact on U.S. culture.

▲ The world-famous trumpet player, Louis Armstrong (center, kneeling), played with King Oliver's Creole Jazz Band.

Cars
Many Americans bought cars. Roads started covering America. ▼

Music
People listened and danced to the new jazz music. ▶

◀ **Women**
Women won the right to vote in 1920.

◀ **Baseball**
Baseball player Babe Ruth became famous.

Flight
Charles Lindbergh was the first person to fly a plane across the Atlantic Ocean alone. ▶

The Roaring Twenties

When peace came after the war, the U.S. **economy** boomed. People danced to new music and sang new songs. Americans made—and spent—more money. The good times of the 1920s became known as the "Roaring Twenties." Many happy, hopeful changes took place in those years.

(TALK AND SHARE) Use the pictures below to tell your partner about the Roaring Twenties.

VOCABULARY
economy—all the business activities of a country

216 UNIT 6 • AMERICA IN TWO WORLD WARS

Activity: Make a Collage

Have students work in small groups. Have them look through newspapers and magazines to find pictures showing typical life in the United States today, just as the pictures here show life in the 1920s. Possible pictures might show cell phones, popular dances, or SUVs. Have students assemble ten to twelve of their pictures into a collage. Then ask students to take turns explaining to their group the importance of each item.

Differentiating Instruction

Beginning
Labeling Pictures Write the words *musicians*, *dancers*, *pilot*, *baseball player*, and *suffragists* on the board and explain them if necessary. Then have students copy these words onto sticky notes and place them appropriately on the pictures.

Intermediate
Dialogue Have students write sentences interpreting the mood and actions of people in the photographs

above. Have teams share their sentences out loud with the class.

Advanced
Sentence Links Have students work with a partner. One student uses a complete sentence to tell something about a picture on pages 216–217. The other student repeats the sentence and adds another idea, linked to the first with the word *and*. For instance, *People liked to dance in the 1920s*, and *they danced to a new kind of music*. Have pairs repeat with another photo.

The Great Depression

Things were not quite as good in the 1920s as they at first seemed. Farmers, for example, were having bad times. Then, in 1929, things got very bad, very fast, for everyone.

THE STOCK MARKET CRASH

Many companies are owned by lots of people. Their shares in the company are called **stocks.** Some people own a few stocks. Others have many.

People can buy and sell stocks on the **stock market.** During the 1920s, stock prices were high. People bought and sold a lot of stocks. Then, one day in 1929, the prices of stocks came tumbling down. All at once, no one wanted to buy stocks. Instead, everyone wanted to sell! Companies lost a lot of money, and millions of people **went broke.**

The crash of the stock market started the Great Depression. Earlier **depressions** were never this bad. As many as 1 out of every 4 workers was **unemployed.** The Depression spread to many parts of the world and lasted throughout the 1930s.

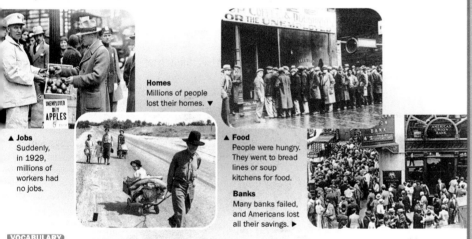

Homes
Millions of people lost their homes. ▼

▲ **Jobs**
Suddenly, in 1929, millions of workers had no jobs.

▲ **Food**
People were hungry. They went to bread lines or soup kitchens for food.

Banks
Many banks failed, and Americans lost all their savings. ▶

VOCABULARY
stocks—shares of a business. Stocks give people a way to own a part of a company.
stock market—the place where people buy and sell stocks
went broke—had no money. A person who went broke couldn't pay bills.
depressions—times when business activity is very slow and people cannot earn money
unemployed—had no job

LESSON 17 • GOOD TIMES AND BAD TIMES **217**

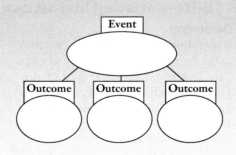

Discuss The Dust Bowl

- Focus students' attention on the photograph at the upper left of page 218. Ask students to describe the scene. Have them talk about how it would be to live on this farm.

- Then ask students what they would do if they lived in the place shown in the picture, and why. Divide the class into pairs. Give each student one minute to explain his or her answer. Have students generate a list of their ideas.

(TALK AND SHARE)

Have students take turns explaining. Suggest that they each choose in advance the two vocabulary words they will use. Use students' discussions as a check of their comprehension of this section.

(Economics)

Depression

Model the cycle shown here. Begin with *Selling* and read each event in turn as you trace your finger twice clockwise around the circle. Make two complete revolutions. Then ask students to predict what could stop the circle and make times better.

▲ The winds blew so hard and long that the area was called the Dust Bowl. The drought lasted from 1931 to 1939.

THE DUST BOWL

A **drought** in the Great Plains added to the **disaster.** Terrible dust storms whipped over the dry plains, blowing away the farmland in thick clouds of black dirt. The area became known as the Dust Bowl.

Farming methods were partly to **blame.** Settlers on the Great Plains had cleared away the grass. They didn't know that the roots of the grass helped hold the soil in place.

(TALK AND SHARE) **Explain to your partner what happened during the Great Depression. Use two or more of the vocabulary words.**

VOCABULARY

drought—a long time without rain. Crops cannot grow during times of drought.
disaster—a terrible event
blame—be at fault; be responsible for something that goes wrong

(Economics)

Depression

In a depression, one bad thing makes other bad things happen. Problems go around in what people call a *vicious* circle. *Vicious* means "very cruel."

Buying
People don't have money to buy things.

Selling
Businesses make fewer goods.

Money
People have less money.

Jobs
Workers lose their jobs.

 Activity: Less and More

Model these sentences: *The less money people have, the less they buy* and *The more money people have, the more they buy.*

Draw students' attention to the constructions *The less... the less* and *the more... the more.* Tell students that these sentences show cause and effect. Have students work in pairs to create sentences of their own that use this form. If necessary, provide prompts such as *The more you read....* or *The less you sleep....*

Differentiating Instruction

Beginning
Generating Words Have students look at the farm pictured on the top of page 218. Tell them the picture is of a farm. Have them tell one another what they know about farms. Generate a list of farm-related words such as *plant, grow, seeds, plows,* and *irrigate.* Write these words on the board to serve as a Word Bank for discussion.

Intermediate
Finding Dates Have partners look through pages 214–219 to find dates.

Have one student ask, *What happened in 1933?* Have the other answer, *Franklin Roosevelt became president in 1933.* Repeat with other years.

Advanced
Press Conference Have students take turns reporting a time in their lives when weather made life hard. Students should use complete sentences. Have other students ask questions about the presentation.

President Roosevelt and the New Deal

President Herbert Hoover and Congress tried to make things better, but they only got worse.

In 1933, a new president, Franklin D. Roosevelt, was **elected.** By then, many Americans were **desperate.** Roosevelt told the people, "The only thing we have to fear is fear itself."

Right away, Roosevelt took action. He set up government programs to pull the country out of depression. He said he had a "new **deal**" for America, so the programs became known as the New Deal. Little by little, the economy got better.

▲ President Franklin Delano Roosevelt talked to Americans on the radio.

The New Deal

Banks New laws changed how banks worked. People's money was once again safe inside banks.

Jobs New government programs created jobs. Workers built roads, airports, and bridges.

Aid Government money was given to the poor.

Social Security New taxes on all workers gave money to **retired** people.

Roosevelt's wife, Eleanor, helped serve food to the poor and hungry. She later became a U.S. representative to the United Nations. ▼

(TALK AND SHARE) **Take turns with your partner telling about the effects of the New Deal.**

VOCABULARY
elected—voted into office
desperate—afraid to the point of having no hope
deal—plan
retired—no longer working, usually because of age

Summary

The United States helped the Allies win World War I. Then, in the 1920s, the country went through good times and bad times. President Franklin Roosevelt's New Deal helped get the economy going again.

Teach About President Roosevelt and the New Deal

■ Invite students to read to find out how Roosevelt helped Americans during the Depression.

■ After students finish reading, have them take turns explaining the New Deal programs.

(TALK AND SHARE)

Have students work with a partner to discuss the topic. Encourage them to use complete sentences in their conversations.

Discuss the Summary

Read the Summary at the end of the lesson, or have a volunteer read aloud while students follow along. Then return to the Big Idea on page 211. Point out the connections between the Big Idea and the Summary.

✓ Assessment

Assess students' comprehension by asking the following questions:

History

• Why did the United States enter World War I?

• What were some of the good times during this period? What were some of the bad times?

• How did the Great Depression affect the United States?

• How did the country recover from the Depression?

Language

Write or say sentences to show how these words are related:

• Economy, unemployment, depression

• Drought, disaster

• Allies, enemies

Assessment Book

Use page 35 to assess students' comprehension.

Teach Summarizing

Explain to students that summarizing means telling not the separate details, but what they mean all together. To do this, students must find the main ideas.

Model the Organizer

- Explain that these Summary Notes tell about the Great Depression.
- Ask a volunteer to read aloud the numbered ideas. Point out that they all share a common theme: they are each an example of the bad economy during the Great Depression.
- Explain to students that the *bad economy* is the Big Idea of these details. Draw students' attention to the statement in the Main Point box.

Give Practice Summarizing

- Tell students that they will now have a chance to practice summarizing history themselves.
- **Draw** Have beginning English language learners work on the Draw activity with a partner.
- **Write** Have intermediate and advanced students complete the Write activity. Have students share their work with a partner and ask volunteers to share their finished work with the class.

Summarizing

Summarizing Events in History

When you summarize, you retell something in fewer words. You tell only the main ideas in a summary. Leave out the small details. Summary Notes can help you. You list the main ideas. Then you support it with important details.

Summary Notes

Title or Topic: The Great Depression

Main Point: The economy was very bad during the Great Depression.
1. Workers lost their jobs.
2. Banks closed.
3. Millions were homeless.

Practice Summarizing

1. Draw Make Summary Notes for the Roaring Twenties. Draw things that show why the 1920s was a good time in America. Use your Summary Notes to tell your partner or group about the Roaring Twenties.

2. Write Summarize the New Deal. First, make Summary Notes to show ways that President Roosevelt helped end the Great Depression. Then, use your notes to write a paragraph. Begin with your summary statement. Use the words in the Word Bank in your paragraph.

Word Bank
president Roosevelt
New Deal government programs Social Security
jobs

220 UNIT 6 • AMERICA IN TWO WORLD WARS

Activity: Internet Resources

Have students work in pairs to research people and events related to the lesson. Students should find examples of photographs, stories and poems, and oral histories. Useful websites include:

- http://www.chicagohs.org/exhibitions/flappers
- http://memory.loc.gov/ammem/fsowhome.html
- http://www.art-ww1.com/gb/visite.html

Differentiating Instruction

Beginning
Giving Help Encourage students to look back at the pictures on page 216 to help them recall what happened during the Roaring Twenties. Have them draw or write three of their ideas in their Summary Notes. Ask them to summarize the Roaring Twenties as *good times* or *bad times*.

Intermediate/Advanced
Writing a Paragraph Have students start with three main ideas and create a summary statement from them. Provide prompts such as *These ideas all show ___*. Suggest students look to the Word Bank for help in creating their paragraphs. Suggest that a topic sentence can come from the Main Point in their Summary Notes. Remind students to make sure they use capital letters and punctuation where they are needed.

Activities

Grammar Spotlight

Telling How Much Use *more, less,* or *fewer* to tell how much.

	What It Means	When to Use It	Examples
more	bigger or greater	With singular or plural nouns	More banks were closed.
fewer	smaller in number	With plural nouns	Fewer Americans had homes.
less	a smaller amount	With singular nouns	They bought less food.

Write two sentences to tell the answers to these questions.

1. Did Americans have *more* or *fewer* jobs during the Great Depression?

2. Did Americans have *more* or *fewer* jobs during the New Deal?

Hands On

World War I Poster With your group, make a World War I propaganda poster. Talk about how to get Americans to sign up for the war. Draw pictures and write a caption for your poster.

Oral Language

The Flapper Song Some young women in the 1920s were called Flappers. As a group, read the "Flapper Song" out loud.

> *I cut my hair,*
> *And bought a car.*
> *I wore my skirts real short.*
> *We danced to jazz,*
> *And razzmatazz,*
> *And Ma went out to vote!*

Partner Practice

Interview with the President With a partner, role-play President Roosevelt talking to a man who is out of work. The man tells the president about his hardships. The president tells the man how he will help.

Activities

Grammar Spotlight

Explain to students that *more, fewer,* and *less* all are words that compare amounts. Pantomime that *more* means an increase and that *less* and *fewer* both mean a decrease.

Call students' attention to the examples, especially the *When to Use It* column. Point out that *more* is used with either a singular or plural noun. It is acceptable to say *more money* (singular) as well as *more jobs* (plural). Point out that *less* is limited to non-count nouns (*less food*) and *fewer* to plural nouns (*fewer people*). Then have students write the sentences to practice using *more* and *fewer.*

Hands On

Have students complete the assignment by sharing their poster with the class and discussing it.

Oral Language

Ask students to speculate on the meaning of *razzmatazz.* Ask students which is more important here, the meaning of the word or its sound.

Partner Practice

Some students may feel more comfortable with this assignment if they write out a short script in advance.

Activity: Extend the Lesson

Karen Hesse's book *Out of the Dust* (Scholastic, 1999) is a series of free verse poems that describe the life of Billie Jo, a young Oklahoma teenager during the Great Depression. The book won the 1998 Newbery Award.

Program Resources

Student Activity Journal

Use page 79 to practice *summarizing.*

Overhead Transparencies

Use 24, Sequence Notes, with page 220.

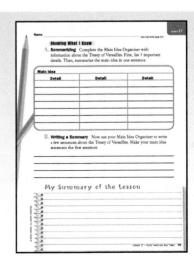

Fighting World War II

STANDARDS CONTENT

History

- Find primary sources on the Internet
- Recognize the causes and course of World War II
- Explain what happened during the Holocaust
- Identify effects of World War II on American life

Language

- Identify the following Key Concepts: *fascism, dictator, central control, nationalism,* and *racism*
- Recognize and distinguish words with multiple meanings
- Practice evaluating

Begin Building Background

- Refer to the statement *My great-grandfather fought in World War II* below the picture of the girl. Ask students if they know anyone who was or is a soldier. Have volunteers tell a little about the soldiers they know. Provide students with words such as *weapon, army,* and *uniform* as necessary.

- Then call students' attention to the photo on page 222. Have them discuss the questions under the photo. Focus students on:

  - The feelings of both soldiers in the picture

  - What might happen next

Fighting World War II

Here you'll learn about World War II. You'll also learn how to find primary sources on the Internet and practice evaluating historic events.

Building Background

▲ My great-grandfather fought in World War II.

- **What words would you use to describe this picture?**
- **Why do you think the soldier is pointing a gun?**
- **How do you think the man with his hands up feels?**

222 UNIT 6 • AMERICA IN TWO WORLD WARS

🏃 Activity: Two-column Chart

Write the word *WAR* in large letters on a piece of posterboard. Divide the board into two columns. Label one *What People Do* and the other *How People Feel.* Have students work in small groups to think of words that belong in these categories, such as *shoot, run,* and *hide* for the first and *proud, tough, scared, sad,* and *angry* for the second. Students should write their words on sticky notes and place them in the correct column. Use Overhead Transparency 29, Two-column Chart.

📖 Differentiating Instruction

Beginning

Using Visuals Use the photos on both pages to help students form short, simple sentences, such as *The man has a hat* or *The child is scared.* Have students pantomime words that are unfamiliar. Then have students point to the picture they are enacting.

Intermediate

Making Comparisons Have students work in pairs. Have them take turns choosing two of the pictures on pages 222–223. Have them use the forms *These pictures are alike because ____* and *These pictures are different because ____* to name one similarity and one difference in the pictures.

Advanced

Describing Pictures in Writing Have students work in pairs to create three to four sentences that tell about one of the pictures on pages 222–223. Then have them share their sentences with another pair.

From 1941 to 1945, Americans helped fight and win World War II. The war was fought to stop the spread of empires in Europe and in Asia. It showed how cruel prejudice can be and how deadly atomic weapons are.

1 Dictators

2 Fighting the Nazis in Europe

3 The Holocaust

4 Fighting the War in the Pacific

LESSON 18 • FIGHTING WORLD WAR II **223**

Introduce the Big Idea

■ Read aloud the Big Idea on page 223. Then call students' attention to the four captions listed on the page. Ask students to predict what they will learn about this period.

■ Tell students that the war happened when some dangerous men called *dictators* got a lot of power and used it to do very bad things. Some students may have firsthand knowledge of dictators in other countries. If so, encourage these students to share what they know about such leaders and how they use their power. Ask students to discuss how they think these and other dictators got their power and how they keep it.

Review

In the last lesson, students learned about World War I. Review the last paragraph on page 215. Ask, *How did Germany feel after losing the war?*

Activity: Role-Play

Prepare a script like the following for students to role-play:

Dictator: *I have a new law. We won't have any more elections. I will be leader for as long as I live.*

Citizen: *That law isn't fair.*

Dictator: *I will make our country safe, you'll see.*

Citizen: *But we want to have a say in our government. We need to get rid of our enemies.*

Dictator: *Yes, yes. That will come later, when the danger is gone.*

Citizen: *No. We need democracy now!*

Dictator (pointing to the Citizen): *That man is a danger. Arrest him!*

Ask students:

• What reason did the dictator give for the new law?

• What did you think of that reason?

• What could a citizen do if he or she wanted to change things?

 Resource Library

***Reader's Handbook* (red)**
Reading on the Internet 514–535

***Reader's Handbook* (yellow)**
Reading on the Internet 390–409

All Write
Using the Internet 227–232

Teach **Key Concepts**

- Read the words aloud, saying each term slowly to model correct pronunciation. Have students repeat the terms. Then read the sentences aloud, emphasizing the words in bold. Point out that some dictators are fascists, but others are not.

- Have students analyze the two illustrations. To focus discussion, ask questions, such as *What do the puppet strings mean?* and *Why is the crowd standing on other people?*

Teach the Visual Aid

World War II Powers and Leaders

- Focus students' attention on the pictures. Explain that the leaders shown on page 224 represented the Allies. Ask students to review the definition of *allies* (page 214).

- Then explain that the three leaders on page 225 worked together against the Allies. Their countries were called the Axis Powers. Tell students that both *Allies* and *Axis* mean *countries that are friendly with each other.* Point out that allies do not always like one another's ideas or form of government. Sometimes they come together because they have a common enemy.

Talk and Explore

Key Concepts

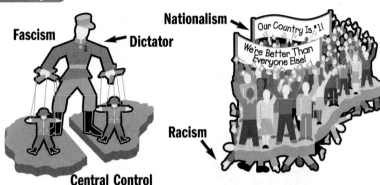

Germany and Italy had a form of government called **fascism.** An all-powerful leader, the **dictator,** had **central control** of the nation.

He appealed to people's **nationalism**—pride in their country—and to their **racism**—the belief that their race was better than others.

World War II Powers and Leaders

The Allies

Britain	United States	Soviet Union	France
Winston Churchill	Franklin D. Roosevelt	Joseph Stalin	Charles de Gaulle

224 Unit 6 • America in Two World Wars

Activity: World Maps

Have students work in pairs. They should use the map on pages 12–13 to locate and identify the countries named in the visual aid. (Point out that the Soviet Union no longer exists; the largest piece of it today is Russia.) Have partners connect the shape or location of the country with words that may help them find the country on the map. Examples might include *Italy is shaped like a boot* or *France looks like it is reaching to the west.*

Differentiating Instruction

Beginning

Describing Pictures Have pairs of students pool the words they know to describe each of the men in the visual aid. Encourage them to use the models *He has a _____* and *He is _____*.

Intermediate

Combining Sentences Put students into groups of three. Have the first two students each make a statement about the same world leader. The third student combines the statements into a sentence with the word *and*,

such as *He has no hair* and *he is wearing a coat.* Then have students switch roles.

Advanced

Nationalism Explore the word *nationalism.* It means *pride in one's country*, and its root is *nation.* Ask partners to decide if nationalism is good, bad, or both. Then have students take one minute each to explain their ideas.

Finding Primary Sources on the Internet

A primary source is a record of an event made by a person who saw it or took part in it. The Internet is a good place to find primary sources. Here's how to do it.

1. Use a search engine such as www.google.com.

2. Type in key words about your subject. For example, you could type in *World War II photographs.*

3. Scan the sites that come up. Click on the one that seems best. Sites that have *.org, .edu,* or *.gov* in the address often have primary sources.

- Explain that this feature tells students how to use the Internet to find information about people and events in history.

- Remind students that *primary sources* include words, pictures, and other objects created by people during a time in history. Generate examples of primary sources, such as diaries, letters, and photographs.

- Read the Skill Building feature aloud, or have volunteers read paragraphs while other students follow along.

- Explain that a *search engine* is like an index. If possible, have a computer available to model the process for students. Show students how they can access search engines, type in key words, and evaluate search results.

The Axis

Italy	**Germany**	**Japan**
Benito Mussolini	Adolph Hitler	Hideki Tojo

LESSON 18 • FIGHTING WORLD WAR II **225**

 Activity: Primary Source

Have students work in small groups to use the Internet to find a primary source about the World War II era. Have them choose from the following list of key words or add others as appropriate: *World War II letters, World War II photo gallery, Churchill's speeches, victory gardens, home front, Navajo Code talkers, war maps.* Groups can report the results of their research to the class.

 Program Resources

Student Activity Journal

Use page 80 to build key vocabulary.

Use page 81 to practice finding primary sources.

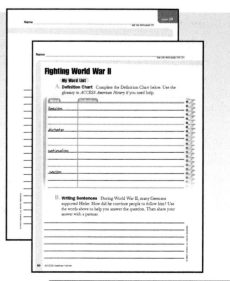

Introduce **Fighting World War II**

- The spread of fascism in Europe triggered the start of World War II. Discuss the difference between attacking countries to obtain land and power and entering a war for defensive reasons.

- Have students preview the pictures, headings, and maps on these two pages. Ask them to predict the events that occurred at the beginning of World War II.

- Encourage students who know about how World War II began to share what they know. Then invite students to read to find out more.

Fighting World War II

In 1939, World War II began. The United States fought in Europe and the Pacific to end fascism. The war took about 50 million lives and was the worst war in history.

World War II Begins

When the German **dictator** Adolph Hitler started to invade nearby countries, World War II began.

▲ Hitler reviews his troops.

DICTATORS RISE TO POWER

World War I left Germans bitter. Germany had lost a great deal in the war, and the worldwide depression made its economy worse. Italy also was hurt by the depression. During the 1930s, both nations turned to dictators for leaders.

In Germany, Adolph Hitler and his Nazi party took control. In Italy, Benito Mussolini and his Fascist party ruled. Both men had the same set of ideas about government, called **fascism.** They believed in a strong central government that managed the economy. They held an extreme view of **nationalism** and wanted to expand their nations through war.

Hitler and Mussolini joined forces in the 1930s. They became known as the **Axis** powers. In 1939, Germany invaded Poland. Immediately, Britain and France declared war on Germany in order to protect themselves.

VOCABULARY

dictator—a ruler with total power. No court or other governing body can check the power of a dictator.

fascism—a political set of ideas that says a strong central government and a very powerful leader are best

nationalism—pride in one's country

Axis—the group of nations, including Germany, Italy, and later Japan, that formed one side in World War II

226 UNIT 6 • AMERICA IN TWO WORLD WARS

 Activity: Definition Game

Divide the class into two groups: *terms* and *definitions*. Using the vocabulary words on pages 226–227, have students write one file card for each term and definition. Collect the cards, shuffle them, and pass them out. Have a student with a term stand and say the term. Ask for the student with the definition that matches the term to stand and read the definition. Continue until all the cards have been read.

 Differentiating Instruction

Beginning

Plural Nouns Have students look for plural nouns in the reading. Remind students that the letter *-s* at the end of a noun often means *more than one*. Point out plural nouns in the reading such as *nations* and *leaders*. Have students use phrases such as *one leader* and *two leaders*.

Intermediate

Finding Answers As students finish reading a paragraph, have them write a *wh-* question about it. The question does not have to have an answer in the text. Once students are through pages 226–227, give them time to work with a partner to research the answers to their questions and share them with the class.

Advanced

Discussion Group Have small groups discuss why the Germans wanted a fascist government in the 1930s and whether it could happen in another country some time in the future.

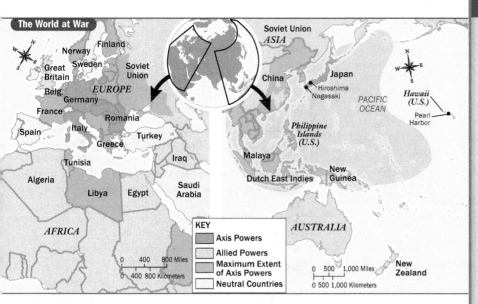

The World at War

KEY
- Axis Powers
- Allied Powers
- Maximum Extent of Axis Powers
- Neutral Countries

0 400 800 Miles
0 400 800 Kilometers

0 500 1,000 Miles
0 500 1,000 Kilometers

NAZIS OVERRUN EUROPE

The German attacks were swift and strong. Poland soon surrendered to the more powerful German forces. After that, other countries fell to the Germans. By 1941, even the great nation of France was under Hitler's power. So were parts of the Soviet Union.

BOMBING OF PEARL HARBOR

At first, America stayed **neutral** in World War II. In 1940, Japan joined the Axis. A year later, Japan bombed the U.S. **naval base** at Pearl Harbor, Hawaii. The attack killed 2,300 Americans. Another 1,100 people were wounded. Quickly, President Franklin Roosevelt asked Congress to declare war. The United States joined the **Allies** to fight the Axis powers. Now Americans, too, were fighting in World War II.

(TALK AND SHARE) With your partner, talk about the start of World War II. Ask yourselves the 5 W's to tell about it: *Who* fought? *What* happened? *Where, when,* and *why* did it start?

▲ The battleship *Arizona* burns in Pearl Harbor after the Japanese attack.

VOCABULARY

neutral—not taking sides in a war
naval base—the headquarters of a navy. The United States lost 21 ships and 188 planes in the attack on its naval base at Pearl Harbor.

Allies—the group of nations, including Britain, the United States, and the Soviet Union, that formed one side in World War II

Teach About World War II Begins

■ Call students' attention to the map on the top of page 227. Help students use the key to determine what section of Europe the Axis controlled. Ask what land the Allies still held (*Britain, much of the Soviet Union*). Tie the map to the subhead *Nazis Overrun Europe.*

■ Discuss the idea of remaining *neutral.* Ask volunteers to tell about a time when they took sides in an argument between friends. Ask volunteers to tell about a time when they did *not* take sides. Tie this discussion to the lesson by explaining that not taking sides is being neutral.

■ Remind students that the United States had been neutral at first in World War I as well. Ask why the United States changed its mind this time. (*It was attacked.*)

(TALK AND SHARE)

Have students work with a partner to discuss the five W's. Use their responses as a check of their understanding of pages 226–227.

Activity: Similarities and Differences Chart

Remind students of what they learned about World War I and the U.S. entry into that war. Make a large chart from posterboard. Label it *World War I and World War II.* Create two columns: *Alike* and *Different.*

Have students think of ways in which the two wars were alike and different. Encourage them to look back at pages 214 and 215 in the previous lesson. Put students' ideas on the chart.

Program Resources

Student Activity Journal

Assign page 82:
- To create study notes for students to review
- To provide reinforcement of key vocabulary

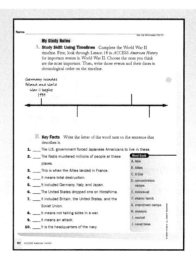

Discuss The War in Europe

- Show students a large map of Europe and Africa, or sketch a rough version on the board. Then use arrows or sticky notes to demonstrate where the Allied armies moved after the United States entered the war in Europe: north from North Africa, east from France, and west from the Soviet Union.

- Explain that places where wars are fought are called *fronts* and that the Allies were attacking Germany on three different fronts. Refer students to the map on page 227. Have them point out where a military leader might attack Germany. Ask them to explain their reasoning.

Language Notes

- Draw students' attention to the Language Notes box. Tell students that they have to read sentences carefully to know which meaning of these words is being used.

- For practice, divide the class into two groups. Assign each group one word from the word pairs. A representative from the group should draw the word, pantomime it, or use the word in a sentence.

Language Notes

Multiple Meanings
These words have more than one meaning.

- **force**
  1. group of fighters
  2. push

- **coast**
  1. land beside the sea
  2. move ahead without using power

- **last**
  1. the end
  2. continue

- **left**
  1. went out of
  2. opposite of right

- **party**
  1. a political group
  2. a get-together for fun

The War in Europe

The Allies had to fight fiercely to turn back the Germans, but victory in Europe lay ahead.

TURNING BACK GERMANY

The Germans had **overrun** many countries. Now that the United States was in the war, President Franklin Roosevelt and British Prime Minister Winston Churchill made plans to win it. First, the Allies drove the Germans out of North Africa. Next, they forced Italy to surrender. The **Soviet Union,** at the cost of millions of its soldiers' lives, drove the Germans out of Soviet lands. Then, the Allies turned their armies toward freeing France from German control.

D-DAY

On June 6, 1944, more than 156,000 Allies landed on a coast in northern France. The soldiers had sailed across the English Channel on 4,000 ships. Another 600 warships and 11,000 planes accompanied them. This huge **invasion**—it was the biggest ever by sea—became known by its code name, **D-Day.**

Allied troops attacked the Germans in France. Winning battle after battle, they kept marching toward the German capital of Berlin. Meanwhile, the Soviet troops were chasing the Germans back home. By April 1945, Hitler could see that the end was near, and he **committed suicide.** Five days later, the Germans surrendered. On May 8, 1945, the war in Europe was declared over at last.

VOCABULARY
overrun—taken over; defeated and occupied by an enemy
Soviet Union—a union of 15 countries headed by Russia
invasion—an attack
D-Day—June 6, 1944, the date when Allied forces landed in France to begin freeing Europe from the Germans
committed suicide—killed himself

228 UNIT 6 • AMERICA IN TWO WORLD WARS

 Activity: Sentence Patterns

Ask students to determine which meaning best fits the sentence.

- He **left** the room. (*went out of, opposite of right*)
- She looked to her **left**. (*went out of, **opposite of right***)
- How long will the movie **last**? (***continue**, the final*)
- I ate the **last** cookie. (*continue, **the final***)

 ## Differentiating Instruction

Beginning
Word Help Generate a list of basic words on this page that seem troublesome for students. Have students write three of these words on cards and draw a picture on the other side related to the word's meaning. Have them go through the cards one by one with a partner.

Intermediate
Multiple Meanings Focus students' attention on the Language Notes box. As students read, have them make a

list of words with multiple meanings. Help them define these words as necessary. Post their lists in the classroom for future reference.

Advanced
Letters of Protest Have students work in small groups to write a letter to the editor telling what is going on in the concentration camps and asking people to do something to stop it.

THE HOLOCAUST

In Germany, the Allies were shocked to find **concentration camps.** These were places where the Nazis had murdered 11 million people—men, women, and children. Among the murdered were 6 million Jews. Also killed were millions of Gypsies, Russians, and Poles. The horrible **slaughter** done in the camps came from Hitler's **racism.** It is known as the **Holocaust,** from a word meaning "total **destruction.**"

(TALK AND SHARE) Explain to your partner two things you remember about World War II in Europe.

▲ The Allies found few survivors at the concentration camps. Most of them were starving.

VOCABULARY
concentration camps—Nazi prisons where millions of people were killed
slaughter—the brutal killing of large numbers of people
racism—the belief that one's own group is the best and the hatred of people who belong to a different group
Holocaust—the Nazi murder of 11 million people
destruction—the act of turning something into nothing

LESSON 18 • FIGHTING WORLD WAR II **229**

Talk About The Holocaust

- Draw students' attention to the photograph of the concentration camp survivors. Have students describe what they see and tell how the picture makes them feel. Explain to students that many prisoners were killed as soon as they arrived at the camps. Others were put to work and died later of overwork and hunger.

- Explain to students that the Jewish people were treated especially cruelly during the Holocaust. Tell students that Hitler unfairly blamed the Jews for most of Germany's problems.

- Call students' attention to the photo of the star. Explain that *Jude* (yoo-da) is the German word for *Jew* and that the six-pointed star is a symbol of the Jewish faith. Explain that the Nazis forced Jews to wear these stars to identify them easily.

- Explain that most Jews who lived in Europe during the 1930s were murdered in the Holocaust but that Jewish religion and culture still survive. Emphasize that the United States is home to several million Jews today.

- More information about the Holocaust can be found on the Internet at http://www.ushmm.org.

(TALK AND SHARE)

Students should review the lesson headings and any notes that they took.

Activity: Internet Resources

Have students work in pairs to research Jewish culture and religion. Partners may use library materials or the Internet. Each pair should find three facts about the topic and report on them to the rest of the class. (Check Internet sites to make sure they are reliable.)

Activity: Personal Response

Tell students that many survivors of the Holocaust were forced to hide or leave their homes in order to stay alive. Read aloud the personal stories of some Holocaust survivors, such as those found on the Internet at http://www.ushmm.org/museum/exhibit/online/phistories/. Warn students that parts of the stories may be upsetting. After the reading, give students a few minutes to talk with a partner about what they learned. Then have students write or draw a personal response to the stories.

Discuss The War in the Pacific

Focus students' attention on the picture of the atomic explosion on page 230. Explain that the atomic bomb helped end World War II in the Pacific but more than 200,000 civilians were killed and thousands more got sick with cancers and birth defects.

Key Connection: Geography

■ Explain that the war in the Pacific was hard to fight because of the geography of the area. Have students look at a globe to get an idea of the distances involved.

■ Ask students why the small and scattered islands of the Pacific would have been useful to both sides. (*Ships and airplanes needed them to refuel and to get supplies.*)

TALK AND SHARE

Have groups think of a few reasons that Truman was right to drop the bombs and a few arguments against his decision.

The War in the Pacific

After winning the war in Europe, the Allies still had to **defeat** Japan.

WAR WITH JAPAN

By 1942, Japan had **conquered** many lands in the Pacific. Some of the lands were British or American colonies. Fighting for these lands was terrible for the Allies. Tens of thousands of U.S. soldiers were killed.

The tide started to turn against the Japanese in the spring of 1942. The Allies began winning battles at sea that were fought by warplanes **launched** from ships. Then they invaded islands that the Japanese held. Inch by **brutal** inch, they began beating back the enemy. By 1945, American troops were close to invading Japan itself.

ATOMIC BOMBS END THE WAR

The United States feared that an attack on Japan would cause a million U.S. troops to lose their lives. President Harry Truman decided instead to use a new weapon—the **atomic bomb.** Truman warned Japan that it would face complete destruction unless it surrendered. Japan refused to surrender. On August 6, 1945, America dropped an atomic bomb on the city of Hiroshima. On August 9, it dropped a second atomic bomb, on Nagasaki. The blasts from these two bombs and the sickness that came afterward killed more than 200,000 Japanese. On August 14, Japan surrendered. World War II— the deadliest war in history—was over.

TALK AND SHARE Talk with your partner about President Truman's decision to drop atomic bombs on Japan. Tell why you think he did it. Tell what you think about it.

▲ When an atomic bomb explodes, it makes a huge mushroom-shaped cloud that spreads cancer-causing gas.

VOCABULARY
defeat—beat in war; conquer
conquered—took control of a nation by force
launched—sent into the air
brutal—very cruel; inhuman
atomic bomb—a hugely destructive weapon

 Activity: Debate

After students read the text, ask them whether they think the United States *should* or *should not* have dropped atomic bombs on Japan. Have students explain their answers.

Encourage students to express their ideas using the form *The United States should/should not have bombed Japan because ___*. If students all support the same perspective, offer alternative viewpoints.

 Differentiating Instruction

Beginning
Summarizing Facts Have students work with a partner to choose two facts they remember about World War II. Have them take turns summarizing these facts while their partner listens.

Intermediate
Using Vocabulary Words Have students work with a partner to look back over the vocabulary words from the lesson. Then have them look at the pictures in the chapter through page 231. Ask them to explain to

each other which words go with which pictures.

Advanced
Role-Play Have students work in groups of four. Two students act out a conversation between a U.S. government official and a Japanese American being sent to an internment camp. Then the other two students take a turn. Students who are not part of the role-play can watch and listen. Then have them question the players about how each role felt.

The War at Home

World War II brought many changes to America. For one, the war helped end the Great Depression. To make war supplies, factories hired new workers. Because so many men were at war, lots of the new workers were women. It was the first time in America that so many women worked for pay.

A sadder result of the war involved Japanese Americans. While at war with Japan, the U.S. government worried that Japanese Americans might not be loyal to America. The government forced many Japanese Americans to move to **internment camps.** The government locked up some of its own citizens, even though they had not done anything wrong. In the 1970s, the U.S. government **apologized** to the Japanese Americans it had treated wrongly and hurt during the war.

The United Nations building is in New York City. The flags of member nations fly outside it. ▼

TALK AND SHARE Take turns with your partner explaining some of the effects World War II had in America.

Government

The United Nations

After World War II, nations knew they must work together to prevent war, so they formed the United Nations.

Today almost all the nations of the world belong to the UN. Each nation has a vote in the General Assembly. Power, however, lies with the 5 Allies who won the war—the United States, Britain, the Soviet Union (now Russia), France, and China.

The UN works for peace. It gives aid to poor nations, helps to control disease, and works for human rights.

VOCABULARY

internment camps—places set up during war to keep people who might be a threat to the safety of a country
apologized—said "I'm sorry" for doing wrong

Summary

The United States played a major role in winning World War II. It was fought in both Europe and the Pacific and was the deadliest war in history.

Teach About The War at Home

■ Ask students to imagine the effects of the war on people in the United States.

■ After students finish the reading, have them discuss the lives of women and Japanese Americans during the war.

TALK AND SHARE

Have students work in pairs to discuss the effects of World War II. Have each pair write down the two effects they think were the most important.

Government

The United Nations

Explain that the word *United* means *becoming one*, just as in *United States.* The United Nations is a group of many countries working and acting together. Ask students to discuss why they think countries thought it was a good idea to form the United Nations.

Discuss the Summary

Have a volunteer read the Summary at the end of the lesson while students follow along. Then return to the Big Idea on page 223. Ask students to make connections between the Summary and the Big Idea.

✔ **Assessment**

Assess students' comprehension by asking the following questions:

History

• What did Hitler and Mussolini do?

• How did the Allies beat the Nazis in Europe?

• What was the Holocaust?

• Why did the United States drop atomic bombs on Japan?

Language
Which word does not belong?

• Dictator, Roosevelt, Hitler, Stalin

• Japan, Italy, Allies, Germany

• Axis, neutral, Allies, invasion

Assessment Book
Use page 36 to assess students' comprehension.

Teach Evaluating

Explain to students that evaluating history means deciding what you think about it. Tell students that a Web can help them form an opinion about what happened. Remind students that *opinions* are different from *facts.* Opinions are personal ideas and cannot be called right or wrong. Point out, however, that opinions based on facts can make other people agree with you.

Model the Organizer

■ Ask volunteers to read aloud the four phrases on the outer circles of the Web. Discuss how these statements all describe something that happened during fascism.

■ Then call students' attention to the evaluation in the center. Read the statement aloud. Explain that this statement is one person's opinion, based on the facts listed in the organizer.

Give Practice Evaluating

■ Invite students to review the information on page 230 to find facts to support their opinions.

■ **Draw** Have less fluent students work on the Draw activity with a partner.

■ **Write** Ask more fluent students to complete the Write activity.

Develop Language

Evaluating

Evaluating Historic Events

When you evaluate, you form an opinion. To evaluate a time in history, think about what happened. Were the effects good or bad? Decide what *you* think about the events. Base your opinion on the facts. It helps to organize your ideas in a Web. This Web evaluates fascism in Europe.

Fascism Web

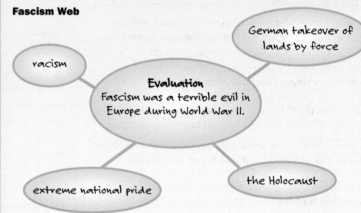

- racism
- German takeover of lands by force
- **Evaluation** Fascism was a terrible evil in Europe during World War II.
- extreme national pride
- the Holocaust

Practice Evaluating

1. Draw What do you think about the decision to drop atomic bombs on Japan? First, find the facts about why they were dropped and what happened. Then, make a Web. Use drawings to show the facts. In the middle of your Web, show your evaluation. Use your Web to tell your partner what you think about this event in history.

2. Write Think about the effects of World War II in America. Were they good, bad, or both? Use a Web to organize your thoughts. Then write your evaluation in a paragraph. Exchange paragraphs with a partner and check each other's work.

Check Your Writing

Make sure you
- ☐ Use complete sentences.
- ☐ Use a period at the end of each sentence.
- ☐ Spell all the words correctly.

Activity: Internet Resources

Have students use the Internet to help them research subjects related to World War II. Students may work in pairs to find some of the items listed below. Encourage them to present a summary of their findings to the class.

- Pictures
- Poems
- Historical fiction
- Personal narratives
- Timelines

Differentiating Instruction

Beginning

Create an Organizer Focus on the words *evaluate, opinions,* and *facts.* Contrast facts, such as *My dog is brown,* with opinions, such as *My dog is cute.* For the Draw activity, have students start with the facts about the bombing of Japan. Then help students write their opinion, or evaluation.

Intermediate

Can a War Be Good? Encourage students to think about some good things that happen in wartime (*a cruel dictator is removed from power, people work together, people do heroic acts to save others*). Invite contrasting opinions. Then have students complete the Write activity.

Advanced

Persuasive Writing Tell students that a paragraph giving their evaluation is a persuasive paragraph. It needs a topic sentence, reasons that support their opinion, and a strong closing sentence that will make the reader agree with them.

Grammar Spotlight

This, That, These, Those   The words *this*, *that*, *these*, and *those* are pronouns. They point out people or things. *This* and *that* refer to one person or thing. *These* and *those* refer to more than one person or thing. All these words can stand alone or be used in front of nouns.

Number	Stands in Front of a Noun	Stands Alone
Singular (only 1)	This <u>date</u> is known as D-Day.	This is known as D-Day.
	That <u>war</u> ended the Great Depression.	That ended the Great Depression.
Plural (more than 1)	These <u>men</u> were dictators.	These were dictators.
	Those <u>bombs</u> ended the war.	Those ended the war.

Write a sentence about the Holocaust. Use *that* in your sentence and let it stand alone. Write another sentence about the new workers in factories. Use *these* before a noun in your sentence.

Oral Language

Words with Multiple Meanings   Each partner says a sentence using one of these 5 words: *left, party, force, coast, last*. The other partner says a sentence in which the meaning of the word is different. The Language Notes on page 228 can help you.

Hands On

December 7, 1941   With a partner or in a small group, find out what President Roosevelt said to Congress about the day the Japanese attacked Pearl Harbor. Roosevelt's speech is a primary source. Use the Internet to find his speech. Decide together what key words you will use in your search. Then tell the class what you found.

Partner Practice

Family History   Find out how your family lived during World War II. With your partner, decide what questions you will ask family members. Then each of you interview your family. Afterwards, talk about what you learned. Give a report to your class.

LESSON 18 • FIGHTING WORLD WAR II   **233**

Grammar Spotlight

Give the following example of the use of pronouns. Draw two circles on the board some distance apart. Stand next to one of the circles. Point to the nearest circle. Say, *Look at <u>this</u> circle*. Then point to the other circle. Say, *Look at <u>that</u> circle*.

Draw students' attention to the examples. Help students understand how the table is organized. Remind students of the differences between *singular* and *plural*.

Oral Language

Have students work in pairs. Encourage students to refer to page 228 and ask each other for help before consulting with an adult.

Hands On

Help students find an appropriate search engine. Remind them to double-check the spellings of their words. Ask them how they will know when they have found a good website.

Partner Practice

Students can use the lesson for guidance when writing questions. Encourage them to ask their families the effects of several different events.

 Activity: Extend the Lesson

Number the Stars by Lois Lowry (Laurel Leaf Books, 1998) is a novel about a young girl growing up in Denmark during World War II. Based on actual events, the story describes how thousands of Danes joined forces to help the country's Jews escape when Germany took over their country.

 Program Resources

Student Activity Journal

   Use page 83 to practice *evaluating*.

Overhead Transparencies

   Use 33, Web, with page 232.

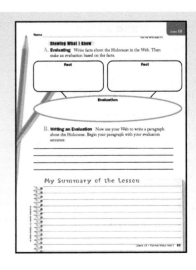

The Cold War

STANDARDS CONTENT

History
- Differentiate between facts and opinions
- Recognize the effects of Soviet communism on world affairs
- Identify ways the conflicts in Korea and Vietnam influenced domestic and international politics
- Identify effects of the Cold War within the United States

Language
- Identify the following Key Concepts: *communism, totalitarian, democracy,* and *Cold War*
- Use verb phrases
- Practice comparing events

Begin Building Background

- Refer to the statement below the picture of the girl on page 234. Ask students what would happen if someone built a wall through their own city or town.

- Then call students' attention to the photo. Explain that this photo was taken in Berlin, Germany, at a time when people really did build a high wall through the city. Discuss the questions. Focus on:
  - The materials used to build the wall
  - Why the soldiers are there
  - What the other people in the picture might be thinking and feeling

The Cold War

Here you'll learn about the time in the 20th century when the two great powers in the world were the United States and the Soviet Union. You'll also learn how to tell facts from opinions and practice comparing events in history.

Building Background

▲ I can't imagine having a wall and guards in the middle of our city.

- **What's happening in this picture?**
- **Why would people build a wall down the middle of a city?**
- **How would you feel if it happened in your city?**

234 UNIT 7 • STRUGGLING FOR PEACE AND JUSTICE

 Activity: Make a Map

Show students a street map of their city or town. Have students use a colored dot sticker to show where they live. Help students locate and mark landmarks (*schools, stores, offices, and parks*). Draw a bold line between the dots to divide the dots into two groups. Explain that this line stands for a wall that cannot be crossed. Have students list three people or places that they could no longer visit if such a wall existed.

Differentiating Instruction

Beginning
Generating Sentences Have students study the pictures on page 235. Ask them to work in pairs to describe all or part of each picture in a brief sentence. Have students compare their sentences with those generated by other groups.

Intermediate
Writing About the Photo Have partners create three sentences about a picture of their choice: who they see, what is happening, and how they feel about it.

Ask students to share their sentences with the class.

Advanced
Asking Questions Have students work in pairs. Ask them to choose one of the pictures on pages 234–235. Have one student ask two questions about the picture for his or her partner to answer. Then have them choose another picture and switch roles.

During the Cold War, the Soviet Union controlled half of Europe. Communism spread into countries in Asia. The United States worked with other nations to stop the spread of communism.

1 **Communism in the Soviet Union**

2 **A Divided Europe**

3 **Wars in Asia**

4 **Effects of the Cold War**

LESSON 19 • THE COLD WAR **235**

Introduce the **Big Idea**

■ Point to the cartoon labeled *1*. Ask students if the face on the octopus looks familiar (*Joseph Stalin, pictured on page 224*). Have students analyze what the cartoon is saying about the term *communism*. Remind students that the Soviet Union was a name for Russia and some of its neighbors.

■ Make the connection between the picture labeled *2* and the picture on page 234. Draw students' attention to the picture labeled *4*. Ask students:

- What are the people on the left doing? (*They are protesting.*)

- Why do you think they are standing there?

Tell students they will learn that Americans did not all agree about how to fight the Cold War.

Review

Review the Soviet Union's role in World War II. Have students discuss some reasons why the relationship between the Soviet Union and the United States might have changed after the war.

Activity: Allies and Enemies

Remind students that countries, like people, can have friends and enemies. Point out that friendly countries are usually called *allies*. Ask students to think about *allies* and *enemies* from earlier lessons. Ask students:

- Which countries have been allies of the United States? When?

- Which countries have been enemies of the United States? When?

- Have any countries been allies of the United States and then enemies, or the other way around?

Have students work with a partner. Encourage them to look back at previous lessons to find information. Have students give their answers in complete sentences if possible, such as *Spain was an enemy of the United States during the Spanish-American War* or *France and the United States were allies in World War II.*

Resource Library

***Reader's Handbook** (red)*
Fact and Opinion 281

***Reader's Handbook** (yellow)*
Fact and Opinion 203

All Write
Using Facts and Opinions 253

Teach — Key Concepts

- Emphasize that democratic and totalitarian countries give power to different groups or individuals.
- Have students describe what they see in the illustration. Help them to connect it to the term *Cold War*.
- Point to the phone that the democratic leader is holding. Ask students what they think it symbolizes.

Teach the Visual Aid — Hot Spots of the Cold War

- Focus students' attention on the maps of the Koreas and Vietnam. Remind students that the United States and the Soviet Union never attacked each other's countries. Explain that the two nations instead encouraged warfare and took opposite sides in wars between other nations. Tell students that this was especially true during two wars in Asia.
- Have students read the legends on the maps of the Korean War and explain what the maps show.
- Have students locate Laos, Cambodia, and North and South Vietnam on the map of Southeast Asia.

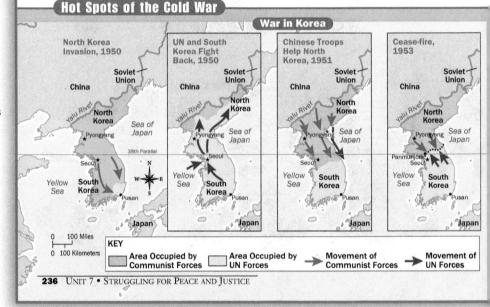

Key Concepts

Communism Cold War Democracy

Totalitarian

In **communism,** all land and property are owned by the nation, and business is controlled by the government.

The communist countries had **totalitarian** governments. All the power was in the hands of the ruling groups.

In a **democracy,** power is in the hands of the people who elect their leaders. The **Cold War** was a war of democracy against communism.

Hot Spots of the Cold War — War in Korea

236 UNIT 7 • STRUGGLING FOR PEACE AND JUSTICE

Activity: "Cold" War

Explain that *Cold War* is figurative. It does not literally mean a war that is fought in a cold climate. Read the following sentences aloud:

- The music left me cold.
- I wanted to enter the contest, but I got cold feet.
- She is a cold-hearted person.

Have students sketch the literal meaning of each sentence. Then have them discuss each meaning of *cold* and guess the meaning of *Cold War*.

Differentiating Instruction

Beginning
Key Terms Have students write the words *communism* and *democracy* on sticky notes and place the notes on the terms where they appear in the Key Concepts picture on page 236. Say, *In communism, a few people have control of the government. In a democracy, everyone gets a vote.* Have students use the sticky notes to highlight these words throughout the chapter.

Intermediate
Creating Sentences Have students work with a partner to use the pictures and definitions in Key Concepts to tell each other simple sentences about communism and democracy.

Advanced
Fact and Opinion Have partners generate sentences using the Key Concepts words, write them on chart paper, and identify which are facts and which are opinions. Then have them share their work with the class.

Skill Building

Telling Facts and Opinions Apart

People have strong ideas about government and history. When they talk about ideas, they use facts to support their opinions. You need to be able to tell facts from opinions. A fact can be shown to be true. An opinion is based on feelings and ideas. These words are clues to opinions: *best, worst, better, good, bad, evil*.

Fact	Opinion
An idea that everyone can agree is true	An idea that some people believe
EXAMPLE	**EXAMPLE**
America is a democracy.	Democracy is the best form of government.

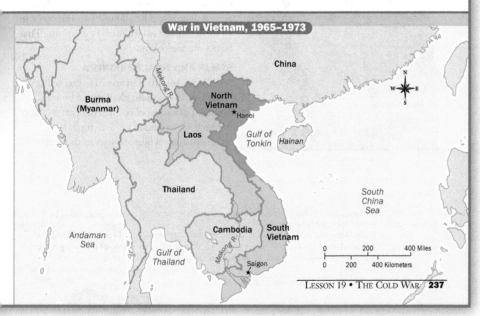

War in Vietnam, 1965–1973

China

Burma (Myanmar)

North Vietnam ★Hanoi

Laos

Gulf of Tonkin

Hainan

Mekong R.

Thailand

South China Sea

Andaman Sea

Cambodia

South Vietnam

Gulf of Thailand

Mekong R.

Saigon ★

0   200   400 Miles
0   200   400 Kilometers

Teach Skill Building

- Explain that this feature tells students how to distinguish facts from opinions.

- Read the opening paragraph of the feature aloud, or have a volunteer read aloud as other students follow along.

- Give an example of facts and opinions from within the classroom, such as the following:
  - Fact: This room has twenty-five chairs.
  - Opinion: This room has the nicest chairs in the school.

- Then read aloud the examples of facts and opinions in the chart at the bottom of the feature.

- Ask volunteers to give examples of facts and opinions related to earlier lessons.

Activity: Tell Fact from Opinion

Have students work in small groups. Assign each group to make a Two-column Chart with the labels *Fact* and *Opinion*. Then have them look for statements of fact and statements of opinion in newspapers and magazines. Have students discuss with group members whether the statements represent facts or opinions. Then have students cut out the statements and glue them in the proper place on the chart.

Program Resources

Student Activity Journal

Use page 84 to build key vocabulary.

Use page 85 to practice telling facts and opinions apart.

Overhead Transparencies

Use 29, Two-column Chart, with page 237.

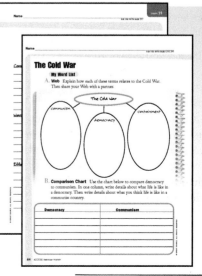

Introduce
The Cold War

- The Cold War differs from the wars described in earlier lessons. Help students understand the nature of the conflict.

- As a class, make a list of reasons that countries might dislike each other.

- Then ask students to think of different ways that countries might handle their differences. Draw out the possibilities of compromise and warfare.

- Explain that even without physical battles, people can show anger toward each other. During the Cold War, the United States and the Soviet Union were unfriendly, but they never invaded each other.

Key Connection: Government

- Point out that countries do not have to be at war with each other to be enemies, but governments of enemy countries do not trust each other.

- Ask students if they know any examples of real-world allies and enemies from personal experience or from news accounts. Their real-life examples need not involve the United States.

Look and Read

The Cold War

From 1946 until the late 1980s, the United States and the Soviet Union clashed in a struggle. Much of Europe lay under Soviet control. Communism spread to Asia, and wars were fought in Korea and Vietnam.

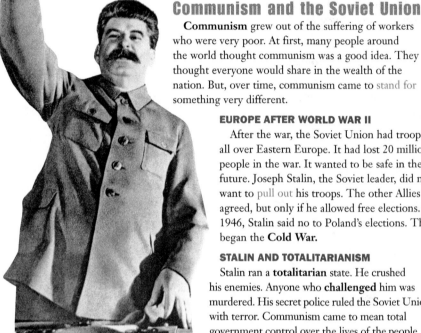

▲ Joseph Stalin

Communism and the Soviet Union

Communism grew out of the suffering of workers who were very poor. At first, many people around the world thought communism was a good idea. They thought everyone would share in the wealth of the nation. But, over time, communism came to stand for something very different.

EUROPE AFTER WORLD WAR II

After the war, the Soviet Union had troops all over Eastern Europe. It had lost 20 million people in the war. It wanted to be safe in the future. Joseph Stalin, the Soviet leader, did not want to pull out his troops. The other Allies agreed, but only if he allowed free elections. In 1946, Stalin said no to Poland's elections. That began the **Cold War.**

STALIN AND TOTALITARIANISM

Stalin ran a **totalitarian** state. He crushed his enemies. Anyone who **challenged** him was murdered. His secret police ruled the Soviet Union with terror. Communism came to mean total government control over the lives of the people.

VOCABULARY

communism—a way of living in which all wealth is owned by everyone together. There is no private property in communism.
Cold War—the conflict between democracy and communism that began after World War II
totalitarian—a kind of government in which all power is in the hands of the ruling group
challenged—spoke or worked against; objected to

238 Unit 7 • Struggling for Peace and Justice

Activity: Word Experts

Tell students they will be "word experts" for certain vocabulary words. For each set of facing pages, assign each student a specific word to learn. Give students time to become comfortable with the words they have been given. Then pair students, making sure each partner has a different word. The word expert teaches a word to the partner. Experts may use their word in a sentence, pantomime, or give a definition.

Differentiating Instruction

Beginning
Choral Reading Read the opening paragraph on page 238 aloud, breaking the text into phrases. Have students follow along in their own books. Then have them repeat what you say in a choral reading. Using the headings, help students understand the major ideas in the text.

Intermediate
Paired Reading Have students work with a partner to read pages 238 and 239. Have them take turns reading

paragraphs aloud as the other student follows along. Then have the listener ask the reader a question.

Advanced
Note-taking Have students make a Two-column Chart to use as they read. After each page, partners should compare their notes and discuss their differences. Then individuals may add to their notes before continuing to read.

A DIVIDED EUROPE

The Soviets set up communist governments all across Eastern Europe. Winston Churchill of Britain said, "An iron curtain has descended across the continent." Stalin said Churchill's words were "a call to war" and ordered his people to start building weapons.

In 1949, the nations of Western Europe joined with the United States and Canada to form the North Atlantic Treaty Organization (NATO). The NATO nations counted on each other for help if the Soviet Union attacked.

THE BERLIN WALL

At the end of World War II, the Allies divided Germany. The Soviet Union controlled East Germany. Berlin—the capital city of Germany—was split in two. In time, the Soviets built the Berlin Wall through the city. It stopped **refugees** from leaving **poverty** in East Germany. Communist soldiers shot anyone who tried to cross the Berlin Wall.

Language Notes

Verb Phrases
These phrases have special meanings.

☐ **stand for:** mean; represent

☐ **pull out:** remove

☐ **count on:** rely or depend on

☐ **back up:** support; help

(TALK AND SHARE)
With your partner, make a two-column chart about what communism means. On one side, show why people liked the idea. On the other side, show what communism came to mean.

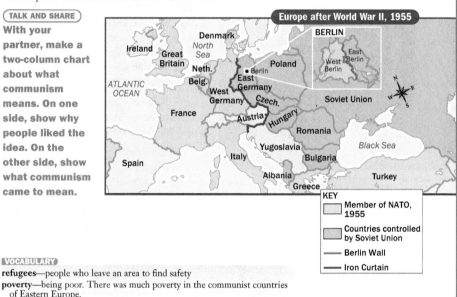

Europe after World War II, 1955

BERLIN

West Berlin · East Berlin

Ireland · Denmark · North Sea · Great Britain · Neth. · Belg. · Poland · • Berlin · East Germany · West Germany · Czech. · Soviet Union · France · Austria · Hungary · Romania · Yugoslavia · Italy · Bulgaria · Black Sea · Spain · Albania · Greece · Turkey

ATLANTIC OCEAN

KEY
☐ Member of NATO, 1955
☐ Countries controlled by Soviet Union
— Berlin Wall
— Iron Curtain

VOCABULARY
refugees—people who leave an area to find safety
poverty—being poor. There was much poverty in the communist countries of Eastern Europe.

Teach About A Divided Europe

■ Refer students to the map of Europe at the bottom of page 239. Point out that the city of Berlin lay well inside Russian-controlled East Germany, even though part belonged to democratic West Germany.

■ Explain that the East German government closed the border between East and West Germany, mostly to keep their own people from leaving.

■ Emphasize that the building of these walls, especially the Berlin Wall, cut off families and friends from one another.

Language Notes

■ Draw students' attention to the Language Notes box. Tell students that many verbs change their meanings when prepositions such as *up*, *out*, and *on* are added to them.

■ Write the verb phrases on the board. Cover up the prepositions. Ask volunteers to define the verb on its own. Then, as a class, discuss the meaning of the entire phrase.

(TALK AND SHARE)

Beginning learners may draw pictures showing what people wanted from communism and what actually happened in Europe.

Activity: Role-Play

Have students create and perform a short imaginary dialogue between two friends in Germany at the time the Berlin Wall was built. Have them imagine that one lives in communist East Berlin and the other in democratic West Berlin. Ask students to consider how the characters would feel about the part of Berlin in which they live and the building of the wall.

Program Resources

Student Activity Journal
Assign page 86:
• To create study notes for students to review
• To provide reinforcement of key vocabulary

Overhead Transparencies
Use 29, Two-column Chart, with the Advanced activity on page 238.

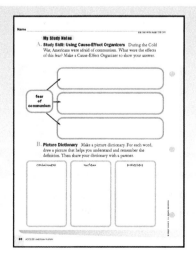

Discuss Wars in Asia

■ Show students a map of Asia or sketch a rough version on the board. Locate the Soviet Union and the peninsula that includes China, Vietnam, and Korea on the map. Make it clear that China and the Soviet Union together took up a large piece of Asia.

■ Explain that on these two peninsulas, the United States fought to contain communism.

■ To help students understand *containment*, explain how a box or can is a *container*. Both words include *contain*, which means *hold inside*. The United States did not want communism to get out of these areas and spread to more of the world.

■ Ask if students have played or watched a soccer game or other sport in which the final result was a tie. Explain that the Korean War was more like a tie than a victory for either side. Tell students that the dividing line between North and South Korea is like the Berlin Wall. It keeps families apart, even today.

Wars in Asia

In Europe, the Cold War enemies did not fight battles against each other. But in Asia, the Cold War turned "hot," and wars were fought.

CONTAINMENT

America feared that communism would spread around the world. To stop it, U.S. leaders made a plan of **containment.** NATO became one key piece of this plan. Another part aimed at stopping the spread of communism in Asia.

COMMUNIST CHINA

In the 1930s, the Chinese fought a civil war. They stopped during World War II to fight the Japanese. After the war, the communist forces of Mao Zedong again fought to control China. In 1949, they won, and China became a communist country.

THE KOREAN WAR

After World War II, communists also took control of North Korea. But the people in South Korea wanted a democracy. So the country was split across the middle at the **38th parallel.**

In 1950, the communist forces of North Korea crossed the 38th parallel into South Korea. This started the Korean War.

The United States asked the United Nations to send troops to Korea, which it did. Communist China came to aid North Korea. Most of the UN soldiers were American, and more than 37,000 Americans lost their lives fighting there. In 1953, a **cease-fire** ended the war, but Korea has remained split into two countries ever since.

▲ The Korean War stopped the spread of communism in Korea, but the country remains divided.

containment—the policy to stop the spread of communism
38th parallel—the latitude line that separates South Korea from North Korea
cease-fire—an agreement to stop fighting

Activity: Facts and Opinions

Tell students to work in small groups to generate facts and opinions about the worldwide spread of communism. Have them create a Two-column Chart to show their ideas. Possible examples of each include:

• Fact: The communists held lands in both Europe and Asia.

• Opinion: The communists would take over the world unless the United States stopped them.

Differentiating Instruction

Beginning
Directional Words Focus on the directional words *north*, *south*, *east*, and *west*, each of which appears in the names of countries in this lesson. Help students locate these directions in the classroom and label the walls with the appropriate directional word.

Intermediate
Acronyms Have students look at such acronyms as NATO and UN. Explain that these words are formed from the first letters of the organizations' names.

Help students look for other examples of acronyms, such as USA.

Advanced
Vocabulary Tic-Tac-Toe Have partners make cards for each vocabulary word and take turns drawing them. One player is *X* and the other *O*. After defining the word, a player marks an empty box. The player to fill three boxes in a row wins.

THE VIETNAM WAR BEGINS

Vietnam also was a divided country. Communists ruled North Vietnam, but South Vietnam had an anti-communist government. Even so, many communists lived in the South. Called the **Viet Cong,** they tried to overthrow the South Vietnamese government. The communist North backed up the Viet Cong with soldiers and other aid. Seeing this, President John F. Kennedy sent military **advisers** and arms to help South Vietnam.

At first, America stayed out of the fighting. That changed in 1964. President Lyndon Johnson did not want to lose another country to communism. He ordered bombs to be dropped on North Vietnam and asked Congress for power to fight to keep South Vietnam free from communism. Quickly, the fighting in Vietnam became worse. Soon America was sending more and more troops to South Vietnam.

TALK AND SHARE Tell your partner about the Korean War. Ask your partner to tell you about the war in Vietnam. Use the Vocabulary words when you tell what happened.

▲ The Vietnam War could not be won. Vietnam became a communist country.

 VOCABULARY

Viet Cong—the communists in South Vietnam who fought to unite with North Vietnam

advisers—people who give advice or tell others what to do

LESSON 19 • THE COLD WAR **241**

Teach The Vietnam War Begins

■ Review past wars in U.S. history. Ask students to recall whether the United States lost or won most of its wars. Ask how the United States' record might influence the decision to enter another war.

■ Tell students that many Americans believed in what they called the *domino theory*, in which communism would spread to one country after another like a row of falling dominoes. Demonstrate by making a short chain of dominoes and knocking the first one over. Many Americans believed if Vietnam became a communist country, the rest of southeast Asia would become communist as well.

TALK AND SHARE

Have students take turns sharing information with their partner. Remind them to use page 240 for Korea and page 241 for Vietnam.

 Activity: Cause-Effect

Have students work in small groups to make a Cause-effect Organizer about U.S. involvement in the Vietnam War through 1969. Have students mark whether the causes and the effects stem from *facts* (F) or *opinions* (O). Have them use a graphic organizer like the following:

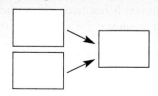

Activity: Make a Prediction

Have students work in pairs. Ask them to use the information on page 241 to predict what happened in Vietnam after 1969. Have partners discuss their ideas with each other. Then have students work together to summarize their ideas in a short sentence, such as *The United States will win the war* or *The communists will take over.* Have students write down their predictions to check them later.

Discuss Effects of the Cold War

■ Have students predict the effects of the Cold War inside the United States.

■ Ask students if they think that communism and nuclear war are still threats to Americans.

Key Connection: Civics

Emphasize that many people during the 1950s wanted to make sure all Americans were loyal to the United States. Explain that some workers were forced to sign "loyalty oaths" and promise that they were not communists. If they did not sign, or if they spoke out against these oaths, they might be fired. Have students discuss this policy in small groups. Ask students to decide if the policy was fair or unfair.

Technology

The Space Race

Explain that the race for space was not just about taking pride in being first to the moon. Tell students that scientists of the time knew that spacecrafts could not only go to the moon, but they could also be used for spying or to shoot weapons. Tell students that as a result, Americans were worried and frightened when they realized that the Soviets had circled the earth in *Sputnik*. Explain that American scientists quickly started to build new and better technologies.

Effects of the Cold War

The Cold War had several effects within the United States. Americans feared the Soviet Union, and they also feared each other. In time they became divided about fighting in Vietnam.

AMERICAN FEAR

People in the United States were afraid. At first, many Americans thought communism was a good idea. Later, people feared that those same Americans were communist spies. Congress began holding **investigations.** Many people were **persecuted** and lost their jobs. Some people even called the investigations a **witch hunt.**

THE ARMS RACE

In 1949, the Soviet Union tested an atomic bomb. That shocked America. An **arms race** with the Soviet Union began. Each side rushed to make more powerful bombs. The world lived in fear of **nuclear** war. U.S. families built bomb shelters in their yards and basements. Children practiced protecting themselves during duck-and-cover drills at school.

▲ Children show what to do during a duck-and-cover drill.

VOCABULARY

investigations—meetings to look very carefully at what people are doing
persecuted—treated badly or unfairly
witch hunt—unfair attack on people to make government officials look good
arms race—a contest over who can build the most powerful weapons
nuclear—related to the power released when an atom is split. A nuclear explosion has enough power to destroy a city.

Technology

The Space Race

One Cold War contest was the race to conquer space. The Soviets led in 1957 when their spaceship *Sputnik* circled the earth. Then when the United States put men on the moon in 1969, the United States was ahead.

The science that let people get to the moon also led to new technologies. Discoveries improved a wide range of things, such as baby food, reading glasses, and even gym shoes. Satellite TV and cell phones also came from the space race.

▲ "That's one small step for man, one giant leap for mankind," said U.S. astronaut Neil Armstrong when he stepped on the moon.

242 UNIT 7 • STRUGGLING FOR PEACE AND JUSTICE

Activity: Write a Poem

Call students' attention to the information about bomb shelters and duck-and-cover drills at the end of page 242. Have students work in pairs to think of words that might tell about the feelings of children at the height of the Cold War. Then have students write short poems using these words. Ask volunteers to read their poetry aloud.

Differentiating Instruction

Beginning
Answering Questions Ask students simple *wh-* questions about the pictures on pages 242–243, such as *Where are the children?* (*under their desks*) or *What is on the top of the Berlin Wall?* (*a flag*) Have students work with a partner to find the answers.

Intermediate
Summary Have students work with a partner. Have them reread the blue headings on pages 242 and 243. Then have them use the headings to help

explain to their partner what the section is about.

Advanced
Talking About Pictures Have students take turns talking about the pictures on pages 242–243. Ask them to discuss what they see in the pictures and what they think the people are feeling. After each student is finished, ask another student to summarize what he or she just heard.

COUNTRY DIVIDED OVER VIETNAM

By 1968, more than 500,000 U.S. troops were fighting in Vietnam. As more and more U.S. soldiers were killed or wounded, large numbers of people turned against the war. **Protesters** marched in the streets. Students on college campuses took over buildings and burned their **draft cards.**

Other Americans were angry with the protesters for not supporting the troops fighting in Vietnam. Veterans returning from the war were not treated like the heroes of other wars. Their **sacrifice** was not **appreciated.** America became so bitterly divided that it had to pull out of Vietnam.

In 1973, President Richard Nixon reached a peace agreement with the Viet Cong and North Vietnam. Within months, all U.S. troops were gone from Vietnam.

COLD WAR ENDS

Over time, the people of the Soviet Union grew to hate their communist leaders. Poland and other Eastern European countries forced out their communist governments. East Germany opened the Berlin Wall. Tired of central control, 15 Soviet republics declared independence in 1991. The Soviet Union was gone. In 1992, Russian leader Boris Yeltsin and U.S. President George Bush declared the end of the Cold War.

(TALK AND SHARE) **With a partner, explain 3 effects of the Cold War.**

VOCABULARY

protesters—people who speak and march against something
draft cards—cards that showed that their owners had registered to go into military service if selected
sacrifice—a giving up of something for an important cause. Many soldiers sacrificed their lives.
appreciated—seen as valuable; thought highly of

▲ People protest in Washington, D.C. One sign reads "Crush the Draft." The draft was the system that sent young men to fight in the war in Vietnam.

▲ People dance on the top of the Berlin Wall. On November 10, 1989, the wall was opened. Soon thousands of people moved into the West.

Summary

The Cold War was a contest between democracy and communism. The Soviet Union controlled Eastern Europe. Communism spread to Asia as well. Wars were fought in Korea and Vietnam to stop communism from growing.

Teach About the Country Divided Over Vietnam and the Cold War Ends

- Draw students' attention to the photograph in the upper right of page 243.

- Explain that people who act against a policy are called *protesters*. Remind students of the colonists' protests against British taxes. Some Americans thought protesting the war was an honorable thing to do, but others believed it made the communists fight even harder and so put U.S. troops in danger.

(TALK AND SHARE)

Have students work with partners to explain the effects of the Cold War. Have each pair choose the effect they think was the most important and tell another pair why they chose it.

Discuss the Summary

Read aloud the Summary and call students' attention to the Big Idea on page 235 to review what they learned.

✓ Assessment

Assess students' comprehension by asking the following questions:

History

- Why did people think that communism was a good idea?
- Why did the Soviet Union build the Berlin Wall?
- Why were the Korean and Vietnam Wars fought?
- How did feelings about communism affect life in the United States?

Language

Match the word to its definition.

Words	Definitions
1. Communism	A. All power is in the ruling group
2. Totalitarian	B. Being poor
3. Poverty	C. Wealth is owned by everyone together

Assessment Book

Use page 37 to assess students' comprehension.

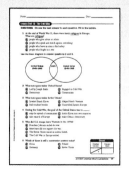

Teach Comparing

When taking tests, students will be asked to compare and contrast historical events. Tell students that a Venn Diagram can help them find similarities and differences.

Model the Organizer

■ Have students read the labels in the three parts of the Venn Diagram. Have them trace the outside of the circle labeled *Korean War.* Be sure they include the section marked *Both.* Tell students that facts about the Korean War will appear inside this circle. Repeat with the second circle and the Vietnam War.

■ Ask students to show you the part of the diagram included in both circles. Facts about both wars appear in this part of the diagram. Have students identify what is true only of the Korean War, what is true only of the Vietnam War, and what is true of both wars.

Give Practice Comparing

■ **Draw** Encourage students to share their drawings.

■ **Write** Ask volunteers to read their paragraphs to the class.

Develop Language

Comparing

Comparing Events in History

When you compare things, you tell how they are alike and different. A Venn Diagram can help you organize your ideas. Use the middle part to show how two things are alike. Use the outside parts to show how they are different. This Venn Diagram compares the Korean War and the Vietnam War.

Venn Diagram

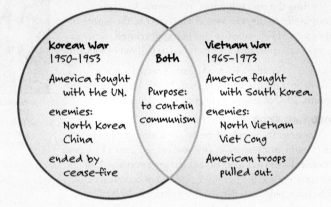

Korean War
1950–1953

America fought with the UN.

enemies:
North Korea
China

ended by cease-fire

Both

Purpose: to contain communism

Vietnam War
1965–1973

America fought with South Korea.

enemies:
North Vietnam
Viet Cong

American troops pulled out.

◄ "No mercy for spies," some people said during the days of the Cold War.

Practice Comparing

1. Draw Make a Venn Diagram to compare democracy to communism during the Cold War. In the middle part, draw pictures to show ways they are the same. In the outside parts, show ways they are different. Use words or pictures in your diagram. Then tell your partner how you compare the two kinds of government.

2. Write Write a paragraph comparing ways that the United States and the Soviet Union were alike and different during the Cold War. Make a Venn Diagram to help you organize your thoughts. The Word Bank can help you with ideas and spellings.

> **Word Bank**
>
> United States
> Soviet Union
>
> democracy
> communism
> totalitarian
>
> outer space
> bombs

Activity: Internet Resources

Have students use the Internet to research subjects related to the Cold War. Students may work in pairs to find examples of items such as photographs, documents, propaganda, and political cartoons. Useful links include:

- http://www.coldwar.org
- http://vietnam.vassar.edu
- http://www.koreanwar.net

Differentiating Instruction

Beginning

Venn Diagram Help students find words for differences between communism and democracy, such as *dictator, free elections,* and *private property,* and words for similarities, like *superpower,* and *troops in Korea.*

Intermediate

Writing Sentences Ask students to write sentences in three lists, rather than in a paragraph for the Write activity. Their lists should reflect the three parts of their diagrams: the Soviet Union Only, both the Soviet Union and the United States, and the United States Only.

Advanced

Paragraph Construction For the Write activity, have students state the similarities in one sentence. They should use the rest of their paragraph to show how the nations differed. Lead students to a concluding sentence, such as *The Soviet Union and the United States were huge, powerful nations with very different ways of life.*

Activities

Grammar Spotlight

Comparative Adverbs Adverbs are words that describe verbs, adjectives, and other adverbs. Many adverbs end in *ly*.

Adverb	Comparing Two Things	Comparing More Than Two Things
	Use *more* plus *than* or add *er* plus *than*	Use *most* or add *est*
quickly	The first soldier moved more quickly than the second.	The third soldier moved most quickly of all.
long	World War II lasted longer than the Korean War.	The Vietnam War lasted the longest of all three wars.

Write a sentence comparing the power of the Soviet Union to the power of Poland. Use the word *powerful* in your answer. Then write another comparison sentence and use the word *short*.

Hands On

Fact Maps Work with your group to make a Cold War Fact Map. Choose Berlin, Korea, or Vietnam. First, draw a map of your place, using the maps in this lesson as models. Then, label your map with facts that tell what happened there.

Oral Language

Fact or Opinion Play the Fact or Opinion game. Each partner writes 4 cards. On two of the cards, write facts about the Cold War. On the other two cards, write two opinions you have about things that happened during the Cold War. Check page 237 for clues to facts and opinions. Then exchange cards. Tell your partner which cards are facts and which are opinions.

Partner Practice

What's the Purpose? Make a chart together. Title it: What's the Purpose? Label two columns.

Berlin Wall   NATO

Complete the chart to show the purpose of each. Then use your chart to tell your class what these things were for.

LESSON 19 • THE COLD WAR **245**

Activities

Grammar Spotlight

- Give the following demonstration. Ask two students to stand up. Say, *Jose stood up quickly, but Jeanne stood up more quickly than Jose.* Point out that *quickly* is an adverb, and *more quickly* is an example of a comparative adverb.

- Explain that short words are more likely to add *-er* and *-est* than longer words, which take *more* and *less*, but tell students that there are no clear rules; the endings have to be memorized.

Hands On

Have students consult maps in the text, online, or in atlases and other library resources. Be sure each student has a chance to share ideas.

Oral Language

Encourage students to look back at the text to help them recall facts.

Partner Practice

Remind students that the *purpose* is the *reason*. Have students work in small groups to complete the chart. Students should discuss each topic and come up with one simple statement for each column.

Activity: Extend the Lesson

America in Conflict (in the Stories in History series, McDougal Littell, 2003) includes an introductory essay and several works of historical fiction involving the Cold War and the Vietnam era. Among the stories are "The Soviets Launch Sputnik," "Black Soldiers in Vietnam," "Heading Toward 'Heartbreak,'" and "The Vietnam Veterans Memorial."

Program Resources

Student Activity Journal

Use page 87 to practice *comparing*.

Overhead Transparencies

Use 31, Venn Diagram, with page 244.

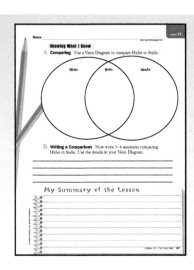

Getting Equality

STANDARDS CONTENT

History

- Find causes in history
- Identify the role of *Brown v. Board of Education* in extending civil liberties to African Americans
- Recognize key events and people in the Civil Rights Movement
- Explain the extension of rights to Hispanics, Native Americans, and women

Language

- Identify the following Key Concepts: *racial prejudice, segregation,* and *discrimination*
- Identify and distinguish confusing word pairs
- Practice explaining events

Begin Building Background

- Direct students to the picture on page 246. Have students answer the questions below the picture. Ask students to consider:
  - Why the people behind the girl are acting the way they are
  - Where the girl in front might be going
  - Where and when this photo might have been taken
- Point out the words below the picture of the boy. Have students explain what he means by *people like us.* Have students talk about why people might have been yelled at.

Getting Equality

Here you'll learn how groups of Americans fought for civil rights. You'll also learn how to find causes and practice explaining events.

Building Background

▲ My uncle told me that people like us got yelled at too.

- **What do you think is happening in this picture?**
- **How do you think the girl in front feels?**
- **Have you ever seen anything like this happen? If so, when?**

246 UNIT 7 • STRUGGLING FOR PEACE AND JUSTICE

 Activity: Getting Equality

Write the word *equality* in large letters in the middle of a sheet of posterboard. Ask students what they think *getting equality* means, and what they think the world would be like if everyone got it.

Distribute large index cards. Have students fill the cards with words, phrases, or pictures that show their ideas of *equality.* Then add the cards to the poster.

Differentiating Instruction

Beginning

Understanding Equality Focus on the concepts *equal, fair,* and *unfair.* Use counters or coins. Distribute an equal number to each student. Say, *Everybody has the same number. It is* equal. *It is* fair. Then redistribute them so some students get more than others. Say, *Now the numbers are different. It is* not equal. *It is* unfair. Repeat several times, asking students to identify whether a distribution is fair and equal or unfair and not equal.

Intermediate

Partner Talk Pair students and have them discuss how people feel when they are not treated equally. Model the use of sentences beginning *People feel ___.*

Advanced

Making Predictions Have students work in pairs to predict what they will learn about how African Americans, women, and other groups used to be treated and what happened.

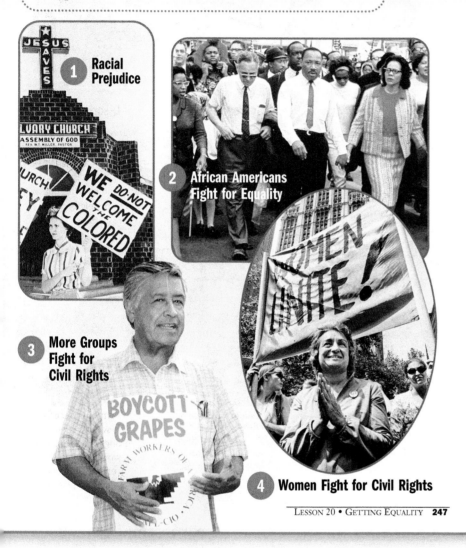

In the mid-1900s, African Americans across the country began a struggle for equality. Soon other groups began fighting for their civil rights too.

1 **Racial Prejudice**

2 **African Americans Fight for Equality**

3 **More Groups Fight for Civil Rights**

4 **Women Fight for Civil Rights**

Introduce the Big Idea

- Read aloud the Big Idea on page 247, or ask a volunteer to read it while students follow along.
- Draw students' attention to the four headings on the page.
- Have students discuss the possible meanings of terms such as *civil rights* and *prejudice*.
- Ask students to use the images and headings to predict the story line of this lesson.
- Tell students that the struggle for equality took place at the same time as the Cold War described in the previous chapter.

Review

Students learned about inequality in past lessons. Ask them to list examples from the text of one group treating another badly because of race, nationality, or religion. Possible answers include the oppression of Native Americans and the Holocaust.

Activity: Make a Timeline

Have students create a timeline to show the sequence of events during the civil rights struggle. Ask students to draw a line along a sheet of paper turned sideways. Then have them use a ruler to mark points at intervals of one centimeter. Have students label these points with years from 1945 (the end of World War II) to 1970.

As students read the chapter, have them mark important events on the timeline according to the year in which they took place. Suggest that

they write simple words and short phrases to stand for an event. As students fill in their timelines, ask them questions, such as *In what year did _____ take place?* and *Which happened first, _____ or _____?* Encourage students to ask one another these types of questions as well. Use Overhead Transparency 28, Timeline.

Resource Library

***Reader's Handbook* (red)**
Looking for Cause and Effect 644–645

***Reader's Handbook* (yellow)**
Looking for Cause and Effect 524–525

All Write
Cause and Effect 270–271

Teach Key Concepts

- Read aloud the three concepts, saying each term slowly to model correct pronunciation.

- Have students repeat the terms after you.

- Next, read the definitions aloud. Explain that the word *prejudice* comes from the roots *pre* (before) and *judge*. Help students see how the word suggests judging a person before getting to know him or her.

Teach the Visual Aid

Civil Rights Leaders

- Focus students' attention on the six people pictured on pages 248–249.

- Draw a K-W-L Chart on the board. Complete it as a class.

  - Ask students to share any information they may already know about these people.

  - Then ask students what they want to learn about these people.

  - After students have finished reading the descriptions under each picture, ask them what they have learned.

Talk and Explore

Key Concepts

Racial Prejudice

Racial prejudice is having a poor opinion of people because of their skin color.

Segregation

Segregation was one result of racial prejudice. It kept people of different races apart.

Discrimination

Segregation is one kind of **discrimination,** or unfair treatment. It goes against people's civil rights—the justice and equality that are owed to people because they are citizens.

Civil Rights Leaders

Martin Luther King, Jr.

CIVIL RIGHTS LEADER FOR AFRICAN AMERICANS
He led peaceful protests against the unequal treatment of African Americans.

Thurgood Marshall

CIVIL RIGHTS LAWYER AND SUPREME COURT JUSTICE
He won a civil rights case that integrated American schools.

Rosa Parks

CIVIL RIGHTS ACTIVIST
She was arrested for not giving up her bus seat to a white man and helped end segregation in public places.

248 UNIT 7 • STRUGGLING FOR PEACE AND JUSTICE

Activity: *-tion* Words

Focus students on the words *discrimination* and *segregation*. Pronounce the suffix *-tion*. Explain that nouns often end with this suffix, and many of these nouns are related to verbs. Draw out the connections between the words and their verb forms: *discriminate* and *segregate*. As a class, generate other *-tion* words, such as *invention*, *addition*, and *imagination*. Help students identify the verb forms.

Differentiating Instruction

Beginning
Cause-Effect Give demonstrations of simple events, such as the snapping of a pencil point, and give one or more causes for each. Say, *The event was that the pencil point broke. The cause was that I pushed too hard.* Have students think of their own events and tell or show what caused them.

Intermediate
Numbers and Directions Have partners ask and answer questions about the pictures using ordinal-number and directional vocabulary. Examples include *Whose picture is fourth from the left* and *Whose picture is second from the right?*

Advanced
Prejudice Discussion Have small groups generate a list of forms of prejudice they know or have heard about, including forms of prejudice other than that against skin color. Then have them report to the class.

Finding Causes in History

A cause—or reason—explains why something happened. Major events in history often have more than one cause. When you read history, ask yourself, *"Why did this event happen? Is there more than one reason?"* Below are 3 causes that led to the Civil Rights Movement.

Cause
African-American children could not go to the same schools as white children.

Cause
African Americans could not use the same seats on buses and trains as whites.

Cause
African Americans could not eat in "whites-only" restaurants.

Event
The Civil Rights Movement

Russell Means

LEADER OF THE AMERICAN INDIAN MOVEMENT (AIM)
He spoke out against broken treaties with Native Americans.

César Chávez

ACTIVIST FOR MEXICAN-AMERICAN FARM WORKERS
He led nationwide boycotts and organized labor unions.

Betty Friedan

FOUNDER OF THE WOMEN'S MOVEMENT IN AMERICA
She wrote and spoke widely for women's rights in the workplace.

LESSON 20 • GETTING EQUALITY **249**

Teach **Skill Building**

- Read aloud the paragraph at the top of page 249.
- Emphasize that most events in history have several different causes.
- Have volunteers read aloud each of the causes in the example as students follow along. Be sure students understand the terms *cause* and *effect*.

 Activity: Civil Rights Chart

Explain that civil rights are the basic freedoms people have because they are citizens. Have small groups decide which are the most important civil rights Americans have and complete Two-column Charts by writing the civil rights on the left and giving examples in drawings or words on the right.

 Program Resources

Student Activity Journal

Use page 88 to build key vocabulary.

Use page 89 to practice finding causes.

Overhead Transparencies

Use 3, Cause-effect Organizer, with page 249.

Use 29, Two-column Chart, with page 249.

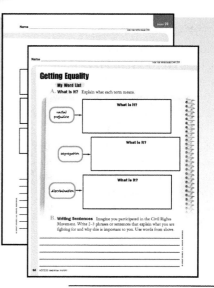

Introduce Getting Equality

Have volunteers take turns reading sentences aloud in the first paragraph below the heading *Racial Prejudice*. Have other students follow along. Then have students take turns reading the rest of the text aloud with a partner while the other follows along. Tell students to pay special attention to the different groups that were being treated unfairly.

Language Notes

- Draw students' attention to the Language Notes box. Explain that these words are easy to confuse.

- Have volunteers use each word in a sentence to demonstrate how different their meanings are.

- Remind students to read these words carefully. Point out that changing a single letter can completely change the meaning of a word.

TALK AND SHARE

Have students work with a partner to discuss the picture. They can read aloud the pictured sign to each other and look up unfamiliar words. Remind pairs to use vocabulary words as they talk.

Language Notes

Confusing Word Pairs
These words are easily mixed up.

- **far:** a long way away
- **fair:** just and reasonable
- **races:** groups of people
- **racist:** being against people of another race
- **step:** stage toward a goal
- **stop:** end or cease

Getting Equality

In the 1950s, African Americans started to fight against racial prejudice and for equal rights. Soon other groups did too.

Racial Prejudice

Discrimination was legal far into the 20th century. Most Southern states had laws that kept the black and white races apart. African Americans, especially in the South, had to use separate **facilities** from white Americans. Racist people called this system "separate but equal."

However, World War II taught people a lesson. When Americans learned of the horrors of the Holocaust, many of them saw the need to end **racism** at home. African Americans who fought in World War II came back to face prejudice at home. They joined with others who believed **segregation** must end.

One early step to end segregation came in 1948. This was when President Harry S Truman ordered the military to stop the segregation of blacks and whites. He ordered, "the armed services of the United States [must keep] the highest standards of democracy, with **equality** of treatment and **opportunity** for all those who serve in our country's defense."

▲ Buses were segregated in the South. *Colored* means African Americans, or blacks. *Patrons* are customers, the people who rode the bus.

TALK AND SHARE **Explain in your own words what this picture means.**

VOCABULARY

discrimination—treating people unfairly because of their race
facilities—places of services, such as restrooms or hotels
racism—the belief that your group is best and the hatred of people who belong to a different group

segregation—the separation of people of different races
equality—having the same rights as all other citizens
opportunity—chance. All people should have an equal opportunity to live a good life.

 ## Activity: Word Webs

Have students work with a partner to make a Word Web. Have them write a vocabulary word in the center of a sheet of paper and then draw four to six lines radiating from it. Have them write or draw related words, phrases, or pictures on each of the lines. For instance, *segregation* might be surrounded with words such as *apart*, *separate*, and *not together*. Invite partners to share their work with the rest of the class.

Differentiating Instruction

Beginning
Learning from Pictures Ask students where the photo on page 250 was taken (*inside a bus*). Help them read the sign. It says that *by law* white and African-American people must sit in different places. (It also says *No smoking*.) Point out that this law was based on racial prejudice.

Intermediate
Partner Quiz After reading each page, have partners write questions about segregation and quiz each other.

Example: *When did President Truman end segregation in the military?*

Advanced
Role-Play Have students create dialogue for a role-play between a bus driver and an African-American rider who wants to sit near the front door of the bus. Have the driver refer to the sign.

African Americans Fight for Equality

By 1954, laws in many places kept African Americans and white Americans apart. This **situation** was not easy to change. The fight for equality was about to start.

THE SUPREME COURT FORBIDS SEGREGATION

Many **public schools** in America were segregated. Often, the schools for blacks were much worse than the schools for whites. The Supreme Court ended that **injustice** in 1954. In the **landmark** case of *Brown* v. *Board of Education of Topeka, Kansas*, the Court ordered the **integration** of all American public schools. Thurgood Marshall, the lawyer in that case, later became the first African-American **justice** on the Supreme Court.

▲ Thurgood Marshall, center, outside the Supreme Court building

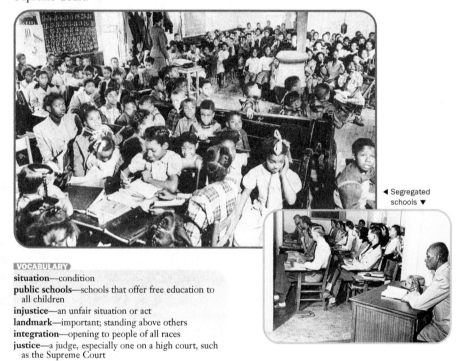

◄ Segregated schools ▼

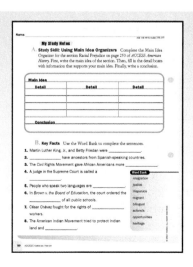

VOCABULARY

situation—condition
public schools—schools that offer free education to all children
injustice—an unfair situation or act
landmark—important; standing above others
integration—opening to people of all races
justice—a judge, especially one on a high court, such as the Supreme Court

LESSON 20 • GETTING EQUALITY **251**

Teach African Americans Fight for Equality

■ Ask students to summarize what they learned about segregation during the years following the Civil War and Reconstruction (Lesson 14).

■ Have students brainstorm a list of the parts of their day that would be different if they lived in a segregated society.

■ Explore the idea of *separate but equal*. Ask students how they would like to learn in a schoolroom that looked like the one pictured on the left and whether they think the black student shown in the picture at the bottom is being treated "equally." Have them explain their thinking.

Activity: Design a Dream School

Explain that a *dream school* means *the best school that you can imagine*. Ask students to draw their dream school. Have them label furniture, equipment, and other important features. Have them explain how the design of the room and the objects inside it will help students.

Then connect to the content of the lesson by having them talk about how the classrooms pictured on page 251 and their ideal school are different.

Program Resources

Student Activity Journal
Assign page 90:

- To create study notes for students to review
- To provide reinforcement of key vocabulary

Overhead Transparencies
Use 33, Web, with page 250.

Discuss The Civil Rights Movement

■ Ask students to think of some ways African Americans could resist segregation.

■ Have students study the pictures on these two pages. Ask, *In what ways are these people fighting prejudice?*

■ Emphasize that most protesters were otherwise peaceful, even when they were attacked by angry crowds or police officers. Ask:

  • How do you think people around the country reacted to these peaceful protests?

  • How would the movement have been different if African Americans had fought discrimination with violence?

Teach the Pictures

The pictures on this page show civil rights activists, many of them college students, trying to integrate schools and lunch counters. Ask:

  • What personality traits would allow someone to face angry mobs?

  • If you saw these images on television, how would they affect your opinion on the Civil Rights Movement?

THE CIVIL RIGHTS MOVEMENT

Protests against segregation grew quickly after that. The massive **resistance** to racial **prejudice**—by both blacks and whites—became known as the **Civil Rights Movement.** The movement forced the passage of the Civil Rights Act in 1964. It made segregation in America **illegal** at last. Hotels, theaters, playgrounds, libraries—all public places—were opened to all races equally.

When black students integrated Little Rock High School in Arkansas, the government sent federal troops to protect them from the angry mob. ▶

▲ Students sit at a lunch counter where they are not being served.

> **VOCABULARY**
>
> **resistance**—the opposing of or saying no to something
> **prejudice**—opinions formed without knowledge of the subject. *Racial prejudice* is hatred of people of other races.
> **Civil Rights Movement**—the effort by millions of Americans in the 1950s and 1960s to win equality for African Americans
> **illegal**—against the law

▲ Civil rights activists march outside a store to protest its segregated lunch counters.

252 UNIT 7 • STRUGGLING FOR PEACE AND JUSTICE

Activity: Round Table Discussion

Remind students that many civil rights protesters were breaking laws. Ask students to discuss whether they think it's OK to break a law to protest unfair laws. Have students form small groups. Give each student one minute to express his or her ideas to the rest of the group. After all students have spoken, ask one student from each group to summarize the group's discussion.

Differentiating Instruction

Beginning
Key Concept Search Have students look for the Key Concepts of *prejudice* and *segregation*, along with the word *integration*, and mark the places where these words appear with a sticky note. Have them use plus signs (+) to mark the appearance of *integration* and minus signs (–) for *prejudice* and *segregation*.

Intermediate
Main Ideas Have students read page 252, stopping after each sentence to discuss its main idea with a partner.

Advanced
Speech Writing Ask students to pretend that they have been invited to speak at an event with Dr. King. Have them write a short speech, telling the class their views on prejudice.

▲ Thousands come from all over the United States to hear Martin Luther King, Jr., give his "I Have a Dream" speech in Washington, D.C. ▶

TALK AND SHARE Work with your partner to make a Cause-effect Chart. Show problems that African Americans had *before* the Civil Rights Movement and how their lives changed *after* it.

Primary Source

"I Have a Dream"

Martin Luther King, Jr., became a voice for African Americans during the Civil Rights Movement. On August 28, 1963, King led more than 200,000 marchers to the nation's capital. There he stirred the hearts of all with his famous speech.

"I have a dream that one day this nation will rise up and live out the true meaning of its creed . . . that all men are created equal."

"I have a dream that my 4 little children will one day live in a nation where they will be judged not by the color of their skin but by the content of their character."

Talk About Martin Luther King, Jr.

■ Ask students to recall what they learned about Martin Luther King, Jr., from the discussion on page 248.

■ Give students this additional background information:

• As a young minister, King helped get rid of segregation on the buses of Montgomery, Alabama.

• King is perhaps most famous for his work leading the march on Washington in 1963.

• His 1968 assassination by a segregationist was a tragedy.

TALK AND SHARE

Have pairs draw or write words and phrases to show the changes. Ask students to explain their work to you.

Primary Source

"I Have a Dream"

Tell students that Martin Luther King's "I Have a Dream" speech is one of the most widely quoted and most frequently viewed of American political speeches. Ask students to describe the photographs of King speaking and the crowd listening to him. If possible, obtain a copy of a videotape showing King speaking and show it to students.

 Activity: Describe Words

Have students work in small groups to imagine they are at the march on Washington in August 1963, somewhere in the picture on the upper right of page 253. Have students take turns describing a sight, sound, or feeling they think they might have experienced. Examples might include:

• It's hot in the sun.

• I can hear people clapping.

 Activity: Choral Reading

Have students give a choral reading of the quotations excerpted here. Help students divide the reading into meaningful phrases (such as *I have a dream . . . that my 4 little children. . . .*). Explain the meaning of the words *creed* and *character*, and ask students where they have seen the words *all men are created equal* before.

Discuss The Struggle for Equality Expands

- Remind students that African Americans were not the only people to suffer from discrimination at this time.

- Have students preview the images on these two pages. Ask them to predict what groups they will read about.

- Have students add the dates listed on page 254 to the timelines they constructed earlier in the lesson.

Teach the Pictures

In the bottom left photograph, AIM leaders Russell Means and Dennis Banks lead a group in a victory song. The grape boycott poster in the upper left corner uses an image inspired by Aztec artwork. Both pictures show how groups maintained cultural identity while fighting for rights. Ask, *Why is it important to stay proud of one's culture and history while struggling for equality?*

César Chávez asked Americans not to buy grapes until the workers who picked them got a fair deal from the land owners. ▶

▲ AIM protesters reminded Americans that Native Americans were not treated fairly.

The Struggle for Equality Expands

Hispanics, American Indians, and women also joined in the fight for civil rights.

MORE GROUPS ORGANIZE

The African-American fight for equality moved other groups, including **Hispanics,** to fight discrimination. In 1962, César Chávez, a Mexican-American leader, started a union to improve the lives of **migrant workers.** Americans from Cuba and Puerto Rico also took steps to get equality. They formed groups to elect Hispanics into government and to pass laws for **bilingual** education.

Native American **activists** united to get better treatment. In 1968, they founded the American Indian Movement (AIM). This group demanded laws to protect Indian **heritage,** land, and their right to self-rule.

VOCABULARY

Hispanics—people whose roots are in Spanish-speaking nations
migrant workers—farm laborers who go from place to place to find work
bilingual—having to do with two languages. In bilingual classes, students can read and study in Spanish and English.
activists—people who take strong actions to get changes
heritage—traditions and skills handed down by parents to children

254 UNIT 7 • STRUGGLING FOR PEACE AND JUSTICE

 Activity: Venn Diagrams

Have students compare the struggles and lives of African Americans to those of Hispanics. Ask students to create a Venn Diagram with a partner. Have them label the left circle *African Americans*, the right circle *Hispanics*, and the central overlap *Both*. Students should write facts about the two struggles in the diagram. Have partners share and discuss their work with another pair. Use Overhead Transparency 31, Venn Diagram.

 Differentiating Instruction

Beginning
Using Pictures Write *Other Groups* on the board and say, *In the 1960s and 1970s, other groups won rights also.* As you work through pages 254–255, invite volunteers to come to the board to create a list, writing *Hispanics* or *Latinos, Native Americans,* and *women* below your heading.

Intermediate
Note-taking Have partners make Two-column Notes to complete as they read through the lesson together,

a paragraph at a time. They can record the group on the left and what it gained on the right.

Advanced
Performing a Skit Call students' attention to the information about César Chávez and the grape boycott. Have partners prepare and present a skit about the grape boycott. Have one student play a shopper and the other an activist or migrant worker asking the shopper not to buy grapes.

THE WOMEN'S MOVEMENT

In 1966, Betty Friedan and other women formed the National Organization for Women (NOW). NOW fought to get women these rights.

- Better child care for working mothers
- Equal **opportunities,** or chances, in education
- Equal opportunities in business and politics
- Equal pay for equal work

By the 1970s, many careers opened to women. More women entered medical and law schools than ever before. More women won elections to Congress. In 1981, Sandra Day O'Connor became the first woman on the U.S. Supreme Court.

TALK AND SHARE With a partner, list what each of these 3 groups fought for during the 1950s and 1960s: Hispanics, women, and Native Americans.

VOCABULARY
opportunities—chances

▲ An amendment to the Constitution, the Equal Rights Amendment (ERA), did not pass. But today, all states give equal rights to women by law.

▲ Sandra Day O'Connor was sworn in to the Supreme Court on September 25, 1981.

Summary

African Americans fought back against unjust laws. That began the Civil Rights Movement of the 1950s and 1960s. Hispanics, Native Americans, and women all soon joined the fight for equality. Over the next 20 years, each group made great gains.

Teach The Women's Movement

- Review the discussion of women's rights in Lesson 10. Ask students, *When did women receive the right to vote in national elections?* (*1920*)

- Ask, *When did women join the work force in large numbers?* (*World War II*)

- Have students speculate on what kinds of rights women wanted by the 1960s.

- Have students add the founding of NOW to their timelines.

TALK AND SHARE

Encourage students to use complete sentences in their conversations, and remind them that they may look back at the Two-column Chart and the Venn Diagrams they created earlier on these two pages. Use student responses to help gauge their understanding of pages 254–255.

Discuss the Summary

- Read the Summary aloud, or have a volunteer read it, while students follow the text.

- Then return to the Big Idea on page 247. Point out that the Summary is more specific than the Big Idea: it names the other groups that sought equality and refers directly to civil rights.

✓ Assessment

Assess students' comprehension by asking the following questions:

History

- What forms of discrimination existed in the 1950s?

- What were some of the strategies African Americans used to fight against unjust laws?

- How were the struggles of women, Native Americans, and Hispanics like the struggles of African Americans? How were they different?

Language

Say or write a sentence using the following word pairs:

- Discrimination, segregation
- Equality, opportunity
- Resistance, activists

Assessment Book

Use page 38 to assess students' comprehension.

Teach Explaining

Students will have to explain events when taking tests and writing papers. Tell students that a Web can help them list reasons or details.

Model the Organizer

■ Read aloud the text *Goals of the Women's Movement* in the center of the sample Web.

■ Tell students that the four smaller ovals each explain a goal of the women's movement. Have volunteers read these reasons aloud.

■ Rephrase each statement in this form: *Women wanted equal pay (better child care, equal opportunities . . .), so they began the women's movement.*

Give Practice Explaining

■ Tell students that they will now have a chance to practice explaining historical events themselves.

■ **Draw** Have beginning English language learners work with a partner on the Draw activity.

■ **Write** Have intermediate and advanced language learners complete the Write activity.

■ Ask students to share their work with a partner. Encourage volunteers to share their finished work with the class.

Develop Language

Explaining

Explaining Events in History

When you explain an event in history, you make its meaning clear. To do this, you often give reasons why the event happened. Sometimes you give details that tell what people were working for. A Web can help you organize details. For example, this Web shows 4 goals of the Women's Movement.

Women's Movement Web

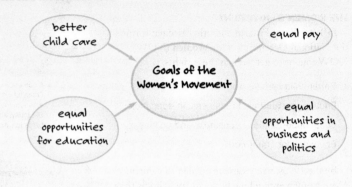

Practice Explaining

1. Draw Make a Web. Draw pictures to show the people who fought for equality during the Civil Rights Movement and the changes they won. Use your Web to explain the Civil Rights Movement to your partner.

2. Write Think about the Civil Rights Movement. What were its causes? What were its main events? Create a Web that shows details about the Civil Rights Movement. Then write a paragraph that explains this important time in history. Be sure to check your writing.

Check Your Writing

Make sure you
☐ Use complete sentences.
☐ Use a period at the end of each sentence.
☐ Spell all the words correctly.

 Activity: Internet Resources

Have students use the Internet to do research related to the lesson. Have students work in pairs to find items such as first person accounts, news articles, and songs. Ask them to summarize what they learned for the rest of the class. Useful websites include:

- http://www.civilrightsmuseum.org
- http://memory.loc.gov/ammem/aaohtml/exhibit/aopart.html

 Differentiating Instruction

Beginning
Web Help Ask students simple questions, such as *Why did African Americans fight?* and *What did they want?* Direct students to place the term *Civil Rights Movement* in the center of the Web and draw pictures in the surrounding ovals. Then have students explain their ideas to their partners.

Intermediate/Advanced
Paragraph Writing Have students use the sample Web as a model for this assignment. Ask them to place the term *Civil Rights Movement* at the center of their Webs and list their ideas in the outside ovals using note form. Encourage students to use a topic sentence to write their paragraphs and call their attention to the Check Your Writing box in the lower right corner of page 256.

Activities

Grammar Spotlight

Infinitives An infinitive is made up of the word *to* plus a verb. Infinitives often follow other verbs.

Infinitives: *to* + verb	**Verbs** often followed by infinitives	**Example**
to get	want	*I want to get more freedom.*
to fight	decide	*They decided to fight for civil rights.*
to go	start	*She started to go on freedom marches.*
to stop	try	*They tried to stop prejudice.*

Write these sentences. Finish them with an infinitive from the chart.

1. Hispanics wanted _____ equality.
2. Women decided _____ civil rights too.

Partner Practice

Struggles of the Civil Rights Movement With your partner, look back at the pictures in this lesson. Make a list of the struggles in the Civil Rights Movement. Then explain what caused people to fight so hard for equality.

Oral Language

We Shall Overcome With a partner or small group, do a choral reading of this famous civil rights song.

> *We shall overcome. (3 times)*
> *We shall overcome some day.*
> *Oh, deep in my heart*
> *I do believe*
> *We shall overcome some day.*

2nd verse uses *We shall walk in peace.*
3rd verse uses *We shall build a new world.*

Activities

Grammar Spotlight

■ Ask students simple questions such as these:
  - Do you like <u>to eat</u> sandwiches?
  - Have you tried <u>to run</u> a mile?
  - Did you ever learn <u>to swim</u>?

■ Write the questions on the board after students answer them. Underline the infinitive in each question.

■ Point out that other verbs (*like, try, learn*) come before the infinitives. Have students generate similar sentences of their own, if possible.

Partner Practice

Encourage students to use a Web to help them explain their ideas. Alternatively, have them construct a Cause-effect Organizer such as the one pictured on page 249. You can also use Overhead Transparency 3, Cause-effect Organizer.

Oral Language

Explain that this song has many verses. Have students make up their own verses to add at the end.

 Activity: Extend the Lesson

The PBS video series *Eyes on the Prize* is a thorough and often moving account of the Civil Rights Movement. The series uses archival photos and movies of civil rights demonstrations, as well as interviews with important figures in the movement. It won many important awards when it first was broadcast in the 1980s.

Program Resources

Student Activity Journal
Use page 91 to practice *explaining*.

Overhead Transparencies
Use 3, Cause-effect Organizer, with page 257.
Use 33, Web, with page 256.

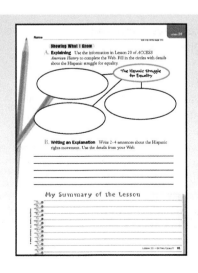

Into the 21st Century

STANDARDS CONTENT

History
- ■ Read a bar graph
- ■ Recognize international events that influenced U.S. foreign and economic policy at the beginning of the 21st century
- ■ Identify the growth of new economic powers
- ■ Explain how globalization and immigration continued to change U.S. society

Language
- ■ Identify the following Key Concepts: *technology, economic strength,* and *globalization*
- ■ Recognize figurative language
- ■ Practice interpreting events in history

Begin ▸ Building Background

- ■ Ask students the questions below the large photo on page 258. Focus students on:
  - • Why someone might cause so much destruction
  - • How the disaster would make people feel about those who caused it
- ■ Ask a volunteer to read aloud the caption below the girl's picture. Encourage students to share their own understanding of the events of September 11, 2001. Provide students with words as needed (*terrorist, disaster, attack*).

Talk and Explore

Into the 21st Century

Here you'll learn about changes in America at the beginning of the 21st century. You'll also learn how to read double bar graphs and practice interpreting events in history.

Building Background

▲ I saw this on TV. It was awful!

- ■ **What does this photo mean to you?**
- ■ **What words would you use to describe what happened?**
- ■ **Why would someone do this?**

258 UNIT 7 • STRUGGLING FOR PEACE AND JUSTICE

 Activity: Facts and Opinions Chart

Have students give words, phrases, and ideas that they think of when they look at the photo on page 258. Ask students to decide if their ideas represent *facts* (such as *the building is burning*) or *opinions* (such as *it is scary*). Create a Two-column Chart with the headings *Facts* and *Opinions*. Help students write their ideas on index cards and tape them to the proper part of the chart.

 Differentiating Instruction

Beginning
Describing Pictures Have students work with a partner. Ask them to tell each other things that they see in the pictures on pages 258–259. Allow them to use either single words or phrases, such as *building, gun,* or *on fire*. Have the partner point to what is being described.

Intermediate
Writing Questions Have students work in pairs to create three *wh-*questions about the picture on page

258, such as *What is happening?* or *Who made this happen?* Ask students to share their questions with the class.

Advanced
Small Group Discussion Have students in small groups discuss how they would feel if a similar attack took place on their community and how they think they would respond. Encourage the use of complex sentences.

Big Idea

As the 21st century began, the world changed even faster. New groups threatened world peace. New powers rose based on economic strength, and businesses worked to create a global economy.

1 Threats to Peace

2 New Powers

3 Facing the Future

- Ask students, *What do these three pictures tell you about the events you will read about in this lesson?*

- Emphasize that the 21st century is not yet complete; students will be a part of deciding what will happen next and how the United States will change and grow.

Teach the Pictures

The picture at the bottom right shows a globe above a picture of the European Union's monetary unit, the euro. Many European countries have given up their own forms of currency and have adopted the euro. Residents of the EU may travel easily among the member countries and use the same form of money. Ask students, *How does the world change when people can more easily travel and buy each other's goods?*

Review

Remind students that the previous two lessons mentioned important changes in the years before 2000. Ask students to look for the themes of turmoil and people's rights as they read this lesson.

Activity: The Future

Point out to students that the events of today are part of history. Emphasize that previous generations of Americans did not know how the events of their time were going to turn out.

Connect this idea to the lesson by explaining that students will help determine what the next steps will be for the United States.

Next, ask students to imagine a future United States in which they would like to live. Ask them to think about technology, jobs, the environment, and anything else they would like to consider. Have them form small groups to talk about their ideas.

Then, pass out large sheets of oaktag or butcher paper. Have students write and draw their vision of a future United States with their groups. Ask one student from each group to present their poster to the class. Encourage students to look for ways to make their ideas a reality.

Resource Library

Reader's Handbook (red)
Bar Graph 549

Reader's Handbook (yellow)
Bar Graph 414, 419, 426

All Write
Bar Graphs 280

Teach · Key Concepts

- Say the three Key Concepts slowly to model correct pronunciation. Have students repeat after you. Then read aloud the Key Concept sentences. Talk about what the words mean.

- Have students connect the Key Concepts to a different historical event, such as linking technology to the development of cars, telephones, and other inventions in the early 1900s.

- Have students write a short description of *economic strength* with reference to the 1920s and 1930s (good times and bad times).

Teach the Visual Aid

The Changing World of the 21st Century

Focus students' attention on the visual aid. Point out that this visual aid is like a poster, not a timeline. The ideas shown were not all separate events and did not occur in sequence. Have volunteers describe each picture in three to five sentences. Ask, *What story do these images tell?*

Talk and Explore

Key Concepts

Technology · **Economic Strength** · **Globalization**

Technology is the use of scientific knowledge that leads to inventions. It changes how people live.

Economic strength is the power that comes when people have jobs and businesses are making money.

Together, technology and economic strength lead to **globalization,** or the coming together of business interests around the globe.

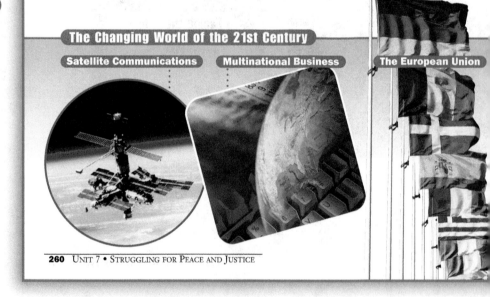

The Changing World of the 21st Century

Satellite Communications · **Multinational Business** · **The European Union**

260 UNIT 7 • STRUGGLING FOR PEACE AND JUSTICE

Activity: Word Swap

Have students preview the Look and Read section on pages 262–267. Have students choose two vocabulary words or phrases they would like to learn and write them on file cards with definitions or pictures on the back.

Then have students find a partner with two different words. Have partners teach each other their words and definitions. If time permits, have students repeat the activity with a second partner.

Differentiating Instruction

Beginning
Studying a Bar Graph Focus on comparing words such as *tallest* and *shortest* or *larger* and *smaller.* Call students' attention to the bar graph on page 261. Ask questions such as *Which bar is highest?* or *Find a bar that is shorter than ____.* Students may answer in words or gestures.

Intermediate
Describing a Picture Have students secretly choose a picture in the visual aid and describe it to a partner. The

partner should guess which picture is being described.

Advanced
Caption Writing Have students work with a partner. Ask them to write one or two sentences to serve as a caption for each picture in the visual aid. Remind them to use complete sentences, including capital letters and punctuation.

Reading Double Bar Graphs

A bar graph shows a series of bars that stand for numbers. A double bar graph shows paired sets of bars. That way, readers can compare two sets of data at a glance. Follow these steps to read a double bar graph.

1. Read the title. It tells you what the graph is about.

2. Read the key. It tells you what the different colored bars stand for.

3. Read the numbers or labels along the bottom and on the left-hand side.

4. Last, study the pattern the bars make. Which ones are larger? Do both sets of bars change the same? What does the graph mean?

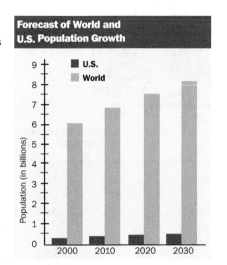

Forecast of World and U.S. Population Growth

■ U.S.
■ World

Population (in billions)

2000 2010 2020 2030

Teach   Skill Building

■ Read aloud the steps in order. Explain that the word *forecast* in the title of the graph means *prediction*.

■ Explain that a forecast is based on past events. It says, in effect, *if* these things keep happening, here's how things will look. Of course, it is possible something—a new medicine, a huge war—could make the prediction not come true.

■ Ask questions such as the following to check students' ability to read and interpret the graph:

 • What was the world's population in 2000? (*six billion*)

 • Will there be more than one billion Americans in 2020? (*no*)

■ Focus students' attention on the overall pattern or trend of the graph. Ask students to compare the rates of U.S. and world population growth. (*World population growth is increasing steadily while the U.S. population grows much more slowly.*)

Terrorism   UN Peacekeeping   Immigrants to the United States

LESSON 21 • INTO THE 21ST CENTURY **261**

Activity: Culture Connection

Invite students to talk about life in their countries of origin. How has life changed in these nations at the beginning of the 21st century? How is it like life in the United States and how is it different? Ask students to focus especially on technological progress and economic strength, if possible. Explain that globalization has had a huge effect on most countries, but has not been felt in all communities.

Program Resources

Student Activity Journal

Use page 92 to build key vocabulary.

Use page 93 to practice reading double bar graphs.

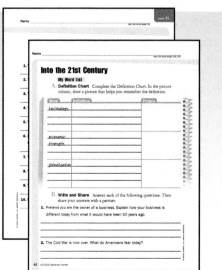

Introduce **Into the 21st Century**

- Remind students of the turn-of-the-century, where the 20th century began in 1900.

- Explain that this lesson will talk about the United States and world affairs at the turn of the 21st century.

Key Connection: Geography

- Show students a world map and have volunteers point out areas of conflict described in the text.

- Develop an understanding of why some groups wanted to break away from larger nations that ruled them. Explain that many nations did not get to draw their own borders:

  - After World War II, the Allies drew boundaries for some countries that put very different groups of people together.

  - Within a country, different groups have different interests and ideas. (Relate this to the U.S. Civil War.)

Look and Read

▲ Chechnyan soldiers are ready to fight for independence from Russia.

▲ UN troops pass by an empty street in Beirut, Lebanon.

Into the 21st Century

New threats, new powers, and major changes in business and technology came as the world entered the 21st century.

Threats to World Peace

As the year 2000 came near, many of the issues that shaped the 20th century were gone. Power struggles between the big European nations were over. The Soviet Union was gone. Communism no longer threatened the free world.

A NEW NATIONALISM

Now threats to world peace came from small groups who wanted **sovereignty** over their own ways of life.

Groups of people who were part of a large nation wanted to control the lands where they lived. In the states that were once Yugoslavia, Serbs battled Croats. Muslims in the Russian state of Chechnya revolted. In the Middle East, the Palestinians fought against the Israelis. Kurds fought in Iraq. Hindus fought Muslims in Kashmir. In many parts of Africa, **ethnic groups** battled each other for control of their countries.

The world watched as small groups fought their larger powers with **unimagined** fierceness. Many times the United Nations debated whether to send in a **multinational** force to help keep the peace. When it did, U.S. forces joined with others to stop the fighting.

VOCABULARY

sovereignty—freedom from outside control and power over their own government
ethnic groups—groups of people who share common ancestors, culture, and history
unimagined—not thought of earlier
multinational—made of many nations

262 UNIT 7 • STRUGGLING FOR PEACE AND JUSTICE

Activity: Teach Vocabulary

Have students keep a list of the vocabulary terms at the end of each page. Have them work with partners to divide their lists into three different groups: nouns (things and ideas, such as *sovereignty*), verbs (action words, such as *loomed* and *hijacked*), and adjectives (describing words, such as *multinational*).

Differentiating Instruction

Beginning

Word Association Focus on the concepts *peace* and *war*. Have students use words or draw pictures to show what peace looks like. Then have them repeat with *war*. Explain that page 262 tells about fighting in the early part of the 21st century, and page 263 tells about a growing kind of warfare called *terrorism*. Have students look for words they associate with war as they read and mark them with sticky notes.

Intermediate

Paraphrasing Have students study the headings in each section. Have them read each section with a partner and then use their own words to explain what the section has to say about the topic in the heading.

Advanced

Summarizing Have students read one paragraph at a time and work with a partner to summarize it. Encourage them to use one complete sentence for their summaries.

NUCLEAR WAR

Nuclear war **loomed** as a possibility. World nations worried about Iraq, Iran, and North Korea developing nuclear weapons. However, the first threats to world peace in the 21st century did not come from these countries, but from terrorists who worked across countries.

TERRORISM

Groups without power turned to **terrorism.** Suicide bombers drove cars full of explosives into restaurants, hotels, and marketplaces. Others **hijacked** planes. The worst attack felt by Americans came on September 11, 2001, when 4 planes were hijacked by Al Qaeda terrorists. They flew the planes into the twin towers of the World Trade Center in New York City and into the U.S. military headquarters building, the Pentagon, in Washington, D.C. Nearly 3,000 people were killed in a single day.

▲ Al Qaeda terrorists (top) flew planes into the Pentagon (middle) and the twin towers of the World Trade Center in New York City (bottom).

VOCABULARY

loomed—could be seen dimly in a threatening way
terrorism—use of great fear and violence as a way of getting control. People who use terrorism are called *terrorists.*
hijacked—took by force

LESSON 21 • INTO THE 21ST CENTURY **263**

Teach About Terrorism

- Ask students to read aloud the definition of *terrorism*. Relate the word to *terror*, or *intense fear*. Emphasize that terrorism usually is carried out by people who want more power.

- Help students understand that terrorism is different from other forms of conflict. Since it usually does not involve governments, terrorism does not use regular armies and formal declarations of war.

- Explain that terrorists do not primarily attack soldiers and military equipment, but they attack unarmed people without warning.

- Ask students to list other ways that the September 11 attacks were different from other forms of warfare in U.S. history.

- Finally, explain to students that the threat and reality of terrorism brought many changes to the United States and other countries. Explore what students know personally about these changes and how they affect immigrants and others.

Review

Have students relate the attack on the World Trade Center and the Pentagon to the attack on Pearl Harbor in 1941. Help them create a two-circle Venn Diagram on the board that shows the differences and similarities.

🏃 Activity: Reflections

Give students time to look carefully at the photos on page 263, as well as at the photo that opens the lesson on page 258. Ask them to form small groups to talk about the feelings and ideas they get from the photos. Then have students create a personal response to the September 11th disaster. Encourage them to use drawing, poetry, collage, or any other medium they enjoy. Ask volunteers to share their work with the class.

📖 Program Resources
Student Activity Journal
Assign page 94:
- To create study notes for students to review
- To provide reinforcement of key vocabulary

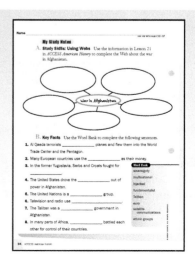

Discuss Wars in Afghanistan and Iraq

- Have students preview the pictures and headings.

- Ask, *What do you know about why the United States fought in Afghanistan?*

- After discussion, encourage students to read the first paragraph.

- Ask volunteers to say what they learned from their reading.

- Repeat the steps above with reasons the United States went to war in Iraq.

- Relate this history to current events in the region.

TALK AND SHARE

Have students discuss the topic with a partner. Encourage them to use vocabulary words from pages 262–264 as they talk. Use their responses as a check of their comprehension of these pages.

Look and Read

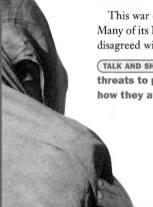

FBI TEN MOST WANTED FUGITIVE

MURDER OF U.S. NATIONALS OUTSIDE THE UNITED STATES; CONSPIRACY TO MURDER U.S. NATIONALS OUTSIDE THE UNITED STATES; ATTACK ON A FEDERAL FACILITY RESULTING IN DEATH

USAMA BIN LADEN

Aliases: Usama Bin Mohammed Bin Laden, Shaykh Usama Bin Laden, the Prince, the Emir, Abu Abdallah, Mujahid Shaykh, Hajj, the Director

WAR IN AFGHANISTAN

A terrorist from Saudi Arabia named Usama bin Laden directed the September 11 attacks. His Al Qaeda terrorist group wanted to drive American **influence** out of the Middle East. In 2001, bin Laden and Al Qaeda worked from the nation of Afghanistan. Afghanistan had a **fundamentalist** government called the **Taliban.** It protected Al Qaeda. Late in 2001, President George W. Bush, with the approval of Congress, sent troops to remove the Taliban from power.

WAR IN IRAQ

The U.S. war against terrorism aimed to keep terrorists from getting weapons of mass destruction. These weapons—such as atomic bombs and poison gases—could kill huge numbers of people at one time.

The U.S. government believed that Saddam Hussein, dictator of Iraq, had weapons of mass destruction. U.S. Secretary of State Colin Powell and others in the government tried to persuade the United Nations to support an attack to end Hussein's rule. When that support did not come, the United States invaded Iraq in March 2003.

This war damaged the **prestige** of the United States. Many of its NATO partners, such as France and Germany, disagreed with the U.S. decision.

▲ Secretary of State Colin Powell, President George W. Bush, Vice President Dick Cheney, and Henry Shelton, chairman of the Joint Chiefs of Staff, meet to discuss U.S. foreign policy.

TALK AND SHARE With your partner, talk about the threats to peace that came in the 21st century and how they affect you.

VOCABULARY

influence—the power of having an effect on others without using force. American influence changed ideas in the Middle East about government, business, and the roles of women.
fundamentalist—very religious and firm in belief
Taliban—the ruling government of Afghanistan from 1996 to 2001. It treated women harshly and helped terrorists.
prestige—honor; reputation

264 UNIT 7 • STRUGGLING FOR PEACE AND JUSTICE

Activity: Right or Wrong?

Ask, *When is it all right for America to send troops into another country?* Have students brainstorm a list of reasons, such as *they attacked us, a friendly country was attacked, people in that country are killing other people, terrorists are there.*

Then divide students into groups to debate the issue. Each group should decide which reasons it would support, and choose a team member to present their views to the class.

Differentiating Instruction

Beginning

Identifying Key People Use the picture and caption information to help students identify the people in government who helped shape U.S. policy in Afghanistan and Iraq. Ask volunteers to provide a definition for *cabinet, president, vice president,* and *secretary of state* (from earlier lessons). Explain the Joint Chiefs of Staff are the top military people in the armed services.

Intermediate

Finding Examples Have partners look for examples of *economic strength* on page 265 and mark them with sticky notes. Partners should discuss how each example shows economic strength.

Advanced

Identifying Problems Ask partners to extend their responses to the Talk and Share activity and create a written list of what they consider the three greatest threats to peace in the 21st century.

New Powers

A new pattern of power took shape in the world. It lay in economic strength, not in military force.

THE EUROPEAN UNION

In 1992, 12 nations signed the Treaty of Maastricht, forming the European Union (EU). Later, more nations joined. The EU is not a union of states, like the United States, but an agreement to work together. In 2002, 12 EU countries agreed to use the same money, and the **euro** became the "dollar" of Europe. The EU promoted free trade among its members. It also worked in areas of law and defense. With the strength of its many countries, the EU became a new force in world power.

CHINA

In 2000, China had the largest population in the world. More than 1.25 billion people lived in China. That is about 5 times as many as lived in the United States. It had the second largest land area. (Russia was first, and the United States was fourth.) The communist economy of China held back its development until the mid-1980s. However, in the 1990s, China had one of the fastest-growing economies in the world.

 TALK AND SHARE With your partner, talk about the new forces in world power and what made them powerful.

VOCABULARY
euro—the money used by many European Union nations

▲ Symbol of the European Union

▲ Euro paper money

▲ Crowd in China

Economics

Free Trade

Governments tax goods from other lands to protect the sale of the same goods their own people make. The taxes make foreign goods more costly than the protected goods. However, nations want to sell their goods everywhere around the world. Free trade agreements remove blocks to trade. In 1992, the United States signed a trade agreement with Canada and Mexico. Called NAFTA (North Atlantic Free Trade Agreement), the agreement took away taxes on most goods traded in North America.

LESSON 21 • INTO THE 21ST CENTURY **265**

Talk About New Powers

- Remind students that nations want strong economies as much or more than they want strong armies.

- Ask students to read this page to learn how changes to the economies in Europe and China changed how strong or weak they were in the world.

TALK AND SHARE

Have students talk about the Talk and Share topic with a partner. Encourage them to use the Key Concept of *economic strength* in their discussion.

Economics

Free Trade

Ask volunteers to review what they learned about tariffs in the age of Jackson, when the South and North disagreed. Ask, *How might arguments about free trade be like the arguments about tariffs?*

Next, review why Theodore Roosevelt broke up monopolies. Ask, *How is a business protected by a tariff like a monopoly?*

Divide students into two groups: For Free Trade and Against Free Trade. Have them brainstorm their arguments and have volunteers present them to the class.

 Activity: Create a Bar Graph

Call students' attention to the population information given for China and the United States on page 265. Have students work with a partner to create a double bar graph comparing the populations of the United States and China. Remind them to include labels and titles for the graph, along with a key that indicates what the bars stand for. Then have students write a sentence that tells what the graph shows.

 Activity: History Notebook

Have students create a history notebook for this lesson. Have students include graphs, pictures, lists, and drawings they have produced to explain and study the events of the lesson. Ask them to show and explain their work to a partner.

Discuss Facing the Future

- Ask volunteers for examples of how earlier inventions, such as the radio, telephone, and airplanes, changed the world.

- Invite students to think about how the Internet and satellite communications affect ways of doing business. Clarify the terms if necessary.

- Tell students these inventions led to globalization, and invite them the read these two pages.

Read the Double Bar Graph

- Call students' attention to the double bar graph on page 266. Have volunteers point out the key, the title, and the labels on the axes.

- Clarify that each pair of bars describes the buying and selling of goods between the United States and another country, a "trading partner." It shows that Canada buys a greater share of our exports than Mexico (or any of the other countries shown). It also shows that we buy more goods from Canada than we buy from any of these other countries.

Look and Read

▲ A business owner sells her products over the Internet.

Facing the Future

More than ever before, America became linked to other nations. The Internet and **satellite communications** brought people together. News and ideas raced around the globe. So did business. Suddenly, a glassmaker in a small town in Mexico could sell to people around the world.

GLOBALIZATION

The economies of the nations of the world became more and more closely connected. People called it **globalization.** Some welcomed it, while others feared it.

In the **global economy,** companies became **multinational.** They traded around the world. This caused new issues of justice to surface. Workers in poorer nations did not get as much pay as workers in the rich nations. They weren't protected by the same safety rules. Some workers in the rich nations lost jobs. Workers in the poorer nations found jobs and gained skills. People debated what was right and what was wrong.

Yet business skyrocketed as nations traded goods. Iowa soybeans went into soy sauce in Taiwan. Americans drove cars made in Japan, drank coffee from Brazil, and ate chocolate from cocoa grown in Indonesia. The global economy had arrived.

Major U.S. Trading Partners at the Turn of the 21st Century

- Percentage of U.S. exports
- Percentage of U.S. imports

Canada, Mexico, Japan, UK, China (0%–25%)

▲ Coffee beans

VOCABULARY

satellite communications—radio, TV, and telephone signals that are sent from the ground to a satellite in space and from there back to the ground, instead of through wires

globalization—the coming together of business interests around the globe. Some people worry that globalization will make everything the same around the world.

global economy—the network of international businesses

multinational—having offices and owners in many nations

266 UNIT 7 • STRUGGLING FOR PEACE AND JUSTICE

 Activity: Made in _____

Have students look at products in the classroom and at home to find out where they were produced. Have students work together to make a tally table and then turn the table into a bar graph showing the origins of these goods. Have them draw a second bar to show their prediction of where most goods would have come from 100 years earlier.

Differentiating Instruction

Beginning

Listing Global Products Using clothing labels, information on objects at hand such as pencils, and their own background knowledge, have students generate a list of products made in one country and sold in another. Have them head their lists *Globalization*.

Intermediate

Study Word Parts Focus on the word *multinational*. Explain that the prefix *multi-* means *many*, and that the word *national* refers to nations, or countries.

Relate the prefix to the word *multiplication*. Help students analyze the meanings of *multiracial, multi-millionaire*, and *international*.

Advanced

Role-Play Have students brainstorm, script, and present (1) a U.S. business person who wants to hire foreign workers, (2) an American worker who could lose his or her job, (3) a foreign worker who might get a job, (4) an American consumer looking for lower prices.

NEW AMERICANS

As the 21st century opened, 1 out of every 10 Americans was born in another land. Immigrants continued to pour in looking for freedom and jobs. Here Muslims and Jews could live peacefully side by side. Here smaller groups did not choose war to get control over their lives. Instead, they worked to elect their people to positions in government.

The U.S. population faced the future together, working to keep democracy strong and its nation safe. Together, Americans looked forward to meeting the challenges of a changing world.

TALK AND SHARE Tell your partner what you think about the United States and the world in the future.

Language Notes

Figurative Language
These words form a picture in your mind.

☐ raced: traveled fast, like people running in a race

☐ surface: rise, like a fish that comes up above the water

☐ skyrocketed: rose to great heights very quickly, like fireworks

☐ pour in: come in a steady stream, like rain

▲ Immigrants keep their heritage alive in the United States. ▶

Summary

As the 21st century began, the world faced new changes. Threats to world peace came from small groups of people with little or no power. Terrorism became the weapon they used. New powers in Europe and China were based on economic strength, not military strength. The economies of the world came together.

Teach About New Americans

■ Remind students that the United States has often attracted immigrants. Students may recall this topic from Lesson 15. Ask students to share stories they know of people who came to the United States.

■ Have students brainstorm reasons that immigrants continued to come to the United States at the beginning of the 21st century.

Language Notes

Call students' attention to the Language Notes. Point out that these words and phrases are used in ways that create images. Explain that a *skyrocket* goes up in the air very quickly. When business (or crime, or anything else) goes up quickly, we say it *skyrockets*.

TALK AND SHARE

Have students discuss the topic with a partner. Encourage them to use the information on pages 266–267 to help shape their answers.

Discuss the Summary

Call students' attention to the Big Idea on page 259. Help students see the connections between the Summary and the Big Idea.

✓ Assessment

Assess students' comprehension by asking the following questions:

History
- How was terrorism different from earlier kinds of fighting?
- What effects did globalization have on the world?
- Why did the European Union and China have growing power?

Language
Which word or phrase does not belong?

- Globalization, global economy, fundamentalist, multinational
- Technology, immigrant, satellite communications
- Terrorism, hijacked, prestige, Taliban

Assessment Book
Use page 39 to assess students' comprehension.

Teach Interpreting

Explain to students that interpreting events is important when reading about history or learning about current events. This page will show them how to develop this skill.

Model the Organizer

- Ask volunteers to read aloud the three headings under the title *Threats to Peace.* Then have volunteers read the individual entries aloud.

- Tell students that a Thinking Tree like this one can help them find the meaning of all the events taken together.

- Explain that the Thinking Tree can also help them understand the relationships among the events.

Give Practice Interpreting

- **Draw** Students can use pictures from newspapers and news magazines to complete their organizers.

- **Write** Students' paragraphs should explain what recent events mean. A good beginning is, *I think that* (whatever is happening) *means that* (things are getting better, worse, are changing, or staying the same). Next comes an example or two. A last sentence sums up how the examples support the interpretation.

Interpreting

Interpreting the Meaning in Events

When you interpret events in history, you tell what they mean. At the turn of the 21st century, many different groups fought. Each fight began with a different event. Together, they meant something. A Thinking Tree can help you gather and organize events. Use the branches of the tree to show how events relate to each other.

Thinking Tree

Threats to Peace

Terrorism	Fight for Sovereignty	Possible Nuclear War
• Usama bin Laden • suicide bombers • Afghanistan	• Yugoslavia • Middle East • Chechnya • Kashmir	• Iraq • Iran • North Korea

Your interpretation might be that 3 kinds of activity threatened world peace.

Practice Interpreting

1. Draw Make a Thinking Tree with pictures that show details about problems in the world today. Show what the United States is doing. Include other nations and what they are doing. Tell a partner your interpretation of what is going on.

2. Write Interpret U.S. action in a current world event. Choose something that is happening now. Make a Thinking Tree to show the event. Make branches for (1) what the United States is doing, and (2) what other countries are doing. Include details in your branches. Then use your Thinking Tree to write a paragraph of 3 to 4 sentences telling how you interpret what is going on. Trade your paragraph with a partner and check each other's writing.

Check Your Writing

Make sure you
- [ ] Use complete sentences.
- [ ] Use a period at the end of each sentence.
- [ ] Spell all the words correctly.

Activity: Internet Resources

Have students use the Internet to find information on key events and ideas from the lesson. Have students work in pairs to find examples of items such as photographs, first-person accounts, speeches, and videos. Ask them to summarize their findings for the class. Useful links include:

- http://cnnstudentnews.cnn.com/fyi/index.html
- http://teacher.scholastic.com/scholasticnews/indepth/911

Differentiating Instruction

Beginning
One Branch Assign the Draw activity to partners and ask them to agree on one current world problem. That is their branch. Then they need to add details about the problem to help interpret what it means.

Intermediate
Small Groups Have students work together to choose an event for the Write activity. That event goes at the top. Help them generate the branches. (There may be only one or two.) Then move to the details within the branches. Students can write a paragraph together on chart paper.

Advanced
Independent Work Explain that the purpose of the Write activity is to relate the event to other events, not just to give an opinion. Students should look for trends. How is the most recent action like or unlike some that came before it. Are things getting better or worse? Does the event move the world closer to peace or toward more violence?

Grammar Spotlight

Phrases with *Who* and *That* A phrase is a group of words that does not have both a subject and a predicate. When the subject is a person, the phrase begins with *who*. When the subject is not a person, the phrase begins with *that*.

Examples of Phrases	What the Phrase Tells About
The bombs that hit hotels hurt many people.	Tells which bombs hurt many people
Usama bin Laden, who headed Al Qaeda, directed the September 11 attacks.	Tells something about Usama bin Laden

Use *who* or *that* to fill in these blanks.

1. The people_____came to America wanted freedom.

2. The attack_____was the worst came on September 11, 2001.

Oral Language

World Trade Take turns with your partner. Each person names something you can buy here that is made in another country. Name as many things as you can think of. One person makes a list of the things named. The other person makes another list that names things that are made in the United States and sold in other countries. Then share your lists with your classmates.

Partner Practice

Reading a Double Bar Graph Work with a partner to interpret this graph. What does it show? Explain to your partner the difference between exports and imports. Then discuss these questions.

1. What happened to U.S imports between 1990 and 2000?

2. What happened to U.S. exports in the same time period?

3. What do you think it means when a country imports more than it exports?

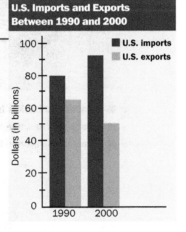

U.S. Imports and Exports Between 1990 and 2000

LESSON 21 • INTO THE 21ST CENTURY **269**

Grammar Spotlight

Explain to students that the words *who* and *that* usually come right after a noun. Emphasize that *who* is used for people and *that* is used for things.

Read aloud the phrases and sentences in the chart. Ask students to repeat after you. Show how the sentence *The bombs hurt many people* is made clearer by inserting the words *that hit hotels*. Have students fill in the missing word in the two numbered sentences.

Oral Language

Ask students to evaluate, or make a judgment about, the value of international trade. When they have finished sharing their lists, ask, *What do you like about international trade? What do you not like about it? Do you think it should grow?*

Partner Practice

Have students start by asking each other simple comprehension questions about the graph, such as *In which year were U.S. imports worth more?* Review the difference between imports and exports. Have students share their responses to the third question with the rest of the class.

Activity: Extend the Lesson

Coming to America: A Muslim Family's Story by Bernard Wolf (Lee and Low Books, 2003) is a photo essay about the experiences of a Muslim family that leaves Egypt for the United States. Simple text combines with photos to portray the struggles and joys of new immigrants to the United States. Particular attention is given to the family's attempt to balance new ways with old ones.

Program Resources

Student Activity Journal
Use page 95 to practice *interpreting*.

Overhead Transparencies
Use 27, Thinking Tree, with page 268.

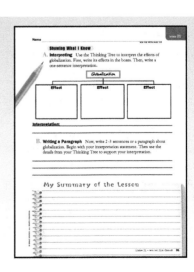

The United States Constitution

STANDARDS CONTENT

History

- Take notes
- Recognize the principles and values of American democracy reflected in the Constitution
- Recognize the functions of the three branches of government
- Identify checks and balances among the branches of government

Language

- Identify the following Key Concepts: *constitution, plan, principles,* and *foundation*
- Recognize words with multiple meanings
- Practice paraphrasing ideas and texts

Begin ⬭ Building Background

- Invite students to read the signs in the picture to identify a state name and a president's name.

- Students should be able to generate such words as *election* and *convention* in response to the first question.

- Use the boy's picture as well as the balloons and confetti in the big picture to elicit that people are excited and celebrating.

- Remind students that the U.S. government that represents people is set up in the Constitution.

Talk and Explore

The United States Constitution

Here you'll learn about the government described in our Constitution. You'll also learn how to take notes and practice paraphrasing parts of the Constitution.

Building Background

▲ People come from every state!

- **What do you think is happening in this picture?**
- **What words describe how these people feel?**
- **What words describe the government of the United States?**

 Activity: It's My Party

Point out that the word *party* has two meanings. Explain that Americans with similar political ideas form a *political party,* such as the Democrats or the Republicans. Contrast this meaning with the kind of *party* that is a celebration. Point out that political parties can have celebration parties, such as the one shown in the picture. Have students tell a partner about a party they attended. Ask volunteers to share their partners' stories with the class.

 Differentiating Instruction

Beginning
Word Cards Concentrate on words related to politics and government, such as *vote, president,* and *laws.* Write these words on cards and provide sentences that use them, such as *The president is the leader of the United States.* Have students copy the words onto cards of their own and draw pictures on the back to help them remember the meanings.

Intermediate
Pantomime Focus on the phrase *checks and balances.* Have students act out how to *check* each other's work and use scales to *balance* objects.

Advanced
Research Help students generate a list of political offices, such as *president, governor,* and *mayor.* Have partners find out who currently holds these offices in the United States and in your area.

Big Idea

The Constitution lays out the plan for the government of the United States. It reflects basic principles and describes 3 branches of government. It also provides checks on the power of government and gives ways to balance power among the different parts of government.

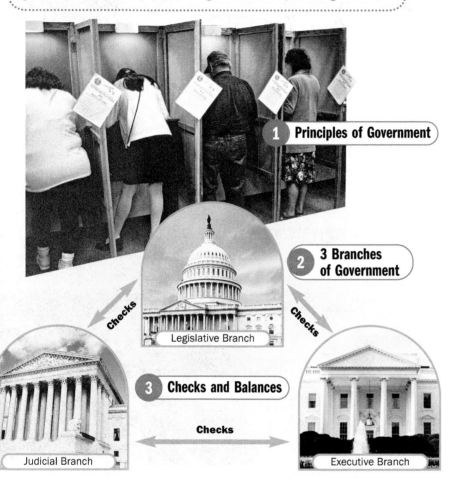

1 Principles of Government

2 3 Branches of Government

Legislative Branch

Checks

Checks

3 Checks and Balances

Judicial Branch

Checks

Executive Branch

LESSON 22 • THE UNITED STATES CONSTITUTION **271**

introduce the Big Idea

■ Read aloud the Big Idea on page 271.

■ Go through the three ideas shown in the headings.

■ Explain that the U.S. Constitution is a very important document that describes how the government works. Tell students that new laws that go against the Constitution can be thrown out by a court. Explain that one of the main ideas of the Constitution is that the powers of government need to be kept separate so that no one part of the government can get so strong it can abuse its power.

Review

Lesson 6 discussed the process used to draft and approve the Constitution. Ask students to recall the problems the new country faced before a Constitution was in place. Then review the Great Compromise.

Activity: Laws

Have students generate a list of laws they know. Write the laws they name, such as *No killing* or *No driving faster than the speed limit* on the board or a sheet of chart paper. Draw out that many laws are expressed as negative statements—that is, they tell people what they may *not* do.

Next, have students form small groups. Ask groups to discuss what would happen if there were no laws against these crimes. Have groups classify the laws into the following categories:

• Laws that they think are absolutely necessary to keep society running

• Laws that they see as important, but not absolutely necessary

• Laws that they believe are bad laws

Have students share their ideas with other groups.

Resource Library

***Reader's Handbook* (red)**
Note-taking 74–76, 646–647, 677

***Reader's Handbook* (yellow)**
Note-taking 526–527, 553, 556

All Write
Note-taking 262–273, 316–317

Teach ▸ Key Concepts

- ■ Say each term slowly to model correct pronunciation. Then have students repeat the term after you. Have volunteers read the Key Concept sentences aloud. Talk about the meanings of these words, relating them to the pictures.

- ■ Have students share what they already know about the structure of the U.S. government. They may use earlier lessons or their own knowledge.

- ■ Have students tell one another how the Constitution is like the plan or blueprint of a building.

Teach the Visual Aid

Powers in the National Government

Focus students on the visual aid. Explain that each picture shows one of the groups that holds power in the U.S. government. Have students read the headings chorally. Then describe each picture. Pay particular attention to the caption that reads *Courts interpret our laws.* Explain that *interpret* means that courts both determine whether an action fits the laws and decide whether the laws fit the Constitution.

Key Concepts

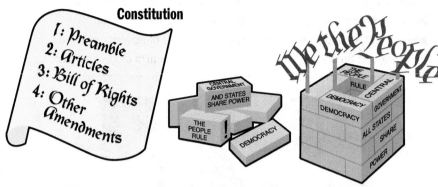

Constitution

1: Preamble
2: Articles
3: Bill of Rights
4: Other Amendments

Plan

A **constitution** is a legal document that lays out a **plan** for government.

Principles

It is built on **principles,** or ideas, about government.

Foundation

These principles are the **foundation,** or base, for the government.

Powers in the National Government

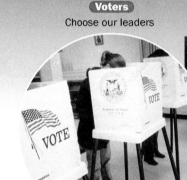

Voters
Choose our leaders

Congress
Makes our laws

VOTE

🏛 Activity: Find the Words

Have students look at the vocabulary terms at the bottom of pages 274–279. Say each term. Ask if students have heard or used it before.

Then divide the class into pairs. Say one of the vocabulary terms at random. Have students scan their texts to find the word where it is used and defined first. Once students find the word, have them read the definition and discuss the word's meaning with their partner.

🔲 Differentiating Instruction

Beginning
Word Work Call students' attention to the pictures in the visual aid. Have students use words they know to describe the pictures. Write some of these words on the board, along with the names of the students who used them. Have the group repeat the words in a choral reading. Ask the student who originally suggested a word to use other words or gestures to explain its meaning.

Intermediate
Partner Talk Have students work in pairs to ask each other about the visual aid. Have them use the form *What does/do (the) _____ do?*

Advanced
Opinions and Reasons Have students talk in small groups about which they think has the most power: the voters, Congress, the president, or the courts. They should give reasons for their opinions.

Taking Notes

Taking notes is a good way to remember something. Take notes when you listen in class and when you read. Your notes will help you later, when you study for a test. Also, just writing the notes helps you remember.

When you take notes, write down the main points. You do not need to write in complete sentences.

A Thinking Tree is a good way to take your notes. Put the main subject at the top. The parts of the subject each have their own places, and you can add the details as you hear or read them.

Three Branches of Government

Legislative Branch
- Makes laws
- Senate
- House of Representatives

Executive Branch
- Carries out laws
- President
- Vice President
- Cabinet

Judicial Branch
- Interprets laws
- Supreme Court
- Other federal courts

President
Carries out our laws

Courts
Interpret our laws

Teach **Skill Building**

- Read aloud the explanation of the note-taking process. Emphasize the idea of writing down just the main points.

- Then tell students that you will read a short newspaper article. Ask students to take notes on what they hear.

- After you read the article, have students share their notes in small groups. Ask them, *What kinds of notes did a good job of summing up the article?* Ask them why they think so.

- Ask students simple comprehension questions about the article and its main points. Have them answer by referring to their notes.

Activity: Culture Connection

Invite volunteers to talk about laws and government of other countries they may know. How are the laws and government like those of the United States? How are they different? Explain that different forms of government are used in the world. Ask students to recall other kinds of governments they have studied (*communist, fascist*). Tell students that even other democracies, such as Canada and France, did not set up their governments quite like the United States did.

Program Resources

Student Activity Journal

Use page 96 to build key vocabulary.

Use page 97 to practice taking notes.

Overhead Transparencies

Use 19, Opinions and Reasons Organizer, with the Advanced activity on page 272.

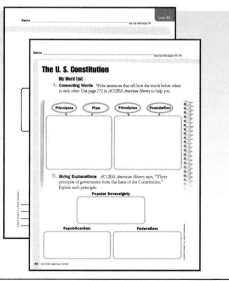

Introduce **The United States Constitution**

- This section reviews the three principles behind the U.S. Constitution. Discuss the form of government that the colonists rebelled against during the American Revolution. Ask, *If you were to form a government for a new country, what ideas would be important to you?*

- Have students read the selection. Ask them to focus on the ideas that form the U.S. Constitution.

Key Connection: Government

- Develop students' familiarity with the terms *democracy* and *republic*, which are critical to understanding the U.S. government. Explain that both words are often used to describe countries in which people elect their leaders. Draw a distinction between *democracies* and *republics* and governments that are *dictatorships*, in which one leader controls everything.

- Have volunteers describe how the governments of other countries they know about do or do not fit the definitions of republics and democracies.

Look and Read

The United States Constitution

The U.S. Constitution is our plan for government. It reflects certain ideas, or principles, about our government. It describes a government with 3 branches that can check each other and balance the power among them.

Principles of the U.S. Constitution

Three **principles** of government form the basis of the Constitution.

1. POPULAR SOVEREIGNTY

Popular sovereignty is the idea that authority for the decisions and actions of a government comes from the people. In history, **authority** for governments came from different sources. The ancient Egyptians, for example, believed the authority for their rulers came from gods. Authority for other governments came from the strength of a ruler and his army. In democracies, authority comes from the people who elect their leaders.

▲ People vote at polling places. These are set up at churches, businesses, and other buildings on election days.

VOCABULARY

principles—the ideas that form a foundation for other ideas
popular sovereignty—rule by the people. A democracy is a government based on popular sovereignty.
authority—the right to rule

 Activity: Word Webs

As students work through the lesson, have them work with a partner to create Word Webs and explain them to classmates. For instance, the word *federalism* could be put in the middle of a Web that includes the words *states, power, government,* and *nation.*

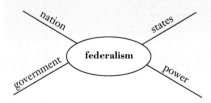

Differentiating Instruction

Beginning

Understanding Principles Direct students to the blue headings on pages 274–275. Have students draw three circles and write the headings in them. Read the sections aloud while students follow along. Use gestures and simpler words, if necessary, to convey the meanings of *popular sovereignty, republicanism,* and *federalism*. After each paragraph, have students write or draw in their circles to show their

understanding of each of the three principles.

Intermediate

Restating Have students read each section below a blue heading and tell a partner what it meant.

Advanced

Note-taking Have students take notes as they read pages 274–275. Remind them that they need not use complete sentences. Have them use their notes to generate two to three questions about the reading.

2. REPUBLICANISM

In some small democracies, the people vote directly on all actions the government takes. That is *direct democracy.* The U.S. government is a **republic.** In a republic, the voters elect people to **represent** them in government. Americans vote for the president, for representatives in Congress, and for leaders in their state and **local** governments.

3. FEDERALISM

Federalism means power is shared between the national and state governments. The Constitution lists the powers of the **federal government.** It also lists some powers that are shared between the national and state governments. All other powers belong to the states.

(TALK AND SHARE) Explain to your partner the 3 principles of government given in the U.S. Constitution.

▲ Senators represent the people of their state in Congress.

VOCABULARY

republic—a system of government in which people elect representatives to make their laws.
represent—speak for. A senator represents the people of his or her state.
local—relating to a certain area or place. A city has a local government.

federalism—a system of government in which power is shared between national and state governments
federal government—the government in Washington, D.C.

Primary Source

The Preamble

The Constitution begins with a section called the Preamble. It gives 6 goals that guided the writers.

"We the people of the United States, in order to (1) form a more perfect union, (2) establish justice, (3) insure domestic tranquility [peace at home], (4) provide for the common defense, (5) promote the general welfare [good], and (6) secure the blessings of liberty . . . do ordain and establish [set up] this Constitution for the United States of America."

Teach About Federalism

■ Ask students to review the definition of *federal.* See page 312 of the Glossary.

■ Have them compare it to the definition of *federalism* on page 275.

■ Ask if students know some responsibilities of states and some responsibilities of the federal government. Students may know that states issue license plates or that only the federal government can declare and fight a war.

■ Explain that the Constitution tells whether the states or the national government has a particular power. Say that some powers are shared.

(TALK AND SHARE)

Have students discuss which of the three principles they think is most important.

Primary Source

The Preamble

Use the information on the Preamble to reinforce the idea of *goals:*

• Have students put the ideas of the six goals into their own words.

• Ask, *If you were in charge of the government, how would you establish justice/ensure peace/provide for defense?*

 Activity: Principles and the Preamble

Divide the class into six groups. Assign each group one of the six goals listed in the Preamble to the Constitution. Have them discuss what laws and policies a government could write that would help meet these goals. Ask students to create a list with three to four different ideas. Plans for *To establish justice,* for instance, might include hiring police officers or giving power to judges.

Program Resources

Student Activity Journal
Assign page 98:
• To create study notes for students to review
• To provide reinforcement of key vocabulary

Overhead Transparencies
Use 33, Web, with page 274.

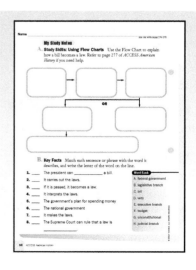

Discuss the
Three Branches of Government

- Have students review the information in the diagram on page 271 and the visual aid on pages 272–273.

- Ask, *What are the three branches of government? What does each branch do?*

- Ask, *Why is it important for the branches to check each other? What might happen if people in one branch could do whatever they wanted?*

- Have students draw three columns in their notebooks. They should label the columns with the three branches of government. They can use the columns to take notes throughout the lesson.

Language Notes

Focus students' attention on the Language Notes box. Point out that these words each have more than one meaning. Read the definitions aloud. Help students decide which meanings of *branches* and *bills* are being used when the words come up in the reading.

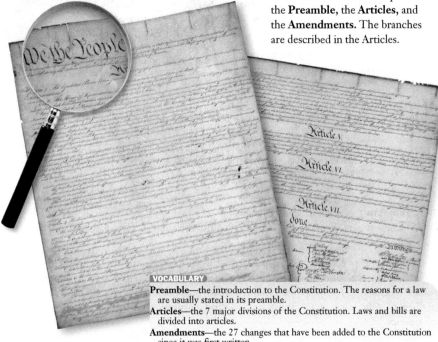

Look and Read

Language Notes
Multiple Meanings
These words have more than one meaning.

☐ **branches**
1. parts or divisions
2. parts of a tree growing out of the trunk

☐ **bills**
1. proposed laws
2. statements of charges and money owed

The Constitution is on display in Washington, D.C. ▼

Three Branches of Government

To keep the federal government from becoming too powerful, the writers of the Constitution divided it into 3 branches. Each branch has its own powers. None of the branches can control the others. This important idea is called *separation of powers.*

The Branches of U.S. Government

Branch	Power
Legislative	To make the laws
Executive	To carry out the laws
Judicial	To interpret the laws

The Constitution has 3 parts: the **Preamble**, the **Articles**, and the **Amendments**. The branches are described in the Articles.

VOCABULARY
Preamble—the introduction to the Constitution. The reasons for a law are usually stated in its preamble.
Articles—the 7 major divisions of the Constitution. Laws and bills are divided into articles.
Amendments—the 27 changes that have been added to the Constitution since it was first written

276 UNIT 8 • CIVICS IN AMERICA

Activity: Words with Multiple Meanings

Have students generate a list of other words besides *bills* and *branches* that have multiple meanings. Encourage students to offer simple definitions for their words and to use these words in sentences that show their different meanings. Write the definitions next to the words. Post the list in a place where students can refer to it easily. Encourage students to add to the list as they find more words with multiple meanings.

Differentiating Instruction

Beginning
Using the Glossary Words such as *federal* and *branches* have been defined in earlier lessons. Encourage students to use the Glossary in the back of their books. In pairs, have students look over each paragraph and write down any words they don't know. Then work together to look up meanings.

Intermediate
Know Your Legislators Have students brainstorm ways to research their senators and member of Congress (*the Web, library, party headquarters*). Then have pairs find information about them and report back.

Advanced
Write a Lawmaker Have students write a business letter inviting a representative to speak to the class.

LEGISLATIVE BRANCH

The **legislative branch** is Congress. It is made up of the Senate and the House of Representatives. The Constitution puts this branch first, in Article 1. It explains how the members of the Senate and the House will be chosen. It lists the **qualifications** people must have to be members of Congress and the length of the **term** they serve. When a term nears its end, the states hold another election. Members of Congress can be elected to many terms.

The Constitution also says how many representatives a state will have in the House and in the Senate. Each state has two senators. The number of representatives from each state in the House is based on the population of that state. For this reason, the Constitution says the government should take a **census** every 10 years.

MAKING LAWS

Congress makes laws. It does this by passing **bills.** Most bills are about spending money to do things, like pay for the military. When Congress wants to do something to help Americans, it must pass a bill to pay for it.

A bill is introduced in the House by a representative or in the Senate by a senator. Laws must pass by a majority vote of both parts of Congress. The bill then is sent to the president, who has **veto** power. If the president signs the bill, it becomes law. If the president does not sign it, Congress can still pass it if two-thirds of both the House and the Senate members vote for it. The bill then becomes law without the president's signature.

VOCABULARY

legislative branch—the part of government that makes the laws
qualifications—the things that make a person able to have the job
term—the length of service in office before another election is held
census—a count of all the people who live in a place
bills—proposed laws
veto—the power to say no

LESSON 22 • THE UNITED STATES CONSTITUTION **277**

Senators

Qualifications
- At least 30 years old
- A citizen at least 9 years
- A resident of the state from which elected

Term
- 6 years

Representatives

Qualifications
- At least 25 years old
- A citizen at least 7 years
- A resident of the state from which elected

Term
- 2 years

Teach the Legislative Branch

■ Point out that the Constitution explains how the legislative branch is set up. As students read page 277, have them look for what the Constitution says about the legislative branch. Ask them to take notes about what they learn.

■ Create a flow chart on the board to show the process for passing a bill. Draw circles to show the House, the Senate, and the president. Put arrows between the various branches to show what happens to a bill after it is introduced and what happens if the president vetoes it. Walk students through the flow chart, using the reading as a reference.

Senators and Representatives

Draw students' attention to the boxes on page 277 comparing senators and representatives. Have students identify the similarities and differences on the lists. Ask students to explain why they think the qualifications and term lengths are different for the two offices.

Activity: Role-Play

Have students act out the process for passing a bill. Choose a volunteer to act as president. Choose about one-fourth of the remaining students to serve as senators. Assign all other students to be representatives.

Ask members of the "House" to introduce a bill, or propose a new law. Students may suggest laws they would like to see the United States pass, or they may concentrate on smaller concerns such as the menu for the school cafeteria. Once a law has been proposed, follow this procedure:

- Invite representatives to discuss, or debate, the bill.

- Have representatives vote.

- If a majority is in favor, repeat the steps with senators.

- If senators also vote for the bill, send the bill on to the president for signature or veto.

If a bill fails, two members of each body form a "joint committee." They should work out a compromise.

Discuss the Executive Branch

■ Have students take notes on what they read about the executive branch.

■ Emphasize that the president's powers are limited. Ask, *What would happen if a president had unlimited power?*

■ Explain that *secretary*, as in *secretary of defense*, means a person in charge of the department rather than an office worker.

■ Ask students if they know where the president lives and works (*the White House*).

President

Point out the feature on the president's qualifications and term of office that appears on the upper left of page 278. Have students compare this information to what they learned on page 277 about the members of Congress. Ask:

• How are the qualifications alike?

• How are they different?

• Why do you think the president must have been born in the United States?

• Why do you think the president may serve only two terms?

Look and Read

President

Qualifications
☐ At least 35 years old
☐ Born in the U.S.
☐ Lived in the U.S. for 14 years in a row

Term
☐ 4 years
☐ May only serve 2 terms

EXECUTIVE BRANCH

Article 2 of the Constitution describes the **executive branch.** It describes the president's qualifications, term of office, and responsibilities and duties.

The president is the head, or *chief executive*, of the federal government. The president is responsible for seeing that all laws passed by Congress are carried out. The president also sends Congress the annual **budget.** This is the president's **proposal** for spending money to keep the government doing all the things people expect it to do. Congress must decide whether to pass it or change it and then pass it.

The president either signs or vetoes bills passed by Congress. The president is commander-in-chief of the Armed Forces and may ask Congress to declare war. The president directs foreign policy and makes **treaties** with foreign countries if the Senate agrees.

▲ President John F. Kennedy begins his term and makes a promise to uphold the laws.

The executive branch is huge. It has many different departments that employ thousands of people. Department heads, such as the secretary of defense, secretary of state, secretary of treasury, and the attorney general all belong to the president's **cabinet.** They advise the president.

The Constitution also gives the United States a vice president. This person becomes president if the president dies or cannot perform his or her duties. The vice president also **presides** over the Senate.

VOCABULARY
executive branch—the part of government that carries out the laws
budget—a plan for getting and spending money
proposal—a formal, detailed suggestion
treaties—formal agreements among nations
cabinet—the group of top advisers to the president
presides—runs the meeting

278 UNIT 8 • CIVICS IN AMERICA

 Activity: Want Ads

Have students work with a partner. Ask them to imagine that they are writing an advertisement for a person to serve in the government. Have them choose either *president, senator,* or *representative.* Assign students to write a want ad for this position, showing the qualifications and the responsibilities for the job. Read want ads to students from the newspaper if necessary. Then have volunteers read their want ads aloud.

Differentiating Instruction

Beginning/Intermediate
Partner Talk Have students share with a partner what they know about presidents.

Encourage them to use simple sentence models such as *George Washington/Abraham Lincoln used to be president* or *The president lives in the White House/makes speeches/is on TV.*

Have partners read through page 278. Have students tell their partners new things that they learned from the reading.

Advanced
Checks and Balances Make three groups of students and ask each to study the checks and balances of one branch of government. Each group should complete a Two-column Chart, showing *Checks* on the left and *Is Checked By* on the right. Then have groups share their charts.

JUDICIAL BRANCH

The **judicial branch** includes the U.S. Supreme Court and the federal courts. These courts decide whether federal laws have been broken. They also can rule that a law passed by Congress or an action of the president is **unconstitutional.** They rule in cases where two states disagree or when the federal government is one of the sides in a case.

The Supreme Court is the highest court in the land. People may appeal the decision of a lower court to the Supreme Court. If the Court agrees to hear the case, it can **override** the decision of the lower court.

CHECKS AND BALANCES

These 3 branches of government share power. The Constitution provides a system of checks and balances to keep the branches from **abusing** power.

TALK AND SHARE With your partner, make a poster of the 3 branches of government. Decide together what to show for each branch.

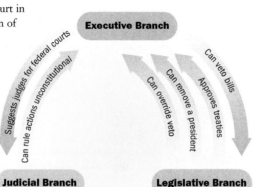

Supreme Court

Qualifications
☐ Nominated by the president
☐ Approved by the Senate

Term
☐ For life

Executive Branch

Suggests judges for federal courts
Can rule actions unconstitutional
Can override veto
Can remove a president
Can veto bills
Approves treaties

Judicial Branch

Legislative Branch

Approves judges for federal courts
Can rule laws unconstitutional

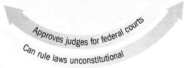

VOCABULARY

judicial branch—the part of government that interprets the laws through its decisions in legal cases
unconstitutional—goes against the Constitution
override—go over. For example, Congress can override a bill the president vetoes if enough people vote for it.
abusing—using wrongly

Summary

The plan for the government in the Constitution is based on principles of popular sovereignty, republicanism, and federalism. The Constitution gives the United States a government with 3 branches and a system of checks and balances to prevent the abuse of power.

Teach Checks and Balances

Walk students through the visual organizer on the right of page 279. Explain how the arrows work. Have students describe each part of the chart using language such as *The legislative branch can override a veto*. Ask key questions, such as *Which branch can veto bills/rule laws unconstitutional?*

TALK AND SHARE

Have partners complete the activity. Encourage volunteers to share their posters with the class.

Discuss the Summary

■ Have students read the Summary at the bottom of page 279.

■ Connect the Summary to the Big Idea on page 271.

✓ Assessment

Assess students' comprehension by asking the following questions:

History

• What are the three principles on which the U.S. Constitution is based?

• How are the legislative and executive branches different from each other?

• How does a bill become a law?

Language

Write or say sentences to show how these words are related:

• Republic, represent

• Legislative branch, bills

• Judicial branch, unconstitutional

Assessment Book

Use page 40 to assess students' comprehension.

Teach Paraphrasing

Students will need to paraphrase readings on tests and when writing papers. Tell the class that this page provides strategies for paraphrasing.

Model the Organizer

- Read aloud the original text of Article 1, Section 1, near the top of page 280.

- Ask students to describe what they think the section means.

- Have volunteers read aloud the paraphrased text in the middle of the page. Point out the different ways of expressing the same ideas, such as *consist of* and *made up of*. Emphasize that the words are different, but the basic meaning remains the same for each excerpt.

Give Practice Paraphrasing

- **Tell** Help students with *entitled* (*allowed*) and *several* (*separate; different*). They should understand: *A citizen of one state has the same rights and protections as the citizens of other states.*

- **Write** Students may need help understanding that *evenly divided* means *tied.*

Develop Language

Paraphrasing

Paraphrasing Parts of the Constitution

When you paraphrase, you put something in your own words. An easy way to do that is to think about how you would explain something to a friend. For example, this is how you might paraphrase Article 1, Section 1, of the Constitution.

Original

"All legislative [lawmaking] powers herein granted [given here] shall be vested [put] in a Congress of the United States, which shall consist of [be made up of] a Senate and House of Representatives."

Paraphrase

Congress has the power to make laws. Congress is made up of the Senate and the House of Representatives.

Practice Paraphrasing

1. Tell Practice paraphrasing this part of Article 4. Say in your own words what this means.

Article 4, Section 2
"The citizens of each state shall be entitled to all privileges [rights] and immunities [protections] of citizens in the several states."

2. Write Write a paraphrase of this part of the Constitution: *The Vice President of the United States shall be President of the Senate, but shall have no vote unless they be evenly divided.* Be sure to check your writing.

Check Your Writing

Make sure you
- ☐ Use complete sentences.
- ☐ Use a period at the end of each sentence.
- ☐ Spell all the words correctly.

Activity: Internet Resources

Have students research the Internet for information on key events from the lesson. Have them work in pairs to find items about lawmakers and presidents. They should present a summary of their findings to the class. Useful websites include:

- http://www.supremecourtus.gov
- http://house.gov

Differentiating Instruction

Beginning
Working Together Have students read Article 4, Section 2 out loud with you. Emphasize *rights* and *protections*.

On the board write *each state* and *several states*. Invite a volunteer to draw an equal sign between the two phrases on the board. Students should understand that the sentence means *Citizens have the same rights and protections no matter what state they live in.*

Intermediate/Advanced
Phrasing Ideas Have students work with a partner to discuss the meanings of unfamiliar words. Remind students to check for proper spelling, punctuation, and capitalization in their finished work.

Activities

Grammar Spotlight

Passive Verbs With active verbs, the subject is doing the action. When an action is done *to* the subject of a sentence, the verb is passive. A form of the verb *be* (*is, are, was, were, been*) comes before the verb. You use passive sentences when you want to emphasize the thing being done, not the thing that did it.

Active or Passive	Sentence	Emphasis
Active	*The Constitution provides for a separation of powers.*	Emphasizes the Constitution
Passive	*Separation of powers is provided by the Constitution.*	Emphasizes the separation of powers
Active	*Congress makes the laws.*	Emphasizes Congress
Passive	*The laws are made by Congress.*	Emphasizes the laws

Rewrite this sentence to emphasize leaders: *People elect their leaders.* Use a passive verb.

Hands On

Constitution Thinking Tree Reread pages 274–275 and take notes. Make a Thinking Tree like the one on page 273. Work with your partner to decide what the main idea is. Decide together how many parts your tree should have. Then fill in the details.

Partner Practice

Checks and Balances Take notes about the ways each branch of the federal government can check the power of the others. Share your notes with a partner and talk about how your notes are the same or different.

Activities

Grammar Spotlight

Explain to students that passive sentences and active sentences use different word orders. Give simple examples from daily life, such as contrasting *Maria read the book* with *The book was read by Maria.* Point out how the words *Maria* and *the book* change places, and how *read* becomes *was read by.*

Read aloud the sample sentences. Have students repeat after you. Then have students rewrite the sentence at the bottom of the section so it is in the passive voice. (*Leaders are elected by the people.*)

Hands On

Remind students of the steps in the note-taking process. Distinguish between *branches* of the organizer and *principles* of the Constitution. Ask students to discuss which details are most important.

Partner Practice

Encourage students to use a method of organization that makes sense to them. Ask questions such as *What can the president do to keep Congress from getting too much power?*

 Activity: Extend the Lesson

Jean Fritz's nonfiction book *Shh! We're Writing the Constitution* (Putnam Publishing Group, 1998) is an engaging and funny account of the Constitutional Convention. Along with describing the people who attended the convention and the political ideas they supported, Fritz explains how the Constitution was put together and how it helped set up a new and different form of government.

Program Resources

Student Activity Journal
Use page 99 to practice *paraphrasing.*

Overhead Transparencies
Use 20, Paraphrase Chart, with page 280.

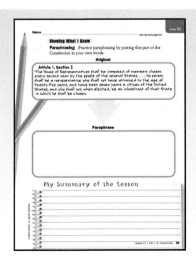

The Bill of Rights

STANDARDS CONTENT

History

- Describe ways to read newspapers critically
- Identify freedoms protected by the First Amendment
- Recognize the protections offered in the Bill of Rights

Language

- Identify the following Key Concepts: *rights*, *freedoms*, and *guarantee*
- Recognize and distinguish homophones
- Practice explaining an idea

Begin   Building Background

- Ask students the questions below the photo. Focus students on:
  - What the people in the picture might be doing
  - What their actions tell about the rights of Americans
- Ask volunteers to talk about any marches or demonstrations they have seen or taken part in. Provide words as needed (*protest, justice, demands*).
- Then draw out key ideas about protests:
  - People protest when they dislike what is happening in the world.
  - Americans have the right to protest peacefully.
  - Protests are only sometimes effective in changing policy.

The Bill of Rights

Here you'll learn about the Bill of Rights. You'll also learn how to read newspapers critically and practice explaining American freedoms.

Building Background

▲ People marched to protest what the Chinese were doing to Tibet. They wanted the U.S. government to help.

- What do you think is happening in this picture?
- What does this remind you of?
- What words would you use to describe these people and what they're doing?

282 Unit 8 • Civics in America

  Activity: Role-Play

Ask students to suggest changes to make the world a safer or fairer place. Have them choose one item from their discussion and decide which world leader might have the power to make this change. Have a volunteer play this person. Then role-play a conversation between the volunteer and the members of the class. Have the class members describe the problem and the volunteer offer a solution. Repeat with other problems and volunteers.

Differentiating Instruction

Beginning

Describing Pictures Have students study the pictures on these two pages. Ask them to generate words that describe the moods or feelings of the people in the photos. Have students show each other faces that are *happy, sad, worried,* or *angry*.

Intermediate

What *Right* Means Have students focus on the various meanings of *right*. Examine the meaning of the word in phrases such as *a right answer, turn*

right, and *the right thing to do*. Introduce the concept of a *right* as something people have a legal or moral claim to. Help students compare the different meanings.

Advanced

Connecting Have students discuss the pictures on page 283 with a partner. Have them identify the freedom illustrated in each picture and predict what it means in their own lives.

The Bill of Rights is the first 10 amendments to the U.S. Constitution. It protects freedoms and guarantees rights to all who live in the United States.

WHO WILL DISARM OUR WEAPONS OF MASS DESTRUCTION?

1 **5 Freedoms of the First Amendment**

Religion

Speech

Petition

Assembly

2 **Protection from the Powers of Government**

Press

Introduce the Big Idea

■ Read aloud the Big Idea on page 283.

■ Go through the two headings.

■ Explain that the Bill of Rights lists the freedoms that are guaranteed/ protected for all people who live in the United States. Emphasize that there are two different kinds of freedoms: freedom *to* act and freedom *from* government power. Tell students that people can be *free* to *do a thing*, and they can also be *free* from *being forced to do a thing*. The latter may be a more difficult concept for many students.

Review

Return to the discussion of the Bill of Rights in Lesson 6 (page 87). Ask students to form small groups. Have them take turns telling one another one fact they remember about their study of the Bill of Rights.

 Activity: Rights Chart

Have students form small groups. Ask group members to generate two lists: the rights they think Americans have and the rights they think Americans do not have.

Have each group create a Two-column Chart to show their ideas. The first column should be headed *Americans have the right*. The second should be headed *Americans do not have the right*.

Accept all answers, but encourage students to express their ideas as broadly as possible. *Americans do not have the right to . . . hurt other people*, for instance, is preferable to a long list reading . . . *kick other people/punch other people/trip other people* and other examples of ways to hurt others.

When groups have completed their work, invite them to share their ideas with the rest of the class. Help students find and note areas of disagreement between groups. Have students refer to their charts as they read through the chapter to see if their ideas of the rights enjoyed by Americans were correct.

 Resource Library

***Reader's Handbook* (red)**
Reading a Newspaper Article 218–233

***Reader's Handbook* (yellow)**
Reading a News Story 144–156

All Write
Evaluating Sources of Information 226

Teach **Key Concepts**

- Say each term slowly to model correct pronunciation. Ask students to repeat after you. Next, read aloud the Key Concept sentences and discuss their meanings.

- Ask students to talk about a time when they or a family member used their rights.

- Explain that a freedom is a kind of right. A freedom is something that can't be taken away, and a right is something that is *owed* to you.

- Rights belong to all people. The Bill doesn't give people rights. It protects them.

Teach the Visual Aid

First Amendment Freedoms

Draw students' attention to the visual aid. Explain that the photos show five of the most important freedoms guaranteed by the Bill of Rights. Ask students to describe each picture. Then briefly explain each freedom.

Key Concepts

Rights	Freedoms	Guarantee
Rights are the things the laws say are owed to you. For example, free education is a right in the United States.	**Freedoms** are things you can do whenever you want without being harmed by the government.	A **guarantee** is a promise. The Bill of Rights guarantees that you are free to say what you think.

First Amendment Freedoms

Freedom of Religion

Freedom of Speech

Freedom of the Press

284 UNIT 8 • CIVICS IN AMERICA

 Activity: Reflection

Ask students to talk quietly with a partner about the five First Amendment freedoms. Have students discuss what each freedom means and how it affects their lives, either now or in the future.

Then have students spend ten to fifteen minutes working on their own. Ask them to produce a personal response to one or more of the five freedoms. They may use pictures, words, or a combination of both.

Differentiating Instruction

Beginning

Word-Picture Associations Focus on building word-picture associations. Have students write the Key Concepts *rights*, *freedoms*, and *guarantee* on sticky notes. Review the meanings of these words. Have students read the Key Concept sentences chorally. Ask them to place their sticky notes in their textbooks to show pictures or sentences that talk about these concepts.

Intermediate

Describing Pictures Have students describe each picture in the visual aid in sequence. Have them use the model sentence *The first/second/last picture shows. . . .*

Advanced

Rights and the News Provide a news article about something of interest to people in your community. Have students discuss it and then consider how freedom of the press matters to them.

Reading Newspapers Critically

The Bill of Rights guarantees freedom of the press so people can find out what's going on. One way to find out is by reading newspapers. However, newspaper articles give both facts and opinions. How do you know if the idea you are getting from an article is true? You need to read critically.

A critical reader asks questions. You can do this in your head, but often it is a good idea to make a Critical Reading Chart.

Questions	My Thoughts
1. What is the main idea?	(Write the "big idea" or opinion.)
2. What facts are given?	(Write the facts that support it. Facts could be information, like numbers given, and quotations from experts or people who saw something happen.)
3. What is the source for those facts?	(People quoted and organizations named are sources. Write where the information came from.)
4. Should I believe those sources?	(A believable source is someone with experience who is fair about the subject.)
5. Is there another side to this story?	(Think about what the writer might *not* be telling you. Use your imagination.)

Freedom to Petition

Freedom of Assembly

Teach Skill Building

- Ask students to share their knowledge of newspapers.

- Pass out newspapers or sections of newspapers. Have students locate and identify such parts of the paper as the editorial page, letters to the editor, and local news stories. Explain that one difference among these parts is whether they provide opinions as well as facts.

- Read aloud the paragraph at the top of page 285. Review the differences between facts and opinions.

- Walk through the questions with students. Explain the meaning of a *source*. Ask students to name people in the class who might be good *sources* of information on movies, baseball, or other topics of interest.

- Sum up the discussion by reminding students that newspapers have the right to publish what they want, and readers have the responsibility to read newspapers carefully and decide what to believe.

Activity: Culture Connection

Tell students that not all countries protect the rights of their citizens. Countries that regularly deny their citizens freedoms and rights include North Korea, Cuba, Sudan, and Myanmar. (See an updated list of repressive governments at http://www.freedomhouse.org.) Have students find an example in one of these or a similar country. Suggest that they use the Internet or resources in the library.

Program Resources

Student Activity Journal

Use page 100 to build key vocabulary.

Use page 101 to practice reading newspapers critically.

Overhead Transparencies

Use 7, Critical Reading Chart, with page 285.

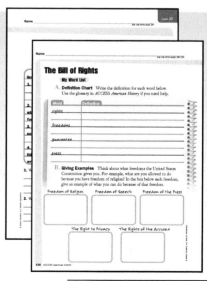

Introduce
The Bill of Rights

- This lesson covers the ten amendments in the Bill of Rights. Pages 286–287 detail the First Amendment. Read aloud the blue headings. Remind students of the visual aid on pages 284–285. Tell them to keep the visual aid images in mind when reading this section.

- Then have students do paired reading, switching turns with their partners after each heading.

Government
The Bill of Rights and the Courts

- Read the feature aloud, or have volunteers read while students follow along. Emphasize that courts decide questions about what the freedoms in the Bill of Rights actually mean.

- Briefly describe the history of religion in American life to put the freedom of religion clause in context:
  - Almost all of America's original colonists were Christian.
  - The founders of the government wanted to ensure that no church, even a Christian church, became too powerful in public life.

- Ask, *Why is it good to keep government separate from religion?*

Look and Read

The Bill of Rights

The Bill of Rights is the first 10 amendments to the Constitution. These amendments protect everyone, whether they are citizens or not.

First Amendment Freedoms

The First Amendment protects 5 freedoms.

1. FREEDOM OF RELIGION

The First Amendment **guarantees** that people in America can **worship** the way they want. It says the government can't have an official religion or support one religion over another. This principle is "separation of church and state."

2. FREEDOM OF SPEECH

The First Amendment guarantees that people can share their ideas without fear of punishment. Free **expression** goes beyond speaking and writing. It also includes making works of art—drawings, music, movies, and so on.

There are some limits to freedom of speech. You can't tell lies that may hurt a person's **reputation** or that cause a **panic.** You can't encourage people to **riot,** destroy something, or do other crimes. You can't give information to an enemy.

VOCABULARY

guarantees—promises that certain things will happen
worship—praise God or gods. Prayers, hymns, and religious services are ways of worshipping.
expression—a telling or exchanging of ideas

reputation—what most people say and think about someone
panic—a fear that spreads through a group of people and makes them lose control of themselves
riot—take part in the wild, violent disturbance of a crowd of people out of control

Government
The Bill of Rights and the Courts

The First Amendment says, "Congress shall make no law respecting an establishment of religion." What does this mean? For example, can the school day begin with a prayer? Can a judge hang the 10 Commandments in a courtroom?

The courts decide these questions. They say the answer is no. Government buildings can't have anything that would make people with a different religion or no religion feel uncomfortable.

286 UNIT 8 • CIVICS IN AMERICA

 Activity: Word Pictures

Have students preview the vocabulary words on pages 286–290. Have them work with a partner to choose three words they would like to learn. Ask them to create "word pictures" in which the word is written in a way that shows its meaning. For example, a word picture for *privacy* might show the word behind a door, or *expression* could be written in a speech balloon. Encourage students to share their work with classmates.

 Differentiating Instruction

Beginning
Learning Terms Focus students' attention on the five blue headings on this spread. Develop an understanding of the terms *religion, speech, the press, assembly,* and *petition.* Use these words in sentences and have students act them out. Have students use the pictures on pages 286–287 to tell partners about the terms.

Intermediate
Paired Reading Have students read one section at a time. Have them discuss what they read with a partner.

Advanced
What I Learned Have partners read about the First Amendment freedoms and make a card for each one. They can turn the cards face down and take turns drawing a card and explaining the new things they learned about the freedom.

3. FREEDOM OF THE PRESS

The First Amendment gives people the right to **publish** their ideas. This means we have a free **press** in America. Adults can read anything they want. They can see whatever other people publish. The government cannot **ban** books or magazines, even when some people find them **offensive**.

4. FREEDOM OF ASSEMBLY

The First Amendment says Americans can gather together anytime. They can discuss and share their opinions aloud, as long as the **assembly** is peaceful. Americans have the right to protest in public. They can form or join groups. The government can't make it a crime to belong to a group.

5. FREEDOM TO PETITION

The First Amendment guarantees the right to **petition** the government. When people petition, they ask for a change in a law or for a new law. This freedom means people can tell the government it is doing something wrong without being punished.

(TALK AND SHARE) Explain to your partner what the 5 freedoms guaranteed by the First Amendment mean.

Language Notes

Homophones
These words sound alike, but they have different spellings and meanings.

- **principle**: idea that forms a base, or foundation, for other ideas
- **principal**: most important; *also* the head of a school

- **some**: part of something
- **sum**: the result of adding numbers

- **aloud**: out loud
- **allowed**: let; permitted

VOCABULARY

publish—make public. Books, TV programs, and writings on the Internet are published.
press—people who make information and ideas known through any of the media
ban—make a law to stop the publication of something
offensive—hurtful, annoying, or disgusting
assembly—a gathering of people
petition—ask formally and in writing that the government do something

Teach About First Amendment Freedoms

- Help students build word associations around each event. For example, write the word *religion* on the board. Have students think of words or phrases that relate to it.

- Help students understand the importance of each amendment. Ask, *What would life be like without freedom of _____?*

- Explore how these freedoms have affected students' own lives and the lives of friends and family members.

Language Notes

Have partners each take one of the words in the three pairs and say or write a sentence using it correctly. Then have students trade words and give different sentences.

(TALK AND SHARE)

After partners have finished their explanations, ask, *Which of the five freedoms do you believe is most important? Why?* Use students' answers and ideas as a comprehension check.

 Activity: Internet Resources

Divide the class into five groups and assign each group one of the freedoms. Ask students to use Internet resources to learn more about the freedom and what it means. Then have them report their findings to the rest of the class.

Useful discussions about the freedoms and the court cases that have helped define them can be found online at http://www.firstamendmentcenter.org.

 Program Resources

Student Activity Journal

Assign page 102:

- To create study notes for students to review

- To provide reinforcement of key vocabulary

Discuss Protection from the Power of Government

- The two pictures on page 288 show differing views on gun laws. Have volunteers read aloud the protest signs and the pictures' caption, which defines the NRA. Ask:
  - Which picture shows the NRA's opinion?
  - Why do you think the other group is opposed to the NRA's views?

- Invite volunteers to explain why the Bill of Rights protects the right to own guns.

- Tell students that when in the 1770s the colonists' protests began to be serious, the British said some Americans had to let British troops stay in their homes. This is why we have the Third Amendment.

▲ People do not agree about guns. The NRA is the National Rifle Association. This group says no to most laws that control gun use.

Protection from the Power of Government

The Bill of Rights also protects people from the government wrongly using its power against them.

THE RIGHT TO BEAR ARMS

The Second Amendment protects the right to keep and **bear arms.** It was included because of the important role of **militias** at the time of the American Revolution. These small armies of citizens helped fight the British. Later, militias helped keep the peace. The farmers and townspeople who made up the militias **volunteered.** They were not **professional** soldiers, so they brought their own weapons.

Many Americans believe that if people didn't have guns, there would be less violence. However, the Founding Fathers believed government should not take away the right of people to have guns. National, state, and local governments cannot take away that right, but they do pass laws to control the use of guns.

Laws in most places say that only adults can own guns. Some kinds of weapons are against the law. Usually, people who own guns must list them with a government official.

NO TROOPS IN PEOPLE'S HOUSES

The Third Amendment says the government can't make people give housing to soldiers in peacetime. In wartime, Congress would first have to pass a law. Only that way could the government put troops in people's homes.

VOCABULARY

bear arms—carry weapons
militias—armies of citizens who are not professional soldiers. Today, the U.S. National Guard is a militia.
volunteered—worked without pay as a way of giving service to the community
professional—working for pay at a job that also is a career

288 UNIT 8 • CIVICS IN AMERICA

 Activity: Persuasive Writing

Have students work in pairs. Have them read page 288 carefully. Ask them to make a Two-column Chart that lists reasons people might want to own guns and reasons people might want to ban guns.

Then have students decide their own opinion on the topic. Have them use the information on their chart to write a persuasive paragraph explaining their views. Encourage students to share their paragraphs with their partner.

 Differentiating Instruction

Beginning/Advanced
Paired Reading Pair beginning learners with advanced English speakers and have the advanced students play the role of coach. Have coaches read pages 288–289 aloud while their partners follow along. Encourage readers to stop to demonstrate concepts with gestures and actions where necessary.

After each paragraph, the coaches should ask their partners one or two *yes/no* questions. Model good questions

for coaches. Have them help their partners find the answers in the text. Afterward, ask what students thought of the activity and what they learned from it.

Intermediate
Read and Respond Have students work in pairs. After each paragraph, have one partner ask the other a question as a comprehension check. Answering partners should show where the answer can be found in the text.

THE RIGHT TO PRIVACY

The Fourth Amendment says people should be "secure in their persons, house, papers, and effects." The principal meaning here is that people have a right to **privacy.** Police and other government officials cannot simply search people or their things. First, they need to show **evidence** of a crime. Many times people in government have looked into the private lives of their enemies to find things they can use to punish them. That is not allowed in the United States.

People today have many records. These include their doctor's records, telephone records, records of what they bought, records of the books they have checked out of the library, and so on. The Fourth Amendment protects all these records from **unreasonable** searches. The government is allowed to look at your records only if it has a **search warrant** from a judge.

Police sometimes have to search for illegal weapons and drugs. However, they must follow the laws to protect people's privacy.

 VOCABULARY

privacy—freedom from other people looking at one's personal life
evidence—things that show what is true and what is not true; proof
unreasonable—without a good reason
search warrant—written permission from a judge to search for evidence. Judges give search warrants when they believe the searchers will find evidence of a crime.

LESSON 23 • THE BILL OF RIGHTS **289**

Talk About The Right to Privacy

- Ask students to think about a time they went to the doctor's office, made a phone call, or rented a movie. Ask them if they would like the government to know what illness they had, whom they talked to, or what they watched. Have students explain why they feel this way.

- Explain that most Americans are uncomfortable having the government know these things about them for no good reason. Draw a distinction between looking at the records of someone accused of a crime and someone the government has no reason to suspect.

Key Connection: Law

Point out that it is not always clear what rights are guaranteed by the first ten amendments. What does *unreasonable* mean in the Fourth Amendment, or *cruel and unusual punishment* in the Eighth? What actions count as speech for the purposes of defining freedom of speech? Explain that it is the job of the courts to decide these matters.

Activity: Newspaper Articles

Collect newspaper and magazine articles having to do with issues stemming from the Bill of Rights. As an alternative, have students find articles of their own in newspapers or magazines that you hand out. Distribute these articles to pairs of students. Have them read the articles slowly, noting unfamiliar words and concepts. Then have students create a Critical Reading Chart for their article similar to the one described on page 285. Have them decide whether the article is trustworthy or not, and explain why.

Finally, have students imagine that they are presenting the information in the article as part of a TV news program. Tell them that they must summarize the information in a few quick sentences. When all students are ready, set up a "TV studio" at the front of the room and have partners come up to give their broadcasts. Use Overhead Transparency 7, Critical Reading Chart.

Discuss The Rights of the Accused

- Explain that one of the strongest powers of the government is the power to punish people for crimes.

- Ask, *Why do we need rights to protect people accused of crimes?*

- Have students read the opening paragraph of page 290. Then go through the Due Process Protections chart with students. Explain the vocabulary terms along with more common words such as *accused*, *trial*, and *innocent*.

- Have students explain to one another why these protections are important.

Teach the Pictures

Students may wonder why the people pictured on this page have their hands in the air. Explain that people who are testifying in court must repeat an oath to tell the truth, and that the oath is traditionally said with the right hand and forearm raised. Explain that it is a crime to lie to a court while under oath.

Look and Read

THE RIGHTS OF THE ACCUSED

The government has the power to put a person in jail or even to take a person's life. The Fifth, Sixth, and Eighth Amendments make sure the government will follow certain steps before punishing anyone for a crime. The steps are called **due process** of law. Due process includes the rules that police and courts must follow. Most of the rules are not in the Bill of Rights but in laws. The Fifth Amendment says police and the government must follow those laws.

Due Process Protections

The Fifth Amendment also says:

In a serious crime, a grand jury has to hear the evidence and agree to a trial.

If you're found innocent of a crime, you can't be tried for it again.

You can't be forced to **testify** against yourself or to answer questions that might make you seem guilty.

Other amendments say that if you are accused of a crime, you have the right:

To know why you were **arrested**

To know who will speak against you in court

To have a speedy, public trial

To have a **jury** of fair people from the same place where the crime happened

To have a lawyer go with you to court

Not to be given a cruel or unusual punishment

Not to have a **ball** or fines that aren't fair

MORE ABOUT THE RIGHT TO JURY

Some court cases are not about crimes. In a **civil lawsuit**, the Seventh Amendment gives people a right to a trial by jury.

VOCABULARY

due process—the steps set out by law
testify—give evidence in court
arrested—taken by force to jail or to court
jury—a group of citizens who listen to a court case and decide what the facts mean
bail—money paid to make sure a person will appear for a trial. People pay bail to stay out of jail while waiting for their trial.
civil lawsuit—a court case about money or property, not about crime

---

 Activity: Amendments and Protections

Distribute copies of the actual text of the Fifth through Eighth Amendments. (The Constitutional amendments can be found online at http://www.house.gov/Constitution/Amend.html, among other places.) Divide students into small groups. Have them match the entries in the chart with the amendments as they summarize. Afterward, ask students which parts were difficult to match, which were easier, and why.

 Differentiating Instruction

Beginning

Role-Play Focus on the words *crime*, *innocent*, and *guilty*. Make two simple stick puppets. Have one "steal" some play money. Say, *He stole the money. Stealing is a crime. He is guilty.* Point to the other puppet. Say, *He did not steal the money. He is not guilty. He is innocent.* Have students make puppets of their own and practice using and demonstrating terms with a partner.

Intermediate

Court Words Have students choose a vocabulary word such as *arrested*, *bail*, or *testify*. Have them explain the word to a partner and use it in a sentence.

Advanced

Critical Thinking Ask students what would happen if there were no protections for people accused of crimes. Have partners make a list of possible outcomes and share their lists with the class.

LIMITS TO FEDERAL GOVERNMENT

The Ninth Amendment explains that we have many other rights besides those stated in the Constitution. These rights include living where we want, traveling freely, working at a job we want, marrying and having children—or not—and choosing a school for our children.

The Tenth Amendment states that powers not given to the federal government belong to the states or the people. This is still another check to protect you from the power of the federal government.

The U.S. Constitution, with the Bill of Rights, has worked for more than 200 years. Today it is the oldest written constitution in the world, and many other nations have made constitutions like it.

TALK AND SHARE Choose one of the rights that protect people from the power of government. Explain to your partner why it is important to you.

People in the United States enjoy the right to live, worship, and go to school in freedom.

Summary

The Bill of Rights is the first 10 amendments to the U.S. Constitution. It guarantees freedoms and protects the rights of all people who live in the United States.

Teach Limits to Federal Government

Tell students that the Ninth and Tenth Amendments explain that the states have some powers and that the people themselves have many more. Remind students that the Constitution is not a list of every single law, or every single right; it simply tells the foundations and principles of government.

TALK AND SHARE

Have partners complete the Talk and Share activity. Ask volunteers to share their responses with the rest of the class.

Discuss the Summary

■ Have students read the Summary on the bottom of page 291.

■ Draw their attention to the Big Idea on page 283. Have students connect the ideas of the Summary to those expressed in the Big Idea.

■ Have volunteers use their own words to explain some of the facts and concepts they learned in this lesson.

✓ Assessment

Assess students' comprehension by asking the following questions:

History

• What are some of the freedoms listed in the First Amendment?

• How does the Bill of Rights protect people from the power of the national government?

Language

Match the word to its definition.

Words	Definitions
1. Guarantee	**A.** Hurtful
2. Ban	**B.** To stop something
3. Offensive	**C.** A promise

Assessment Book

Use page 41 to assess students' comprehension.

Teach Explaining

Tell students that this page will help them learn a skill that they will need to pass tests and write papers in school.

Model the Organizer

■ Read aloud the opening paragraph while students follow along. Point out that the organizer has two columns, each of which gives details about a free press.

■ Have volunteers read the details about a free press given in the chart's left-hand column. Then ask volunteers to read the second column, telling what happens when the press is not free. Be sure students understand the difference between the two columns.

■ Tell students that the details in the organizer can help them explain why a free press is a good thing.

Give Practice Explaining

■ **Draw** Students may use photos from newspapers or magazines to complete their notes.

■ **Write** Encourage students to include a topic sentence and a conclusion.

Explaining

Explaining American Freedoms

When you explain something, you give details that allow you to make your point. Two-column Notes can help you gather and keep track of the important details. These Two-column Notes list 3 details about a free press. They also give 3 details about what happens in countries without a free press.

Two-column Notes

With a Free Press	Without a Free Press
The press can report on things that government officials do wrong. Also, it can tell a different side of events from the government explanation.	The press can report only official versions of events.
The public can read and see whatever people choose to publish and perform. All people are free to publish or perform their ideas.	The government can make certain books and other forms of communication illegal.
People can get lots of information and hear many different points of view.	People can get only the information the government wants them to have.

Practice Explaining

1. Draw Make Two-column Notes about freedom of religion. Show freedom of religion on the left. On the right, show what happens when freedom of religion is denied. Draw pictures to show what you mean. Use your Two-column Notes to explain freedom of religion to your partner.

2. Write Make Two-column Notes for freedom of speech. Show 3 details about freedom of speech on the left. On the right, tell what would happen if there wasn't freedom of speech. Then use your notes to write a paragraph of 3 to 4 sentences explaining freedom of speech. Use words from the Word Bank in your explanation.

Word Bank
ideas
expression
communication

writing
music
art

ban

 Activity: Internet Resources

Have students research the Internet for further information on the Bill of Rights. Have students work in pairs to find one of the types of items below and present a summary about it to the class:

- Pictures
- Court cases
- Quotations about freedoms and rights
- Comparisons with other cultures and countries
- Newspaper stories

Differentiating Instruction

Beginning
Adding Labels to Pictures Encourage students to use words and short phrases for captions on the pictures they draw in their Two-column Notes for the Draw activity.

Intermediate
Partner Practice Have partners work together on a Two-column Notes chart for the Write activity. They should agree on the details and work to write one sentence about each. Then they can link their sentences into a paragraph and write one summarizing sentence for the end.

Advanced
What Free Speech Means to Me
Invite students to make their paragraphs personal by telling what the freedom of speech means in their own lives. Urge them to use an example.

Activities

Grammar Spotlight

Clauses with *Because* and *Although* A clause is a group of words that has a subject and predicate. Some clauses express a complete thought. They are *independent clauses*. Some clauses do not express a complete thought. They are *dependent clauses*.

A dependent clause can be joined with an independent clause to make a sentence. Note how these clauses are joined by the words *because* and *although*.

Independent Clause	**Dependent Clause**
The police could search the house	*because they had a search warrant.*

Dependent Clause	**Independent Clause**
Although he said he was innocent,	*the police arrested the man.*

Write a sentence about police making a search. Use a dependent and an independent clause in your sentence. Use *because* or *although* to join the clauses in your sentence.

Partner Practice

Bill of Rights Scrapbook Together with your partner gather 3 newspaper articles that show the Bill of Rights in the news. For each article, make a Critical Reading Chart as shown on page 285. Agree on an opinion about each article. Then make a scrapbook. Paste in your articles and charts. Write your opinions about each article and include them in your scrapbook. Share your scrapbook with a friend.

Hands On

Taking the Bill of Rights Home Make 5 folds in a piece of paper. Label each column with 1 of the 5 freedoms of the First Amendment. Then draw illustrations in each column to show what that freedom means. Fold your paper back along the creases so you have a blank cover showing. Label it First Amendment Freedoms. Take it home to show your family what you have learned.

COVER

Grammar Spotlight

Explain to students that there are two types of clauses—dependent and independent. Remind students that *independent* means *free* or *able to stand alone.* Explain that *dependent* means *not able to stand alone.* Tie these meanings to the description of dependent and independent clauses in the paragraph at the top of page 293.

Read aloud each example. Point out the function of the words *because* and *although* in the sentences. Ask students to identify which clauses are independent and which are dependent.

Partner Practice

Have students write the various freedoms of the first ten amendments on cards or sticky notes to help them evaluate whether or not articles discuss the Bill of Rights. Have less fluent students work with more advanced partners, or have them find one or two articles instead of three.

Hands On

Have students begin by folding their papers in half lengthwise and then have them fold each half into thirds. You may wish to make a model to demonstrate the folding process to students.

Activity: Extend the Lesson

In Defense of Liberty: The Story of America's Bill of Rights by Russell Freedman (Holiday House, 2003) is a clear description of the first ten amendments and their impact on American society. The book is targeted mainly toward middle school students. Freedman describes the historical reasons for the Bill of Rights and summarizes some of the compromises and debates connected with the amendments' freedoms.

Program Resources

Student Activity Journal
Use page 103 to practice *explaining.*

Overhead Transparencies
Use 29, Two-column Chart, with page 292.

Responsible Citizenship

STANDARDS CONTENT

History

- ■ Demonstrate ways to separate fact from opinion
- ■ Explain the role of the citizen in American democracy
- ■ Recognize duties of citizens
- ■ Recognize responsibilities of citizens

Language

- ■ Identify the following Key Concepts: *duty*, *citizen*, and *responsibility*
- ■ Recognize words with multiple meanings
- ■ Practice persuading people to your point of view

Begin ⟨Building Background⟩

- ■ Ask students the questions below the photo. Focus students on:
  - • Who the food is for
  - • How the man is helpful to others
- ■ Encourage students to talk about similar activities they have taken part in. Provide students with words as needed (*homeless*, *needy*, *hungry*).
- ■ Draw out key ideas about charitable work:
  - • It can help people in need.
  - • It can make the people who do the work feel good.
  - • Helping other people is part of being a responsible citizen.

Talk and Explore

Responsible Citizenship

Here you'll learn about U.S. citizenship. You'll also learn how to separate fact from opinion and practice persuading others.

Building Background

▲ Our group makes sandwiches for a homeless center once a month.

- ■ **What is this man doing?**
- ■ **Why do you think he is doing it?**
- ■ **When in your life did you ever do something like this?**

 Activity: Making a Difference

Have students form small groups. Explain that helping people who are in need can make the world a better place. Tell students that some people call this *making a difference.*

Ask each group to brainstorm ways that they can make a difference by helping others. Assign one student from each group to record the group's ideas. Then have students from each group present their lists to the class.

Differentiating Instruction

Beginning
Volunteering Focus on the picture above and provide help with such vocabulary as *volunteer, mission, neighborhood, outdoors, homeless,* and *hungry.* Invite short answers to such questions as *What is the man showing?* (*food*) *Where is the mission?* (*outdoors*)

Intermediate
Sharing Vocabulary Have partners make lists of all the words they associate with citizenship. Then compile a master list for the class.

Advanced
Oral Sharing Assign small groups one of the pictures on pages 294–295 and have students discuss what they think it has to do with being a citizen. Then have groups choose a representative to tell the class their ideas.

Big Idea

For the United States to stay strong and free, its citizens must do their duty and meet their responsibilities.

1 Citizenship

2 Duties of Citizens

3 Responsibilities of Citizens

Introduce the Big Idea

■ Read aloud the Big Idea on page 295.

■ Call attention to the three headings.

■ Explain that citizens are people who are members of a country. Tell students that people can become citizens in different ways. Emphasize that people get some important advantages by being citizens, but that citizens also must do some things that might be hard or unpleasant.

Review

Remind students of the previous lessons on the Constitution and the Bill of Rights. Review vocabulary terms such as *rights*, *freedoms*, and *principles*. Explain that the job of being a citizen includes helping to protect those rights and freedoms for everyone.

Activity: Role-Play

Ask students to imagine what might happen if people only wanted the easy parts of being a citizen.

Explain to students that you will pretend to be the U.S. government. Ask them to play the parts of citizens who only want the advantages of being a citizen, and don't want to do things that are hard or dangerous.

Say, *There is an important election coming up. Are you planning to vote?*

Have three to five students answer in character, using complete sentences such as *No, I'm too busy that day* or *No, voting is boring*.

Continue with other questions:

• There is a big trial next week. Will you be a member of the jury?

• An enemy has attacked us. Will you join the army?

Then discuss the role-play with students.

Resource Library

Reader's Handbook (red)
Fact and Opinion 281

Reader's Handbook (yellow)
Fact and Opinion 203

All Write
Using Facts and Opinions 253

Teach [Key Concepts]

- Point out the Key Concepts. Say each term slowly to model the correct pronunciation. Ask students to repeat after you. Next, read aloud the Key Concept sentences, or have a volunteer read them for the rest of the class. Talk with students about what the words and sentences mean.

- Point out that *duty* and *responsibility* have similar meanings. Ask students if they can see the difference. (*A duty is a thing you must do. A responsibility is a thing you should do.*)

- Explain that the word *citizen* has a legal meaning. Tell students that people may feel they belong to a nation, but that does not make them citizens.

Teach the Visual Aid
[Active Citizenship]

Call students' attention to the visual aid. Point out that these photos all show ways in which citizens fulfill their duties and responsibilities. Ask students which activities look like they might be fun and which look more like work. Then briefly explain each duty or responsibility. Have students look for these six activities as they read through the lesson.

Talk and Explore

[Key Concepts]

Duty   **Citizen**   **Responsibility**

Laws describe the duties of **citizens,** or what they must do. For instance, citizens have a **duty** to pay their taxes.

A **responsibility** is owed to the other people in the nation. Citizens count on each other to meet their responsibilities.

[Active Citizenship]

Voting

Serving on a Jury

Paying Taxes

296 UNIT 8 • CIVICS IN AMERICA

 Activity: Duties and Responsibilities

Have students work with a partner. Ask them to make a list of the duties and responsibilities they have at home. Give examples if necessary, such as preparing meals, sweeping floors, or helping younger siblings with homework.

Then have students use the list to make a Venn Diagram. Each circle shows one student's duties and responsibilities. The overlap shows those shared by both students.

 Differentiating Instruction

Beginning
Identifying Facts and Opinions Have each student label one card *fact* and one card *opinion*. Have students hold up a card in response to your saying sentences such as *Today is Monday* and *Cookies are good.*

Intermediate
You Decide Have students write the words *fact* and *opinion* on either side of an index card. In small groups, have students take turns telling a fact or an opinion, and have the others hold up the side of the card that shows which it is.

Advanced
Finding Facts and Opinions Have students look at a book for facts and opinions. Have them write each fact or opinion in their own words, or mark each fact with a sticky of one color and each opinion with a sticky of another color. Have them tell a partner whether facts or opinions were easier to find.

Separating Fact from Opinion

When you read or listen to someone who is trying to influence you, you need to know whether you are being given facts or opinions. A *fact* is a statement that can be proven through such sources as a dictionary, almanac, or encyclopedia.

An *opinion* is a personal feeling, belief, or attitude. Words that express judgments or evaluations usually signal opinions. These signal words include *best, worst, believe, think, favorite,* and *boring.*

Topic	Fact	Opinion
PLEDGE OF ALLEGIANCE	The Pledge of Allegiance was written by Francis Bellamy and was first published in 1892.	The Pledge of Allegiance is the best statement ever written.
POLITICAL PARTIES	Americans can join a political party.	Working to get someone elected is my favorite way to be a good citizen, and it's not boring. It's fun.

Participating in Community Life

Staying Informed by Reading the Newspaper

Serving in the Armed Forces

Teach Skill Building

- Read with students the discussion of how facts and opinions are different.

- Call students' attention to the signal words mentioned in the text. Have students read through the chart.

- Be sure that students understand the following academic vocabulary: *prove, statement, belief, attitude, judgment.*

- Pick up a book. Give a fact about it (such as the title or author) and an opinion about it (such as *It is exciting* or *It is easy to read*). Have students identify which is the fact and which is the opinion. Ask them to tell how they know. Repeat if desired with other objects or ideas.

- Ask students to share some facts that they know. Then ask them to share some opinions.

Activity: Teach Vocabulary

Have students look through pages 298–303, paying close attention to the vocabulary words at the bottom of each page. Ask partners to choose six to eight terms they would especially like to learn. Have them write each term on one side of a card and a picture or a definition on the other. Next, have them create a simple mobile frame out of straws and yarn. As students learn the words, have them add the cards to their mobile frames.

Program Resources

Student Activity Journal

Use page 104 to build key vocabulary.

Use page 105 to practice separating fact from opinion.

Overhead Transparencies

Use 31, Venn Diagram, with page 296.

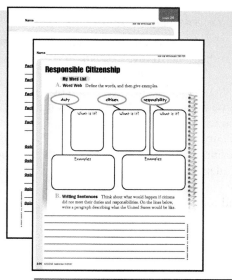

Introduce Responsible Citizenship

- Ask students to preview the headings and chart in the reading. Ask, *What do you think this reading will be about?*

- Walk through the chart on page 298 with students. Be sure they understand that the left column refers to *who* can become a citizen and that the right column explains *how* people can become citizens.

- Tell students that while many Americans are pleased that many immigrants become new citizens each year, others believe that the country already has more people than it can manage. Explain that some countries have much stricter requirements for becoming a citizen.

TALK AND SHARE

Have students work in pairs to discuss the topic. Use their responses as a comprehension check of the material on page 298.

▲ New citizens

Responsible Citizenship

Citizens need to meet their responsibilities and do their duties in order to protect their rights.

U.S. Citizenship

Most Americans get their **citizenship** by birth. They are **citizens** because they were born in the United States or have parents who are citizens. People born in the U.S. **territories** of Puerto Rico, Guam, the Virgin Islands, or the Northern Mariana Islands are also U.S. citizens.

Other people can become U.S. citizens too. The Office of Citizenship runs **naturalization.** The office is part of U.S. Citizenship and Immigration Services (USCIS) in the Department of Homeland Security. The process has many details, but this chart shows how someone can become a U.S. citizen.

Becoming a Naturalized Citizen

The Person	The Process
Must be at least 18 years old	Fill out an application form
Must have entered the U.S. legally	Be approved in an interview with an agent from the Office of Citizenship
Must have lived in the U.S. at least 5 years	Pass a test on U.S. government and history
Must be of good moral character	Recite an **oath of allegiance** in a ceremony for new citizens
Must be able to read, write, and speak English	

TALK AND SHARE
Explain to your partner how a person born outside the United States can become a U.S. citizen.

VOCABULARY
citizenship—the state of being a citizen
citizens—members of a nation
territories—lands under the control of the United States
naturalization—the way people become U.S. citizens if they weren't born as citizens
oath of allegiance—a promise to be true to the nation

298 UNIT 8 • CIVICS IN AMERICA

 Activity: Expert Testimony

Suggest that students decide together who to invite to talk to the class about his or her experience becoming a citizen. This would be a good opportunity to build a strong connection with students' homes, so encourage students to invite a parent, grandparent, or other relative. Students should plan the questions they want their "expert" to answer and make a list.

 Differentiating Instruction

Beginning
Choral Reading Have students read the bulleted list below the heading *Obey Laws.* Before each phrase, insert the word *laws,* so it reads *Laws protect rights, Laws keep people from hurting each other,* and so on. Ask volunteers to act out or demonstrate the meaning of each phrase.

Intermediate
Partner Practice Have students read aloud one paragraph at a time. Have them mark unfamiliar words with sticky notes and discuss their meanings. Then have them summarize what they read.

Advanced
Talking About Taxes After reading the selection, have partners discuss why taxes are needed.

Duties of Citizens

U.S. citizens have several duties that are required by law.

OBEY LAWS

The first duty of all Americans is to obey the laws. Laws help a society. Here are some things laws do.

- Protect rights
- Keep people from hurting each other
- Protect property
- Solve problems between people
- Protect health and safety
- Give fair **punishments** to people who break laws

PAY TAXES

The U.S. government provides many services to its citizens. A list of all services would be enormous. Here are some government services.

- A military to protect people
- Social Security money to help when people get older
- Schools to educate people
- Parks for people to enjoy
- Highways for travel
- Courts, judges, and lawyers to keep people safe and free

Taxes pay for everything the government does. Each year, people pay **income tax.** In most states and cities, people pay **sales taxes** nearly every time they buy something. In some states, people who own land or buildings also pay a **property tax** every year. Paying taxes is a duty. It is something people must do to keep the society running.

VOCABULARY

punishments—fines, jail terms, and other penalties
income tax—a tax paid on the money earned at a job
sales tax—a tax paid on things people buy
property tax—a tax paid on land, buildings, or big things like boats or cars that people own

▲ Police enforce traffic laws.

Language Notes

Multiple Meanings
These words have more than one meaning.

break
1. not obey
2. make something come apart

services
1. helpful, useful, or necessary acts
2. work done for others

states
1. large divisions of the country
2. says

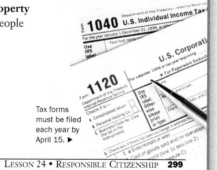

Tax forms must be filed each year by April 15. ▶

Teach About
Duties of Citizens

- After students read the text under the subhead *Obey Laws*, ask them questions about what would happen if there were no laws.

- Point out the subhead *Pay Taxes*. Ask students what they know about taxes. Emphasize that noncitizens who live or work in the United States must pay certain kinds of taxes, too.

- Then go over the kinds of taxes with students. Explain that some taxes go to the federal government, while others go to state and local governments.

- Invite students to research sales tax rates through the Sales Tax Clearing House, Inc. at the following website: http://thestc.com/Strates.stm

Language Notes

- Draw students' attention to the multiple-meaning words in the box. Pick two volunteers for each word. Have them use the word in a sentence, using one of the two definitions.

- Point out the words in the text. Ask students which definition matches each word in context.

 Activity: Tax Dollars at Work

Ask students to list government activities they think are especially useful. The bulleted list under the heading *Pay Taxes* could be a starting point. Other services might include fire protection or school lunches.

Then ask students to imagine that they have to pay $100 in taxes. Have them draw a circle graph to show how much of this tax money they would like to go to each of the programs on their list.

Program Resources

Student Activity Journal

Assign page 106:

- To create study notes for students to review
- To provide reinforcement of key vocabulary

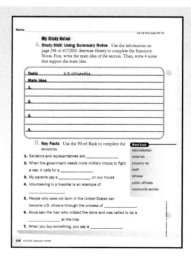

Teach About More Duties of Citizens

Ask students to generate a list of wars they remember from earlier lessons. Point out that each of these wars was fought by soldiers, some of whom sacrificed their lives to help protect their nation and people. Emphasize that some soldiers were volunteers, and others were drafted.

Discuss the Branches of the Military

- Have students read the branches of the military chart.
- Have them tell what they know about these branches and their duties.
- Explain that although the branches are separate, they often work together to help resolve conflicts.

Teach the Pictures

Ask students to describe the pictures of people in the military. Ask, *How are these people different from soldiers we saw in earlier lessons?* Tell students that weapons have changed and the people have changed, too. Emphasize that the military needs not just fighters but also computer technicians, linguists, pilots, cooks, and other specialists. Explain that women have gained an increasingly important role in the military.

▲ The U.S. military is one of the strongest armed forces in the world. ▶

HELP DEFEND THE COUNTRY AGAINST ENEMIES

Citizens help protect the nation in many ways. The forces of the military respond when enemies attack. They also serve when the UN calls for troops to help bring peace to areas around the world.

Military Forces
- Army
- Navy
- Air Force
- Marines
- U.S. Coast Guard

Today, service in these forces is **voluntary.** People choose to serve because they believe they can make a difference in the world. They can protect freedom. Also, military service can be a good career. However, the nation sometimes needs to call up a large number of troops in a **draft.** Responding to a draft is not something you can refuse to do. It is a duty.

VOCABULARY
voluntary—done of one's own free will; not forced or required
draft—the selection of troops to serve in the military

300　Unit 8 • Civics in America

 Activity: Internet Resources

Draw up a list of Americans who have served in the military. Possible names include Ulysses S. Grant, Colin Powell, George Washington, and Dwight Eisenhower. Invite students to add to the list. Then, have students form small groups and choose one person from the list. Have them list five to six questions about this person. Then have them use Internet resources to find out answers and share their work with the class.

 Differentiating Instruction

Beginning
Partner Talk Have students use the pictures on pages 299–301 to talk with a partner about the duties of citizenship. Ask them to use words and gestures to help them explain.

Intermediate
Group Work Have students form small groups. Ask them to take turns telling one another why it is important for citizens to attend school when they are young. Have each group appoint a secretary to record their ideas.

Afterward, have groups share their work with one another.

Advanced
My Choice Have students write a five-sentence paragraph explaining how they would choose to serve their country. Ask them to explain what they would like to do, where, and why.

SERVE ON A JURY

Citizens have a duty to serve on a jury. The Constitution gives all Americans the right to a trial by jury. When you appear for **jury duty,** you help protect someone's right to a fair trial. Citizens also have a duty to serve as a **witness** at a trial if they are called to do so.

ATTEND SCHOOL

From age 5 until their mid-to-late teens, Americans have a duty to attend school. There you gain the knowledge and skills needed to be a good citizen. These skills will help you make informed choices later when voting for **public officials.** The skills also will let you help society through your job.

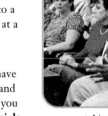
▲ A jury must weigh facts to be fair.

(TALK AND SHARE) Choose one of the duties of citizenship. Explain to your partner why it is important to the nation.

Students work hard to stay informed. ▼

VOCABULARY

jury duty—the call to be part of a group of citizens who listen to a court case and decide what the facts mean

witness—a person who answers questions in a trial

public officials—people elected to work in government

opportunity—a chance

level best—very best effort

constituents—the people an elected official represents

Government

Serving the Public

California Congressman Tom Lantos, a native of Hungary, survived the death camps of World War II. But he lost his whole family in the Holocaust. He became a naturalized American citizen in 1953. Lantos talked about his job in government service. He said, "I really felt I had an **opportunity** to do my **level best,** not only on behalf of my **constituents,** but for the millions of people who have been allowed to come to this country, to repay the freedom and opportunity we gained by becoming American citizens."

LESSON 24 • RESPONSIBLE CITIZENSHIP **301**

Talk About Other Duties

■ Have students read the headings on page 301. Ask them to explain to a partner what they know about serving on a jury or attending school.

■ Then have students read through the two paragraphs. Ask them to explain each paragraph in their own words.

(TALK AND SHARE)

Review effective note-taking practices, such as the process outlined on page 273. Then have partners discuss the Talk and Share activity. Ask students to take notes on their partners' answers.

Government

Serving the Public

■ Ask students *wh-* questions about the feature on Representative Tom Lantos. Questions might include:
- What job does Lantos have?
- When did he become a naturalized citizen?
- Why did he want to go into government service?

■ Point out that quoted words such as *repay* and *opportunity* show Lantos's belief that government service is a way of helping his new country.

Activity: Summarize an Opinion

Point out that the five headings on pages 299–301 describe five important duties of U.S. citizens. Write these headers on the board as a list labeled *Citizens Must*. Have volunteers read items on the list aloud.

Ask students to silently decide which of the five duties they think is most important. Ask a volunteer to express his or her opinion for the class to hear, including a brief reason for the opinion. For instance, a student might say, *Serving in the*

military is most important because *that keeps the country safe.*

Have another student summarize the previous opinion and then give a new reason for choosing the same duty, or explain why a different duty is most important.

Go around the room until everyone has had a turn to speak and summarize. Wrap up the activity by asking the first speaker to summarize the opinion of the last.

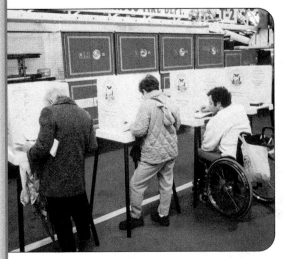

Discuss Responsibilities of Citizens

- Review the connection between responsibilities and duties. Remind students that duties have the force of the law behind them, while responsibilities usually do not.

- Read aloud the opening paragraph or have a student volunteer read aloud while others follow along.

- Call students' attention to the blue headings on pages 302–303. Then have students read through the text.

- Discuss the phrase *Life, Liberty, and the pursuit of Happiness.* Ask students to say a sentence for each word to show how it relates to them personally.

Key Connection: Government

Ask, *What bad things could happen if we don't pay attention to what our representatives in government are doing?* (*They could use our tax money to make themselves rich. They could help their friends and hurt people they don't like.*) Then invite volunteers to persuade the group that voting is important.

Responsibilities of Citizens

Citizens have **responsibilities** as well as duties. Responsibilities are just as important as duties. American democracy depends on people meeting their responsibilities.

RESPECTING THE RIGHTS OF OTHERS

You expect people to **respect** your rights, and you must respect the rights of others. Sometimes this means respecting the rights of people with whom you disagree. According to the Declaration of Independence, people have a right to "Life, Liberty, and the **pursuit** of Happiness." All Americans have these rights, and they should receive the same respect and **treatment,** regardless of race, religion, beliefs, or other differences.

VOTING

U.S. citizens have the right to vote when they reach the age of 18. Voting is one of the most important responsibilities of citizens. Sometimes people think their votes won't make a difference, so they don't vote. This is a mistake. Throughout history, many people have fought hard to earn the right to vote, some even giving their lives. When you vote for a **candidate** for **public office** or for a new law, you are helping to guide the government. If you don't like the job the government is doing, you should help elect other people in the next election.

VOCABULARY
responsibilities—actions you owe to others in society. Meeting your responsibilities is voluntary. Laws do not make you do these things, but people depend on them.
respect—show care or consideration for
pursuit—the getting of or chasing after. Many people have died in the pursuit of freedom.
treatment—actions; dealings; considerations
candidate—a person who is working to get elected
public office—a job—like mayor, governor, or senator—that a person is elected to

 Activity: Real-world Connection

Remind students that power is held partly by people in government, such as senators and presidents, and partly by the voters.

If possible, have a local government official come in and speak to the class. Encourage the official to talk not only about his or her duties and responsibilities but also about how politicians are responsive to—and dependent on—the people of the community.

 Differentiating Instruction

Beginning
Studying Meanings Focus on the two pictures above. Point to a picture. Ask, *What is happening? How does this help America?* Have students answer with words, phrases, or gestures.

Intermediate
Multiple Meanings Have students explore the meanings of the words *strong* and *free*. Point out that *The United States is strong* may mean something different from *That man is strong.* Have students discuss the

meanings with a partner and share their ideas with the rest of the group.

Advanced
Writing a Letter Have students in small groups talk about adults they know who participate in community life. Their list may include politicians, community organizers, or members of volunteer groups. Have students write a letter to one person on their list asking what he or she does and why.

PARTICIPATING IN AMERICAN LIFE

All citizens have a responsibility to contribute to community life. You can contribute by helping in your local hospital or by **participating** in a local park cleanup. You can volunteer to be a tutor or a friend to someone in need. When you volunteer for **community service**, you are being a good citizen. You are helping to make your community and nation a better place to live.

Ways to Participate

Take responsibility for your actions.	Stay informed.
Support your family and friends.	Use information to make judgments and decisions.
Give leadership to groups.	Form your opinions and express your views in public.
Do volunteer service.	Vote.
Do military service.	Join with others to work for changes you believe in.

(TALK AND SHARE) Choose one of the responsibilities of citizenship and tell your partner how you would go about doing it.

VOCABULARY

participating—being part of; working in
community service—volunteer work that helps the people in the place where one lives

Summary

By doing their duties and meeting their responsibilities, citizens make the nation strong and help keep the people free.

Teach About Participating in American Life

- Explain to students that the term *participating* includes many different kinds of activities. Have students read through the chart with a partner. Ask them to mark unfamiliar words with sticky notes. Then have students share the words they marked with the class. Encourage classmates to try to explain the meanings of words for those who weren't sure.

- Relate the ideas in the chart to the picture on page 294. Ask students how the man is participating in American life.

(**TALK AND SHARE**)

Have partners carry out the Talk and Share activity. Ask volunteers to share their responses with the rest of the class.

Discuss the Summary

- Have students read the Summary at the bottom of page 303.

- Then return to the Big Idea on page 295. Draw language and concept connections between the Summary and the Big Idea. Ask students to explain one duty or responsibility that they learned.

 Assessment

Assess students' comprehension by asking the following questions:

History

- How does paying taxes help the United States?

- Why is it important to vote?

- What might happen if citizens do not carry out their duties and responsibilities?

Language

Say or write a sentence using the following word and phrase pairs:

- Taxes, duty

- Citizen, naturalization

- Candidate, public office

Assessment Book

Use page 42 to assess students' comprehension.

Teach Persuading

Read aloud the opening paragraph. Explain to students that persuading simply means trying to get other people to think as you do. Have students tell about times when they tried to persuade a friend, teacher, or family member to agree with them.

Model the Organizer

- Read aloud the opinion at the top of the Argument Organizer.

- Tell students that the supporting details listed in the organizer explain why the opinion makes sense.

- Have students express the opinion and one of the supporting details in a sentence using *because*, such as *We need to clean up the vacant lot because it is a mess.*

- Show students how the opinion and the order of the details lead to the conclusion.

Give Practice Persuading

- **Draw** Have beginning and intermediate language learners complete the Draw activity. Encourage intermediate students to include written words and phrases in their posters as well as artwork.

- **Write** Advanced language learners should complete the Write activity.

Develop Language

Persuading

Persuading People

To persuade people, you need to give reasons why they should agree with your point of view. You need to add details that support your argument. Some details can be facts, and others can be opinions. You organize the details in a way you believe will be effective. One way to build a strong argument is to put your best idea last.

An Argument Organizer can help you. Notice how it has 3 parts: (1) your opinion, (2) the details that support your argument, or opinion, and (3) the conclusion you want others to reach.

Argument Organizer

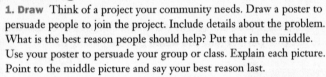

Opinion: We need to clean up the vacant lot.

Supporting detail:	**Supporting detail:**	**Supporting detail:**	**Supporting detail:**
The vacant lot on the corner is a mess.	There are broken glass and rusty cans on the lot.	Your little sister could get hurt if she fell there while she was playing.	We're all going to get together and clean it up. It will be fun.

Conclusion: You should join us.

Practice Persuading

1. Draw Think of a project your community needs. Draw a poster to persuade people to join the project. Include details about the problem. What is the best reason people should help? Put that in the middle. Use your poster to persuade your group or class. Explain each picture. Point to the middle picture and say your best reason last.

2. Write Persuade people that knowing the news is important. Gather details about how knowing the news can make you a better citizen. Make an Argument Organizer to organize the details. Use it to write a paragraph of 4 to 6 sentences persuading people to stay informed. Exchange paragraphs with a partner and check each other's writing.

Check Your Writing

Make sure you
- Use complete sentences.
- Use a period at the end of each sentence.
- Spell all the words correctly.

Activity: Internet Resources

Have students research the Internet for information on key ideas from the lesson. Have students work in pairs to find one of the types of items below and present a summary about it to the class:

- Pictures of volunteers, soldiers, or jurors
- Biographical sketches and first-person accounts
- Voters' guides
- Information on naturalization

Differentiating Instruction

Beginning
Drawing a Poster Have students begin the Draw activity by deciding on a project and forming an opinion about it. Help them put this opinion at the top of the poster. Then have them list supporting details and write or draw them on the poster as well.

Intermediate
Creating a Diagram Have students start the Draw activity by determining a project and an opinion. Then have them make an Argument Organizer to

list their supporting details and conclusion. Have students use words and sentences as well as pictures in their poster.

Advanced
A Reminder Remind students that their most effective arguments should come last. Have them use the Check Your Writing box when they are finished.

Grammar Spotlight

Verbs with Can The word *can* is a verb you might put in front of another verb. *Can* adds to the meaning of the verb that comes after it.

What It Means	Example
Has the ability to	*A citizen can vote.*
Tells what's possible	*I can vote after 6 o'clock.*
Asks a question	*Can you meet me after I vote?*

The verb *can* does not change. Do not add *s* to verbs that follow *can*.

Write 3 sentences about volunteering. Use a different use of *can* in each one.

Hands On

Citizenship Comic Book As a small group, make a 4-page comic book about citizenship. Make your book tell a story. Create at least 3 characters. Choose the things you will show. If you choose 12 things a citizen should do, you could show 3 on each page. Draw pictures. Use speech balloons. Make copies of your book to take home and show your family what you have learned.

Oral Language

Duties and Responsibilities Say a sentence to your partner about one of the 5 duties of citizens. Then ask your partner to say a sentence about a way to meet 1 of the 3 responsibilities of citizens. Each of you should talk about a different duty and responsibility. You can look back in this lesson for help.

Partner Practice

Facts and Opinions Work with a partner to list facts about citizenship. Then, together make another list. This time write your opinion about what makes a good citizen. Share your lists with others and make a group list of all the different facts and opinions.

LESSON 24 • RESPONSIBLE CITIZENSHIP **305**

Activities

Grammar Spotlight

Explain to students that *can* is a helping verb that goes in front of other verbs.

Have students generate simple sentences using *can*. Ask them to use both questions and statements. Then have students complete the assignment by writing the sentences about volunteering.

Hands On

Before students start to draw, have them make a rough outline of their comic book. They should list the basic ideas they plan to cover and the order they will show them. Glance through students' outlines to make sure they include enough ideas.

Oral Language

Students may use the forms *One duty of citizenship is _____* and *You can be a responsible citizen by _____.*

Partner Practice

Advanced language learners can use complete sentences to persuade partners to include items on their list.

 Activity: Extend the Lesson

Becoming a Citizen by Sarah E. De Capua (Childrens Press, 2002) describes the process of naturalization in clear, straightforward prose and illustrations. De Capua explains the procedures and requirements for citizenship, and she also describes how a typical naturalization ceremony might work.

Program Resources

Student Activity Journal

Use page 107 to practice *persuading*.

Overhead Transparencies

Use 1, Argument Chart, with page 304.

GLOSSARY

Pronunciation Key

ă	pat	ĭ	pit	ôr	core	ŭ	cut
ā	pay	ī	bite	oi	boy	û	urge
âr	care	îr	pier	ou	out	th	thin
ä	father	ŏ	pot	ŏŏ	took	*th*	this
ĕ	pet	ō	toe	ŏŏr	lure	zh	vision
ē	be	ô	paw	ōō	boot	ə	about

A

abolitionist (ăb′ə lĭsh′ə nĭst) *n.* a person who worked to end slavery. *The **abolitionist** helped many slaves escape.* (p. 134)

abuse (ə byōōz′) *v.* use wrongly. *If we **abuse** our computer time, the teacher will take it away.* (p. 279)

activist (ăk′tə vĭst) *n.* a person who takes strong action to get changes. *The **activist** gave a speech about protecting our forests.* (p. 254)

adobe (ə dō′bē) *adj.* sun-dried brick made of clay and straw. (p. 27)

advantage (ăd văn′tĭj) *n.* a good thing that can cause success. *Mia's strength gives her team an **advantage.*** (p. 167)

adviser (ăd vī′zər) *n.* a person who gives advice about how to solve problems. *My **adviser** told me which classes I need to take.* (p. 94)

alliance (ə lī′əns) *n.* an agreement between two countries to help each other fight a common enemy. *The **alliance** helped us win the war.* (p. 73)

allies (ăl′īz) *n.* nations that join together to fight an enemy. *The **allies** helped each other to defeat their enemy.* (p. 214)

Allies (ăl′īz) *n.* the group of nations, including Britain, the United States, and the Soviet Union, that formed one side in World War II. *The **Allies** fought against Germany, Japan, and Italy.* (p. 227)

amendment (ə mĕnd′mənt) *n.* a change to a document. *The Constitution has 27 **amendments.*** (p. 87)

Americas (ə mĕr′ĭ kəz) *n.* the continents of North and South America. (p. 36)

annex (ăn′ĕks) *v.* add territory to one's land. *The ruler wanted to **annex** the island to make the country larger.* (p. 204)

annexation (ăn′ ĭk sā′ shən) *n.* adding land or property. *American sugar planters called for U.S. **annexation** of Hawaii.* (p. 200)

answerable (ăn′sər ə bəl) *adj.* responsible; must explain itself. *Politicians are **answerable** to the people who elect them.* (p. 121)

antislavery (ăn′tē slā′və rē) *adj.* against slavery. ***Antislavery** groups tried to stop slavery.* (p. 156)

apologize (ə pŏl′ ə jīz′) *v.* say *I'm sorry* for doing wrong. *I want to **apologize** for being mean to you yesterday.* (p. 231)

appreciate (ə prē′shē āt′) *v.* see as valuable; think highly of. *I **appreciate** your help with my math homework.* (p. 243)

argue (är′gyōō) *v.* persuade people by giving reasons. *I will **argue** for a longer lunch period at the next student council meeting.* (p. 62)

arms race *n.* a contest over who could build the most weapons. *Fear caused the **arms race** between the United States and the Soviet Union.* (p. 242)

arrest (ə rĕst′) *v.* take by force to jail or to court. *The police officer will **arrest** the man for stealing.* (p. 290)

Articles (är′tĭ kəlz) *n.* the 7 major divisions of the Constitution. *Laws and bills are divided into **articles.*** (p. 276)

Articles of Confederation *n.* the document that described the first government of the United States. *The U.S. Constitution replaced the **Articles of Confederation** in 1779.* (p. 82)

assassinate (ə săs′ə nāt′) *v.* kill. This word is used for the murder of a public leader. *A gun was used to **assassinate** Abraham Lincoln.* (p. 178)

assembly (ə sĕm′blē) *n.* a gathering of people. *A school **assembly** was held to welcome new students.* (p. 287)

atomic bomb *n.* a hugely destructive weapon. *The **atomic bomb** killed many people.* (p. 230)

attract (ə trăkt′) *v.* draw or bring people in. *The color yellow will **attract** bees.* (p. 50)

authority (ə thôr′ĭ tē) *n.* the right to rule. *The principal has **authority** in the school.* (p. 274)

Axis (ăk′sĭs) *n.* the group of nations, including Germany, Italy, and later, Japan, that formed one side in World War II. *The **Axis** nations lost the war.* (p. 226)

B

bail (bāl) *n.* money paid to make sure a person will appear for a trial. *People pay **bail** to stay out of jail until their trial is over.* (p. 290)

balance (băl′əns) *n.* an equal division. *The **balance** of opinions in our group made it easy to work together.* (p. 111)

ban (băn) *v.* make a law to stop the publication of something. *Some **governments ban** books because of what they say.* (p. 287)

battle (băt′l) *n.* a large fight between armed forces. *Many soldiers died in the **battle.*** (p. 71)

bear arms *v.* carry weapons. *The U.S. Constitution gives Americans the right to **bear arms.*** (p. 288)

beyond (bē ŏnd′) *prep.* on the far side; past. *The top shelf is **beyond** my reach.* (p. 107)

big business *n.* the group of large businesses that control their industries. ***Big business** often forces small companies to close down.* (p. 195)

bilingual (bī lĭng′gwəl) *adj.* having to do with two languages. *Anita is **bilingual** because she can speak Spanish and English.* (p. 254)

bill (bĭl) *n.* a proposed law. *If Congress approves the **bill,** it will become a law.* (p. 277)

Bill of Rights *n.* the first 10 amendments to the Constitution. *The **Bill of Rights** protects the basic rights of people.* (p. 87)

bitterly (bĭt′ ər lē) *adv.* with anger and disappointment. *Kevin **bitterly** served his detention.* (p. 154)

bitterness (bĭt′ ər nəs) *n.* a deep, painful, feeling of anger. ***Bitterness** in the South lasted long after the Civil War.* (p. 178)

blame (blām) *n.* have the responsibility for something wrong. *The storm was to **blame** for the damage.* (p. 218)

boom (bōōm) *v.* grow very large, like a loud explosion. *The cellular phone industry began to **boom** in the late 1990s.* (p. 193)

border (bôr′dər) *n.* the official line that separates two lands. *Ciudad Juarez, Mexico, is across the **border** from El Paso, Texas.* (p. 145)

border state *n.* a Union state on the border with a Confederate State. (p. 166)

Britain (brĭt′n) *n.* the name of the country that includes England, Scotland, and Wales. *The people of **Britain** are British.* (p. 58)

broke (brōk) *adj.* without any money. *I can't buy the CD because I'm **broke.*** (p. 217)

brutal (brōōt′l) *adj.* very cruel, not human. *The beating was so **brutal** the victim was put in the hospital.* (p. 156)

budget (bŭj′ĭt) *n.* a plan for getting and spending money. *On our **budget,** we save $25 a month.* (p. 278)

buffalo (bŭf′ə lō′) *n.* a large animal, like a cow; also called *bison. Plains Indians hunted **buffalo** for food and clothing.* (p. 23)

C

cabinet (kăb′ə nĭt) *n.* the group of top advisers to the president. *The **cabinet** met with the president to talk about the war.* (p. 94)

California Trail *n.* a pioneer trail leading southwest from Missouri to California. (p. 109)

canal (kə năl′) *n.* a waterway that is dug between bodies of water. *The boat traveled through the **canal.*** (p. 108)

candidate (kăn′dĭ dāt′) *n.* a person who is working to get elected. *Each **candidate** gave a speech about what he would do if elected.* (p. 144)

canyon (kăn′yən) *n.* a narrow valley with steep sides and a stream at the bottom. *It's a long way to the bottom of the **canyon.*** (p. 27)

carpetbagger (kär′pĭt băg′ər) *n.* a Northerner who moved south after the Civil War for financial gain. The name came from the idea that he carried all his things in a bag made from carpets. (p. 179)

cavalry (kăv′əl rē) *n.* the part of an army that fights on horseback. *The army does not need the **cavalry** anymore because it uses tanks.* (p. 203)

cease-fire (sēs′fīr′) *n.* an agreement to stop fighting. *The battle ended in a **cease-fire.*** (p. 240)

census (sĕn′səs) *n.* a count of all the people. *The government takes a **census** to find out how many people live in each city and state.* (p. 277)

central control *n.* a concentration of planning and decision-making. ***Central control** means that decisions are all made at the capitol or headquarters by people who may be far away from where things are happening.* (p. 224)

century (sĕn′chə rē) *n.* a period of 100 years. *1900 to 1999 is the 20th **century.*** (p. 190)

ceremony (sĕr′ə mō′ nē) *n.* an event held at a special time, such as when people marry or die, or when a new leader is chosen. *The graduation **ceremony** lasted 4 hours.* (p. 24)

challenge (chăl′ənj) *v.* speak or work against; object to. *Activists **challenge** things that don't seem fair.* (p. 238)

cheap (chēp) *adj.* not expensive. *I like this store because it has **cheap** clothes.* (p. 106)

Cherokee Nation *n.* a Native American group. *The government forced the **Cherokee Nation** to leave Georgia.* (p. 123)

Christianity (krĭs′chē ăn′ĭ tē) *n.* the religion based on the teachings of Jesus Christ. (p. 37)

citizen (sĭt′ĭ zən) *n.* a member of a nation. *Luz is an American **citizen.*** (p. 298)

citizenship (sĭt′ĭ zən shĭp′) *n.* the state of being a citizen. *Immigrants can get U.S. **citizenship.*** (p. 298)

civil lawsuit *n.* a court case about money or property, not about crime. (p. 290)

civil rights *n.* the rights of citizens. *The Constitution protects our **civil rights.*** (p. 179)

Civil Rights Movement *n.* the effort by millions of Americans in the 1950s and 1960s to win equality for African Americans. *The **Civil Rights Movement** changed many lives.* (p. 252)

civil war *n.* a war between parts of the same country. *The **Civil War** between the North and South ended slavery in the United States.* (p. 169)

claim (klām) *v.* say that something belongs to you. *If someone doesn't **claim** the lost dog, Mom said I could keep him.* (p. 36)

cliff dwellers *n.* Native Americans of the Southwest who built their houses on the sides of cliffs. (p. 27)

Cold War *n.* the conflict between democracy and communism that began after World War II. *The Soviet Union and the United States feared each other during the **Cold War.*** (p. 238)

colony (kŏl′ə nē) *n.* an area that is ruled by another country. *People who live in a **colony** are called* colonists. (p. 46)

colored (kŭl′ərd) *adj.* black; African American. *People do not use the word* **colored** *anymore because it is offensive to African Americans.* (p. 154)

commit suicide *v.* kill oneself. *The man said he would **commit suicide** if he lost his job.* (p. 228)

common (kŏm′ən) *adj.* like most people, not rich and powerful. *The **common** people did not like their ruler.* (p. 118)

communication (kə myōō′nĭ kā′shən) *n.* the way people exchange news and ideas. *Technology makes **communication** easier.* (p. 193)

communism (kŏm′yə nĭz′əm) *n.* a way of living in which all wealth is owned by everyone together. *There is no private property in **communism.*** (p. 238)

community service *n.* volunteer work that helps people in the place where one lives. *Many schools require students to do **community service.*** (p. 303)

compass (kŭm′pəs) *n.* a tool for finding direction. It uses a magnetic needle that points north. *When we were lost, we used a **compass** to find our way back to camp.* (p. 36)

compete (kəm pēt′) *v.* take part in a contest. *Eddie will **compete** in the race.* (p. 120)

competition (kŏm′pĭ tĭsh′ən) *n.* a contest. *Businesses are in a **competition** for customers.* (p. 194)

compromise (kŏm′prə mīz′) *n.* a way of settling a disagreement in which each side gets part of what it wants. *We finally reached a **compromise** that made us both happy.* (p. 85)

concentration camp *n.* a Nazi prison where millions of people were killed. *Nazis forced the Jewish people into **concentration camps.*** (p. 229)

Confederacy (kən fĕd′ər ə sē) *n.* the states that left the union. *The **Confederacy** fought against the Union in the Civil War.* (p. 166)

Confederate States of America *n.* the Confederacy, the nation formed in 1861 by Southern states that left the Union. *The **Confederate States of America** fought the Union in the Civil War.* (p. 159)

conflict (kŏn′flĭkt′) *n.* a long struggle. *The leaders discussed a plan to end the **conflict** between their nations.* (p. 145)

Congress (kŏng′grĭs) *n.* the lawmaking part of government. ***Congress** includes both the Senate and the House of Representatives.* (p. 106)

conquer (kŏng′kər) *v.* take control of a nation by force. *Saddam Hussein tried to **conquer** Kuwait in 1990.* (p. 230)

constituent (kən stĭch′ōō ənt) *n.* a voter represented by an elected official. *Each of us is a **constituent** of the president.* (p. 301)

constitution (kŏn′stĭ tōō′shən) *n.* a legal document that describes the functions of government. *The U.S. **Constitution** describes 3 branches of government.* (p. 272)

Constitutional Convention *n.* the meeting that decided what should be in the Constitution. (p. 83)

containment (kən tān′mənt) *n.* a policy to stop the spread of communism. *Part of the U.S. **containment** plan was in Asia.* (p. 240)

continent (kŏn′tə nənt) *n.* one of 7 large bodies of land. *The **continents** are Africa, Antarctica, Asia, Australia, Europe, North America, and South America.* (p. 24)

Continental Army *n.* the American army in the American Revolution. (p. 71)

Continental Congress *n.* a group of men who led the American colonists to independence from Britain. *The **Continental Congress** became the first government of the new nation.* (p. 60)

control (kən trōl′) *n.* the power to rule or direct. *The British had **control** over business activities in the colonies.* (p. 56)

convention (kən vĕn′shən) *n.* a meeting. *My doctor went to a medical **convention.*** (p. 84)

cowman (kou′mən) *n.* a farmer who raises cattle (cows, bulls, and steers). (p. 183)

craftsman (krăfts′mən) *n.* a man who uses skill to make things. *A shipbuilder or printer is a **craftsman**.* (p. 70)

create (krē āt′) *v.* build or make. *I think we should **create** an after-school book club.* (p. 50)

crew (kro͞o) *n.* a group of workers. *The construction **crew** worked on the building.* (p. 183)

crime (krīm) *n.* an act against the law. *Michael committed a **crime** when he stole the video game.* (p. 181)

crisis (krī′sĭs) *n.* a time of great difficulty. *Jasmine handled the **crisis** of her mother's death very well.* (p. 83)

cruel (kro͞o′əl) *adj.* causing pain and suffering. *The **cruel** man kicked the dog.* (p. 51)

culture (kŭl′chər) *n.* a way of life. ***Culture** includes language, foods, beliefs, and ways of doing things.* (p. 22)

custom (kŭs′təm) *n.* a way of doing something, such as eating, talking to elders, worshipping God, and so on. *The American **custom** of shaking hands is new to some immigrants.* (p. 133)

cut off (kŭt ôf) *v.* separate. *The army **cut off** supplies to the enemy.* (p. 71)

D

dangerous (dān′jər əs) *adj.* not safe. *Driving fast is **dangerous**.* (p. 35)

D-Day *n.* June 6, 1944, the date when Allied forces landed in France to begin freeing Europe from the Germans. (p. 228)

deal (dēl) *n.* a plan. *I made a **deal** with my parents to improve my grades.* (p. 219)

debate (dĭ bāt′) *n.* a formal talk between people who have different opinions. *Our class held a **debate** to discuss school uniforms.* (p. 84)

debt (dĕt) *n.* an amount of money owed. *I can't buy anything new until I pay my credit card **debt**.* (p. 83)

decision (dĭ sĭzh′ən) *n.* a ruling. *A judge made the **decision** to let me live with my father.* (p. 157)

Declaration of Independence *n.* the document that said the colonies were free from British rule. (p. 63)

declare (dĭ klâr′) *v.* say in an official way. *The referee will **declare** an end to the fight.* (p. 63)

defeat (dĭ fēt′) **1.** *v.* beat; win against the enemy. *I hope we **defeat** their team in the tournament.* (p. 71) **2.** *n.* a lost battle. *Our **defeat** hurt the team's pride.* (p. 74)

defend (dĭ fĕnd′) *v.* fight to protect. *We went to war to **defend** our freedom.* (p. 143)

delegate (dĕl′ ĭ gāt′) *n.* a person sent to a meeting to represent others. *Each neighborhood sent a **delegate** to the town meeting.* (p. 83)

demand (dĭ mănd′) *v.* say firmly. *I **demand** an apology.* (p. 166)

democracy (dĭ mŏk′rə sē) *n.* a system of government that gives power to the people. *People vote for their leader in a **democracy**.* (p. 236)

democratic (dĕm′ə krăt′ĭk) *adj.* like a democracy, where people get to vote on important things. *In a **democratic** society, people vote for their leaders.* (p. 155)

department (dĭ pärt′ mənt) *n.* a part of the government that reports to the president. *The Secretary of State heads the **Department** of State.* (p. 94)

depression (dĭ prĕsh′ən) *n.* a time when business activity is very slow and people cannot earn money. *Many people lose their jobs during a **depression**.* (p. 217)

desperate (dĕs′pər ĭt) *adj.* afraid to the point of having no hope. *The starving man was **desperate** for food.* (p. 219)

destiny (dĕs′tə nē) *n.* what will happen; fate. *My **destiny** is to become rich and famous.* (p. 122)

destruction (dĭ strŭk′shən) *n.* the act of turning something into nothing. *The **destruction** of the building angered the town.* (p. 229)

dictator (dĭk′tā′tər) *n.* a ruler with total power. *No court or other governing body can check the power of a **dictator**.* (p. 143)

disaster (dĭ zăs′tər) *n.* a terrible event. *The hurricane was a **disaster**.* (p. 218)

discrimination (dĭ skrĭm′ə nā′shən) *n.* unfair treatment of people because of their race, age, or disability. *Women face **discrimination** in many parts of the world.* (p. 250)

document (dŏk′yə mənt) *n.* a written paper. *When you get married, you sign a **document** to make it legal.* (p. 63)

draft (drăft) *n.* the selection of troops to serve in the military. *During the Vietnam War, some men avoided the **draft**.* (p. 300)

draft card *n.* a card that showed a person had registered to go into military service. *A protester burned his **draft card**.* (p. 243)

drought (drout) *n.* a long time without rain. *Crops die during a **drought**.* (p. 218)

due process *n.* the steps set out by law. *The courts must follow **due process**.* (p. 290)

duty (do͞o′tē) *n.* something you cannot refuse to do. *Citizens have a **duty** to pay their taxes every year.* (p. 296)

E

economic strength *n.* the power that comes when people have jobs and businesses are making money. *The **economic strength** of the U.S. makes it a powerful nation.* (p. 260)

economy (ĭ kon′ə mē) *n.* all the business activities of a country. *When people have money to buy things, the **economy** is strong.* (p. 167)

elect (ĭ lĕkt′) *v.* vote into office. *We will **elect** a new president in November.* (p. 219)

electricity (ĭ lĕk trĭs′ĭ tē) *n.* a kind of power, or energy. ***Electricity** moves inside wires.* (p. 193)

emancipation (ĭ măn′ sə pā′shən) *n.* a release from restraint or control. *President Lincoln gave the slaves their **emancipation**.* (p. 164)

empire (ĕm′pīr′) *n.* a group of lands or countries under one government. *India was once part of the British **Empire**.* (p. 37)

equal (ē′kwəl) *adj.* the same in size or value. *He divided the cake into 8 **equal** pieces.* (p. 207)

equality (ĭ kwŏl′ĭ tē) *n.* the condition of having the same rights as other people. *Women fought to gain **equality** in the workplace.* (p. 250)

equip (ĭ kwĭp′) *v.* supply with the things needed. *The coach will **equip** us with uniforms before the first game.* (p. 167)

escape (ĭ skāp′) *v.* get free from. *The prisoner tried to **escape** from jail.* (p. 132)

ethnic group *n.* a group of people who share common ancestors, culture, and history. *Latinos form an **ethnic group**.* (p. 262)

euro (yo͝o′rō) *n.* the money used by many European Union nations. *The **euro** makes it easier to do business in Europe.* (p. 265)

event (ĭ vĕnt′) *n.* something that happens. *The Senior Prom is the biggest **event** of the school year.* (p. 59)

eventually (ĭ vĕn′cho͞o ə lē) *adv.* in the end; finally. *If you keep trying, you will **eventually** achieve your goal.* (p. 134)

evidence (ĕv′ĭ dəns) *n.* the things that show what is true and what is not true; proof. *The chocolate on Hector's mouth was **evidence** that he ate the cookie.* (p. 289)

excite (ĭk sīt′) *v.* stir up strong feelings. *A ringing doorbell will **excite** my dog.* (p. 72)

executive branch *n.* the part of government that carries out the laws. *The president heads the **executive branch**.* (p. 278)

exist (ĭg zĭst′) *v.* be present. *The original documents still **exist** today.* (p. 158)

expand (ĭk spănd′) *v.* grow; take up more space. *The sponge will **expand** if you put it in water.* (p. 155)

expedition (ĕk′spĭ dĭsh′ən) *n.* a trip made by a group of people for a definite purpose. *The scientists on the **expedition** made many new discoveries.* (p. 97)

exploration (ĕk′ splə rā′ shən) *n.* a trip taken to search for something. *The Spaniards saw Mexico on their **exploration** of the New World.* (p. 32)

explorer (ĭk splôr′ər) *n.* a person who travels or searches an area to discover something. *The **explorer** found a new kind of plant in the rainforest.* (p. 35)

export (ĕk′ spôrt) **1.** *n.* a good or product sold to other countries. (p. 116) **2.** *v.* send (goods) to another country for sale.

expression (ĭk sprĕsh′ən) *n.* a telling or exchanging of ideas. *An artist's painting is a form of **expression**.* (p. 286)

extend (ĭk stĕnd′) *v.* Make something larger in area or longer in time. *Do you think Ms. Kwan will **extend** the deadline for our essays?* (p. 144)

F

facility (fə sĭl′ĭ tē) *n.* a place of service, such as a bathroom or a hotel. *Our school has a separate bathroom **facility** for teachers.* (p. 250)

factory (făk′tə rē) *n.* a building where things are made with machines. *My cousin works in a **factory** that makes chocolate.* (p. 130)

factory system *n.* a way of making products in which each worker does only a part of the work. *The **factory system** makes products fast.* (p. 131)

familiar (fə mĭl′yər) *adj.* known. *This place looks **familiar** even though I've never been here.* (p. 167)

famine (făm′ĭn) *n.* a serious lack of food in a place. *The **famine** caused many deaths.* (p. 132)

fanatic (fə năt′ĭk) *n.* someone whose support for a belief is taken to an extreme. *The terrorist was a religious **fanatic**.* (p. 156)

fascism (făsh′ĭz′əm) *n.* a political set of ideas that says a strong central government and a very powerful leader are best. *Adolf Hitler believed in **fascism**.* (p. 226)

fear (fîr) *v.* be afraid of. *I **fear** that I will make a mistake.* (p. 144)

federal (fĕd′ər əl) *adj.* about a kind of government in which power is shared between state governments and a central government. *The government in Washington, D.C., makes **federal** laws.* (p. 121)

federal arsenal *n.* a building where the national government keeps weapons. (p. 156)

federal government *n.* the central government that unites the states. *The **federal government** is in Washington, D.C.* (p. 83)

federalism (fĕd′ər ə lĭz′əm) *n.* a system of government in which power is shared between national and state governments. (p. 275)

ferocious (fə rō′shəs) *adj.* fierce, like an animal. *The **ferocious** dog bit the child.* (p. 168)

fiercely (fîrs lē) *adv.* very hard, with much anger and violence. *The soldier fought **fiercely**.* (p. 202)

filthy (fĭl′thē) *adj.* very dirty. *Do not use that **filthy** sponge to wash the dishes.* (p. 131)

flee (flē) *v.* run away from. *The boy tried to **flee** the burning house by jumping out the window.* (p. 171)

fleet (flēt) *n.* a group of ships. *The **fleet** left the harbor.* (p. 75)

force (fôrs) **1.** *n.* violence; soldiers and guns. *The government took over the courthouse by **force**.* (p. 60) **2.** *n.* forces; groups of people organized to fight. *Our **forces** include the army and navy.* (p. 71)

foreign (fôr′ĭn) *adj.* from another country. *Which **foreign** language do you speak?* (p. 120)

foreign policy *n.* the plan a country makes for how it will act toward other countries. (p. 99)

foreign trade *n.* doing business in and with another country. *Modern technology makes **foreign trade** easy.* (p. 207)

forty-niner *n.* a person who moved to California in 1849 in search of gold. (p. 146)

foundation (foun dā′shən) *n.* base. *The **foundation** of the house is strong because it's made of concrete.* (p. 272)

freedom (frē′dəm) **1.** *n.* liberty from slavery (p. 164) **2.** *n.* the ability to act without being harmed. *The Pilgrims wanted religious **freedom**.* (p. 164)

frontier (frŭn tîr′) *n.* the area on the edge of a settled region. *Many Americans moved to the **frontier** in search of more land.* (p. 97)

Fugitive Slave Act *n.* an 1850 law that made people return runaway slaves to their owners. (p. 154)

fundamentalist (fŭn′də mĕn′tl ĭst) *adj.* very religious and firm in belief. *A **fundamentalist** parent is very strict with children.* (p. 264)

G

global economy *n.* the network of international business. *Technology makes a **global economy** possible.* (p. 266)

globalization (glō′bə lĭ zā′ shŭn) *n.* the coming together of business interests around the globe. *Some people worry that **globalization** will make everything the same around the world.* (p. 266)

goal (gōl) *n.* an objective or desired end. *The writer's **goal** is to finish his book before next year.* (p. 128)

goods (go͝odz) *n.* things for sale. *The truck brought the **goods** to the store.* (p. 34)

gradually (grăj′o͞o əl lē) *adv.* over a long time. *My cold **gradually** improved.* (p. 131)

Great Plains *n.* a dry, treeless region in the middle of the United States. *Oklahoma and Texas are in the **Great Plains**.* (p. 107)

guarantee (găr′ən tē′) *v.* promise that certain things will happen. *If you study, I **guarantee** you will get a good grade.* (p. 286)

H

hardship (härd′shĭp′) *n.* a difficulty, a problem. *The **hardship** of losing his father made Robert a stronger person.* (p. 169)

harsh (härsh) *adj.* cruel and severe. *My **harsh** comment upset Teresa.* (p. 154)

harvest (här′vĭst) *n.* the gathering of food crops at the end of the growing season. *During the **harvest**, Juan's parents need his help.* (p. 24)

head (hĕd) **1.** *v.* lead. *A general will **head** the army.* (p. 94) **2.** *n.* the top person in an organization. *Mr. Sanchez is the **head** of the company.*

hemisphere (hĕm′ĭ sfîr′) *n.* one half of the earth's surface. *North and South America are in the western **hemisphere**, and Europe, Africa, and Asia are in the eastern **hemisphere**.* (p. 99)

herd (hûrd) *n.* a large group of one kind of animal. *The loud noise scared the **herd** of sheep.* (p. 26)

heritage (hĕr′ĭ tĭj) *n.* traditions and skills handed down by parents to children. *I am proud of my Mexican **heritage**.* (p. 254)

hijack (hī′jăk′) *v.* take by force. *The terrorists tried to **hijack** a plane.* (p. 263)

Hispanic (hĭ spăn′ĭk) *n.* a person whose roots are in Spanish-speaking countries. (p. 254)

Holocaust (hŏl′ə kôst′) *n.* the Nazi murder of 6 million Jews from 1933 to 1945. (p. 229)

homeland (hōm′lănd′) *n.* the land where a person is born; the country a people call home. *The war in my **homeland** forced my family to move.* (p. 191)

horrify (hôr′ə fī′) *v.* shock. *If I dyed my hair green, it would **horrify** my parents.* (p. 191)

hotbed (hŏt′bĕd′) *n.* a place where anything grows and develops quickly. *The cafeteria is a **hotbed** of school gossip.* (p. 156)

House of Burgesses *n.* the lawmaking body in the Virginia Colony. (p. 47)

houses (hou′sĭz) *n.* parts of the legislature. *The **houses** of Congress are the House of Representatives and the Senate.* (p. 85)

humiliated (hyo͞o mĭl′ē āt′əd) *adj.* lowered in pride and dignity; ashamed. *Tony felt **humiliated** after losing the fight.* (p. 215)

I

idol (īd′l) *n.* a hero; someone admired. *The firefighter became the boy's **idol** when he rescued him from the fire.* (p. 72)

illegal (ĭ lē′gəl) *adj.* not allowed by law; against the law. *Stealing is **illegal**.* (p. 110)

imbalance (ĭm băl′əns) *n.* a condition of not being equal. *Carmen's arrival created an **imbalance** between boys and girls in our gym class.* (p. 142)

immigrant (ĭm′ĭ grənt) *n.* a person who comes to a new country to live. *My father is a Haitian **immigrant**.* (p. 132)

imperialism (ĭm pîr′ē ə lĭz′əm) *n.* the plan of a country for getting control over other countries. *American **imperialism** caused the Spanish American War.* (p. 202)

import (ĭm pôrt′) **1.** *n.* a good or product brought in from another country. (p. 116) **2.** *v.* bring in (goods) from another country for sale.

imported (ĭm pôrt′əd) *adj.* brought into the country for sale. *People argue about taxing **imported** goods.* (p. 120)

income tax *n.* a tax paid on the money earned at a job. ***Income tax** comes out of your paycheck.* (p. 299)

independence (ĭn′dĭ pĕn′dəns) *n.* the freedom from control. *Mexicans won their **independence** from Spain on September 15, 1810.* (p. 62)

independent (ĭn′dĭ pĕn′dənt) *adj.* free from outside control. *College students are more **independent** than high school students.* (p. 202)

Indian (ĭn′dē ən) **1.** *n.* a name for a native person of the Americas; a Native American. (p. 22) **2.** someone from the Asian country of India

industry (ĭn′də strē) **1.** *n.* the business of making and selling goods. ***Industry** in the town grew rapidly.* (p. 130) **2.** *n.* all the companies in a business. *The textile **industry** makes, sells, and ships cloth.* (p. 194)

influence (ĭn′flo͞o əns) *n.* the power of having an effect on others without using force. *My mother's **influence** made me go to college.* (p. 264)

injustice (ĭn jŭs′tĭs) *n.* an unfair situation or act. *Sending someone to jail without a trial is an **injustice**.* (p. 251)

inspection station *n.* a place where people are inspected—looked over—to be sure they meet the rules. (p. 190)

integration (ĭn′tĭ grā′shən) *n.* the opening of public places and services to people of all races. ***Integration** of U.S. public schools happened in 1954.* (p. 251)

internment camp *n.* a place set up during war to keep people who may be a threat to the safety of a country. *My great-grandmother was sent to an **internment camp**.* (p. 231)

invade (ĭn vād′) *v.* lead an army into a land to take it over. *We need to stop them before they **invade** another country.* (p. 168)

invasion (ĭn vā′zhən) *n.* an attack. *The general carefully planned the **invasion**.* (p. 228)

invent (ĭn vĕnt′) *v.* make for the first time. *I want to **invent** a machine that will do my homework for me.* (p. 35)

invention (ĭn vĕn′shən) *n.* a new tool or idea created out of the imagination. *The **invention** of the Internet changed communication.* (p. 193)

invest (ĭn vĕst′) *v.* put money into business to make a profit. *You should **invest** your money in the stock market.* (p. 202)

investigation (ĭn vĕs′tĭ gā′ shən) *n.* a meeting to look carefully at what people are doing. *An **investigation** proved the man was innocent.* (p. 242)

island (ī′lənd) *n.* a land surrounded by water. *We took a boat to the **island**.* (p. 204)

isolationism (ī′sə lā′shə nĭz′əm) *n.* a policy of not getting involved in the wars of other countries. ***Isolationism** is not a good policy anymore.* (p. 98)

J

judicial branch *n.* the part of government that interprets the laws through its decisions in legal cases. *A system of state and federal courts make up the **judicial branch**.* (p. 279)

jury (jo͝or′ē) *n.* a group of citizens who listen to a court case and decide what the facts mean. *After listening to all the facts, the **jury** decided the man was innocent.* (p. 290)

jury duty *n.* the requirement of citizens to serve on a jury. *I did not go to work today because I had **jury duty**.* (p. 301)

justice (jŭs′tĭs) *n.* a judge, especially one on a high court. *Thurgood Marshall was the first African-American Supreme Court **justice**.* (p. 251)

K

kidnap (kĭd′năp′) *v.* take away by force. *My mother fears someone will **kidnap** me.* (p. 51)

L

labor (lā′bər) *n.* **1.** workers. *Farm workers are cheap **labor**.* (p. 110) **2.** the work people do. *It takes hard **labor** to build roads with shovels.*

laissez-faire (lĕs′ā fâr′) *n.* an economic policy in which the government doesn't make rules about business. *Monopolies grew under **laissez-faire**.* (p. 195)

landmark (lănd′märk′) *adj.* important. *African Americans won a **landmark** victory when the Civil Rights Act was passed.* (p. 251)

lately (lāt′lē) *adv.* recently; not long ago. *Ms. Gomez has not given us much homework **lately**.* (p. 182)

launch (lônch) *v.* send into the air. *We watched them **launch** the rocket on TV.* (p. 230)

legislative branch *n.* the part of government that makes the laws. *Congress is the **legislative branch**.* (p. 277)

legislature (lĕj′ĭ slā′chər) *n.* the part of government that makes laws. *In the federal government, the **legislature** is called Congress.* (p. 82)

level best *adj.* very best effort. *Dominique gave her **level best** but still didn't make the team.* (p. 301)

liberty (lĭb′ər tē) *n.* the freedom to act without control. *The colonists fought for their **liberty** from English rule.* (p. 164)

local (lō′kəl) *adj.* relating to a certain area or place. A city has a local government. ***Our local** government makes the town's laws.* (p. 275)

log cabin *n.* a simple house made from logs. *The old man lived in a **log cabin**.* (p. 118)

longhouse (lông′hous′) *n.* a long, wooden Iroquois house. (p. 24)

loom (lo͞om) *v.* can be seen dimly in a threatening way. *Worry will **loom** over me until I get my test back.* (p. 263)

loss (lôs) *n.* a death. *The death of the President was a terrible **loss** to the country.* (p. 169)

Louisiana Purchase *n.* the 1803 sale by France of much of western North America to the United States. (p. 96)

loyal (loi′əl) *adj.* faithful, true. *The **loyal** dog followed his owner everywhere.* (p. 70)

Loyalist (loi′ə lĭst) *n.* a colonist who stayed loyal, or true, to Britain. *The **Loyalist** joined the British army.* (p. 70)

M

mainland (mān′lănd′) *n.* a country's biggest piece of land. *America's **mainland** does not include the states of Alaska and Hawaii.* (p. 145)

majority (mə jôr′ĭ tē) *n.* an amount greater than half. *The **majority** of kids in my school play sports.* (p. 158)

Manifest Destiny *n.* the idea that the United States had the right to own and settle lands from the Atlantic to the Pacific Oceans. *Native Americans suffered as a result of **Manifest Destiny**.* (p. 122)

manual (măn′yo͞o əl) *n.* a small book of instructions; a handbook. *The **manual** showed me how to set up my computer.* (p. 73)

manufacturing (măn′yə făk′chər ĭng) *n.* the business of making goods by hand or by machine. ***Manufacturing** provides many jobs in this town.* (p. 95)

Massachusetts Bay Company *n.* a business with power from the king of England to set up a colony, pay for it, and make money from it. *The **Massachusetts Bay Company** brought the people to America who founded Boston.* (p. 49)

massacre (măs′ə kər) *n.* the killing of a large number of people who can't defend themselves. *We held a service for the people who died in the **massacre**.* (p. 58)

mercantilism (mûr′kən tē lĭz′əm) *n.* a way nations grew wealthy. They used the resources of colonies to make and sell more goods than they bought. *Getting colonies was part of **mercantilism**.* (p. 46)

merchant (mûr′chənt) *n.* a business person who makes a living buying and selling things. *The **merchant** sold us an antique chair.* (p. 46)

migrant worker *n.* a farm laborer who goes from place to place to find work. *The **migrant worker** never lived in one place for more than a few months.* (p. 254)

migrate (mī′grāt′) *v.* move from one region to live in another. *Some farm workers **migrate** to find work.* (p. 22)

military (mĭl′ĭ tĕr′ē) *adj.* relating to the armed forces. The army, navy, air force, and marines make up the U.S. military. *The army sent **military** supplies by train.* (p. 167)

military officer *n.* a person of high rank in the armed forces, such as a captain, an admiral, or a general. *The **military officer** commanded the soldiers to attack.* (p. 72)

militia (mə lĭsh′ə) *n.* an army of citizens who are not professional soldiers. *The National Guard is a **militia** that exists today.* (p. 288)

minuteman (mĭn′ĭt măn′) *n.* a colonist who was ready to be a soldier. *The **minuteman** fought bravely against the British in the Battle of Lexington.* (p. 61)

mission (mĭsh′ən) *n.* a church or other building where priests live and teach their religious beliefs. *The priest left his home to work in an African **mission**.* (p. 37)

missionary (mĭsh′ə nĕr′ē) *n.* a person who goes to another country to spread his or her religion. *The Christian **missionary** told the children a story about Jesus.* (p. 204)

mob (mŏb) *n.* a large crowd that is out of control. *It took over 100 police officers to control the angry **mob**.* (p. 95)

monopoly (mə nŏp′ə lē) *n.* a business that completely controls the making and selling of a product. *Standard Oil forced its competitors out of business and became a **monopoly**.* (p. 194)

Monroe Doctrine *n.* the idea that Europe should not set up new colonies in the Americas and that the United States would stay out of European problems. (p. 99)

mound builders *n.* the Native American cultures of the Ohio and Mississippi rivers who built large hills made of earth. (p. 25)

movement (mo͞ov′mənt) *n.* a group of people working together to reach a goal they all share. *People joined the Civil Rights **Movement** to fight for racial equality.* (p. 135)

mule (myo͞ol) *n.* an animal like a horse that can be trained and used to pull or carry things. *The **mule** pulled a wagon.* (p. 108)

multinational (mŭl′tē năsh′ə nəl) *adj.* **1.** made of many nations. *The **multinational** group discussed a Middle East peace plan.* (p. 262) **2.** having offices and owners in many nations. *The computer company grew and became **multinational**.* (p. 266)

N

nationalism (năsh′ə nə lĭz′əm) *n.* pride in your country. *Americans fly American flags to express their **nationalism**.* (p. 226)

naturalization (năch′ər ə lĭ zā′ shən) *n.* the way people become U.S. citizens if they weren't born as citizens. *When I turn 18, I'll go through the process of **naturalization**.* (p. 298)

naval base *n.* the headquarters of a navy. *Japan attacked the **naval base** at Pearl Harbor.* (p. 227)

naval fleet *n.* a group of ships used to fight on the ocean. *The United States sunk all of the ships in the Spanish **naval fleet**.* (p. 203)

negotiate (nĭ gō′shē āt′) *v.* talk in order to settle a conflict. *I decided to end the fight and **negotiate** with my mother.* (p. 195)

neighborhood (nā′bər ho͝od′) *n.* an area in a city. *This **neighborhood** has many good Thai restaurants.* (p. 191)

neutral (no͞o′trəl) *adj.* not taking sides in a war. *Sweden remained **neutral** during World War II and did not fight on either side.* (p. 215)

New World *n.* the name Europeans gave to the continents of North and South America. (p. 32)

newcomer (no͞o′kŭm′ər) *n.* a person who has just come into a place. *The **newcomer** did not know her way around the city.* (p. 190)

nuclear (no͞o′klē ər) *adj.* related to the power released when an atom is split. *A **nuclear** explosion can destroy a city.* (p. 242)

nullification (nŭl′ə fĭ kā′shən) *n.* the idea that a state could decide not to obey a national law. ***Nullification** is about states' rights.* (p. 121)

O

oath of allegiance *n.* a promise to be true to the nation. *I swore an **oath of allegiance** when I became an American citizen.* (p. 298)

obey (ō bā′) *v.* follow as an order. *You should **obey** your parents when they tell you to do something.* (p. 121)

offend (ə fĕnd′) *v.* cause hurt feelings and anger. *I'm worried that I will **offend** Caroline if I tell her that the dress is ugly.* (p. 156)

offensive (ə fĕn′sĭv) *adj.* hurtful, annoying, or disgusting. *Many people complained that the songs had **offensive** language.* (p. 287)

official (ə fĭsh′əl) *adj.* from the government or other authority. *We're waiting for an **official** response.* (p. 73)

opportunity (op′ər to͞o′nĭ tē) *n.* a chance. *A college education will give you the **opportunity** to find a good job.* (p. 106)

Oregon Trail *n.* a pioneer trail leading northwest from Missouri to Oregon. (p. 109)

organize (ôr′gə nīz′) *v.* put together; arrange. *I need to **organize** my messy closet.* (p. 135)

orphan (ôr′fən) *n.* a person whose parents are dead. *The **orphan** missed her parents.* (p. 118)

outnumbered (out nŭm′bərd) *v.* had fewer people. *The boys at our school are **outnumbered** by the girls.* (p. 75)

outraged (out′rājd) *adj.* angered by something wrong. *My parents were **outraged** by my low math grade.* (p. 155)

override (ō′vər rīd′) *v.* go over. *Congress can **override** a presidential veto.* (p. 279)

overrun (ō′vər rŭn′) *v.* take over; defeat and occupy. *The army will **overrun** the city by morning.* (p. 228)

P

panic (păn′ĭk) *n.* a fear that spreads through a group of people and makes them lose control of themselves. *The smoke caused a **panic** in the building.* (p. 286)

Parliament (pär′lə mənt) *n.* the highest lawmaking group in Britain. *Members of **Parliament** voted to tax the colonists.* (p. 58)

participate (pär tĭs′ə pāt′) *v.* be part of; work in. *I would love to **participate** in the school play.* (p. 303)

passenger (păs′ən jər) *n.* a person who travels in a ship, plane, train, or bus. *Over 100 **passengers** died in the airplane crash.* (p. 48)

Patriot (pā′trē ət) *n.* a colonist who wanted independence from Britain. *The **Patriot** shot the British soldier.* (p. 70)

peninsula (pə nĭn′syə lə) *n.* a point of land that sticks out into the sea. *Florida is a **peninsula** because the ocean surrounds it on 3 sides.* (p. 75)

permanent (pûr′mə nənt) *adj.* lasting; not going away. *The nail left a **permanent** mark on the wall.* (p. 23)

permission (pər mĭsh′ən) *n.* an agreement from someone with power. *Did you get **permission** from your dad to use the car?* (p. 51)

persecute (pûr′sĭ kyōōt′) *v.* treat badly and unfairly, usually because of religion, politics, or race. *You should not **persecute** people for their beliefs.* (p. 48)

persecution (pûr′ sĭ kyōō′ shən) *n.* the harm people suffer because of who they are. *Religious **persecution** forced the Pilgrims to flee England.* (p. 44)

persuade (pər swād′) *v.* cause someone to do something by giving strong reasons. *I hope I can **persuade** Anna to come with us.* (p. 134)

petition (pə tĭsh′ən) *v.* ask formally and in writing that the government do something. *I will **petition** the mayor for money to buy school computers.* (p. 287)

Pilgrim (pĭl′grəm) *n.* a *Mayflower* colonist. *The **Pilgrim** became friends with an Indian.* (p. 48)

pioneer (pī′ə nîr′) *n.* a person who settles an area and gets it ready for others who come later. *The **pioneer** built a house for his family.* (p. 107)

pit (pĭt) *v.* set to fight. *The competition **pit** me against my best friend.* (p. 169)

Plains Indians *n.* the Native Americans who lived in the flat parts of the western United States. (p. 23)

plan (plăn) *n.* a scheme; a strategy. *Marisa's **plan** for going to college involves saving money.* (p. 272)

plantation (plăn tā′ shən) *n.* a large farm. *Slaves picked cotton on the **plantation**.* (p. 50)

point of view *n.* an opinion. *I would like to know your **point of view** on gun control.* (p. 95)

policy (pol′ĭsē) *n.* a plan of action that a government makes. *Foreign **policy** changed as a result of the war.* (p. 98)

political party *n.* a group of people who share ideas about government and who work to get their members elected. (p. 95)

politics (pŏl′ ĭ tĭks) *n.* the activities related to government; also the activities of government. *Armando wants to go into **politics** and run for senator.* (p. 119)

popular (pŏp′yə lər) *adj.* well-liked by many people. *We waited an hour for a table at the **popular** restaurant.* (p. 118)

popular sovereignty *n.* the rule by the people. *Americans believe in **popular sovereignty**.* (p. 274)

population (pŏp′yə lā′shən) *n.* all the people who live in an area. *As the **population** of the city grew, it got harder to find an apartment.* (p. 25)

port (pôrt) *n.* a place where ships stop to load and unload goods. *The ship left the **port** after unloading all the food.* (p. 108)

poverty (pŏv′ər tē) *n.* the condition of being poor. *Many children who live in **poverty** do not have enough food to eat.* (p. 239)

power (pou′ər) *n.* the strength or force that can make people do things. *The king of England had **power** over the colonists.* (p. 56)

prairie schooner *n.* a strong wagon covered to keep out wind and rain and pulled by animals. *Mother and I rode in the **prairie schooner** with all of our things.* (p. 109)

Preamble (prē′ăm′ bəl) *n.* the introduction to the Constitution. *The reasons for a law usually are stated in a **preamble**.* (p. 276)

prejudice (prĕj′ə dĭs) *n.* bad and unfair ideas about people based on a group they belong to. *Racial **prejudice** is hatred of people of other races.* (p. 191)

prejudiced (prĕj′ə dĭsd) *adj.* having a bad opinion of people because of the group they belong to. ***Prejudiced** people wouldn't hire African Americans.* (p. 133)

preside (prĭ zīd′) *v.* run a meeting. *Nadia will **preside** over the meeting today.* (p. 278)

presidency (prĕz′ĭ dən sē) *n.* **1.** the time a person serves as president. *George W. Bush led the country in a war during his **presidency**.* (p. 94) **2.** the job of the president—its duties and functions. *The **presidency** has changed over the years.* (p. 118)

presidential election campaign *n.* the series of activities to get a person elected to be president. *The candidate visited 50 cities during his **presidential election campaign**.* (p. 158)

presidential election year *n.* the year that Americans vote for a new president. *I will be old enough to vote in the next **presidential election year**.* (p. 144)

press (prĕs) *n.* the people who make information and ideas known through any of the media. *The **press** reported what the president said.* (p. 287)

prestige (prĕ stēj′) *n.* honor; reputation. *The award increased the **prestige** of our school.* (p. 264)

prime (prīm) *adj.* the very best. *I love to eat **prime** ribs.* (p. 122)

principle (prĭn′sə pəl) *n.* an idea that forms a foundation for other ideas. *Democracy is an American **principle** of government.* (p. 274)

prisoner of war *n.* a person captured by the enemy and held until the war is over. *Our soldiers rescued a **prisoner of war**.* (p. 74)

privacy (prī′və sē) *n.* being free from other people looking at your personal life. *I close my bedroom door when I want **privacy**.* (p. 289)

product (prŏd′əkt) n. a thing made to be sold. *The ad made me want to buy this **product**.* (p. 130)

professional (prə fĕsh′ə nəl) *adj.* working for pay doing a job that is also a career. *Maya dreams of becoming a **professional** soccer player.* (p. 288)

propaganda (prŏp′ə găn′də) *n.* booklets, movies, and posters put out by a government to push an idea onto society. *The government used **propaganda** to gain support for the war.* (p. 215)

property (prŏp′ər tē) *n.* things that are owned. *My rich uncle owns a lot of **property**.* (p. 51)

property tax *n.* a tax paid on land, buildings, or some big items like boats or cars, that one owns. *We pay a **property tax** on our house.* (p. 299)

proposal (prə pō′zəl) *n.* a formal, detailed suggestion. *The principal rejected our **proposal** for a longer lunch period.* (p. 278)

proslavery (prō slā′və rē) *adj.* supporters of slavery. ***Proslavery** Southerners fought to preserve slavery.* (p. 156)

protection (prə tĕk′shən) *n.* the act of keeping something safe. *My father has a large dog for **protection**.* (p. 206)

protectorate (prə tĕk′tər ĭt) *n.* a weak country under the protection and control of a strong country. *Cuba was a U.S. **protectorate** until it became independent in 1901.* (p. 203)

protest (prō′ tĕst′) *v.* publicly show strong opinions against something. *The people marched in front of the White House to **protest** the war.* (p. 58)

protester (prə tĕst′ər) *n.* a person who speaks, or acts to show he or she is against something. *The **protester** marched outside the store with a sign that told people not to shop there.* (p. 243)

public office *n.* a job—like mayor, governor, or senator—that a person is elected to. *My mother ran for **public office** last year and was elected.* (p. 302)

public official *n.* person elected to work in government. *The president is a **public official**.* (p. 301)

public school *n.* a school that offers free education to all children. (p. 251)

publish (pŭb′lĭsh) *v.* make public. Books, TV programs, and writings on the Internet are published. *I hope to **publish** a book one day.* (p. 287)

punish (pŭn′ĭsh) *v.* make someone suffer for doing wrong. *My parents will **punish** me if I stay out too late.* (p. 60)

punishment (pŭn′ĭsh mənt) *n.* a fine, a jail term, and other penalties. *Jordan received a severe **punishment** for starting the fight.* (p. 299)

Puritan (pyŏŏr′ĭ tn) *n.* a member of an English religious group who came to the colonies to get religious freedom. (p. 49)

pursuit (pər sōōt′) *n.* the getting of or chasing after. *Many people have died in the **pursuit** of freedom.* (p. 302)

Q

qualification (kwŏl′ə fĭ kā′shən) *n.* a thing that makes a person able to have a job. *I might not get the job because I don't have that **qualification**.* (p. 277)

R

racial prejudice *n.* having a poor opinion of someone because of his or her skin color. ***Racial prejudice** led to unfair treatment of minorities.* (p. 248)

racism (rā′sĭz′əm) *n.* the belief that your group is the best and the hatred of people who belong to a different group. *We're working to get rid of **racism** in our society.* (p. 229)

radical (răd′ĭ kəl) *adj.* extreme, or far to one side. *Most people don't like my **radical** idea.* (p. 178)

rage (rāj) *v.* speak or act with great anger. *The man **raged** about the dent in his car.* (p. 147)

raid (rād) *n.* a sudden attack. *We surprised the enemy with a **raid** on their camp.* (p. 156)

ratify (răt′ə fī′) *v.* make into law; approve formally. *The senate needs to **ratify** the treaty.* (p. 86)

reaction (rē ăk′ shən) *n.* response. *His **reaction** to the sad news was to cry.* (p. 176)

rebel (rĭ bĕl′) *v.* fight against the one who rules. *If the king does not listen to the people, they will **rebel**.* (p. 143)

rebellion (rĭ bĕl′yən) *n.* a fight against one's own government; a revolt. *The army put down the **rebellion**.* (p. 83)

Reconstruction (rē′kən strŭk′shən) *n.* the series of steps that Congress took to bring the Southern states back into the country. *Federal troops enforced laws in the South during **Reconstruction**.* (p. 178)

Redcoats (rĕd′kōts) *n.* a name for British soldiers during the American Revolution. *The **Redcoats** fought the Patriot army.* (p. 61)

reform (rĭ fôrm′) *n.* a change for the better. *The teachers called for **reform** in the school system.* (p. 195)

reformer (rĭ fôrm′ər) *n.* a person who works to improve life and get rid of things that cause people harm. *The **reformer** worked to end slavery.* (p. 134)

refugee (rĕf′yŏŏ jē′) *n.* a person who leaves an area to find safety. *The **refugee** left his war-torn country.* (p. 239)

refuse (rĭ fyōōz′) *v.* say no. *I **refuse** to pay that much money for a shirt.* (p. 159)

region (rē′jən) *n.* an area of land where many things are the same. *I live in a mountain **region**.* (p. 22)

register (rĕj′ĭ stər) *v.* sign or fill out a record. *I will **register** for this class.* (p. 190)

regulate (rĕg′yə lāt′) *v.* control a group by giving it rules. *Teachers must **regulate** the classroom so that students can learn.* (p. 195)

religion (rĭ lĭj′ən) *n.* a belief in and worship of God or spirits. *In my **religion**, we pray to God in a church.* (p. 26)

religious (rĭ lĭj′əs) *adj.* believing in God or spirits. *The **religious** woman prays daily.* (p. 37)

religious freedom *n.* the ability to worship as one chooses without being hurt. *The colonists left England because they wanted **religious freedom**.* (p. 44)

represent (rĕp′rĭ zĕnt′) *v.* speak for. *Americans elect people to **represent** them in government.* (p. 275)

representation (rĕp′ rĭ zĕn tā′shən) *n.* having someone in government speak for you. (p. 58)

representative (rĕp′ rĭ zĕn′tə tĭv) *n.* a lawmaker; somebody in government elected by the voters in a state to speak and vote for them. (p. 47)

representative government *n.* a government run by elected officials. *The United States has a **representative government**.* (p. 47)

republic (rĭ pŭb′lĭk) *n.* a nation that has a system of government in which people elect representatives to make their laws. *The United States is a **republic**.* (p. 275)

Republican Party *n.* one of the main political parties in the United States. *The **Republican Party** won more votes than the Democratic Party.* (p. 158)

reputation (rĕp′yə tā′shən) *n.* what people say and think about someone. *Those kids have a **reputation** for getting into trouble.* (p. 286)

resistance (rĭ zĭs′təns) *n.* the opposing of or saying no to something. *His **resistance** to authority got him in trouble.* (p. 252)

resource (rē′sôrs′) *n.* something in a place that people use to help them live. *Water is a **resource** that we use everyday.* (p. 22)

respect (rĭ spĕkt′) *v.* show care or consideration for. *You should always **respect** your elders.* (p. 302)

responsibility (rĭ spŏn′sə bĭl′ĭ tē) *n.* an action owed to others in society. *You have a **responsibility** to be honest.* (p. 302)

retired (rĭ tīrd′) *adj.* no longer working because of age. ***Retired** people have more time for their families.* (p. 219)

retreat (rĭ trēt′) *v.* go away from the fighting. *The captain ordered his soldiers to **retreat** because he knew they could not win the battle.* (p. 143)

revenge (rĭ vĕnj′) *n.* the act of getting even. *Chris got **revenge** for what Steven did to him.* (p. 143)

reversal (rĭ vûr′səl) *n.* a turning backward; a change to the opposite. *When Carla lost her job, she experienced a **reversal** of fortune.* (p. 181)

revolt (rĭ vōlt′) *n.* a fight against a government. *The government stopped the **revolt**.* (p. 206)

revolution (rĕv′ə lōō′shən) *n.* a war against your own government. *The people fought a **revolution** to gain freedom.* (p. 61)

right (rīt) *n.* the things laws say are owed to you. *People have the **right** to practice any religion in the United States.* (p. 284)

riot (rī′ət) *n.* a wild, violent disturbance caused by a crowd of people out of control. *The people broke store windows during the **riot**.* (p. 286)

ruins (rōō′ĭnz) *n.* what is left after buildings fall to pieces or are destroyed. ***Ruins** of Mayan cities in Mexico still stand today.* (p. 171)

S

sacrifice (săk′rə fīs′) *n.* a giving up of something for an important cause. *Death in battle is a **sacrifice.*** (p. 243)

sales tax *n.* a tax paid on things you buy. *There is a 5 cent **sales tax** on this candy bar.* (p. 299)

satellite communication *n.* radio, TV, and telephone signals that are sent from the ground to a satellite in space and from there back to the ground, instead of through wires. (p. 266)

scalawag (skăl′ə wăg′) *n.* a white Southerner who worked with the federal government during Reconstruction. *People called him a **scalawag.*** (p. 179)

search warrant *n.* a written permission from a judge to search for evidence. *Judges give **search warrants** when they believe the searchers will find evidence of a crime.* (p. 289)

season (sē′zən) *n.* one of 4 times of the year: spring, summer, fall, or winter. *Summer is my favorite **season** because it is hot outside.* (p. 26)

secede (sĭ sēd′) *v.* leave the United States and form a new country. *South Carolina threatened to **secede** from the United States.* (p. 121)

sectionalism (sĕk′shə nə lĭz′əm) *n.* caring more about one's own part of the country than about the country as a whole. ***Sectionalism** drove the North and the South apart.* (p. 110)

segregation (sĕg′rĭ gā′shən) *n.* the separation of people of different races. ***Segregation** kept black people from going into many restaurants.* (p. 181)

self-government *n.* a government that gets its power from the people, not from kings or from force. (p. 48)

separate (sĕp′ə rāt′) *v.* move away from or leave. *I need to **separate** myself from my sister because we always fight when we're together.* (p. 62)

settle (sĕt′l) *v.* move into a place; make a home there. *The people decided to **settle** near the lake.* (p. 22)

settlement (sĕt′l mənt) *n.* a place where people live. *One British **settlement** was at Plymouth.* (p. 37)

settler (sĕt′lər) *n.* a person who moves into a new area and makes a home there. *The **settler** planted crops on his land.* (p. 46)

sharecropper (shâr′krŏp′ər) *n.* a person who lives on someone else's land and farms it for them. *A **sharecropper** is usually poor.* (p. 180)

side (sīd) *v.* support in a fight or quarrel; be on the same side. *My parents always **side** with my sister when we fight.* (p. 202)

silk (sĭlk) *n.* a fine, shiny cloth. *My scarf is made of **silk.*** (p. 34)

situation (sĭch′ōō ā′shən) *n.* a condition or combination of circumstances. *In this **situation,** we need to be careful.* (p. 251)

skyscraper (skī′skrā′pər) *n.* a very tall building. *We rode the elevator to the top of the **skyscraper.*** (p. 193)

slaughter (slô′tər) *n.* a killing of large numbers of people; a massacre. *I felt sick about the horrible **slaughter.*** (p. 143)

slave (slāv) *n.* a person who is owned and forced to work by someone else. *The man bought a new **slave** to work on his farm.* (p. 50)

slave trade *n.* the business of buying and selling slaves. *The **slave trade** made some white people rich.* (p. 51)

slum (slŭm) *n.* the crowded, dirty part of a city where the buildings are old and need repairs and the people are poor. (p. 191)

soar (sôr) *v.* rise; grow higher. *I watched the balloon **soar** above the trees.* (p. 146)

sovereignty (sŏv′ər ĭn tē) *n.* the freedom from outside control and power over one's own government. *Confederate soldiers fought for the **sovereignty** of the Southern states.* (p. 262)

Soviet Union *n.* a union of 15 countries headed by Russia. *The **Soviet Union** ended in 1991.* (p. 228)

spice (spīs) *n.* a plant like pepper, ginger, or cinnamon that adds flavor to food. *This **spice** makes the chicken taste delicious.* (p. 34)

spike (spīk) *n.* a large, strong nail. *A worker drove the **spike** into the ground.* (p. 183)

spirit (spĭr′ĭt) *n.* a supernatural being. *Angels are **spirits.*** (p. 27)

spy (spī) *n.* a person who finds out or carries secret information in wartime. *The **spy** found out the enemy's plan.* (p. 166)

starvation (stär vā′shən) *n.* death from not having enough food. *The stray dog died of **starvation.*** (p. 46)

starving (stär′vĭng) *adj.* dying from not having enough to eat. *The **starving** children stood in line to get food.* (p. 132)

statehood (stāt′hŏŏd′) *n.* being a state. *Texas achieved **statehood** in 1845.* (p. 142)

states' rights *n.* the idea that the states joined together freely and had power in government. *Southerners argued that **states' rights** meant they could keep slavery.* (p. 167)

steamboat (stēm′bōt′) *n.* a ship powered by a steam engine. *The **steamboat** traveled up the river.* (p. 108)

stock (stŏk) *n.* a share of a business. ***Stocks** give people a way to own a part of the company.* (p. 217)

stock market *n.* the place to buy and sell stocks. *My older brother made a lot of money buying and selling stocks on the **stock market.*** (p. 217)

stood for *v.* was on the side of; represented. *The organization **stood for** animal rights.* (p. 119)

stronghold (strông′hōld′) *n.* a strong or safe place, like a fort. *Once we capture the enemy's **stronghold,** we'll win the war.* (p. 171)

sue (sōō) *v.* ask a court to rule about a law. *Hector will **sue** the man who hit his car.* (p. 157)

suffer (sŭf′ər) *v.* feel pain or loss. *I hope the dog didn't **suffer** before it died.* (p. 37)

suffragist (sŭf′rə jĭst) *n.* a person who works to get more people the right to vote. *The **suffragist** believed that women should be allowed to vote.* (p. 135)

Supreme Court *n.* the highest court in the United States. *The case went all the way to the **Supreme Court.*** (p. 157)

surrender (sə rĕn′dər) *v.* declare that an enemy has won and that fighting can stop. *Since we can't win, we should just **surrender.*** (p. 75)

T

take the risk *v.* maybe lose something; take a chance. *Carlos is willing to **take the risk** of losing his job to help his friend.* (p. 35)

Taliban (tăl′ĭ băn) *n.* the ruling government of Afghanistan from 1996–2001. *The **Taliban** did not allow women to go to school.* (p. 264)

tariff (tăr′ĭf) *n.* a tax on goods from other countries. *The **tariff** made American products cheaper than foreign products.* (p. 120)

tax (tăks) *n.* the money people must pay to a government. *I paid the sales **tax.*** (p. 58)

technology (tĕk nŏl′ə jē) *n.* the use of new knowledge to make new machines. *Computer **technology** makes our lives easier.* (p. 108)

temple (tĕm′pəl) *n.* a building for religious activities. *I prayed inside the **temple.*** (p. 25)

tension (tĕn′shən) *n.* a feeling of fear or nervousness. *The argument between my parents created **tension** at dinner.* (p. 147)

term (tûrm) *n.* the length of service in office before another election is held. *The president only served one **term** in office.* (p. 277)

territory (tĕr′ĭt ôr′ē) *n.* a land under the control of the United States that is not a state. *People wanted their **territory** to become a state.* (p. 106)

terror (tĕr′ər) *n.* a great fear. *Groups use **terror** to punish people or to try to force changes.* (p. 181)

terrorism (tĕr′ə rĭz′əm) *n.* the use of great fear and violence as a way of getting control. *American fear of **terrorism** increased after the September 11 bombings.* (p. 263)

testify (tĕs′tə fī′) *v.* tell under oath what happened. *Robert went to court to **testify** that he saw the man take the woman's purse.* (p. 154)

textile mill *n.* a factory where cloth is made. *The girls worked in a **textile mill.*** (p. 130)

thief (thēf) *n.* a person who steals; a robber. *The **thief** went to jail for stealing money.* (p. 35)

38th parallel *n.* the latitude line that separates South Korea from North Korea. *You can see the **38th parallel** on a map.* (p. 240)

tipi (tē′pē) *n.* a tent. *A **tipi** is made from animal skins.* (p. 26)

totalitarian (tō tăl′ĭ târ′ē ən) *adj.* a kind of government in which all power is in the hands of the ruling group. *The people were not free under their **totalitarian** government.* (p. 238)

trade (trād) *n.* the business of buying and selling goods. *The railroad increased **trade** in our town.* (p. 108)

trade route *n.* a path across land or water that traders travel to buy and sell goods. *Christopher Columbus wanted to find a new **trade route** to India.* (p. 34)

trader (trā′dər) *n.* a person who buys and sells things. *I bought cloth from a **trader** who stopped in our town.* (p. 34)

Trail of Tears *n.* the trip in which the Cherokee people were forced to go west. *Many Cherokee died on the **Trail of Tears.*** (p. 123)

transcontinental railroad *n.* a rail line reaching across the nation. *The **transcontinental railroad** made it much easier to send goods across the United States.* (p. 183)

transport (trăns pôrt′) *v.* move goods or people by a vehicle, such as a train. *We will **transport** our belongings by truck.* (p. 183)

transportation (trăns′pər tā′shən) *n.* ways of getting from one place to another. *The city's **transportation** system makes it easy to get downtown.* (p. 193)

treatment (trēt′mənt) *n.* actions; dealings; considerations. *The kids in my family receive equal **treatment** from my parents.* (p. 302)

treaty (trē′tē) *n.* a formal agreement among nations. *The nations' leaders signed a **treaty** to end the war.* (p. 75)

turning point *n.* an event that changes the direction of events. *At the **turning point** in the war, the Confederacy stopped winning and started losing.* (p. 168)

tyrant (tī′rənt) *n.* a ruler who is cruel to his or her people. *The **tyrant** ordered the people to be shot.* (p. 95)

U

unconstitutional (ŭn′kon stĭ tōō′shə nəl) *adj.* goes against the Constitution. *The court decided that the law was **unconstitutional.*** (p. 157)

Underground Railroad *n.* a system that helped slaves escape. It was not a real railroad. *Slaves escaped north on the **Underground Railroad.*** (p. 134)

unemployed (ŭn′ĕm ploid′) *adj.* had no job. *The **unemployed** man read the help-wanted ads in the newspaper.* (p. 217)

unemployment (ŭn′ĕm ploi′mənt) *n.* the situation of people being out of work. *High **unemployment** occurs during a depression.* (p. 212)

unfortunately (ŭn fôr′chə nĭt lē) *adv.* sadly. ***Unfortunately,** I can't go to the party because I have to study for a test.* (p. 131)

unimagined (ŭn′ĭ măj′ĭnd) *adj.* impossible; not able to be thought of. *Computers work with **unimagined** speed.* (p. 262)

union (yōōn′yən) *n.* a group of workers who join together to make business owners change things. *The **union** went on strike to get better pay.* (p. 131)

Union (yōōn′yən) *n.* the United States. *The Southern states left the **Union.*** (p. 111)

United States Constitution *n.* the law that sets up the federal government and gives power to the states and rights to the people. (p. 86)

unreasonable (ŭn rē′zə nə bəl) *adj.* without a good reason. *I think my detention is **unreasonable** because I didn't do anything wrong.* (p. 289)

V

Valley Forge *n.* Washington's army camp in Pennsylvania. *Many soldiers died during the harsh winter at **Valley Forge.*** (p. 72)

veto (vē′tō) *adj.* having the power to say no. *The president has **veto** power.* (p. 277)

victory (vĭk′tə rē) *n.* a winning. *Our team celebrated the **victory.*** (p. 203)

Viet Cong *n.* the communists in South Vietnam who fought to unite with North Vietnam. (p. 241)

violence (vī′ə ləns) *n.* physical force used to cause damage and harm. *The **violence** at my school makes me feel unsafe.* (p. 95)

voluntary (vol′ən tĕr′ē) *adj.* done of one's own free will; not forced or required. *Participation in this event is **voluntary.*** (p. 300)

volunteer (vol′ən tîr′) *v.* work without pay as a way of giving service to the community. *I **volunteer** at an animal shelter.* (p. 288)

voyage (voi′ĭj) *n.* a long journey or trip. *The **voyage** to America took 3 months.* (p. 36)

W

War of 1812 *n.* the last war the Americans fought against the British. *Andrew Jackson fought in the **War of 1812.*** (p. 118)

wave (wāv) *n.* a movement of many people coming in, like an ocean. *A **wave** of Irish immigrants came to America.* (p. 190)

weapon (wĕp′ən) *n.* a tool of hunting and war, like an arrow or a gun. *The police found the murder **weapon** in the garbage.* (p. 26)

went at *v.* attacked; fought. *My brothers **went at** each other and broke the T.V.* (p. 75)

went broke *v.* had no money. A person who went broke couldn't pay bills. *The man **went broke** after he lost his job.* (p. 217)

went on strike *v.* stopped working. A strike is a group action taken to make a business owner change things. *The workers **went on strike** until the owner decided to pay them more.* (p. 131)

wilderness (wĭl′dər nĭs) *n.* the land in its wild, natural state where few or no people live. *Many animals live in the **wilderness.*** (p. 96)

witch hunt *n.* a persecution of people to make government officials look good. *The senator was engaged in a **witch hunt.*** (p. 242)

witness (wĭt′nĭs) *n.* a person who answers questions in a trial. *The **witness** told the court what she saw.* (p. 301)

Woodland Indians *n.* the Native Americans who lived in the forests east of the Mississippi River. *The **Woodland Indians** built houses of wood.* (p. 23)

worship (wûr′shĭp) *v.* praise God or gods. *Prayers, hymns, and church services are forms of **worship.*** (p. 286)

wounded (wōōnd′əd) *v.* injured or hurt. *The girl was **wounded** in the basketball game.* (p. 168)

SKILLS AND FEATURES

Acknowledgments

PHOTOS AND ILLUSTRATIONS

T4 *left* ©Christopher J. Morris/CORBIS **T5** *upper right* ©CORBIS **T5** *lower right* ©Howard Sochurek/Time Life Pictures/Getty Images **18** *upper left* ©John Schaefer, Director, Children's Media Workshop **18** *center* ©Bettmann/CORBIS **19** *upper left* ©National Museum of Natural History ©2004 Smithsonian Institution **19** *lower right* ©Nathan Benn/CORBIS **19** *upper right* ©Bettmann/CORBIS **19** *lower left* ©Courtesy of Library of Congress **20** *top* ©Carla Kiwior **20** *lower left* ©Woodland Cultural Centre **20** *lower right* ©Ohio Historical Society **20** *bottom center* ©DK/American Museum of Natural History **21** *bottom center* ©Corbis **21** *lower right* ©Wolfgang Kaehler/CORBIS **22** *upper left* ©National Museum of Natural History ©2004 Smithsonian Institution **23** *center right* ©Christopher J. Morris/CORBIS **24** *upper left* ©Lee Snider; Lee Snider/CORBIS **24** *lower left* ©DK/American Museum of Natural History **25** *top* ©Cahokia Mounds State Historic Site, painting by Michael Hampshire **26** *upper left* ©Michael Bad Hand Terry **26** *lower left* ©Courtesy of Library of Congress **26** *lower left* ©Courtesy of Fermilab **26** *lower right* ©Courtesy of the Sioux City Public Museum, Sioux City, IA **27** *upper right* ©Courtesy of National Park Service **27** *lower right* ©Buddy Mays/CORBIS **28** *lower left* ©National Museum of Natural History ©2004 Smithsonian Institution **29** *lower right* ©John Schaefer, Director, Children's Media Workshop **30** *upper left* ©John Schaefer, Director, Children's Media Workshop **30** *center* ©The Granger Collection, New York **31** *lower right* ©Courtesy of Library of Congress **31** *lower left* ©North Wind Picture Archives **32** *top* ©Carla Kiwior **33** *upper right* ©Rick Gomez/CORBIS **34** *upper left* ©Bettmann/CORBIS **34** *center* ©William Whitehurst/CORBIS **34** *lower left* ©Spencer Jones/Picture Arts/CORBIS **35** *center right* ©Corbis **36** *upper left* ©Snark/Art Resource, NY **36** *center left* ©Reuters/CORBIS **36** *lower right* ©The Victoria and Albert Museum, London/Art Resource, NY **37** *lower right* ©James L. Amos/CORBIS **38** *lower right* ©Werner Forman/Art Resource, NY **39** *upper right* ©The Granger Collection, New York **40** *lower left* ©Museum of Mankind, London, UK/Bridgeman Art Library **41** *lower right* ©John Schaefer, Director, Children's Media Workshop **42** *upper left* ©John Schaefer, Director, Children's Media Workshop **42** *center* ©Bettmann/CORBIS **43** *upper left* ©Getty Images **43** *upper right* ©Brian A. Vikander/CORBIS **43** *lower left* ©Courtesy of Library of Congress **43** *lower right* ©Courtesy of the Library of Virginia **44** *top* ©Carla Kiwior **44** *lower left* ©Courtesy of National Park Service **44** *bottom center* ©The Granger Collection, New York **44** *lower right* ©Hulton/Getty Images **45** *upper right* ©Bettmann/CORBIS **45** *lower left* ©Bettmann/CORBIS **45** *lower right* ©Bettmann/ CORBIS **46** *center left* ©National Park Service **46** *upper left* ©Courtesy of The Association for the Preservation of Virginia Antiquities **47** *top* ©National Park Service **48** *upper left* ©Burstein Collection/CORBIS **48** *bottom center* ©Bettmann/CORBIS **49** *upper right* ©North Wind Picture Archives **49** *lower right* ©North Wind Picture Archives **51** *upper right* ©The Granger Collection, New York **51** *lower right* ©Adam Woolfitt/CORBIS **52** *lower left* ©North Wind Picture Archives **53** *lower right* ©John Schaefer, Director, Children's Media Workshop **54** *upper left* ©John Schaefer, Director, Children's Media Workshop **54** *center* ©Bettmann/CORBIS **55** *upper right* ©Bettmann/CORBIS **55** *center left* ©North Wind Picture Archives **55** *lower right* ©The National Archives and Records Administration **56** *top* ©Carla Kiwior **56** *bottom center* ©Bettmann/CORBIS **56** *lower*

right ©Hulton/Getty Images **56** *lower left* ©Bettmann/CORBIS **57** *upper right* ©Colonial Williamsburg Foundation **57** *lower left* ©Bettmann/CORBIS **57** *lower right* ©The National Archives and Records Administration **57** *bottom center* ©North Wind Picture Archives **58** *upper left* ©Bettmann/CORBIS **58** *center left* ©Corbis **59** *bottom* ©Bettmann/CORBIS **60** *center* ©Courtesy of The Historical Society of Pennsylvania Collection, Atwater Kent Museum of Philadelphia **61** *bottom* ©Hulton/Getty Images **61** *upper right* ©North Wind Picture Archives **62** *upper left* ©Hulton/ Getty Images **62** *lower right* ©Courtesy of Library of Congress **63** *upper right* ©Courtesy of Library of Congress **63** *center right* ©Courtesy of Library of Congress **64** *lower left* ©Painting by Don Troiani, www.historicalartprints.com **65** *lower right* ©John Schaefer, Director, Children's Media Workshop **66** *upper left* ©John Schaefer, Director, Children's Media Workshop **66** *center* ©North Wind Picture Archives **67** *upper left* ©North Wind Picture Archives **67** *upper right* ©Bettmann/CORBIS **67** *lower left* ©Bettmann/CORBIS **67** *lower right* ©Bettmann/ CORBIS **68** *top* ©Carla Kiwior **68** *lower left* ©Bettmann/ CORBIS **68** *lower right* ©North Wind Picture Archives **69** *upper right* ©The Corcoran Gallery of Art/CORBIS **69** *lower left* ©North Wind Picture Archives **69** *lower right* ©The National Archives and Records Administration **70** *upper left* ©Colonial Williamsburg Foundation **70** *lower left* ©North Wind Picture Archives **70** *lower right* ©North Wind Picture Archives **71** *upper right* ©North Wind Picture Archives **71** *center left* ©North Wind Picture Archives **72** *upper right* ©Bettmann/CORBIS **72** *bottom center* ©North Wind Picture Archives **73** *upper right* ©Courtesy of Library of Congress **73** *center left* ©Bettmann/ CORBIS **73** *lower right* ©Courtesy of Library of Congress **74** *bottom* ©Getty Images **75** *center right* ©North Wind Picture Archives **76** *lower left* ©James P. Rowan **77** *lower right* ©John Schaefer, Director, Children's Media Workshop **78** *upper left* ©John Schaefer, Director, Children's Media Workshop **78** *center* ©Courtesy of Library of Congress **79** *center* ©Courtesy of Library of Congress **79** *lower right* ©The National Archives and Records Administration **79** *upper right* ©Courtesy of the Federal Reserve Bank of San Francisco **80** *bottom* ©Carla Kiwior **81** *upper right* ©The National Archives and Records Administration **81** *far upper right* ©The National Archives and Records Administration **80/81** *bottom* ©Ron Mahoney **82** ©Courtesy of the Federal Reserve Bank of San Francisco **83** *upper right* ©Bettmann/CORBIS **84** *upper right* ©Bettmann/ CORBIS **84** *center right* ©Casmir Gregory Stapko, Collection of The Supreme Court of the United States **84** *lower left* ©Courtesy of Library of Congress **85** *lower left* ©National Portrait Gallery, Smithsonian Institution/Art Resource, NY **86** *upper left* ©Courtesy of The Secretary of the Treasury **86** *center left* ©Courtesy of Library of Congress **87** *upper right* ©Najlah Feanny/CORBIS SABA **87** *center right* ©The National Archives and Records Administration **88** *lower left* ©Courtesy of The White House **89** *lower right* ©John Schaefer, Director, Children's Media Workshop **90** *upper left* ©John Schaefer, Director, Children's Media Workshop **90** *center* ©Gilcrease Museum, Tulsa, Oklahoma **90** *lower right* ©Courtesy of the U.S. Mint **91** *top* ©Carla Kiwior **91** *lower right* ©Ron Mahoney **92** *top* ©Carla Kiwior **92** *lower left* ©SuperStock **92** *lower right* ©SuperStock **93** *bottom center* ©Courtesy of The White House **93** *lower right* ©SuperStock **93** *lower left* ©Courtesy of Library of Congress **94** *upper left* ©Bettmann/CORBIS **95** *upper left* ©Courtesy of Library of Congress **95** *upper right* ©Courtesy of Library of Congress

97 *upper right* ©Hulton/Getty Images 97 *center right* ©American Philosophical Society 97 *lower right* ©Missouri Historical Society, St. Louis 98 *bottom* ©Ron Mahoney 99 *upper right* ©Bettmann/CORBIS 101 *lower left* ©John Schaefer, Director, Children's Media Workshop 102 *upper left* ©John Schaefer, Director, Children's Media Workshop 102 *center* ©Courtesy of Library of Congress 103 *upper right* ©Special Collections Research Center, University of Chicago Library 103 *center* ©NY Public Library/Art Resource, NY 104 *top* ©Carla Kiwior 104 *bottom* ©Courtesy of Library of Congress 105 *lower left* ©Courtesy of Library of Congress 105 *lower right* ©North Wind Picture Archives 107 *bottom* ©Albert Bierstadt, Emigrants Crossing the Plains, 1867, 67x102 (framed), 72.19, National Cowboy & Western Heritage Museum, Oklahoma City, OK 108 *upper right* ©Bettmann/ CORBIS 108 *lower left* ©Lee Snider/CORBIS 109 *upper right* ©Museum of the City of New York/CORBIS 109 *center left* ©Courtesy of Library of Congress 109 *lower right* ©Royalty-Free/Corbis 110 *upper left* ©North Wind Picture Archives 110 *center left* ©Corbis 110 *center right* ©Corbis 110 *lower right* ©Courtesy of Library of Congress 113 *lower right* ©John Schaefer, Director, Children's Media Workshop 114 *upper left* ©John Schaefer, Director, Children's Media Workshop 114 *center* ©CORBIS SYGMA 115 *upper right* ©Chicago Historical Society P&S-X 45 115 *upper left* ©Collection of the New-York Historical Society #8838 115 *lower left* ©Ron Mahoney 115 *lower right* ©Troy Anderson/ Amonsoquath Tribe 116 *top* ©Carla Kiwior 116 *bottom center* ©Courtesy of The Cherokee Nation 116 *lower right* ©Courtesy of Library of Congress 117 *bottom center* ©Peter Harholdt/ CORBIS 117 *lower left* ©Courtesy of Library of Congress 118 *upper left* ©The National Archives and Records Administration 118 *lower right* ©Courtesy of Library of Congress 119 *center* ©North Wind Picture Archives 120 *upper left* ©Corbis 120 *bottom* ©Carla Kiwior 121 *upper right* ©Courtesy of Library of Congress 121 *center right* ©Profiles in History/CORBIS 121 *lower right* ©The Granger Collection, New York 123 *upper right* ©Woolaroc Museum Bartlesville Oklahoma 124 *lower left* ©Tony Arruza/CORBIS 125 *lower right* ©John Schaefer, Director, Children's Media Workshop 126 *upper left* ©John Schaefer, Director, Children's Media Workshop 126 *center* ©John Ferguson Weir (1841–1926), The Gun Foundry (1866) Use or reproduction of this work permitted solely by prior written permission of The Putnam County Historical Society and Foundry School Museum, Cold Spring, New York 127 *top* ©Corbis 127 *center left* ©Museum of the City of New York/CORBIS 127 *center right* ©Courtesy of Library of Congress 127 *lower left* ©Bettmann/CORBIS 128 *lower left* ©Bettmann/CORBIS 128 *lower right* ©Bettmann/CORBIS 129 *bottom center-left* ©Corbis 129 *bottom center-right* ©North Wind Picture Archives 129 *lower left* ©Courtesy of Library of Congress 129 *lower right* ©Courtesy of Library of Congress 130 *upper left* ©American Textile History Museum, Lowell, MA 130 *center left* ©North Wind Picture Archives 131 *center right* ©Bettmann/CORBIS 132 *lower left* ©Corbis 133 *center right* ©Bettmann/CORBIS 134 *upper left* ©Bettmann/CORBIS 134 *upper left* ©Corbis 134 *center left* ©renowned artist Paul Collins-collinsart.com 135 *upper right* ©Bettmann/CORBIS 135 *center right* ©Courtesy of The U.S. Mint 136 *lower left* ©Schomburg Center/Art Resource, NY 137 *lower right* ©John Schaefer, Director, Children's Media Workshop 138 *upper left* ©John Schaefer, Director, Children's Media Workshop 138 *center* ©Bettmann/CORBIS 139 *upper left* ©Courtesy of Library of Congress 139 *center left* ©Royalty-Free/CORBIS 139 *center left* ©D. Boone/CORBIS 139 *upper left* ©Courtesy of Library of Congress 139 *center right* ©Courtesy of Ben Cahoon 139 *lower right* ©Courtesy of Library of Congress 140 *top* ©Carla Kiwior 140 *bottom center* ©Courtesy of Library of Congress 140 *lower left* ©Schalkwijk/Art Resource, New York 141 *bottom center* ©North Wind Picture Archives 141 *upper right* ©Courtesy of Library of Congress 141 *lower right* ©Polak Matthew/ CORBIS SYGMA 141 *lower left* ©Courtesy of Library of Congress 142 *upper left* ©Courtesy of Library of Congress 143 *upper right* ©The Center for American History, The University of Texas at Austin 143 *center* ©Getty Images 143 *lower right* ©Art Collection, Harry Ransom Humanities Research Center, The University of Texas at Austin 144 *upper left* ©Texas State Library and Archives Commission 144 *center left* ©Bettmann/CORBIS 144 *center right* ©Courtesy of Library of Congress 144 *center right* ©Adam Woolfitt/CORBIS 144 *center right* ©Adam Woolfitt/ CORBIS 145 *upper right* ©The Corcoran Gallery of Art/CORBIS 146 *upper right* ©Polak Matthew/CORBIS SYGMA 146 *upper left* ©Bettmann/CORBIS 146 *lower right* ©Nevada Historical Society 147 *center right* ©Courtesy of Library of Congress 149 *lower right* ©John Schaefer, Director, Children's Media Workshop 150 *upper left* ©John Schaefer, Director, Children's Media Workshop 150 *center* ©Kansas State Historical Society 151 *upper left* ©Courtesy of Library of Congress 151 *upper right* ©Courtesy of Library of Congress 151 *lower left* ©Bettmann/CORBIS 152 *top* ©Carla Kiwior 152 *center right* ©Missouri Historical Society, St. Louis 152 *bottom center* ©Getty Images 153 *bottom center* ©Bettmann/ CORBIS 153 *lower left* ©Courtesy of Library of Congress 154 *center left* ©The Granger Collection, New York 156 *upper left* ©Bettmann/CORBIS 156 *lower left* ©Courtesy of Library of Congress 157 *upper right* ©Courtesy of Library of Congress 157 *center right* ©Courtesy of Library of Congress 158 *upper left* ©Chicago Historical Society Alexander Hesler ICHi-22037 158 *center left* ©Getty Images 159 *upper left* ©Chicago Historical Society ICHi-20265 159 *center left* ©The Museum of the Confederacy, Richmond, Virginia, Photography by Katherine Wetzel 159 *lower right* ©Courtesy of Library of Congress 160 *center left* ©Bettmann/CORBIS 161 *lower right* ©John Schaefer, Director, Children's Media Workshop 162 *upper left* ©John Schaefer, Director, Children's Media Workshop 162 *center* ©Chicago Historical Society ICHi-07774 162 *lower left* ©Corbis 162 *lower right* ©Corbis 163 *center* ©The National Archives and Records Administration 164 *top* ©Carla Kiwior 164 *lower right* ©Corbis 164 *lower right* ©Courtesy of Ben Cahoon 165 *lower right* ©The Museum of the Confederacy, Richmond, Virginia, Photography by Katherine Wetzel 165 *lower right* ©The Granger Collection, New York 166 *upper left* ©The Granger Collection, New York 166 *center right* ©Courtesy of Library of Congress 167 *upper right* ©Corbis 167 *bottom* ©The National Archives and Records Administration 168 *upper left* ©Painting by Don Troiani, www.historicalartprints.com 169 *upper right* ©Corbis 169 *bottom* ©Royalty-Free/CORBIS 170 *bottom* ©Bettmann/CORBIS 170 *lower right* ©Courtesy of Library of Congress 171 *center right* ©North Wind Picture Archives 172 *lower left* ©James P. Rowan 173 *lower right* ©John Schaefer, Director, Children's Media Workshop 174 *upper left* ©John Schaefer, Director, Children's Media Workshop 174 *center* ©Courtesy of Library of Congress 175 *top* ©Courtesy of Library of Congress 175 *lower right* ©Bettmann/CORBIS 175 *lower left* ©Nebraska State Historical Society Photograph Collections 176 *top* ©Carla Kiwior 176 *bottom center* ©Courtesy of Library of Congress 176 *lower left* ©Courtesy of Library of Congress 176 *lower right* ©Hulton/Getty Images 177 *top* ©Corbis 177 *lower left* ©Courtesy of Library of Congress 177 *lower right* ©Courtesy of Library of Congress 178 *upper left* ©Bettmann/CORBIS 179 *upper right* ©Courtesy of Library of Congress 180 *upper left* ©Courtesy of Library of Congress 180 *center left* ©Bettmann/CORBIS 181 *upper right* ©Bettmann/